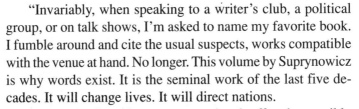

"Invariably, when speaking to a writer's club, a political group, or on talk shows, I'm asked to name my favorite book. I fumble around and cite the usual suspects, works compatible with the venue at hand. No longer. This volume by Suprynowicz is why words exist. It is the seminal work of the last five decades. It will change lives. It will direct nations.

Unlike the firm big-government hand, offered ostensibly to hoist us out of the mire of day to day indecision (while leading us deeper into the swamp), the hand of Suprynowicz only points. But it points to the high ground. It points to hope and the brilliant possibilities alive in the human heart. It points past race and religion, past dogma, and past atomizing welfare-state dependency. It does what words were meant to do: inspire and teach. This book works a slow magic. Suprynowicz has given us the lyrics to freedom's song. It is up to us to make the music."

— Bill Branon, author of *Let Us Prey* (a *New York Times* Notable Book of the Year), *Devil's Hole*, and *Timesong*

SEND IN THE WACO KILLERS

SEND IN THE WACO KILLERS

Essays on the Freedom Movement, 1993-1998

BY
VIN SUPRYNOWICZ

A Mountain Media Book

Send in the Waco Killers—
Essays on the Freedom Movement, 1993-1998

Published by
   Mountain Media
   P.O. Box 4422
   Las Vegas, NV 89127-4422
   e-mail at vin@lvrj.com.

ISBN 0-9679259-0-7

Cover Design: Jeanne Suprynowicz

In Beloved Memory
of Jeanne—
whose love, laughter,
and exuberant spirit of freedom
were the lights of my life—
this book is gratefully dedicated.

The cover design of this book was her last project.

ACKNOWLEDGEMENTS

I didn't "think up" the Libertarian philosophy. As a newspaper columnist, I merely apply it to ongoing developments, checking to see if the paradigm of free will offers a clearer explanation of what's going on—and a more accurate predictor of outcomes—than the Catechism of the Omnipotent State.

With impressive regularity, it does.

In this, I have stood on the shoulders of giants. Some of their works are listed at the back of this book, though easily worth separate mention are Ludwig von Mises, Ayn Rand, my late friend Murray Rothbard, Stephen Halbrook (from whose *That Every Man Be Armed* I have pilfered shamelessly), John Taylor Gatto, Dr. Thomas Szasz, and Aaron Zelman.

The life work of Jim Bovard and Jacob Hornberger, or Larry Dodge and Lew Rockwell, or Marshall Fritz and Larry Pratt have also been inspirations.

My editors at the *Las Vegas Review-Journal*, Sherman Frederick, Tom Mitchell, and John Kerr, have shown endless patience with my literary trouble-making, standing firm when many others might have been less forceful in their defense of my right to publish unpopular opinions. And, of course, the editor of this book, Deke Castleman, recognized coherence in the snarl of a chaotic manuscript, and brought it forth from the darkness into the light. Without his singleness of purpose, this book would not now rest in your hands.

The steady hand of my best friend among many, Rick Tompkins, the Johnny Appleseed of Arizona Libertarianism, can be found here. The support and help, in trying times, of D.J. Shoemaker and the great Bill Branon also proved invaluable. As did that of many a teacher, among whom John Frazer, Charlie Blanchard, and the late Lew Covert are only a representative sample.

(Which is not to say that any person mentioned here shares responsibility for any errors of commission or omission that may follow, those being mine alone.)

I must acknowledge the great good fortune bestowed upon me when Magdalene Waronowicz and Lucille Clark accepted the suits of Wincenty Suprynowicz and Clarence Edward Higginbotham (in 1903 and 1924) in Paterson, N.J., and St. Clairsville, Ohio, respectively, raising fine children who in turn taught me to seek out and defend the truth—though likely never guessing where that credo might lead.

And finally, I feel obliged to acknowledge the inspiring if still wondrous courage of Rear Admiral C.A.F. Sprague, commander of the northern escort carrier group of the Seventh Fleet off Samar, and the tireless competence in maneuver of Lt. Commander A.F. Bayer, Jr., captain of the little escort destroyer *Raymond.*

Commanding only a screening force of escort destroyers and carriers, completely devoid of capital ships, Admiral Sprague looked up from his breakfast on the morning of Oct. 25, 1944, to find bearing down upon him out of the morning mist what was arguably the most powerful surface force afloat, pride of the Japanese Navy, the battleship *Yamato,* with full cruiser escort, straddling his tiny command with thousand-pound shells at a range of 15 miles. Naval historians have since estimated that escort group— including CPO and radioman Vincent Suprynowicz of the

Raymond, my father—were within five minutes of utter destruction when Admiral Sprague gave the still-astonishing order that arguably won the Battle of Leyte Gulf, the greatest naval battle in history.

Admiral Sprague attacked.

Knowing no mere handful of escort carriers and destroyers would dare challenge the most powerful battleship afloat, actually disbelieving his own eyes, Admiral Kurita took it into his head that he was facing a fresh force of aggressive fleet carriers and heavy cruisers, and withdrew. The beachhead at Leyte was preserved; air power finished off the retiring *Yamato* at leisure.

In many ways, this book attempts to answer the question, "What shall we do?" But as new battles for freedom loom, perhaps there is still a lesson for us in the decision of Admiral Sprague, who hesitated not a moment to ask "What shall I do?"

CONTENTS

February 1999

I am proud to be retained as an editorial writer and author of occasional signed commentaries by the *Las Vegas Review-Journal*, Nevada's largest newspaper. When it comes to honoring the principles of liberty and the free market on its editorial page, the *Review-Journal* is one of the top twenty newspapers in the country. However, the opinions expressed and positions taken in this book are entirely my own. They have not been reviewed or endorsed by the editors or proprietors of the *Review-Journal*, or any of the other newspapers that carry my nationally syndicated column.

Vin Suprynowicz
Las Vegas, Nevada

INTRODUCTION

Americans are taught from childhood, by the unionized bureaucrats in the public schools, that we control our own government.

The way it's currently taught, if an American sees an injustice and develops a rational reform that will return our society to a more sensible balance of liberty and civility, all he or she need do is locate a political party that will agree to include the proposal in its platform. Failing that, the concerned American simply starts a new party from scratch.

Want to eliminate the arrogant sneering IRS and its invasive income tax? Want to end the vicious and counterproductive War on Drugs, with its airport body-cavity searches and its SWAT teams battering down your neighbors' doors in the middle of the night? All you have to do is organize a political party, find a candidate articulate enough to voice your views, and throw your time and money into the electoral fray.

You may not win the first time, but as your ideas are heard—and providing they *are* sensible—the number of officeholders you elect will increase over time, until your "radical new ideas" become the political status quo. It worked for the Republicans in 1860, didn't it? It worked for the suffragettes.

As America enters the 21st century, though, most American adults have put away such childish things. They long ago realized the political process is the most cynical of shams. They're not staying away from the polls in droves because they're apathetic, as our talking heads annually coo, but because they're tired of playing a rigged game.

The Libertarian Party has been America's third-largest party since 1972. Since then, the Libertarian Party has entered a viable candidate in every presidential election and raised millions to get its message out.

That money is drained into ballot-access petition drives that cost—guess what?—millions of dollars each election cycle. For what? Just to qualify for something that's automatically handed to *any* Republican or Democrat free of charge: their name on the ballot.

But then, having jumped the million-dollar hurdle and won ballot access, what do the Libertarians discover?

Like patient Negroes attempting to register to vote in the Old South, informed with a snicker that the polling place "just closed" minutes before they arrived, the Libertarians learn that as soon as you get on the ballot, the rules immediately change.

Previously, everyone on the ballot got to take part in candidate debates. But suddenly, the Libertarians are informed, being on the ballot no longer automatically qualifies your candidate to take part in the televised proceedings. No, that's reserved for the viable candidates, where "viable" is defined by some outfit like the League of Women Voters—a virtual subsidiary of the incumbent Republicrat Party.

Why? Because more than two candidates would be "too confusing," of course. We can't confuse the voters with new ideas—no matter how much they cry out against campaigns that turn into personal mud-wrestling matches, an inevitable side effect of Republicrats and Demopublicans pretending to debate when they both agree on every issue of importance. (More taxes, more police, more gun control, more regulations, more drug war, more invasion of privacy, and on and on.)

And what about the rare case where only *two* candidates end up on the ballot: a Libertarian and *either* a Republican or a Democrat? Why, the TV debate on the local tax-supported television station is simply canceled, of course, for a "lack of credible opposition."

Shut out of the TV debates, the Libertarians—like virtually any third party with real issues to discuss—must then depend on the courtesan collectivist press to relay its case to the voters.

But do mainstream media reporters then immerse themselves in the Libertarian platform, calling back with follow-up questions until they understand the Founding Fathers' philosophy of a sharply limited government and expansive personal liberties well enough to explain it in long detailed articles and features?

Of course not. That would be *work*, and it would be *boring*. The readers and TV viewers just want to know who's in the lead and who might have to drop out of the race over that "love-child" charge: you know, the supermarket tabloid stuff. Or, at least, so the voters are told.

Thus the Libertarian candidates are rebuffed with a few dismissive references—or, if they're less lucky, ominous warnings about "fringe candidates of the right-wing militia sort."

This, in spite of the fact that public opinion polls during those 27 years since 1972 have shown Libertarian ideas growing in popularity like weeds—public resentment of the IRS and its income tax, for example, soaring, while the legalization of marijuana (once considered among the most *extreme* and unrealistic

3

of Libertarian proposals) passes by huge margins in virtually every state where voters can wrangle a public referendum on the topic (though the federals and their courts quickly squelch any such popular groundswell. So much for "self-government." Insert bitter laugh here).

And meantime, after 27 years, how many Libertarians now hold seats in the United States Congress? One: former LP presidential candidate Ron Paul, who only won a House seat from Texas by switching his registration to "Republican." And how often is *he* allowed a 30-second sound bite on nationwide TV, do you suppose?

Leaving aside Mr. Paul, the exception who proves many rules, how many times since 1972 have Americans voted overwhelmingly for the candidate and party that promised a smaller government, lower taxes, and less bureaucratic meddling in their lives? Virtually every chance they got.

And how many times have the results been a bigger and more intrusive government, funded by higher taxes extracted via a financial snoop-and-spy network that would have put the East German Stasi to shame?

Why, every time.

Welcome to the freedom movement in America as we approach the millennium: high and dry, socking away survival supplies, and oiling its guns.

Political activism has not worked. What will?

That is the question that gives rise to this book.

Let's not beat around the bush: A lot of patriots and freedom lovers and just plain desperate victims of government oppression figure if the ballot box won't work, the only remaining solution is the cartridge box.

Will freedom return to North America only at the point of a

gun?

At the risk of appearing to split hairs, the question demands that we separate the role of fortune-teller from that of a good-faith advisor.

I believe that, in the end, the insatiable monster state will never allow its claws to be trimmed, nor its slipped collar and leash to be tied back in place. Freedom will return to this continent only through a series of desperate and costly wars of rebellion and secession, leaving Washington City to rule over a truncated slave state approximately equaling the Tyrant Lincoln's old Union, but probably without Maine, Vermont, and New Hampshire.

Educated for generations to believe that redistribution of wealth and the heavy hand of federal "guidance" toward nice-sounding goals of "equality" are the natural way of things, the vast mass of the American public, particularly in the Northeast and southern California, won't get it until taxmen and federal judges and DEA agents swing from every lamppost and the trains bearing beef and wheat as tribute from the subject states simply stop arriving.

Don't get me wrong. The fact that I fear this is inevitable is very different from recommending that folks now take up arms and start shooting federals. To know anything of war is to know that it is not just the bad guys who die, to know the randomness and the mercilessness of the desolation, to know that *everything else* must be tried first.

And the slight glimmer of good news is that there are still a few unexplored avenues through which to seek change, *other* than by electing professional politicians who will swear to see things our way, but only return next year to condescendingly explain, "This is the best compromise we could work out this time around.

You only have to give up a *few* more of your liberties, and submit to fingerprinting each time you pick up your groceries. But you have to understand how the system works."

What are the "unconsidered" routes through which to goad the monster of the omnipotent state in its lair? And can any of them work *without* horse-trading for 218 votes in Congress?

Now you're talkin', brother.

What if people could be made to understand the role the public schools play in their own dumbing down? What if they could be convinced to withhold their children from this form of human sacrifice and teach them the true principles of liberty at home or in private academies, starving the government schools of victims till they stand abandoned and in ruins, scorned by a newly literate nation?

What if the average American could be taught how one of the major safeguards of all our liberties, our inherited thousand-year-old Anglo-Saxon system of trial by jury, has been corrupted and castrated by government lawyers and judges working in concert to stack juries sworn in advance to convict? It only takes one juror in 12 to hang every jury from here till doomsday. What if every one of the 90 percent of suspects arrested for victimless crimes started to walk free, until the cops just gave up, left us in peace in our homes and cars, and went back to staking out real burglars and armed robbers?

What if Americans could be made to realize there's no *need* to legalize drugs—that all drug use is protected under the Ninth Amendment, that all drug laws are already null and void, that all they need to do is wait for inviolate citizen juries to laugh them out of court?

What if only six percent of Americans—the same fraction that fought the War for Independence—could be made to under-

6

stand the importance of proudly owning and bearing military-style arms, not because we hope for war, but because (with the same logic through which the United States won the Cold War) we understand the value of superior force as a deterrent to would-be tyrants?

What if books with such subversive ideas—this one and others like it— could be slipped into the hands of 20,000 Americans, and then 40,000, and then 60,000, who would each see to it that they found two more readers, and then four, and then eight?

That would be a brave new journey toward freedom and away from the paralysis of fear. And like every journey, it begins with a single step.

A step you've already taken.

Because you've just read the first 1,800 words of *Send in the Waco Killers*. And that was the hard part.

Now comes the good stuff.

I

WHERE WE WENT WRONG

A Real Mandate For Change

When Russian President Boris Yeltsin met his opposite number, newly elected American President Bill Clinton, in early 1993, he came away with a positive impression. "I like him," said the longtime member of the Communist Party of Russia. "He's a socialist."

By June 1993, having watched young Mr. Clinton in action for five months, Nobel economic laureate Milton Friedman, an American free-market capitalist, confirmed that this judgment was much more than an off-hand remark, calling Mr. Clinton "a socialist" in public and in writing.

The response to such a straightforward observation in polite American society today is to ignore it and move on as though nothing has happened. Press the point and you may hear a derisive snort.

As every schoolchild knows, "socialist" is now a totally out-of-date term, used only by doddering right-wing racists with ill-fitting hairpieces in a laughable attempt to insult today's moderate, progressive, social democrats.

After all, is it "socialist" to be in favor of racial and gender equality? To be in favor of quality public schools and a compassionate "social safety net" for the unfortunate?

Those same schoolchildren could tell you that the Stone Age vision of a dog-eat-dog free market, unsupervised by any caring government bureaucracy, was rejected by the American electorate in the watershed election of 1932. In that year, in the depths of the Great Depression with unemployment at record levels, Americans were faced with a clear choice.

One party—let's call it Party "A"—called for "immediate governmental relief of the unemployed by the extension of all public works." This party's far-sighted platform called for a "system of unemployment insurance" and a "system of health and accident insurance and of old age pensions."

"For the proper support of government and as a step toward social justice," the platform went on, "we propose an increase of taxation on high income levels, of corporation taxes and inheritance taxes, the proceeds to be used for old-age pensions and other social insurance."

This plan advocated "public development of electrical energy," and "as a further means of agricultural relief ... insurance against losses due to adverse weather conditions."

Surely all right-thinking Americans can be glad the above platform prevailed over the discredited reactionary notions of the competing campaigners—let's call them Party "B"—who ploddingly insisted, "We believe that a party platform is a covenant with the people to be faithfully kept by the party when entrusted with power, and that the people are entitled to know in plain words the terms of the contract to which they are asked to subscribe. ... We advocate an immediate and drastic reduction of governmental expenditures by abolishing useless commissions and offices, consolidating departments and bureaus, and eliminating extravagances to accomplish a savings of not less than 25 percent in the cost of the federal government. ... We favor maintenance of the national credit by a federal budget annually balanced. ... We advocate the removal of government from all fields of private enter-

10

prise except where necessary to develop public works. ... "

Any graduate of today's government schools will surely have learned enough to tell you that the first platform is that of Franklin Delano Roosevelt and his victorious Democratic coalition, while the discredited second platform was that of Herbert Hoover and his "robber baron" Republicans.

But that graduate would be wrong. All the pledges and demands of Party "A" are actually excerpted from the 1932 platform of Socialist Norman Thomas, which Roosevelt and the Democrats savagely reviled as "fantastic and un-American," a platform that was repudiated with a popular vote of only 884,781 in 1932, fewer votes than the Socialists garnered in 1912.

On the other hand, that sober "covenant" of Party "B" to reduce the size of the federal government by 25 percent was the linchpin of the 1932 Democratic platform, a paean to free markets and pared-down government that even in the desperate days of the dust bowl won the support of 22,821,867 Americans, more than Thomas' 885,000 and Hoover's 15,761,841 together.

As a side note, Hoover, a classic economic meddler, was not called the "Great Engineer" just for building a few dams. The term "social engineer" was already well-established, and the notion that Hoover "did nothing" about the deepening Depression because of his supposed laissez-faire philosophy is a purposeful "Big Lie" of almost Hitlerian proportions.

In fact, the activist Hoover burned the White House midnight oil—and burned up the phone lines—actively cajoling, blackmailing, and arm-twisting American industry into keeping wages high, which could have no effect but to throw *everyone* out of work during a deflationary spiral, as Murray Rothbard demonstrated in his classic book *America's Great Depression*.

Hoover, with the "best of intentions," thus managed to extend what could have been a minor economic correction into a major worldwide Depression, by precisely the kind of centrally

planned, IMF-style interventions that are again so heartily recommended to us today.

Yet by the 1990s, the only presidential candidates appearing
on the ballots in all 50 states who pledge to actually reduce the
size of the federal government—the Libertarians—are considered
such far-out radicals that they aren't even allowed into the televised national debates.

Socialists? I dare Bill and Hillary Clinton to find a thing in
the Socialist platform of 1932 that they disagree with. Even better, if they'd like to initiate some really dramatic "change," I dare
them to institute the *Democratic* platform of 1932.

No one else ever used it.

With Tweezer Regulation,
Once Laissez-Faire Nevada Joins The Morass

Nevada is booming. Due to its traditional low taxes and
laissez-faire business climate, it's been booming a long time.

That reputation brings a lot of people here looking for work.
Some arrive with adequate skills and a good work ethic, but nearly
penniless. They find a room, eat the last of the stale crackers in
the car, and set out bright and early looking for work.

What awaits them?

Let's say our penniless new arrival is a skilled hair stylist.
Knocking on doors, he quickly learns he can't immediately start
plying his trade in an established Nevada salon. Salon workers
must have state licenses and shop owners are dragooned into enforcing that state regulation by a provision of the law that exposes them to a $1,000 fine should they employ anyone who
doesn't.

But, being resourceful, our willing worker soon finds a few

places where he can practice his skill "around the edges" of this regulated industry, earning enough money to put food on the table until he can save enough to acquire the stipulated state licenses.

Although barbers and cosmetologists require licenses in Nevada, the folks who style your hair before you get your picture taken at a portrait studio have so far avoided any licensing, since they don't actually cut the hair. Likewise, "hair designers" can take honest work styling wigs or hairpieces—after the owner has removed said appliance—without going through the onerous licensing requirement.

Well, never fear, the Nevada Legislature has put an end to that!

With only days to go before the end of the 1995 biennial legislative session in Carson City, and with legislative leaders insisting only the most pressing bills could now be heard, both houses of the Legislature OK'd Assembly Bill 531, which outlaws the employment of unlicensed "hair designers"—even for wigs!

Has anyone heard a rash of complaints about serious injuries sustained by consumers who allow unlicensed "hair designers" to work on their unoccupied hairpieces? Of course not. Yet this extension of the existing protection racket for barbers and stylists—an undisguised attempt to protect such "professionals" from low-priced competition—passed the state Senate by a vote of 16-5, and the Assembly by a vote of 40-1, with only Doug Bache, D-Las Vegas, in opposition. (I was prepared to elevate Mr. Bache, a government schoolteacher, to hero status for his lone resistance, but it turns out he voted "nay" only after 15 barbers in his district called to complain that the new measure wasn't restrictive *enough*.)

These days, all that seems necessary in most any state capital to win approval of new restrictions on the right of honest Americans to earn a living is the mere assertion that a profession has been discovered that *isn't yet regulated.*

Were it not for the fact that it will throw yet more economically marginal Nevadans—Nevadans who would rather be work-

13

ing, I rush to add—onto the welfare rolls, this bill would be an absolute hoot. Regulated now is the act of "cleansing or beautifying the hair by the use of cosmetic preparations, antiseptics, tonics, lotions, or creams." Regulations also apply to "arranging, dressing, curling, waving, cleansing, singeing, bleaching, tinging, coloring, or straightening the hair of any person with the hands or mechanical or electrical apparatus or appliances."

Also regulated under this fine new protective measure are "aestheticians," defined as folks who offer skin-care assistance, or who "apply make-up or eyelashes to any person, tinting eyelashes and eyebrows and lightening hair on the body except the scalp," as well as "removing superfluous hair from the body of any person by the use of depilatories, waxing, or tweezers. ... "

To take the examination for licensure, an applicant must be not less than 18 years of age, "of good moral character," and have "successfully completed the 10th grade in school or its equivalent."

Allow young women who get pregnant and drop out of school in the ninth grade to earn milk money for their children by washing and curling hair? Not in newly progressive Nevada.

Worst of all, although the requirement can be waived for hair designers who have been licensed four years in another state, to even *take* the new state exam young aspirants must have received "training of at least 1,200 hours, extending over a period of seven consecutive months, in a school of cosmetology approved by the board."

So, it's a cosmetology instructor's full-employment act, as well!

Laissez-faire, indeed. May we see your work papers, please?

How does a boa constrictor kill a pig? The snake doesn't really have sufficient strength to crush the ribs of any good-sized prey. But it doesn't need to. Once it has its body coiled around the victim, it simply waits. As the victim struggles, the poor thing uses up oxygen, even as its bloodstream continually transports

14

more carbon dioxide from the struggling muscles to the lungs. Eventually, the piglet must exhale that exhaust gas, partially collapsing its lungs. Then it quickly tries to inhale again, to replace the vented carbon dioxide with fresh life-giving oxygen.

But it's not fast enough. As it exhales, the snake tightens its grip. The pig can't inhale. It struggles harder, which only forces it to try to breathe again, leading to a further tightening of the coils.

In precisely the same manner does government—once it is allowed to escape from the cage of a written Constitution that once allowed it to fund and do only a specific *limited* number of things—coil around us, watching for any crisis or problem as an opportunity to create a new "program," hire new "agents," institute "reforms."

It may be patient, but it never backs off. Someday, it knows, it will have finally grown large enough for the big meal it has in mind. Propose reducing a tax and you'll be aggressively asked, "How are we going to pay for that?" What this really means is, "How are we going to raise the same amount of revenue elsewhere, since government can never be allowed to grow smaller, only bigger?"

Meantime, each complaint that "there ought to be a law" is welcomed by our cheerful helpers in government with the same contented smile the giant snake displays each time it feels its victim try to breathe.

Nor can there be any doubt about the final result.

Why This Book Seems So Strange

There be ideas here.

You don't have to embrace them all. In this day and age, compared to the products for which most publishers are willing to kill

15

an acre of trees, having any ideas at all is a pretty daring example of product differentiation.

We are taught to hide our ideas now, for a similar reason that earlier generations were taught to hide every inch of their bare flesh below the neck, every hint of their sexuality.

Sex is a powerful force. Unbridled, it can evoke violent passions. Society seeks to wall off the sex drive. This makes sense, up to a point: The pathological effects of too much sexual repression hardly need any repetition here.

Raw and naked ideas have a similar power to shock, to infatuate, to explode the decadent social conventions with which generations of frightened, mincing, little perverts have tried to embalm and mummify and neuter their power. Like the harpooned whale, the idea is more powerful than we are; we're not sure where it will take us. Just as the sexually repressed—taught to feel shame rather than exultation at the contemplation of their bodies—are afraid to let go and enjoy the exhilaration of carnality even when it's appropriate, so is the power of a big naked idea too bright and frightening a thing to contemplate for those who cannot come to it honest and unafraid, who instead cower in fear that its radiance will expose them for the twisted self-hating frauds that they are.

Today, our society suffers from idea repression. Try to express one bold, pure, unadulterated thought and everyone around you—especially those who wish to help you—will rush to point out, "Oh, but of course you don't mean to go that far. You were only exaggerating for effect. Obviously, everything is relative. Every idea has to be adjusted, modified, blunted, pared down, and adapted to meet current conditions. Oh yes. Of course, we all realize that. In fact, if you'll stop to think about it, you'll realize that wasn't a new idea you had at all. Upon further examination, it's only a minor variant on the previously established idea, isn't it?"

What is new is not the approach, but the thing being denied. Not too many years ago, young gentlemen were taught that, should

16

they slip on the ice in a crowd of Christmas shoppers and catch themselves by unwittingly grabbing at the bosom of some strange woman in front of them, the appropriate thing to say was, "Oh, I'm sorry to have grabbed your elbow, madam, but I slipped on the ice." Both parties were thus allowed to avoid confronting an unthinkable event.

Today, you're free to gyrate your hooters in public. But please, keep those ideas tightly wrapped.

"But I hear new ideas all the time," many will insist. "Turn on the all-news television channels and there are people there expressing new ideas about 22 hours a day. It's *dizzying*, there are so many ideas!"

No. How to make low-calorie snacks for the kids out of Shredded Wheat and Velveeta is not the kind of "idea" I'm talking about, nor are all the shouted urgent viewpoints on whether the latest congressman to get caught with his zipper down will be forced to resign.

Here are a few *ideas*:

1) Juries have the right, the power, and the duty to acquit a defendant, regardless of the evidence, if they judge the law under which the defendant is charged to be unconstitutional, or otherwise repugnant to their conscience.

The Constitution guarantees all defendants in criminal matters a trial by a randomly selected jury. Any government judge or prosecutor who participates in voir dire "stacking" of a jury—removing any juror who knows about this crucial historical right and duty simply because that juror refuses to agree in advance not to exercise it—thus violates his or her oath to protect and defend the Constitution. This is a crime, punishable as treason. Just as Alfred the Great hanged judges who replaced obstinate jurors with others more willing to convict, so should our judges today face the death penalty for this same betrayal of their sacred trust.

2) Not only is the "War on Drugs" hopeless and counterproductive, not only does it afford would-be fascists at all levels of government unprecedented opportunities to trample our Constitution and Bill of Rights, not only does it represent an interference, banned by the Ninth Amendment, into consensual commerce and medical liberty, but it also amounts to an official government "establishment of religion" (Puritanism) in blatant violation of the *First* Amendment.

The very first chapter of the book of *Genesis* reports that God gave man every flower and seed-bearing herb and tree for his use. At the same time the Creator gave us the freedom to decide whether and how to use the medicinal herbs (including those that can alter our consciousness or provide a religious experience). He also made us responsible to suffer the (natural) consequences if we make foolish decisions about the use of these plants. Any government with the arrogance to think it can take away both our freedom to make such decisions and our responsibility to live with the consequences—answering for those consequences before that Higher Power, not their jumped-up tribunals—is insufferable.

This does not mean that, "Marijuana should be available by prescription." It means that morphine sulfate should be available in five-pound bags at the supermarket for a couple of bucks, like sugar ... but probably in a different aisle, to avoid confusion.

3) Free men and women have a God-given individual right to bear arms of a sort that can be used to defend their homes, property, and families against bandits, thieves, assailants, and the armies of tyrants. Today, such arms specifically include shaped-charge anti-tank missiles, shoulder-launched heat-seeking anti-aircraft missiles, large mortars, 57mm recoilless rifles, and belt-fed machine guns. Law-abiding citizens must be allowed to buy such weapons (and a thousand rounds of ammo) over the counter for cash from any store that wishes to sell them, without having to "show ID." Any government agent who attempts to turn this right

into a "conditional privilege" by asking us to "apply for a permit" thus violates his or her oath to protect and defend the Constitution. This is a crime, punishable as treason.

4) No government has any right to involve itself in education, which is a sacred right and prerogative of parents—though said parents are of course free to voluntarily hire others to help educate their children. Anyone who has ever voted for or enforced a law that makes attendance "mandatory" at a government youth propaganda camp has committed the crime of conspiracy to execute a kidnapping, which is punishable as a felony.

I didn't originate these ideas. Most of them have been around for at least 300 years.

Assuming they can refrain from jumping in with the aforementioned, "Oh, but of course you don't mean to go that far. I'm sure what you really mean is that we should *study* some modest reform of our drug laws blah blah blah," most Americans would doubtless describe the ideas above as radical.

They are. "Radical" comes from the Latin stem for "root." To return to these ideas—which would not have seemed at all foreign to folks like Jefferson, Washington, and Franklin, or even Madison and Hamilton—would be to go to the root of the problems with our modern society, which today is almost terminally ill.

Why do ideas so broad and unblemished appear so strange to us? Why is our "public debate" now as constrained as the practice speech-making of a high-school student council debating what color of crepe paper to use in decorating the gym for the fall dance?

Why do we limit *ourselves* to suggesting a few cosmetic changes around the edges? Is it some deep-seated sense of guilt, a belief that we don't really deserve the relative peace and prosperity we now enjoy, that if we draw too much attention to ourselves some anonymous celestial agent will suddenly widen his eyes and announce: "Wait a minute, Pilgrim, you don't belong here on the planet of peace and plenty. You're supposed to be on the planet of endless slavery, quagmires, and disease! And you've been here *how* long? Man, wait till the Boss hears about this screw-up!"

When did radical become a term of disapproval? If you have a thorn bush and you'd rather have an apple tree, the cosmetic approach is to get some string and tie a bunch of ripe apples on the thorn bush, so it looks like an apple tree.

Of course, a week later all the rotted apples will fall off. But that only shows you haven't hired enough trained specialists, and given them a large enough budget, to keep hanging apples on the thorn bush.

Today, such a scheme would be described as "sensible moderate reform, by working within the existing system."

If I propose to simply dig up the thorn bush by the roots, throw it away, and plant a real apple tree where it stood, that is judged radical. It's an "unrealistic, childish, and perhaps even mentally aberrant refusal to acknowledge reality and work within the existing system."

I said our society is ill. I mean that the people can find no satisfaction. They work hard, but the fruits of their labors are seized from their mouths. The poor do not thank them for their charity, but instead shout and picket in front of the Capitol, insisting that the government loot them more handouts from our paychecks, in a manner that conveys no warmth or grace to the soul of either the recipient or the "donor"—who is held down, mewing piteously, to be shorn once again.

We crave truth, and our masters patiently explain that their euphemisms, misdirections, and evasions are actually a superior *form* of truth. It sounds good while they're talking, but later we can't remember why it seemed so convincing or why we couldn't think of what to ask next. It never occurs to us to blame the "nice" high-school teachers who were supposed to teach us how to test or refute a logical proof, but who instead filled our time with "classroom projects" involving the recycling of different colored bottles, while cutting pictures of toucans out of magazines to demonstrate our empathy for the plight of the rainforest.

We are told to "pursue happiness" by using what wealth we are allowed to retain to buy fancier televisions, to drive fancier cars, to take ever more exotic vacations—on credit.

Is this satisfying? In fact, as with refined cocaine or casual sex or almost any other fast-acting drug, most of the pleasure lies in the anticipation. The experience itself is almost always a disappointment, leaving us either less happy than when we began, or else compulsively trying again and again to recreate the pleasure of "the first time," like a caged animal humping its treadmill.

What is satisfying is to return to your house after a hard day of work, justified. To know that what you have earned or made with your own hands no one can take away, because you own it free and clear, not merely "rent" it from its true owner, the government, which can take it away any time the tax collectors judge you have not paid "enough." To know that you are free to gradually accrue a reliable store of wealth, which you will be free to turn over to your children or grandchildren, so that they will have some protection against unforeseen adversity.

What is satisfying is to know that you've built a solid family, that your children have not been propagandized every day for years to sneer at the values you hold true, to dismiss you as a troglodyte, even to pick up the phone and turn you in to the government as a "potential child abuser" if you own guns or engage in unorthodox medical practices or dare to discipline them—till you live in fear of your own children, just as adults spoke in whispers in Germany in the 1930s lest the strutting Hitler Youth, who had once been their own children, "turn them in."

Americans keep droning their little propaganda slogans they learned in government school that this is a "free country."

Really? With the highest incarceration rate in the world? With

21

the highest tax collections in the world?

When you see a police car pull up behind you on the highway, knowing the officer is "running your number" to learn more about you than you'd ever tell your next-door neighbor, do you feel happy and free? Or do you feel dirty, guilty, and frightened?

Is that a nice feeling? What have you done that you deserve to be made to feel that way?

A free country? John Hay once observed, "The evils of tyranny are rarely seen but by him who resists it." Of course, you're "free" to buy a six-pack and watch the game on TV. To go watch another car-chase movie where the wisecracking, straight-shooting, government agents are always the good guys.

But are you free to attend a non-traditional church whose sacrament is peyote? Receive a religious vision to stockpile food and arms and ammunition against a coming flood? Pull your children out of the mandatory government youth propaganda camps and school them at home? Adopt any non-traditional style of family life?

"Oh, I wish you'd stop harping on Waco and Ruby Ridge," I hear more and more now. But those were televised lessons provided by our masters, to demonstrate to us what happens to folks who get the wrong idea about what they're still "free" to do in this "free country."

Where did we go wrong? Anywhere we trusted a "government expert" who told us he or she knew better than our parents, our family, our instincts born of 100,000 years and grafted into our genes. The first time we put a crying child on a bus to the mandatory government school, hiding our own tears because we were told it was for the best, that we must instruct our child it's "time to act grown-up now." The first time we ignored our child's screaming because, "Everyone has to get their DPT shots." The first time we allowed some crass politician in a black robe to tell us what to do in a jury room. The first time a parent did what he'd been told, calling the police and turning in his own son for smoking hemp, an herb far less dangerous or addictive than tobacco, with the result that the son went to prison to be gang-raped and given AIDS, while the family was destroyed.

Everything they told you was a lie.

But the truth shall set you free.

The Collectivist History of the United States

W.D., from Georgia Tech in Atlanta, writes:

In the course of a dinner table discussion with my grandfather about my libertarian views, he asked me if I knew about the period of the "robber barons" in the late 1800s, when "big business had more power in this country than the government did," and whether government regulation and control of industry weren't necessary to prevent that from happening again.

When I got home, I pulled out the *Pocket History of the U.S.* I'd bought a few months before, but never got around to reading.

I found its 22-page chapter on "The Rise of Big Business" and read about the transition from the corporation to the pool and then to the trust, about the Standard Oil Company, "the greatest monopoly in the country," about the effect of trusts on the average man's community, how "local industry dried up, factories went out of business or were absorbed, and neighbors who worked not for themselves but for distant corporations were exposed to the vicissitudes of policy over which they had no control."

23

It certainly came out sounding pretty dire. What is the libertarian answer to this type of situation? What can I tell my grandfather? ... I might guess that it was government's intrusion or regulation that allowed this situation to develop, but according to the *Pocket History* there wasn't much regulation:

"Government authorities took a complacent attitude toward land grabbing, timber cutting, cattle grazing on the public domain; numerous fortunes were founded on the exploitation of the property of the nation."

Is the *Pocket History's* depiction of the time period fair, or biased?

Well, W.D., The "robber baron" myth is one of the most pervasive in the fantastic socialist version of our history still being shamelessly promulgated in our government schools.

Far from taking a "complacent attitude," government caused enormous problems starting as far back as the 1840s. For example, the federals voted subsidies to monopoly enterprises like the grossly inefficient steamships of Edward K. Collins, which failed *despite* their subsidies in open competition with real entrepreneurs like Cornelius Vanderbilt. Later, having learned nothing from that failure, they supported the political hucksters who raced to build shoddy rail lines on ill-prepared ground, mainly to capture per-mile federal subsidies (usually in the form of checkerboarded 640-acre sections of free land)—lines so ill-planned they mostly went bankrupt as soon as free-market competition arrived.

"Free of regulation"? The Interstate Commerce Commission was set up to regulate the railroads immediately after the Civil War. It quickly became a captive of the major players in the industry supposedly to be "regulated," and was thus far more effective in protecting the big boys from upstart competitors than anything else. This pattern of federal regulation has been repeated

24

over and over again ever since.

Note the underlying assumption in young W.D.'s *Pocket History*, that wealth and power concentrated in the hands of a few entrepreneurs is bad, whereas concentration of vast billions and monopolistic power in the hands of government agencies like the public schools—or even the EPA—is wise and beneficent.

Yet neither the Mellons, nor the Fords, nor Andrew Carnegie, nor Jim Hill ever had the power to draft a single boy into the Army and send him to his death in France, nor to outlaw a competitor the way Congress has outlawed non-Federal Reserve banks and non-allopathic doctors, nor to force a consumer to buy a single piece of their merchandise on pain of prison, the way we're forced to "purchase" government programs.

Standard Oil, at the height of its "monopoly," never controlled more than 25 percent of the market.

Also note tell-tale phrases such as "the property of the nation," "land-grabbing," and "the public domain." Not until our history started to be rewritten during the so-called Progressive Era (circa 1912) were such collectivist phrases seen. Prior to that—and again today, everywhere but in Washington—the unsettled lands were always presumed to belong to the first settler who could make a living off them, not to "the government acting on behalf of the social collectivity," the kind of phrase the intellectual Trotsky used to dream up to justify the raw land grabs of his buddy Lenin, before they had that little falling-out.

Why were the family fortunes built on "land-grabbing" in the late nineteenth century in the West any more evil than the family fortunes built on "land-grabbing" in the 1600s, 1700s, and early 1800s in Massachusetts, New York, Georgia, and Illinois? Why wasn't that "the exploitation of the property of the nation"? Why aren't we taught that the period 1781-1846 was the era of the greedy and evil "robber agriculturalists"?

What does "the property of the nation" mean, anyway? How

does that differ from the now-discredited notion of who owned the land in the Soviet Union?

• • •

Meantime, what about the evils of "the distant corporation"?

In his *Pocket History of the U.S.*, remember, W.D. read about the effect of trusts on the average man's community, how "local industry dried up, factories went out of business or were absorbed, and neighbors who worked not for themselves but for distant corporations were exposed to the vicissitudes of policy over which they had no control."

Hmm. "Factories went out of business or were absorbed." But isn't the charge against the "robber barons" that they got rich by *building* nasty factories? Henry Ford paid unheard-of high wages because he figured out ways to increase the value of the time of each worker, hundreds of times beyond what their fathers could have accomplished in a blacksmith's shop—the technology the "Progressives" would apparently like to send us all back to.

Do you have any idea what your car would cost if it were hand-made by blacksmiths—by "neighbors working for themselves instead of some distant corporation"? Any idea what you'd pay for a spare part? Or how long you'd wait while your blacksmith tried to hammer it into just the right shape to fit into your one-of-a-kind transmission?

If millions of new jobs were being created, such that half the population of Europe was anxious to sleep in steerage to get here, what does it mean to whimper that "factories went out of business or were absorbed"? That some blacksmith who used to make nails by hand at $1 a bucketful lost his job when the Scrantons figured out how to build a machine that would produce them for five cents a barrel?

26

Oh, boo-hoo. I'm so sorry I bought a house that I could afford because of the mass production of nails and two-by-fours. I promise not to buy another house that isn't built with lumber hand-hewn and nails hand-forged by worthy local carpenters and blacksmiths, even though today's $80,000 house would thus cost me something over $2 million.

What the "greed" of the robber barons made possible was an unprecedented concentration of wealth to fund research labs and develop prototypes and assemble the huge machine tools that no lonely local craftsman could ever have financed—the tools that built our modern world.

W.D. might ask his granddad if he'd really like to go back to those wonderful days when neighbors worked for themselves in muddy hamlets without any sewage disposal except the cesspit out back. Would he prefer simpler times when the average lifespan was 45 and we suffered 20 percent infant mortality from diseases that we shrug off nowadays with a couple of penicillin pills—marketed by huge and distant pharmaceutical corporations?

The cry of the "trust busters" was always that the robber barons were practicing concentration in hopes of eventually ripping off the public by raising prices. But John D. Rockefeller's efficiencies drove the price of kerosene down from 26 cents a gallon in 1870 to eight cents a gallon in 1880. He kept driving down the price all his life, and he lived to be 98.

Rockefeller, of course, knew that he had to get prices down to defeat the competition of new oil from the Russian fields in the Crimea and the Caucasus. He then passed on those savings through lower prices, improving the standard of living of the entire world.

Yet today, one of the recommended classroom exercises in our new national "America 2000 education standards" is a "mock classroom trial of John D. Rockefeller" for organizing the Standard Oil trust "against the best interests" of the American people.

Has the industrial revolution really turned out so badly? I

27

don't sweat in a stinking mill, do you? Here I sit, tapping away on a little electronic keyboard designed and built by a "distant corporation," which greedily puts at my fingertips for a few hundred dollars a technology that would have cost millions just 40 years ago, that never would have been invented at all without five generations of robber barons.

Young W.D. needs to buy his granddad a slim volume called *The Myth of the Robber Barons*, by Burton Folsom (see "Appendix II"), *Capitalism and the Historians*, edited by F.A. Hayek, is a second choice.

Anyway, we now have thousands of times more regulation than we did in 1912. So, does granddad think everything is finally OK? Can the legislators all go home? Or are they, in fact, proposing even more new business-crippling regulations this year than they did last year?

My goodness, why? If they've had 84 years to pass all the regulations they could think of, I would think by now their control of the greedy businessman would be fine-tuned about to perfection.

I wonder what granddad thinks of von Mises' law—that every government intervention causes new and unforeseen problems, which lead to calls for *more* government regulation, et cetera, ad infinitum?

The War of 1912

T.C. writes in from Seoul with an inquiry about my repeated call for the repeal of every law enacted since December of 1912.

"How did you select 1912 as the date for which all necessary laws had been enacted?"

R.M. in Colorado expands the inquiry: "What is 'magic' about

28

the year 1912? Behold says 1862, some groups say 1866/1871, and others say 1933/1938. This is entirely new to me, and I would like to hear whatever you have that makes 1912 important."

I responded:

Yes, the reign of the tyrant Lincoln really started the destruction of the Founders' guarantee of a "weak limited" federal government. Let's talk about suspending habeas corpus, jailing Chicago newspaper editors for criticizing the president's war policies, introducing an unconstitutional income tax and equally unconstitutional military conscription—not to mention shelling civilian populations, burning American cities to the ground, and generally using murderous force of previously unimagined proportions to conquer by the sword states that had never been warned their admission into the union was irrevocable.

Imagine paying $3 to tour the Halloween House of Horrors at the state fairgrounds, only to be chained up and kept as a slave inside that darkened charnel house for the rest of your life, your screams for mercy being used to entertain each successive year's crowd, told, "Gee, we can tell from your ticket that you voluntarily paid to get in, but we can't seem to find anything written down here that says you're free to ever leave."

Going back to the 1860s, however, leaves room for hysterics to cry that we're looking to reverse the liberation of black folks and return to slavery times—patently absurd, but why invite such a red herring?

Although the federal income-tax amendment (the Sixteenth) was proposed by Congress in 1909, it was declared ratified (possibly with some degree of fraud, though I think that argument is profitless) in February 1913, just as Professor Wilson and the "Progressives" were being sworn into office after their victory in 1912.

Despite the fact Prof. Wilson did not receive the majority of the vote (the Republican vote of 7.6 million was split between

29

Bull Moose Teddy Roosevelt and incumbent William Howard Taft, while Wilson drew only 6.3 million), the Democrats ignored their lack of a "mandate" and promptly rushed in the graduated income tax—a main tenet of the 1912 *Socialist* platform—which of course has provided expanded funding for every federal regulatory and police agency we have come to know and hate ever since.

The federal flood after this initial dam failure of 1912 was rapid. The first federal regulation of drugs and narcotics came quickly in 1914, after outrageously racist testimony before Congress, in which local sheriffs were allowed to present unchallenged anecdotal "evidence" that blacks, Mexicans, and "Chinese" were widely known to take on the strength of 10 men, and to assault and deflower white women in the streets, upon consumption of cocaine, marijuana, and opium, respectively.

Direct popular election of U.S. senators was rushed through between 1912 and 1913, turning them into nothing more than senior congressmen out grubbing for popular votes—destroying the indirect but vital veto power that the state legislatures had held over enactments by the populist House of Representatives.

Nationalization of virtually the entire economy got an enormous boost when Wilson promptly broke his re-election promise and took the nation into World War I, buying with doughboys' lives the seat he wanted at the peace table—the long-awaited entrée for the American "elite" into the first line of world powers.

Oh, the Progressives were ambitious! With all that stick-in-the-mud stuff about "limited federal powers" finally swept away, suddenly their campaign to ban alcohol—to boost the nation's hygiene and productivity by banishing the Demon Rum—no longer had to proceed county by county and state by frustrating state. No, there would be no more "driving across the line into the wet county" once alcohol Prohibition became the law nationwide in 1919.

That police-state failure was repealed in 1933, of course. But few now remember that the National Firearms Act of 1934 was justified by the spectacle of bootleggers shooting up the streets of Chicago and Kansas City with their Tommy guns during the late 1920s.

How odd, to ban a behavior the year *after* you've eliminated its root cause. Gangsterism was plummeting in 1934, despite the Depression. And of course, said law had no impact on Clyde Barrow's ability to haul around a sawed-off Browning Automatic Rifle. It only makes it mighty difficult and expensive for law-abiding folks like you or me to buy a B.A.R—John Browning's classic "militia weapon" of the 20th century, too nasty and "modern" a native engineering masterpiece for anyone but cops and rich hobbyists to be trusted with, as it now celebrates its 80th birthday.

Is it one of history's little ironies—or the result of something more closely resembling a conspiracy—that in their rush to *suppress* Reds, anarchists, and racial minorities who "didn't know their place," the table-pounders of 1912-1914 handed us our current collectivist welfare-police state? I leave that question for another day.

• • •

My response to T.C. in Seoul, in turn, brought two addenda. Novelist L. Neil Smith wrote from Colorado:

"Vin—You forgot the 1913 Federal Reserve Act, arranged at the infamous Jekyll Island meeting (some say 'conspiracy'). When I was looking for the pivotal event around which to drape [the 1980 novel] *The Probability Broach*, several people suggested changing history by having somebody drop a biplane load of dynamite on that meeting."

From Phoenix, long-time Libertarian political strategist

George O'Brien added:

"Another point about 1912 and Wilson: WW I brought the first vestiges of central economic planning (what is now called 'industrial policy') to America.

"In the short 18 months the U.S. was in the war, the federal government forced all the railroads to operate as if they were one big railroad. Competition between industrial firms was limited, if not eliminated, and there were huge subsidies to specified businesses.

"This program of cartel mercantilism was far more extensive than anything the U.S. had ever seen before. All of a sudden, the big businesses that were being ravaged by competition could relax. Their tiny competitors were crushed for the sake of efficiency and their profits guaranteed.

"Warren G. Harding's return to 'normalcy' in the early 1920s was a big letdown to the business leaders who imagined they had found heaven. All that was needed to bring back the heady days of WW I was another crisis and they could expand industrial policy anew. In October of 1929, they got their chance."

Thanks for the help, chums. It turns out I knew more than I could even remember!

Poisoned By The Lie

I was browsing the Autumn 1994 edition of *Policy Review*, the quarterly magazine of the Heritage Foundation (see "Appendix II"), when I stumbled across a piece called "Russia's Spiritual Wilderness," by German author Barbara von der Heydt.

Von der Heydt does an excellent job explaining why what passes for a free market has been unable to bring prosperity to Russia.

"Confiscatory tax rates have not only stunted entrepreneurial impulses," she writes, "they serve as a serious inducement to tax evasion and collusion with the mafia. Businesses pay at least 55 percent of net income, and can incur rates as high as 120 percent. ... A contract for mafia protection is cheaper than counting on corrupt police or the choked courts for justice. ... "

(Interestingly, financial writer and analyst Doug Casey, editor of the *International Speculator* newsletter, sees things exactly the same way: "Putting aside arbitrary legal distinctions, the [Russian] government and the mafia are the same in that they use force to extract revenue from society; they're different in that there's actually a better exchange with the mafia.")

This is a recipe not for the kind of healthy economic growth seen in the United States through 1912, but rather for the perpetual poverty of cultures where it's considered better to destroy wealth than to expose it to seizure—places like Sicily.

Nor can the 18th century American model be easily exported to such a place. Again, Ms. von der Heydt: "As Russell Kirk eloquently explained in 'The Roots of American Order,' the concepts of democracy from Greece, of civic virtue from Rome, and redemption and higher law embodied in Judeo-Christian teaching merged with Anglo-Saxon common law, property rights, and a market economy." The combination gave birth to American notions of democracy and economic freedom.

"Edmund Burke observed that those who are not governed from within must be governed from without. No laws can create good citizens or a good society. ... It was always understood by the American Founding Fathers that the moral law written in the heart and the code of law written by a nation must be in harmony with a higher law. ..."

In Russia, on the other hand, the very souls of the people have been poisoned by 70 years of what Alexander Solzhenitsyn calls "the culture of the lie." Out in the provinces in Prague, Vaclav

Havel said in 1990, "We have become morally ill because we have become accustomed to saying one thing and thinking another," a condition that George Weigel called "moral schizophrenia."

The result? Valery Orlov, deputy director of the Russian prison system, tells von der Heydt that people who have never faced the consequences of their own decisions retain no inner compass. Now that the strong state structure is gone, "there's a moral vacuum" that crowds Russian detention facilities with more than a million prisoners. There were 25,000 assassinations and a half-million thefts in Moscow last year—car thefts are up to 250 per day and juvenile crime is up 300 percent.

"Envy is common," von der Heydt reports. "There is a widespread belief that wealth can only be accumulated at the expense of another, an impression sadly confirmed by the success of the most rapacious and least scrupulous. Many people throughout the former communist empire yearn for the old security of the 'nanny state.'"

What does this sound like? With the exception of parts of the rural West and South, where 19th century American values of honesty, self-reliance, and neighborliness still thrive, it sounds a lot to me like Bill Clinton's America, where hypocritical drug laws, along with taxes and regulatory restrictions on even legal start-up businesses, make gangsters the only symbols of capitalism visible to inner-city youth, while the president himself preaches envy of those "greedy" enough to save, invest, and create jobs.

"Moral schizophrenia"? We all know the "War on Drugs" is allowing the federal government to shred the Constitution to confetti without preventing a single junkie from getting high. Yet let motor-mouth Joycelyn Elders state this obvious fact, and the dedicated cocaine Hoovers in the White House (25 percent of White House staff have permanent drug-test waivers) cover their ears and run about like creatures from Alice in Wonderland, shrieking "Horrible! Horrible! Stop her from saying such things! Politically

34

unclean!"

Why this fear of the truth? Because Washington rules by a lie. Bureaucrats know that once plain speaking gets started, it's hard to stop.

Ernie Hancock and others of the Arizona Libertarian Party have succeeded in pressuring the government schools there to allow Libertarians into the schools one day a year, providing them equal time with the Republicrats and Demopublicans to attempt to explain to young "social studies" classes how the parties differ. Ernie and his pals take the kids through the kind of simple moral discourse they've likely never heard before:

"What do we call someone who robs from the rich to give to the poor?"

"A thief?"

"That's right. And what if 60 percent of the people vote that it's OK for him to take our money? What do we call him then?"

"A thief?" the children always answer.

"That's right. And what do we call an agent of the government who uses an income tax to steal from the rich and give to the poor?"

"A thief."

From the mouths of babes.

It's hard to blame the Russians for failing to understand and adopt principles they never knew. How much sadder for the nation that invented them to throw away such a freedom- and wealth-producing legacy in a single generation.

Losing Our Way

Disguised by day as an editorial writer at a major metropolitan newspaper, I have the opportunity every other fall to sit down and help interview several dozen incumbent and would-be state lawmakers.

I first noticed the curious lack of fire in the 1996 crop of candidates, though it got no better in '98. Right wrongs? Comfort the afflicted? With droning consistency we heard: "Oh, probably just continue on the way things are going ... one legislator can't have that big an impact ... you're lucky to be able to shift a budget item by as much as two percent ... I'm not familiar with those issues because they didn't come before my committee ... I'd have to study that."

Even the Republican incumbents—supposedly such radical ax-wielders—mostly declined to name a single state program they'd cut or kill, hesitant to offend the remotest outpost of the powerful unionized bureaucracy.

But what really proved revealing was to ask the candidates a question any 10th grader ought to be able to answer: "What is the purpose of government?"

"Government has a role to take care of people who can't take care of themselves," responded a prominent Republican running for the state Senate.

"It's there to establish policies for assistance to communities when the resources or programs are not available. We have a responsibility to help make people's lives better," explained one prominent Democrat. (Not only did this pretty schoolmarm and former union chief blame all the current problems in our government schools on the parents, she even had a solution: "Why don't we look at some responsible training for parenting?")

"To satisfy the living standards of the American people," said another schoolteacher.

"Government is there to serve the people, to see tax money is spent in the right ways," responded a Republican incumbent, who went on to explain that police officers supplementing their departmental budgets by seizing the houses and planes of suspects before they're convicted of any crime is "OK, if they're serving a function. We should have a committee come in and study that."

(We endorsed this incumbent's opponent. It worked. The incumbent lost.)

Another incumbent schoolteacher-lawmaker perhaps best summarized the bureaucratic role most of our modern delegates see for themselves: "It [government] provides a variety of services: police, fire protection, education," he explained. "At the state level, the state administers the federal programs, like welfare and education."

Does no one recall how Tom Jefferson warned that we would know we had descended into Bonapartist tyranny if ever our once-sovereign states (originally 13, now 50) were reduced to the role of mere "administrative jurisdictions" for the central authority, "like the Departments of France"?

In fairness, my question about the purpose of government seemed to catch most candidates off guard. Many appeared to be struck speechless for a time, darting their eyes from side to side, or opening and closing their mouths in dumb puzzlement like spiny fish hauled suddenly to the surface from the dark and silent depths.

Many readers—educated in the same government schools— may even wonder what's wrong with the above replies. Surely it's true that our state legislators spend most of their time deciding how tax revenues shall be "fairly" divided to provide "services otherwise unavailable," isn't it?

Sure. It's also true that soldiers, for the most part, shine boots, march around in squares, and perform equipment maintenance. But I hope that if someone were to ask the Joint Chiefs to define the purpose of the Armed Forces, they would refer not to spit-shines and tautly made bunks, but rather to defending the Republic from invasion. To lose sight of the *purpose* is to lose all.

The purpose of government on this continent, the Declaration of Independence reminds us, is different from the purpose of many a European or Third World satrapy, which may well be to

37

divide up the tax loot according to some proto-feudal hierarchy of special interests who prop up the throne.

Not so long ago, our delegates still realized their main role was not placing a measured dollop of succor into the mouth of each whining constituency, but rather guarding our liberties against the assaults of the insatiable petty tyrants of the bureaucracy, who can always be counted on to cloak their power-grabs in pious mewlings about the widows and orphans.

The Declaration reminds us that governments are "instituted among men" for the sole purpose of "securing the unalienable rights" with which men are "endowed by their Creator," rights which include but are not limited to "Life, Liberty, and the Pursuit of Happiness" ... including the right to private property and the vital right to keep and bear arms.

This is the standard against which each proposed government enactment should be measured—in Washington City or Carson City, in Austin or Lansing—not merely whether it will please a majority of the suppliants who have traveled to the capital to bow and scrape and present their offerings at court.

Let the Impeachments Begin

Leaders of 76 national, state, and local bar associations issued a joint letter to House Speaker Newt Gingrich April 6, 1997, urging the Speaker to resist any efforts to impeach federal judges over disagreements with their rulings.

The lawyers' groups wrote: "The genius of the American system of government is the careful balance created by the Founders between the three branches of government. Moving to impeach judges for individual decisions—a kind of legislative referendum on judicial decision-making—threatens to destroy this delicately crafted balance."

The bar associations' letter apparently comes in response to a call the month before from House Majority Whip Tom DeLay, R-Texas, that Congress should indeed impeach federal judges whose rulings are "particularly egregious."

It's a striking image: a star chamber assembly-line for the removal of judges, systematically defrocking the ministers of the bench for making up the law as they go along.

Let's get concerned when they've dismissed the first 50 or so—with no pensions.

More interesting is this oft-repeated assertion that the "delicate balance of powers" is now operating as intended by the Founders.

How absurd.

Mightier than any federal authority, in the scheme of the Founders, were the sovereign state legislatures, empowered to appoint U.S. senators to veto any federal attempt to assume coercive powers over the states beyond those specified in the 431 words of Article I Section 8 of the Constitution.

That "check and balance" went a-glimmering in 1913, of course. Shall we now count the number of things our state legislatures need federal permission to undertake? Or alternatively, the number of things on which they are required to spend looted tax money, by federal mandate?

But even above the states were the people, authorized by the Second Amendment to keep their arms, not for "sporting use," but as a specific guarantee that any potential federal tyrant would always face the prospect of a populace too well-armed to tolerate any usurpation of our liberties.

Beyond that, the people were granted the final veto over any attempt by government to deprive a fellow citizen of his life or liberty, when the Sixth Amendment guaranteed that "in all criminal prosecutions," the defendant could be convicted only by unanimous vote of an "impartial jury," randomly selected from the local populace.

Does anyone still believe our federal officials have no intention of disarming citizens who might resist federal tyranny? How many of the 20,000 gun-control laws enacted in the past 65 years have been tossed out by these proud courts? How many armed militiamen have been summarily set free on a plain reading of the Second Amendment?

Are we still better armed than the federals—or do we now cower in fear of the knock on the door by the ATF, the DEA, the FDA, the FBI, the USFS, the BLM, the IRS?

How many federal agents who swarmed out to murder armed but peaceful citizens at Ruby Ridge and Waco have been indicted and tried for those crimes, by these attorneys and judges who now blubber so earnestly about the "delicately crafted" balance of powers?

Under current Supreme Court rulings, do defendants still get their guaranteed jury trial "in *all* criminal prosecutions"?

When we now accept, as routine, weeks of careful pre-screening of prospective jurors (witness the Oklahoma City bombing case) to make sure all will agree in advance to employ the death penalty, does this encourage jurors to enter the jury box with open minds, and under a "presumption of innocence"?

Can a jury still be said to be a "random and impartial" cross-section of the community, when anyone honest enough to admit he despises federal gun controls, or the federal tax system, or the government murders at Waco, is summarily dismissed; when the panel is carefully stacked to contain only those who will swear in advance an oath of obedience to the federal judge, to "accept and enforce the law as I give it to you"—when they're sifted so fine that they must even explain the meaning of the bumperstickers on their cars?

Ah, this proud federal judiciary. How long has it been since they performed their most basic Constitutional duty, ruling that *any* expansion of the federal welfare/police state exceeds Constitutional authority—that *any* gang of federal bureaucrats must be immediately disbanded and turned out to fend for themselves? Sixty years? How wonderful, that the federal government could grow to 20 times its previous size, without ever assuming a single power not specified in the 431 little words of Article I Section 8—that section of the Constitution that alone delineates and thus sharply limits the Powers of Congress.

As impeachment is the only means by which a judge can be held accountable, would it really be such a bad thing if a few hundred ambitious lawyers were thus called down from their high seats, put under a hot light, and asked to explain how their rulings to date reflect the sacred oath they all took to protect and defend our inconvenient Constitution?

We'd just be making up for lost time.

Driving Them to Drugs

The only people who complain about Byzantine tax laws and excessive business regulation—according to the common wisdom—are greedy rich Republicans out to hoard even more of their ill-gotten gains.

What a sad rebuttal to find in the March/April 1996 edition of *American Enterprise* magazine a recounting of the testimony before the National Commission on Economic Growth and Tax Reform of Steve Mariotti, who runs a non-profit program teaching entrepreneurial skills to inner-city youth around the country, in hopes they'll someday start their own legitimate small businesses:

"We put special emphasis on making the business legal," Mariotti testified, "and we try to familiarize our students with basic federal tax forms, stressing the importance of complying with all applicable taxes. ...

"However, the number-one obstacle to potential economic development of our low-income communities is the present tax code, which is so complex and confusing we could spend virtually all of our 80-hour entrepreneurship program teaching tax compliance.

"A related and equally troublesome problem is the morass of small-business licensing regulations and permits that engulfs anyone trying to start an honest business on a shoestring—especially in our large cities.

"The result is that our students often feel alienated, intimidated, and hopeless," Mr. Mariotti explained to the commission members. "They can see very clearly that for people who already have money, confusing paperwork and regulations are no problem. They hire accountants and lawyers to deal with them.

"But for an inner-city resident without the luxury of spare cash, three days lost in dealing with a bureaucracy or having to pay a seemingly modest fee of, say, $300 to a CPA, can make the difference between cutting through red tape or buying groceries for the week. ...

"These same young people can see that an illegal business, drugs first and foremost, provides quick cash and no paperwork at all. The temptation is great to drop out into the underground economy. ... In short, the tax code and other small-business regulations basically have the counterproductive effect of reducing the tax base instead of increasing it."

Sniveliberals often whine: "But if we cut welfare, what will the people dooooo? How do you expect them to feed their chillllldren?"

Although skipping meals in freedom is indeed infinitely preferable to slavery on a full stomach, that answer will hardly win over many of these "compassionate" government-school ruminants to the cause of liberty. It may be far better to acknowledge that eliminating all government handouts, cold turkey, will indeed do some harm, unless we're careful to eliminate government restrictions on entrepreneurship and self-employment without a stinking license, at the same time.

Of course, it should be noted that this really leaves us debating the wrong question: merely to ask whether or not we should stop funding the current welfare state blithely assumes the premise that we can go on this way indefinitely.

In fact, our federal and many of our state governments will be effectively bankrupt within the decade, either cutting off many of these "entitlements" on short notice or fulfilling them with paper scrip so valueless as to make no difference.

The real question before us, then, is whether we shall acknowledge this quickly enough to allow the few who are paying attention a little time to make alternative plans, or whether we wish to go over the waterfall together, all still singing our happy songs about "drifting down the lazy river with you."

Those who would continue rushing to disaster at 80 miles an hour are the kind of socialists who prefer to be called Democrats. Those who would reduce our forward speed to 55, while contending that's the same thing as "putting her in reverse," are the kind of socialists who prefer to call themselves Republicans.

Those who make themselves very unpopular indeed by pointing out that the roaring noise is a waterfall up ahead, and there's no longer any way to safety without getting wet, are called Libertarians.

We don't really expect anyone to listen. It's just that our daddies taught us never to tell a lie.

II

THE FEARLESS
DRUG WARRIORS

No Such Thing as 'Innocent'

Most Americans probably figure that if you manage to get a dispute with a government regulator into court, and if 12 good men and true then proceed to unanimously acquit you, that's an end to the matter. You walk out of the courtroom a free man; the bureaucrats slink back to their burrows licking their wounds; justice is triumphant.

America, meet Dr. Dietrich Stoermer.

A native of Konigsberg (now Kaliningrad) in East Prussia, Dietrich Stoermer escaped to the West with his family while still a youngster, in 1947, under fire by the Red Army. Though he still speaks with a discernible German accent, the family actually emigrated to Australia, where Dietrich received his medical degree, after which he served a stint with an Australian M.A.S.H. unit in Vietnam, suffering honorable wounds. His brother is also a doctor. They both practice in Las Vegas. At least, Dietrich Stoermer did until recently.

Dietrich Stoermer is a general practitioner. But over the years, he developed a bit of a specialty as most GPs will. He began treating more and more patients with acute non-cancer pain. "I've talked to his patients, and they say, 'This is the most wonderful doctor; he'll spend so much time with me,'" says Las Vegas attorney David Crosby, one of a slew of lawyers with whom Dr. Stoermer is obliged to spend a lot of his time these days, instead of with his patients. "But he does prescribe based on what he sees their needs as, and that has got him set up for some trickery, for some skullduggery, by the government."

Dr. Stoermer's problems with the federal Drug Enforcement Administration (DEA) began in 1990, when a secretary in his employ was caught calling in unauthorized prescription renewals to local pharmacies. Stoermer says there's no doubt the young woman was carrying on the activity on her own, as a profitable sideline. But the employee apparently told investigators she was acting on Stoermer's orders, and accepted a deal to turn informant, feeding state and federal drug police information about Stoermer's practice. The narcotics police believed they saw a pattern they're trained to look for: Dr. Stoermer seemed to be writing more painkiller prescriptions than is typical for a GP.

Asked at a later date why he believes he was singled out for persecution, Stoermer says a DEA investigator in southern California told him over the phone: "We don't like the way you practice medicine." The DEA wouldn't let me ask the agent in question about that. A PR spokesman for the drug police asked whether I was going to take Dr. Stoermer's word or a government agent's. I pointed out it was hard to take the agent's word if I wasn't allowed to talk to him.

Dr. Stoermer responds: "He never set foot in my office. He never saw the misery of these people. They stereotyped me. They said there couldn't possibly be a GP in this little town treating all these complicated patients. They said I ought to be just treating sniffles and hemorrhoids."

Government regulators moved against Stoermer on several fronts. The state medical board held hearings, contacting dozens of his patients. The IRS audited his business and his tax returns. And, most invasively, the DEA sent undercover agents into his office on numerous occasions in 1991 and 1992, pretending to be patients and asking to be written prescriptions for painkillers—though of course Dietrich Stoermer didn't know that at the time.

"The medical board was calling people who said they had no complaints. They brought in six patients at one hearing, one with a spine curved ninety degrees from spinal arthritis, four others in chronic pain, and the last one was a forty-year-old patient with cancer of the testicles. And these members of the medical review board, none of whom will even touch a chronic pain patient, are going to decide if I'm overprescribing painkillers," Stoermer says.

Finally, in the spring of 1993, federal drug agents arrested Dietrich Stoermer, charging him with 16 counts of improperly distributing prescription drugs. He went on trial in December in Las Vegas, on charges of illegally prescribing Valium, Xanax, and Percodan to undercover agents. Prosecutor Anthony Murry told the jury Stoermer was not so much in the business of medical treatment as he was in the business of "supplying drugs on demand." The $55 per office visit was "easy money," Murry contended.

But defense attorney Lamond Mills successfully pointed out that transcripts of secret tape recordings made by the agents showed Stoermer often questioned the government plants about their symptoms.

"What they had in there was a guy begging him for painkillers, and he kept saying 'No, we don't do things that way,'" adds attorney Crosby, who has acted as a general legal adviser to Stoermer, referring him in turn to each of the expensive specialist attorneys he needs to fight each of the layered government actions.

The jury deliberated for only a few hours before acquitting Dr. Stoermer on all 16 counts. "Merry Christmas," prosecutor Murry told Stoermer Dec. 15 after the verdict was read.

"No hard feelings," responded Dr. Stoermer as he shook

Murry's hand.

But the government did harbor hard feelings. Indeed it did.

• • •

Dr. Stoermer believed he'd be allowed to go back to the practice of medicine. After all, the jury had spoken, and none of his patients had any problem with their doctor; he has never been sued for malpractice in 20 years as an M.D.

But suddenly, in February 1994, a pharmacist called Stoermer's office to report he could not fill a routine prescription. He'd been informed by the government that Stoermer's DEA license number—required to write prescriptions for any "controlled" drug, including even mild pain medication—had been lifted. Pulled. Canceled.

"I was never notified. That's how I found out, from the pharmacies," Stoermer says. "What they claim is I filled out the form wrong when I sent in my license renewal the year before. But they cashed the two-hundred-and-seventy-dollar check in June. They let me practice for nine months on that number, which is the same number I've had for twenty years. Then suddenly, just three weeks after the trial, they discover this clerical error."

"What happened," according to attorney Mills, "is that the DEA sent him another form to fill out, and he filled it out without paying close attention to it, so when they got it back they said 'Oh, you filled out a form to apply for a new number rather than to renew an old number, so we're considering it an application for a new number, and it's being challenged.' They did this many months after they cashed his check with the original renewal application. They absolutely are trying to get back at him, because they not only got hammered, they got embarrassed in court."

"I think a lot of the doctor, but he's a little bit disorganized," explains attorney Crosby. "A lot of doctors are like that. Their paperwork is a mess. That's why they hire people to do it. They have other things on their minds, like doctoring."

Ralph Lockridge, media spokesman for the Drug Enforcement Administration in Los Angeles, responds that Dr. Stoermer's "application for a new license to write for controlled substances is still in process. It hasn't been OK'd or denied."

The chronology goes like this, Lockridge says, "A show-cause request to revoke his license was issued in February of nineteen-ninety-three, so it wasn't after the trial, which was in December of ninety-three. He didn't respond to the show-cause order; he let it lapse."

But Stoermer contends he sent in a check to renew the license as usual and it was cashed in early 1993.

"Does he have the proof?" Lockridge asks.

(Yes; Stoermer acquired a copy of the cancelled check from his bank and showed it to me, at my request.)

"Then he submitted another new application instead of showing cause why his initial number should not be allowed to lapse," Lockridge continued. "I imagine what happened was, after the trial went his way, he changed his mind and decided to try and get a number back.

"I understand what he's saying," Lockridge continues, "that it's all a punitive vindictive act by the government, which is not the case."

"But he was found innocent by a jury."

"Not 'innocent'; he was found 'not guilty.' There's a difference," Agent Lockridge said.

"What?" I asked, sensing we were nearing the heart of the matter.

"They don't use the word 'innocent' in the legal process. It's 'not guilty.' It doesn't necessarily mean the defendant didn't do it. 'Not guilty' can be based on a technicality. I'm not talking about this case in particular, but maybe a confession is thrown out because the defendant wasn't Mirandized. That doesn't mean he didn't do it, it just means he's found 'not guilty.' Now there's a different evidentiary standard for an administrative process than there is at trial. Just like a cop can be found innocent at trial, but there can still be administrative disciplinary action taken against him."

"But the policeman has voluntarily entered into a contractual arrangement with the department," I suggested.

"Yes, and a doctor has entered into a contract concerning the safe handling of drugs as part of a public trust, as well," Agent Lockridge responded.

• • •

I hope you're following this, Legionnaires. Our government bureaucrats no longer consider a not guilty verdict at trial to be the end of the matter. In their view, such results don't mean defendants are innocent. They don't constitute a rebuke from a higher authority—a jury—and an instruction to knock it off and go after someone else. "Not guilty" just means the slimeball got off on some technicality. This time. After all, why would the government have put him on trial if he wasn't guilty?

No, an innocent jury verdict is now seen as nothing more than a minor speed bump on the way to the predetermined bureaucratic end. When a court trial doesn't produce the results they seek, these guys just keep on coming, relentlessly, with the entire wealth and manpower of the federal government behind them. They proceed to the "administrative procedures" level, where there's a "different evidentiary standard" for the review and cancellation of all their licenses and permits, where ideas like double jeopardy and the presumption of innocence are so much less troubling.

And how do they justify this? With the interesting premise

that all the licensing procedures they subject us to—procedures to which we must submit if we are to practice our chosen professions at all—constitute "voluntary contracts" under which we agree to submit to their brand of quasi-military justice, like soldiers or police officers in some new kind of state organized not along the lines of the old English common law, but along some system much more reminiscent of Prussia or the Red Guards.

Voluntary? How long are we to suppose a doctor would be allowed to practice medicine, without being handcuffed and jailed, if he simply said, "No thanks. Now that I understand all your medical licensing procedures are 'voluntary,' I've just decided not to 'volunteer.' Don't worry, all my ads will say, 'declined to submit to state licensing procedures'"?

"For some reason, the feds have it in their mind that they want this guy," says David Crosby. "Dr. Stoermer has bucked the system. He has a different way of dealing with pain patents. Everyone else is afraid to write prescriptions, and he's not. You want to know why pain is undermedicated in this country? The doctors are afraid to write prescriptions because they'll get crucified, that's why.

"The DEA really burned him," Crosby says. "I think he can beat them; he's got a case that can be won. But I don't know if he can make it now. They may have broken his spirit."

A local physician who has known and admired the doctor for years says the effects of his year-long ordeal have changed Dietrich Stoermer.

"He's a totally different man than he used to be," says Dr. Carl Novack, himself a pain specialist. "He's lost a lot of weight—he was a hale and hearty fellow. He was big, burly. He was not the gaunt, nervous, eyes- darting-around, always-looking-around-and-digging-in-his-pocket-for-a-news-clipping sort of guy that you see now. The experience has changed him completely."

"It's a totally unnecessary insane witch hunt," says Dr.

Dietrich Stoermer. "Young doctors believe pain is non-measurable so it's non-existent. Half of the uninsured are in chronic pain. They're not working because of chronic pain. We send these people in for three, four back operations and it doesn't do any good. They use up all their insurance coverage, so after that the medical profession doesn't want anything to do with them; they abandon them.

"Why do we just talk about cancer pain? Thirty million people in this country have non-cancer-related chronic pain. Very few can get any treatment covered by insurance, because it's a pre-existing condition. The answer is like in England, where it's legal to prescribe. Let patients register with one doctor. The doctor starts to get the feeling of what's going on. He figures out what that patient needs to carry on a normal life, and the government doesn't interfere.

"The medical boards are responsible for fifty percent of the drug problem in this country. Nine states have decided medical boards should not interfere with doctors who write scrips for painkillers. The people buying most of those pilfered drugs are chronic pain patients. The drug problem is becoming definitely worse. There are thousands in jail. They get a scrip for ten pills, they need more, so what do they do? They break into a house, and they end up in jail. The chronic pain patients, in my opinion, are the most dangerous people. They flip out, they commit suicide, or they hold up a pharmacy. They are desperate, and no one helps them."

Dr. Carl Novack: "I absolutely agree the War on Drugs does contribute to the problem of trying to get adequate medication for pain. The default setting used to be in favor of the patient; now it's in the interest either of the third-party payer or the government regulator. ... In California, on triplicate prescriptions (the kind required for serious painkillers), a doctor is allowed three hundred per month. You exceed that and your practice is scrutinized."

Many Drug Myths Down, One To Go

Of course, Dr. Stoermer's expertise was in the treatment of *non*-cancer pain.

In a study of *cancer* pain and resulting new guidelines for its treatment, the Agency for Health Care Policy and Research (AHCPR)—a division of the U.S. Department of Health & Human Services—disclosed in March 1994 that 42 percent of cancer patients surveyed received inadequate medication for their pain, despite the availability of adequate drugs to make 90 percent of them comfortable.

The agency then proceeded to debunk many myths that lead to this scandalous result. Perhaps the most persistent barrier to effective pain control is the unfounded belief that using opium derivatives will lead to addiction, the study found. In fact, patients almost never become psychologically hooked on pain pills, and withdrawal symptoms turn out to be easily avoided if medications are tapered off.

But the AHCPR balked at the opportunity to confront head-on our most dangerous drug myth.

Although their report contains the finding, "Physicians are reluctant to prescribe high doses of morphine for fear of drawing attention, and possible punishment, from agencies that regulate narcotics," AHCPR spokesmen chose to ignore this proverbial bloody knife at the crime scene when doing the TV talk show circuit in the days following the release of their report.

Instead, on the "Today" show on the morning following the report's release, Ada Jacox of Johns Hopkins School of Nursing, a member of the AHCPR panel, opted to stick with the tried-and-true nonsense of good drug-bad drug dualism. "'Just Say No To Drugs' refers to the illegal use of recreational drugs," she declared. "It has no place in a discussion of medicating cancer pain."

What a tragic loss of opportunity to point out that the artificial distinction between illegal drugs and valuable medicines is the problem.

In New York state, dying cancer patients must be registered with police as "drug addicts" as though they were young hopheads visiting methadone clinics between liquor-store heists.

How on earth is some local cop supposed to know how much codeine a dying patient needs to spend a final comfortable day with the grandkids?

And how precisely would Jacox have us explain to kids the difference between the drugs they're supposed to "Just Say No" to, and the medicines whose underutilization she rightly decries?

"Call the cops, Mommy. Grandma's using morphine."

"No, honey, that's not a drug, that's a prescription medicine. The drugs we 'Just Say No' to are bad drugs, like marijuana and cocaine."

"But can't marijuana help with vomiting like Grandma gets from chemotherapy?"

"Yes, marijuana used to be a medicine. But since 1933 it's been a 'dangerous drug.'"

"Just like the law changed for alcohol? It used to be dangerous, but now it's not."

"No dear, alcohol and tobacco kill hundreds of thousands of people every year. Just because we made them legal doesn't mean they're safe."

"Oh. But Grandma's morphine is good medicine."

"That's right, dear."

"Can I have some when I get back from the dentist?"

"No. If you take morphine without a prescription it's an illegal drug."

"The prescription makes it legal?"

"That's right."

"But Sean's father got put in jail for writing a prescription for painkillers."

"That's different, dear. That undercover DEA agent wasn't really in pain."

"How was Sean's father supposed to know?"

"Well, dear, when someone goes to the doctor and says they're in pain, the doctor is supposed to assume they're lying to get drugs. Otherwise the doctor goes to jail. Now do you understand?"

Make no mistake about it: All those millions of suffering hospital patients, unable to sleep, writhing in agony, their teeth clenched in unnecessary pain, have been paying an unacknowledged part of the bill for our War on Drugs. I hope it makes the drug warriors proud.

February 7, 1997—
Press Release From the Libertarian Party

WASHINGTON, D.C.—More than 134,000 sex criminals are roaming the streets of America—preying on innocent women and children—thanks to the War on Drugs, the Libertarian Party charged today.

"How many women and children will be raped or sexually molested because, instead of keeping sexual predators behind bars, politicians have filled our nation's jails with nonviolent drug users?" asked Steve Dasbach, the party's national chairman.

His question followed a report released this week by the Department of Justice, which revealed that 134,000 violent sex criminals were released on parole or probation in 1994. Astonishingly, only 99,300 sex criminals remained behind bars meaning the government set free more rapists and molesters than it kept in jail.

"Why were those 134,000 sex criminal released?" asked Dasbach. "Because the government's War on Drugs is filling the nation's prisons at a rapid rate—while acting as a 'get-out-of-jail-free card' for rapists. ... "

Dasbach noted that one year after releasing the 134,000 sex criminals, the government arrested 589,000 people for marijuana possession. And more than 400,000 Americans are locked up on nonviolent drug charges. ...

The 1994 exodus of rapists is partly attributable to that year's Crime Bill, he noted, which mandated life terms for many drug-law violators, compelling prison officials to set more sexual predators free to relieve prison overcrowding.

"It's ironic that the Crime Bill, which Bill Clinton bragged would put 100,000 new cops on the beat, actually helped put 134,300 rapists on the street," he said.

The Great Lightbulb Conspiracy

Gary Tucker, his wife Joanne, and Gary's brother Steve didn't grow marijuana. They didn't buy or sell marijuana. Yet when I began researching their case in 1994, Joanne Tucker found herself awaiting sentencing for "conspiracy to manufacture" marijuana in amounts likely to land her a prison term of 10 years to life, while her husband—an infantry veteran of Vietnam—and his brother sat in a federal pen in Atlanta, awaiting the imposition of sentences which will likely see them doing hard time well into the 21st century, or until we end the War on Drugs, whichever comes first.

What the Tuckers did was operate a store in Norcross, Georgia, called Southern Lights. They sold hydroponic and special fluorescent bulbs for people who wanted to grow plants indoors. Some of their customers—a tiny minority—used that equipment to grow marijuana.

The amount of money the federal Drug Enforcement Admin-

56

istration, the Georgia Department of Investigation, and various other action-hungry government agencies spent to nail the Tuckers remains untallied. But the following numbers may give us some idea.

The narcs staked out the Tuckers' store for two years. At times there were as many as 15 government personnel involved in videotaping people as they went in and out of the store, and writing down the license numbers of customers. The government ran some 1,000 license-plate numbers. Then they started investigating the 1,000 people who owned those cars. But since in Georgia a car can retain its license plate after it is sold, in at least one case they spent time and money investigating a woman who bought a car two weeks *after* it was spotted in the Tuckers' parking lot.

They used high-tech government equipment to take "thermal-imaging" pictures of these suspects' homes, hoping "hot spots" would show up to indicate where indoor marijuana was being grown. They sorted through these people's garbage. They subpoenaed their electric bills, without their knowledge, to see who might be using suspiciously large amounts of electricity.

(Of course, the reason people grow marijuana indoors in Georgia, which has a soil and climate ideal for *outdoor* hemp cultivation, is that the government already takes sophisticated aerial thermal images to determine what crops are growing on private property. Apparently this no longer constitutes *enough* of an invasion of Georgians' privacy.)

Finally, the government raided 80 homes. They made 29 federal cases for growing marijuana. Although some of the remaining 51 were turned over to state authorities for disposition, a fair number turned out to be people who had bought their "grow lights" to raise African violets or tropical fish. That means 36 percent of those raided, and fewer than 3 percent of those investigated, turned out to be worth prosecuting for this heinous federal crime.

But it was enough to make the conspiracy case against the

Tuckers, if only a few of those 29 could be convinced to testify that the Tuckers had talked with them about growing marijuana.

Why would anyone testify to such a thing? Simple. They were promised reduced sentences, or even that charges would be dropped entirely, in exchange for their testimony. Dropping the charges was "absolutely" part of the deal that motivated government witness Andrea Williams, who was busted growing pot for her AIDS-patient husband, according to defense attorney Nancy Lord. Williams cut the deal, then testified that Joanne Tucker knew she was growing the marijuana, according to Lord, whose popularity with Judge William O'Kelly apparently did not improve when he found out Lord had been the Libertarian Party's 1992 vice presidential candidate.

"What they ought to require is that when these government witnesses testify, they put them on the stand and have a U.S. marshal stand right there with a gun to their heads," says Harvey Wysong of the Georgia chapter of the Fully Informed Jury Association, himself a Marine Corps combat veteran. "That's the only way the jury would get a clear picture of their motivation."

But why would the feds sacrifice real "marijuana criminals"— people who were actually caught with the goods—just to nail some lightbulb salesmen? Why would the government expand the definition of "conspiracy" so near the breaking point, contending people who sell grow lights and potting soil "conspire" to grow all the pounds of marijuana that may sprout under those lights over the years?

"Because the Tuckers dissed them," says a source familiar with the case, using the current ghetto slang to indicate a purposeful demonstration of disrespect. Instead of quietly closing their business and slipping out of town when they learned they were under surveillance, the Tuckers stayed open for two years while they were staked out. They called the newspapers, they called their congressman, they went on (the CBS Evening News') 'Eye on America.'

It's not the harm you do, since of course marijuana consumption harms no one. It all comes down to whether you're considered a "friend of the government." And U.S. Attorney Jim Harper told Judge O'Kelly that Joanne Tucker is "no friend of the government."

There's plenty more about this case. The judge and prosecutor pre-screened the jury pool for any citizen who might be fed up with the War on Drugs, for instance, and systematically removed them. The judge refused to allow testimony about the DEA's violation of civil rights or to let the jury know how serious a sentence the defendants faced if convicted. The Tuckers' attorney, Nancy Lord, got the court to release its federal seizure order on the Tuckers' house, only to have it immediately seized by Georgia *state* tax authorities.

But for now, residents of cities where drive-by shootings make the nightly news can certainly be glad their federal government opted to ignore such transitory phenomena in favor of going after as dangerous a menace as lightbulb dealers Gary and Joanne Tucker, a few of whose graying customers grew marijuana for private use in the basements of suburban Atlanta.

'Libertarians Are the Only Ones Who Would Listen'

On St. Patrick's Day 1996, following a campaign appearance in New Jersey, Libertarian presidential hopeful Rick Tompkins of Arizona drove to Brighton Beach, the Russian immigrant enclave in Brooklyn, N.Y., to meet with Anna and Eli Zhadanov.

Anna and Eli are the wife and son of Sam Zhadanov, a 69-year-old Russian-immigrant plastics engineer who, at any other time in our history, would have been considered proof that the American dream lives on.

Sam Zhadanov settled in Brooklyn and set up his own little plastics manufacturing business, first on his own, then hiring one employee, then two, then three. Some of the products he invented and patented himself, including a hypodermic syringe that retracts the needle as it's withdrawn, so a nurse can't prick her finger and risk infection.

What Sam enjoyed most, his son explains, was the challenge of figuring out how to manufacture a desired object more cheaply than anyone else, by reducing the number of steps required to produce the object via extrusion molding—substituting mental work in the design stage for extra finishing work on the factory floor.

So it was the technical challenge that intrigued him most when he was approached by some customers who wanted him to manufacture a large number of tiny perfume sample bottles. The plastic samples they showed him were even labeled for various kinds of perfume. Sam solved the engineering problem, came in with a lower bid than the customers had ever seen, and landed the contract. Soon, his little New Jersey factory was cranking out plastic bottles by the truckload.

But then the customers started acting strangely. Their volume stayed high, and they always paid their bills, but they started asking for the shipments to be sent out at night, or delivered to out-of-the-way locations, where the product would be transferred to different unmarked trucks.

Sam Zhadanov may have been naive, but he wasn't an idiot. He approached a local lawyer in New Jersey, going so far as to ask for a legal opinion in writing. What if someone were to later re-sell his plastic bottles for an illegal use, like holding crack cocaine? Even though Sam Zhadanov had never bought, sold, used, seen, or possessed any cocaine, could he be held in any way legally responsible for how his bottles were used after he sold them? Attorney Martin Spritzer correctly informed old Sam that manufacturers of such generic containers are specifically exempted from the federal definition of "drug paraphernalia." Otherwise, the folks who manufacture various sizes of Glad and Zip-Loc plastic sandwich bags would be in a world of hurt.

But the federals don't care what the law says. They arrested Sam and charged him with "conspiracy to transport" all the cocaine they figured could have fit in all the little plastic bottles he manufactured over the years (two-and-a-half tons.) They seized his $800,000 life savings out of his safe at home. (Survivors of Stalin's Soviet Union don't trust banks—but Sam's cash savings were taken as further evidence of his criminal character.) They seized his Social Security checks. They harassed his other customers until he was forced to sell the Metuchen, N.J., plastics factory he'd personally built up over the years. Then they seized that money, too.

Sam's lawyer—who until four months earlier had worked as a federal prosecutor in New York—told Zhadanov he was sure he could "work something out" with the prosecutors.

"He worked something out, all right," says Sam's son, Eli. Penniless, and facing the prospect that his 58-year-old wife would be on the streets should he be convicted, the elder Zhadanov accepted a "deal" to plead guilty to *all charges* in exchange for a promise of "no hard time," and the return to his wife of half the value of his factory.

But the wife never got a penny.

"It was a trick," son Eli says. "It was a scam from the very beginning. The IRS came in and seized the other half that was supposed to be returned to her. They said, 'We're not prosecutors; we're another branch of government. So a deal you made with them doesn't apply to us.'"

Then came the "no-hard-time" part—five years in Allenwood.

It turns out the federals had kept Zhadanov's factory under observation almost from the first day he accepted the contract to manufacture the plastic perfume bottles. "Factory gates were always open allowing unobstructed view of the manufacturing process from the street," Zhadanov writes from prison. "It was obvious to agents that people inside are not aware of any illegal ... use of their product. Yet ... instead of preventing the crime, their plan was to create the crime and make it flourish!"

Zhadanov's son Eli says police initially considered the old man's role "minor." But that changed, and prosecutors grew enraged, when he refused the "deal" to forfeit all his family and business assets and "cooperate" against his customers.

"To break my father's resolve, prosecutors openly vowed to destroy what was especially precious to him—his business, which he literally built over twelve years with his own hands. They started a methodical harassment of his remaining customers and employees, until the plant had to shut down and employees were laid off.

"So instead of working on his life-saving medical devices," says Eli Zhadanov, "my father is in Allenwood. A man who is the most law-abiding man I ever met—he wouldn't get a traffic ticket.

"You know, my father says he came to this country thinking he was going to escape the gulag, and he ended up in the gulag. You come here and you kind of relax. You say, 'Oh, they'll see it's a mistake. It's not the KGB, it's the federal government. I can talk to them. ... '"

Zhadanov writes that he has been surrounded in prison for the past year by "doctors, lawyers, publishers, professionals, and intellectuals, mostly first-time offenders, who are in many ways victims like myself." Most of them are guilty of violating bureaucratic edicts, not felonies. "Yet some are serving prison terms of up to 15 years. That's longer than served by many murderers and rapists!"

Such victims are singled out, "so that they can be stripped of their property and savings. ... We are turning into a new type of totalitarian state and we don't even know it. ... For much of my life I endured the oppression of the former Soviet Union. Now I am reliving the experience in my new home where I came in search of Justice and Liberty."

• • •

Compare any 1940s detective film with the TV cop-and-court dramas of the 1990s. Our heroes used to be private detectives who discovered who really done it, while the cops sat on their fat behinds, playing cards in their shirtsleeves and smugly holding the wrong man in jail. Today, cops, attorneys, and audiences all know beyond a doubt that the arrested scumbag did it. The only question is whether government prosecutors will be able to successfully navigate the arbitrary and Byzantine obstacle course of court evidentiary procedure and clever defense "motions" far enough to get the crook to "plead out."

I'll believe that network dramatic programming remains anything but extremist pro-government propaganda when I see a made-for-TV movie portraying Randy Weaver or David Koresh or Donald Scott as flawed but tragic heroes, and their government murderers as, well, murderers.

Till then, I refuse to believe it's a coincidence that the "new realism" of 1990s television portrays all cops as heroes (albeit sometimes angst-ridden), all drug dealers as drooling psychopaths (didn't Ambassador Joseph Kennedy used to deal in illegal drugs?), and all arrested suspects as unquestionably guilty.

Rick Tompkins, the Fully Informed Jury activist, 20-year Vietnam-era Air Force veteran, and three-time chairman of the Arizona Libertarian Party, says Brighton Beach is hardly New York's swankiest address, but that the modest apartment of "drug moll" grandma Anna Zhadanov is nicer inside than out.

63

"Eli came over with his son, a beautiful little boy of about six or seven with dark hair and bright eyes. We talked for awhile, then Anna served a beautiful spread of ethnic Russian foods.

"It was an incredible feeling sitting and talking to these eminently nice respectable people. These are not criminals. I reiterated the shame I felt for my country. As [Libertarian political strategist] George O'Brien says, the government is hurting people every day.

"The phone rang, and it was Sam. Apparently he calls from prison every day.

"They still can't deal appropriately with his dental problem, which was in large part caused by the way he was treated by the government. He'd spent $20,000 on dental implants just days before they descended on him. They refused to give him the opportunity to go back to his dentist, so the implants began to deteriorate. He's in a special medical facility now in Kentucky, but even there they don't have the special expertise to deal with his problem. And it looks like they'll ship him back to Allenwood soon."

Son Eli decided to close his small but successful 10-year-old New York ad agency to reopen his father's business in smaller rented quarters. "He decided to revive his dad's business in large part to keep his spirits up. They manufacture mainly devices his father had patents on, some life-saving medical devices he'd invented. Eli managed to get some of the products onto one of the home shopping networks, so now he actually has more back-orders than they can fill. Of course, he still has cash-flow problems.

"Anna and Eli Zhadanov pretty much think the press is worthless," Tompkins reports. "Anna said more than once: 'Libertarians are the only ones who would listen to us.' Even a lot of people they thought of as their friends pulled away."

In a recent letter to Rick, Eli Zhadanov writes:

"Dear Mr. Tompkins: On behalf of my father, my mother, and myself please accept our warmest gratitude and appreciation to you and Kathy for your support. All of us have been deeply touched by your outrage and concern over my father's situation. More importantly, your letter gave us a sense of hope and strength from a realization that the spirit of America is alive and well in people like you. In your words one hears the voice of a true American patriot.

"We admire your courage to speak the truth and stand up against the government terror and oppression. Unfortunately, most Americans are blind to the greatest threat to this country since the American Revolution: their own government raging out of control.

"To us, immigrants from the former Soviet Union, the symptoms are too clear, the prospects are too horrifying. It is essential to our struggling democracy that your voice and those of your supporters be heard. It is not a matter of politics, it is a matter of survival."

• • •

Filling Our Jails With Dangerous Entrepreneurs

In *The Sign of the Four*, Conan Doyle has Sherlock Holmes explain that, once all other possibilities have been eliminated, whatever remains—no matter how improbable—must be the truth.

Since the only sane course now open is to end the Drug War and restore complete medical liberty, totally and overnight (studying the problem doesn't count; substituting treatment for incarceration doesn't count), the only possible conclusion—no matter how improbable—is that every last federal officeholder now ensconced in Washington, D.C., belongs to one of two groups: either they're lying soulless charlatans, willing to enthusiastically endorse policies that they *know* are homicidal, racist, useless, promoters of crime, terror, and urban decay, and destructive in the long term to American life and liberty, or else they are, indeed, homicidal racist maniacs.

This most definitely includes all these so-called "conservative" Republicans, elected since 1994 on a pledge to sharply reduce government interference in our lives.

In July 1995, Speaker of the House Newt Gingrich stood before a big meeting of the Republican National Committee and uttered the bravest-sounding, most hideously cynical, and carefully positioned statement on the Drug War that I can ever remember hearing.

"We should either legalize drugs entirely, or we should get serious," said the Speaker of the House. Since his listeners want nothing to do with legalizing drugs, they most likely heard only the second half. But at a later date, when the polls inevitably show a majority in favor of legalization (just as they did with alcohol in 1932), who do you think will re-run that tape and smugly remind us, "See, I proposed legalization back in ninety-five"?

In the same breath, Mr. Gingrich said something even more perverted. He said, "We must tell anyone who wants to bring drugs into this country to poison our children: We will kill you."

Libertarians would also favor harsh punishment for those who "poison children." But how many drug dealers actually tie down young children and inject them with cocaine or heroin against their will? Someone's been watching *Reefer Madness*. In real life, why give drugs away to kids when there's plenty to be made selling to well-heeled consenting adults? Statistically, the crime of poisoning children with consciousness-altering drugs doesn't exist.

(If, on the other hand, by poisoning children we simply mean facilitating a free market in which an underage child in another country might be able to choose to consume an addictive drug, we must then ask if Mr. Gingrich has ever voted for a budget that contained tobacco subsidies, allotments, and price supports, as well as federal subsidies to facilitate the advertising and market-ing of addictive American tobacco overseas. If so, does he mean to say the governments of those nations have every right to send assassins to Washington, to shoot down Mr. Gingrich and every tobacco-state congressman in the street, like dogs?)

But this either/or stuff is far more corrosive than that. Mr. Gingrich is saying that either there's a Constitutional right to put any drugs or medicines we please into our own bodies, or else we should murder people who put drugs and medicines into their own bodies without government permission. Either/or, he doesn't care, just pick one by majority vote and let's go.

Imagine for a moment the Speaker took a similar either/or position on our other freedoms. Either there's a God-given right to practice whatever religion we choose, or else we should round up and burn at the stake anyone who practices a religion not ap-proved by the majority. It doesn't matter to him which option we choose, just choose and let's get moving.

Either there's a God-given right, confirmed in the Bill of Rights, to freedom of speech, or else anyone who offends the majority of the populace by spouting loathesome hate speech about race or militias or any other anti-government position should be quick-marched to an internment camp. It doesn't matter to him whether we vote to retain that free speech business or get rid of it, let's just put it to a vote and get moving.

This is principled leadership?

In fact, the ever-expanding Drug War now reaps more and more victims who have never touched or seen a drug, let alone fed any to innocent children.

Look at Gary and Joanne Tucker, sentenced to federal peni-tentiaries in Georgia for selling fluorescent lightbulbs.

Look at 69-year-old Russian emigre Sam Zhadanov, now serv-ing five years at Allenwood because his little plastics factory manufactured plastic bottles that the government claims could be used to store cocaine.

Since actual Colombian drug kingpins have their own armies and battalions of well-heeled Miami lawyers far more capable than your average baggy-pants federal prosecutor, the federal government doesn't bother much with them.

No, when you're looking to put on a show for the press, you go after the easy targets: the Dietrich Stoermers, the Joanne Tuckers, the Sam Zhadanovs. *These* are the kind of "drug dealers" who are being locked away in our names so that prosecutors can build careers on the "War on Drugs."

But now, it turns out, ruining their lives, bankrupting them, driving them out of the country, or locking them up for half a decade isn't enough.

Newt Gingrich thinks we should kill them.

Travel Papers, Please?

In one of the frequent sarcastic e-mails I receive from uniformed bully-boys, a particularly challenged Ohio state trooper ridiculed an assertion of mine. In discussing the kinds of tyranny we now routinely accept so long as someone tells us it's to help with the War on Drugs, I noted that Americans are required to show an "internal passport" to authorities upon demand, without any showing of cause, and that we'll soon be required to show our "racial identity cards" on demand, as well.

The good soldier smirked that he'd never seen an "internal passport." He also wondered if I knew where one could apply for any "racial identity card"—without which one might be subject to arrest—from the United States government.

Our "internal passports" are now called "drivers licenses," of course—the computer monitor in the Ohio state trooper's car will tell him more about how many guns you own and whether you owe back child support payments than a Nazi Gestapo officer could ever have dreamed of learning from the flimsy cardboard versions German citizens used to be required to carry around when they traveled. (And just try telling the man with the flashing red-and-blue strobe lights that you have a right to travel the roads anonymously and in peace, and aren't obliged to show him any stinking license to thus exercise your rights. In fact, if it's merely a "drivers" license, why do I need to show it to get on a commercial airplane, which I have no intention of "driving"?)

Has the trooper really never demanded to see one of those little laminated documents? I leave you to judge.

But as to his second question—could I tell him how one might acquire a "racial identity card" from the United States government, a card without which one might actually be subject to arrest—I replied that I certainly could, and forwarded him the following column, which I wrote way back in 1992, and to which (of course) he never responded further.

Government Registration by Race and Religion—Could It Happen Here?

Three members of a racial minority are traveling down a lonely road in the countryside. As it happens, they are returning from a peaceful mission to purchase supplies for a religious ceremony planned at their home village the next day. From the dust behind them emerges a police car, its lights flashing.

The three law-abiding men pull over to await the officer's inquiries. He determines that they have, indeed, purchased supplies necessary for their religious observance, and asks to see their government travel papers.

The driver produces the required government travel permit, listing his own name and date of birth, his race, and his percent of non-white blood. The name and official racial registration number of one of the passengers are also listed. But the space is blank where the proof of the third man's racial purity is required. The three men are thus hauled in for questioning, since the government currently in power in their country allows the practice of their religion only by those who have been certified by the government to be of the required "degree of racial blood."

Is this scene taking place in 1) Nazi Germany in 1938; or 2) the Union of South Africa in 1964?

Try the State of Texas in 1992.

Under regulations adopted in February 1992 by the Texas Department of Public Safety, Controlled Substances Section, with the consent and cooperation of representatives of seven branches of the Native American Church from Arizona to Wisconsin, Texas police may demand to see just such uniform "Peyote Authorization Permits" listing such information vital to the exercise of religious freedom in America today as "Tribe; Degree of Blood; NAC Membership Card Number; and BIA Agency Where Enrolled," from any citizen attempting to purchase or transport the peyote cactus for religious use.

The United States government permits an exemption from the War on Drugs for the religious use of peyote—which grows naturally only in Mexico and two Texas counties—only to those who can prove "25 percent Indian blood." In many cases, this means a father and son may practice their traditional religion, while the mans' wife—the boy's mother—is excluded due to her bloodlines.

A similar exemption from alcohol Prohibition during the years 1919-1933 for the religious use of communion wine required no proof of the communicants' "percentage" of Irish or Italian heri-

70

tage, of course.

In perhaps the saddest aspect of this adoption of "government travel papers"—a concept so un-American that armed guards on German trains once had only to demand such documents to bring a rousing chorus of jeers from American movie audiences —the actual motion to accept the draft "authorization permit" proposed by the Texas narcs in Austin in the winter of 1992 was made by Elmer Blackbird of the Omaha Tribe and seconded by Robert Whitehorse of the Native American Church (NAC) of Navajoland.

It's easy enough for those of us who require no government pass to attend our house of worship to condemn these men for cooperating with their overseers—their religion is one of the last vestiges of their traditional culture, and they are obviously aware how tenuous is the extension of government "permission" for them to continue practicing it at all. (Less than a century ago, their great-grandparents were shot by federal authorities for practicing a precursor religious ceremony, the Ghost Dance, because it frightened the wives of the Indian agents.)

But citizens of western states like Nevada, Arizona, and New Mexico, where state law still allows the legitimate practice of the peyote religion by any and all regardless of "racial bloodlines," should be aware that a Navajo legislator in Phoenix tried and failed in 1992 to revise state law to permit the practice of the religion only by "Native Americans" under the federal definition of "25 percent blood."

Only a small percentage of those in search of spiritual guidance are ever likely to consume the bitter and nauseating peyote cactus. The harrowing night-long ritual of the NAC sacrament hardly lends itself to those seeking some "quick high." But that's hardly the point.

The continuous erosion of our Constitutional rights in the name of the bizarre, hypocritical, and counterproductive $70 bil-

lion "War on Drugs" has gone far enough. No Native American—
no American of any description—should have to prove his or her
"purity of racial blood" (whatever that means, anyway) to government agents in return for "permission" to practice his religion
of choice.

E-mail, I Get Lots and Lots of E-mail

One well-meaning correspondent writes she "might be able
to go along with legalizing marijuana, but not the hard drugs like
heroin, cocaine, etc.

"Addicts are generally not employable," she adds. "What provision would you submit to make sure that if people make the
choice to fry their brains, they and their families aren't laid at the
taxpayers' feet to support?"

Hm. While "addicted" does have some medical meaning, it's
become almost a magical incantation of the War on Plants.

Virtually all tobacco smokers are "hooked on a drug,"
which many Indian tribes considered their most potent and
sacred narcotic. Dr. Andrew Weil of the University of Arizona
and others classify this drug as a near twin to heroin at the top
of the "addictiveness" list, above cocaine and far, far above
the hallucinogens. Yet we all know tobacco addicts are employable (despite their need to slip outside in the worst of
weather, to "fix" far more frequently than your average heroin
addict), so we get around this inconvenient fact by calling tobacco a "soft" drug.

But "soft" (a very imprecise term, generally now meaning
"more acceptable," but stemming from its use in a recognizable
plant form, rather than as an injectable white powder) is used to
describe tobacco precisely because it's legal.

When cocaine was legal, it was most commonly ingested as a more "natural" component syrup in Coca-Cola, and no one contended Coke drinkers were "unemployable." In fact, older folks tell me they generally arrived for work rarin' to go.

When the opiates were legal, they were generally consumed by drinking laudanum or smoking thick brown opium, a much "softer" form than injectable heroin. Some opium addicts did have trouble holding a job, no doubt. But Samuel Coleridge, James Joyce, and others reported drinking prodigious quantities of laudanum with breakfast and still kept up a busy schedule. I suspect the ratio of those who could consume legal opiates in moderation and still function—to those who lost control—was no worse than our current experience with alcohol, most of whose users today remain responsible and productive.

Tobacco addicts, who up till recently favored the Drug War (now that Miss Hillary is making good headway toward outlawing *their* drug of choice, a few are starting to see the light), have long argued that their habit doesn't produce the physical changes and withdrawal cravings of *bad* drugs.

In fact, marijuana and the hallucinogens are not addictive at all, in any medical sense. And if tobacco smokers think their drug of choice can't create any of the startling physical side effects of heroin addiction, they need only try one simple experiment: Quit, cold turkey.

Why did powdered heroin and cocaine grow popular only after Drug Prohibition in 1934? To maximize smuggling profits.

I submit that if coca syrup, opium paste, and laudanum had been left legal, and tobacco prohibited, we would now have a massive problem with people shooting, snorting, or smoking a purified, buffered, white derivative of nicotine (the stuff is quite toxic in its natural form—a potent natural insecticide), derivatives cheaper and safer to transport in bulk without falling afoul of tobacco-sniffing dogs. Our inner cities would be nightmares of nicotine-addicted zombies sortieing forth from their shag houses only long enough to steal, beg, or turn tricks for the money needed for their next fix, outcast former thrill-seekers now converted into shambling reservoirs of disease, blamed for our current huge crime wave, the gang warfare in our cities, etc. And folks would be assuring us that nicotine is nothing like our familiar "soft" drugs, laudanum and Coca-Cola, because of course *their* legal users are solid citizens with jobs, while scabby, thieving, nicotine addicts are completely unemployable.

Furthermore, anyone so bold as to advocate the re-legalization of tobacco would doubtless be asked how much looted tax money he's prepared to allocate to support the families of all the people who would thus be freed to "fry their brains on nicotine."

The Big Lie

If these points need further proof—if the failed Drug War needs another nail in its coffin—the 60-page report "Illicit Drugs and Crime," by Bruce L. Benson and David W. Rasmussen, professors of economics at Florida State University, should do the job.

Professors Benson and Rasmussen studied crime rates in Florida, which poured vast resources into a beefed-up drug war in the years 1984-89, and in Kansas, which did not. In their report, released in August 1996 by the Independent Institute, they report: "In hindsight, it appears that Kansas's relatively modest involvement in the nationwide drug war during the 1984-89 period has resulted in its citizens being relatively safe from crime. This assertion will come as a surprise to many people, but reality mandates that when scarce resources are used to do one thing, they cannot be used to do something else. ... "

74

One consequence of shifting resources to the drug war is that "violent and property criminals are not caught until they have committed a relatively large number of crimes, if they are caught at all."

Then, as jails and prisons clog up with non-violent drug offenders, those violent felons "can be forced out of prison relatively early ... freeing them to commit new crimes"

The "drugs-cause-crimes" analysis fails utterly, according to the Florida economists' research. Most drug users who also commit crimes against person or property reported in interviews that they turned to crime *before* they started using drugs, not the other way around. In fact, it was the higher disposable income and unsavory new connections produced by a life of crime that made it possible for them to buy drugs. "Crime leads to drug use, not vice versa," the professors found.

Because the diversion of resources into the drug war led to a "reduced probability of arrest" for robbery or burglary, "the property crime rate in Florida rose 16.3 percent" from 1983 to 1989.

Violent crime also increased markedly, as dealers displaced from neighborhoods where they had long confined themselves "invaded the turf of established dealers, and residents of previously untapped markets fell prey to violent criminals. Since 1989, Florida has reduced its drug-enforcement efforts, and its property crime rate has fallen."

The drug war has even uglier unintended consequences.

Drug entrepreneurs who run into trouble at the border develop domestic sources of production. "It is now estimated that marijuana is the largest cash crop in California," the professors report.

When the government started looking for domestic marijuana via aerial infrared reconnaissance, California growers moved indoors, switching to "more potent strains" that can produce a $75 million profit out of a $1 million investment in a single year, professors Benson and Rasmussen determined.

And when interdiction started to show some success in California, some growing shifted to the mountains of Kentucky, "involving people whose cultural roots included moonshining and a history of violence, making the trade rougher than it had been before."

Of course, because marijuana is bulky and easy to detect, customers are urged to try "harder" drugs like crack cocaine and heroin, which represent higher profit per volume. And to reduce their chances of ever dealing directly with police informants who may infiltrate their way up through the distribution network, dealers "lengthen drug distribution chains and use younger drug pushers and runners," who are known to be treated far more leniently by the courts.

Well, the politicians did promise us new "opportunities for our young people."

As Americans quickly figured out during alcohol Prohibition in the 1920s, the pathologies of the illicit drug culture are caused not by drugs, but by drug *prohibition*. Alcohol is just as addictive and intoxicating a drug today as it was in 1928. But no one goes blind from drinking bad alcohol, because there's no profit incentive for a legitimate distiller—the kind who proudly puts his name on his product, the kind who can be sued in court—to sell bad stuff. Nor is there any reason for Anheuser-Busch distributors to engage in Tommy-gun shootouts with Miller Lite distributors over distribution territories, when such contract disputes can be effectively resolved in court, at far less cost. Legalization solved these problems, without changing the chemical nature or effects of alcohol (or the desire of users to get stoned) by one iota.

"Illicit Drugs and Crime" only bears out what anyone with open eyes should already know—with the War on Drugs, we've allowed Big Brother to tear up our Constitution and use it for toilet paper. In return, the fearless drug warriors promised that our streets and our children would be safe. They lied.

Half-Steps to Freedom Only
Lend Our Endorsement to Tyranny

A common argument is that urging the instant legalization of all drugs is "just too radical," that it will "turn off too many people who otherwise might be willing to listen" to the call of liberty on less emotion-laden issues.

The problem with this theory, of course, is that liberty is indivisible. Once you tell the authorities, "OK, you can suspend some of our rights, as long as you assure us it's to catch a drug dealer," they'll simply swear out an affidavit that they believe the Branch Davidians (for example) have a methamphetamine lab hidden in the church at Waco where they live with their children, and use that affidavit to lay hold of military tanks and helicopters for their assault—military equipment banned for civilian police work "unless there are drugs involved"—without ever paying any price when their sworn statement turns out to have been invented out of whole cloth. (No evidence of any methamphetamine lab was ever found, of course. The ATF agents made it up out of thin air.)

Or, they'll just swear out an affidavit that a federal officer has seen marijuana plants "growing under the trees" on the mountain property of Malibu millionaire Donald Scott—property that park rangers had previously attempted without success to buy and annex to a neighboring park.

Before the early-morning raid on the Scott ranch in October 1992, agents from various jurisdictions gathered quietly to review maps of the fine lands they'd be able to seize under drug-related civil-asset seizure laws if marijuana were found. The plainclothes thugs—no uniforms, no badges in sight—then cut the lock on the gate and swarmed in, tackling Scott's wife in the kitchen.

When Mrs. Scott screamed that strangers were attacking her, her retired millionaire husband came running down the stairs with his handgun, and was promptly shot and killed by the drug police.

No "marijuana plants" were ever found "under the trees," of course. Not so much as a nickel bag of pot ever turned up, anywhere on the grounds.

Months later, Parks Police declined to let fire engines cross their property when the widow Scott's house caught on fire. It burned to the ground.

And needless to say, no agents were ever disciplined for the murder of Donald Scott. Just another day of "business as usual" for the fearless drug warriors.

Open a loophole in our liberties "just for drugs," and you'll soon find your Second Amendment rights eroded, too. "We have to ban such-and-such type of gun, along with anything we can get away with labeling 'dangerous cop-killer ammunition,' to keep the drug dealers from getting it."

Pretty soon, our First Amendment rights will have to be curtailed—our phones tapped and our e-mail scanned—"just to catch any drug dealers" who happen to nefariously use these means of communication, you understand.

To catch the one percent of the populace who may be dealing in drugs, all our bank transactions greater than $2,500 are now under surveillance and are reported to federal authorities.

As the famous German churchman Dietrich Bonhoeffer could well have warned us 50 years ago, "When they came for the drug dealers I didn't protest, because I was not a drug dealer. When they came for the gun owners I didn't protest, because I was not a gun owner ..."

If you want *your* favorite liberty protected, you *must* protect the liberties of the homosexual, the pornographer, the "greedy profiteering robber baron," the drug dealer, the tax resister, and the gun owner. That's the way it works. Surrender any of these natural allies—allow government more power "just to go after the greedy polluter" or "just to nail the vicious drug dealer" or "just to protect the children from porn on the Internet"—and it's like trying to defend a castle with one gate open.

Then too, once you give up defending one liberty that you feel a little uncomfortable about, and move on to another that's an "easier sell," the opposition will sense that you're moveable, and they'll soon have you scampering like a rabbit, looking for a safer hole in which to hide.

But dare to fight them—let them know you're going to proudly stand your ground, laugh off their hysterical drum-beating and their ridicule, not surrender your principles on the issue that seems *least* popular—and it's astonishing how quickly the opponents of liberty are reduced to the last pitiful whines of an eight-year-old losing an argument on the school playground: "Oh, you think you're so *perfect*. Well, wouldn't it be nice if we could all be *perfect*, if the rest of us didn't have to be *practical*, and occasionally endorse just a reasonable amount of theft or fraud or murder in order to maintain *order*. Wouldn't that be so nice."

An exhilarating freedom flows from shrugging off this ant-farm groupthink we're taught in our government youth propaganda camps, worrying what the others might say if we stray too far from the mainstream consensus, which no one really believes, anyway.

What does the term "leadership" mean? As often as not, a leader is simply the one who's brave enough to say what most folks already know—that the emperor has no clothes—and then to keep saying it, no matter how many times he's told that he's a clown (if not outright insane).

Compromising our principles to win the votes or approval of moderates is certainly not moral. But it turns out it's not useful, either.

The American Socialists—though they were no freedom-lovers—never compromised their principles, with the result that they never, in this century, won more than one or two seats in Congress. Their 1932 presidential-campaign platform demanded federal crop-disaster insurance, government-run old-age pensions, unemployment insurance, inheritance taxes, and a sharply graduated income tax. These ideas were publicly reviled by Franklin Roosevelt and every other Democrat during the 1932 campaign as "fantastic and un-American." Yet, as we know, they've now been enacted in almost every detail.

Norman Thomas' 1932 platform is all law now, simply because their plan was ready to go when a desperate Franklin Roosevelt sent out the word to "try anything."

The Republicans present the opposite case. Opting for sure electoral victory over principle by nominating Dwight Eisenhower over Robert Taft in 1952, the GOP abandoned forever its long-standing promise to hose out Roosevelt's New Deal ant farms. To this day, Republicans still spout the rhetoric of freedom, but their lying game is just about up.

Compromise is always sold as practical, but it's not.

And the Drug War is the great example.

We all know the Drug War is an utter failure at reducing drug use. It does, however, provide the best opportunity since the 16th century witch-hunts for the forces of tyranny and oppression to squat and defecate all over human decency and the U.S. Constitution.

The only solution is to legalize all drugs. Any adult has the right to medicate him or herself with any drug, without prescription, government license, or any other form of permission.

But the moderates quail at such a solution. "We'll be perceived as extremists," they stutter. "What will we do when the opposition accuses us of wanting to see young children on heroin? There must be some half-step we can offer."

So, they increasingly whine: "The purpose of the Drug War is good, but it's just not working. Why don't we study alternatives? Prison is expensive; can't we divert the arrestees into treatment programs?"

Such moderation is worse than what we've got now. I'll tell you why:

1) Government has no right to spend looted tax dollars studying whether it should allow people to exercise their rights.

The right of Americans to self-medication is guaranteed by the Ninth Amendment, which states, "The enumeration in the Constitution of certain rights shall not be construed to deny or disparage other [rights] retained by the people."

Throughout the 18th and 19th centuries, adult Americans were perfectly free to buy and self-administer marijuana, cocaine, and opium without government approval. Because these commodities were not controlled, prices were equivalent to those of parsley or sugar. There were no reported crime waves caused by drug addicts. There was a similar unenumerated right to consume alcohol.

So, when Congress decided to outlaw alcohol, they realized the Ninth Amendment stood in the way, requiring them to pass the addle-brained Eighteenth Amendment, overruling the Ninth for alcohol only.

When they got ready to outlaw drugs, on what date did Congress enact, and the states ratify, a Constitutional amendment authorizing Drug Prohibition?

Never.

Any law that violates the Bill of Rights is null and void. While it would be nice to repeal all our current drug laws, it isn't really necessary. All that's needed is for jurors to start doing their Constitutional duty and setting free anyone accused of a drug crime. This is precisely how jurors helped end alcohol Prohibition.

2) The second reason the moderate compromise position on drugs is bad is that it creates a fallback position for the War on Plants zealots. Why help them? When we're done creating the lesser of two evils, all we've done is impose on our fellow men a brand new evil.

3) Finally, the notion of "treating" people for exercising a liberty is more insidious than just locking them up.

To see this more clearly, just substitute the freedom of religion.

If a government wants to make it illegal for citizens to be Latter-day Saints, or Hutterites, or peyotists, that's evil. (Hutterite conscientious objectors were tortured and killed by our government as recently as 1918. Mormon polygamists were rounded up in internment camps as recently as 1952. Native American Church members can lose their jobs to this day for consuming their church sacrament, peyote. And that's the single peyote church that's been legally recognized and "established" by the federal government, in violation of the First Amendment. Members of any *other* peyote church—like Arizona's Peyote Way Church of God, which admits members and clergy regardless of race—can go to jail if caught buying or transporting their sacrament. But at least such defendants retain the thin hope of appealing any such laws to a politicized Supreme Court full of former drug prosecutors.)

What if, instead, we declared that folks who want to practice these banned religions are mentally ill, subjecting them to government-mandated medical treatment?

When first detained, it would be pretty obvious that such internees are prisoners of conscience. But as time goes by, that would change. Treated with drugs and electroshock therapy, they'd probably appear shambling and incoherent when interviewed days or weeks later, "proving" the state's case. Neither would they serve any fixed sentence—the government can hold someone forever "for his own good" if he's mentally ill.

We do not "treat" people for exercising a Constitutional right.

Besides, in any sane practice of medicine, the patient is assumed to be truthfully describing his complaint. After checking to make sure there's no lesion, trauma, or infection that could be masked by painkillers—in short, after a physician determines the patient is correct in describing his pain as chronic—the correct treatment for someone asking for codeine is to give him codeine.

But the kind of treatment the anti-drug zealots have in mind instead requires doctors to say: "If you're asking for a painkiller, I must assume you're lying because you want to get high. Let's discuss why you either lie to get drugs, or else imagine you're in pain. Did your parents beat you when you wet the bed?"

In any sane society, a pain clinic would be a store that sells opiates, not an Alice-in-Wonderland enterprise based on the premise: "Let's pretend we haven't known for 1,000 years that opiates cure pain. Now, what scheme, no matter how hare-brained, can we try on this patient?"

Anyone with an ounce of concern for human dignity must embrace a complete government retreat from drug control and regulation. Anything else is tyranny.

If freedom seems extreme, it means the same thing as if you find daylight too bright. It simply means you've been in prison so long that you've forgotten it *is* a prison.

We must stop giving the fearless drug warriors the convenient cover of insincerely acknowledging, "Your purposes are good, but we just need to reform your approach a little."

This is a lie. Why lie to cover up for murderers?

Instead, tell them the truth: "You're insane. You are homicidal maniacs. Every day you pursue this drug war exposes you to dozens *more* personal felony indictments—of the death penalty kind—for crimes against humanity."

People have a right to ingest anything they want, to alter their consciousnesses in any way they please. If the opposite is true— that the majority has a right to impose their chosen state of consciousness on the minority, then we could vote to dose you with LSD right here and now, against your will, so long as we outnumbered you ... couldn't we? That's what "democracy" is, in the absence of any unalienable rights.

83

The moderates tell us, "Don't make the drug warriors afraid. Then they'll never compromise."

Wrong. Remember, their clerks and secretaries and dispatchers and cafeteria fry cooks—without whom their enterprise would grind to a halt—are *also* indictable for the war crime of mass murder, as accessories before the fact. Let them know. Like Geena Davis in the remake of *The Fly*, tell the mousy little functionaires to "Be afraid; be very afraid." Shine the spotlight on them. Demand their home addresses, for when the time comes to serve the warrants.

Then watch the little roaches run for cover.

'For Your Own Reasons Turn Into Your Bosoms, as Dogs Upon Their Masters'

Top government officials like Janet Reno and Bill Clinton have publicly pronounced that they "accept full responsibility" for the deaths at Waco or—in the president's case—the deaths likely to ensue from his intervention in Bosnia.

What they mean by the phrase, of course, is the opposite of what it would mean to anyone else. If you or I plant land mines in the backyard, ask the yard man to go back there, and then call the police and say, "I accept full responsibility for the yard man's death," what would happen?

We'd be arrested and tried. Our confessions could and would be used against us. Throwing ourselves on the mercy of the court, we might or might not avoid the death penalty. But we would, in all likelihood, lose our home and our life savings, and end up doing some hard time.

If you accept all this without complaint or protest, you are, indeed accepting full responsibility.

Janet Reno accepted full responsibility for the agonizing fiery deaths of dozens of innocent women and children. Yet she didn't lose her job, or even a night's sleep. She didn't resign, she wasn't arrested, she didn't stand trial. Under these circumstances, it's hard to discern how the phrase, "I accept full responsibility," differs in real content from, "I exterminated the subhuman vermin because that's the unpleasant task I was given; I would do it again tomorrow."

It is in this context Bill Clinton announced in November 1995 that he will accept full responsibility for any American servicemen lost in Bosnia. In his lingo, this pronouncement in no way limits him from saying, three or four years later, "How was I to know it wouldn't work out? You didn't think I meant I'd be *personally* responsible? If you'll check the transcript I think you'll find I did not say the word 'personally.'"

The whole American police state, from top to bottom, works because those who devour our Constitutional rights know they will never be held *personally* accountable.

Look at the fearless drug warriors, most of whom will laughingly admit in private that they know marijuana (at least) is less dangerous than alcohol and that none of these efforts will ever reduce the level of voluntary drug use.

They say, "That's the law," and we let them get away with it. They fully believe that when the drug laws are finally abandoned with an embarrassed shrug—just as the witch trials petered out in the early 1700s—they'll be allowed to retire and take the boat out for a quiet day of bass fishing.

"Hey, we did our best; it was the law," they imagine they'll be free to smile as they invest another chunk of tax-paid pension in fishing tackle and beer.

But by persecuting their fellow Americans under laws that are unconstitutional on their face, all sworn officers of the state violate their oaths to protect and defend the Constitution. We have a name for depriving one's fellow citizens of their rights—or even their lives—under color of law. The word is "felony."

These vicious rodents, who fatten themselves and their pay-rolls off this hypocrisy, must be advised that the day will come when anyone who has ever served as a drug cop, drug prosecutor, or drug judge will be submitted to a fair trial by jury, a jury drawn randomly from a pool containing many of their former victims. The obvious precedent—and a helpful guide for how we should deal with the plea "I was only following orders"—is Nuremberg.

Given that most of these felons would be convicted on the basis of their own recorded statements alone, this only leaves the question of appropriate punishment, one that will make these en-emies of liberty think twice about going back to work next week spying on, seizing the homes and bank accounts of, arresting, and jailing those who do no more than engage in consensual com-merce in medicinal plant extracts.

Perhaps the sentence should be something like this:

"The defendant having been found guilty of depriving his fellow Americans of their rights and liberties under color of law, such verdict having been rendered by a randomly selected jury, including many drug users whose civil rights have been right-fully restored, and given that this defendant has long and publicly and incorrigibly held that it is not the right of the individual to determine how he shall alter his consciousness by use of certain drugs, but rather that it is the sole right and prerogative of the state to determine how each individual's consciousness may or may not be altered, it is therefore the sentence of this court that the condemned be remanded to the nearest federal penitentiary to serve the maximum sentence allowed by law, during which sen-tence he is to be subject to the involuntary administration by the state of precisely those drugs that he has in the past persecuted his fellow Americans for using.

"Let the wardens further be instructed that the timing and

order of administration of these various drugs shall not be known to the prisoner, so that each day may bring him a new and surprising realization of just how pernicious is this notion that the state can or should have any control over the medication and internal states of consciousness of any individual. And may God have mercy on his soul."

Once the Drug Warriors Are Defeated, What Shall We Do With the Prisoners?

My proposal that the jackbooted drug warriors should be sentenced to forced dosing with a random array of consciousness-altering drugs, against their will, for the rest of their lives, was apparently too much for correspondent R.H., who e-mailed me in March 1997, sputtering:

"You are delusional, angry to the point of blindness, and just foolish if you think that those who've enforced a policy that they're employed to enforce should be subjected to a 'forced dosing.' I do hope you were kidding. If you have a problem with the policy, which those enforcement officers didn't create, that's fine, but to say that they should be subjected to inhumane treatment in the name of 'your cause' is callous, in flagrant disregard of human rights and respect, and vicious."

I responded:

Gosh, I certainly hope we didn't hang anyone at Nuremberg for "enforcing a policy that they were employed to enforce," and "which those enforcement officers didn't create." I'm sure our policy there was not to punish anyone for depriving another of his or her God-given human and civil rights, so long as he first donned a uniform and "followed orders" … wasn't it?

Go ahead. Compile the statistics for all the deaths caused by opium and cocaine combined—even given the adulteration and poor dose control encouraged by prohibition. Let me know if you can document more than a few hundred per year in this country.

Then we'll start looking at those who die while driving drunk (or being struck by alcohol-besotted drivers), who are otherwise killed or maimed by violent drunks, who lose their families, emotionally cripple their kids, or die years prematurely due to chronic alcohol use.

I think you're going to lose this statistical contest ... big-time.

Yet those who fought a "War on Alcohol" were finally forced to acknowledge—in 1933, and to the benefit of all—that their police-state efforts had never succeeded in manufacturing anything but massive social pathologies. When do *you* plan to stop torturing, beating, murdering, imprisoning, and impoverishing others (or hiring surrogates to do so) for their personal choices, to placate your own personal demons?

Do you believe that the majority has the right to employ its police powers to enforce or restrict the altered states of consciousness that others may choose to experience, or not?

If you do *not* believe the majority has such a right to impose its will on others through armed force, then I welcome your vote to legalize all drug use immediately, including heroin and LSD by the pound, without prescription.

If you *do* believe the majority has such a right, then what possible objection can you have to my proposing that—if and when those who believe as I do attain majority control—we have a precisely similar right to *force* unwanted drug use on all you benighted "straights"?

Cheer up ... maybe you'll *like* the effects of being surprised by 800 micrograms of LSD in your morning cereal.

Of course, you have an alternative. You can embrace the case for personal liberty—to do drugs, or to remain free not to do drugs—*now*.

• • •

The problem with these fearless drug warriors—like so many who fall in love with the uniforms and the adrenalin rush of "night exercises" against the defenseless and the unprepared—is that they never stop to think what usually happens to folks who start a war of aggression ... and lose. Throughout history, what has generally happened to the losers of wars—especially to those who actually launched wars of aggression—is that they are all killed, sold into slavery, or (if the victors are feeling particularly charitable) locked up in prisoner-of-war camps while the victors get children from their women and teach the resulting tots to play baseball.

We have for far too long allowed these life-hating zealots to proceed on the unchallenged assumption that if they lose their War on Drugs they'll be allowed to simply shrug, say, "What the heck, we meant well," and live out their years—on pensions funded by our tax dollars—fishing on the lake.

Instead, we must impress on these characters a replacement paradigm. They have launched and fought an aggressive war against a peaceful people who wanted only to control their own bodies, their own medical practices, their own states of consciousness.

They have violated our Bill of Rights. They have attacked us, by surprise, in our homes in the dark of night. They have shot us, jailed us, terrorized us, seized our homes, bank accounts, and property. They have ruined our lives and our peace of mind. They have made "registered criminals" of dying cancer patients and the doctors who dare to prescribe them enough opiates to soothe their pain and allow them a few peaceful final days with their families.

If killing them, locking them up in prisoner-of-war camps while we seize their bank accounts and their women and children, or dosing them against their will with today's illegal drugs (as they now dose our own children into docile compliance with Ritalin in their mandatory government youth propaganda camps) are all too vicious for e-mail correspondent R.H. and his ilk, then I propose that we offer them a limited window of opportunity to drop to their knees, apologize for the trouble their insane religious zealotry has caused us all, and plead for amnesty.

What's vicious about that?

III

VOIR DIRE
A FRENCH TERM
FOR JURY STACKING

A Juror On Trial

Laura Kriho, of Gilpin County, Colo., was summoned for jury duty May 13, 1996. She was the 12th juror seated in the case of a 19-year-old woman charged with possession of drug-taking "paraphernalia" and methamphetamine—the diet-pill drug, a standby for college kids pulling all-nighters, issued by the handful to Air Force pilots to help them stay awake on long flights, and technically illegal without a prescription.

According to Ms. Kriho's attorney, Paul Grant, the jurors seated earlier in the day had been subjected to extensive "voir dire" (pronounced vwah-deer) questioning, the process by which the defense and (especially) the prosecution attempt to exclude jurors they believe might be prejudiced against their case.

(A few decades ago, such questioning was limited to asking if one was a blood relative of a principal in the case to be tried. These days, jurors can be asked to fill out questionnaires seeking hundreds of intrusive details, from what model car they drive to what bumperstickers adorn the back end—and are occasionally jailed for contempt of court should they figure it's none of the government's damned business what magazines they read or what church they attend.)

But it was late in the day and everyone was tired. The prosecutor and judge simply asked Laura Kriho whether she could think of any reason she should not be seated.

Laura Kriho had been active in political campaigns to legalize hemp—the marijuana plant—in Colorado. Twelve years earlier, she had received a deferred sentence on a minor drug charge, herself, but had been assured it would be expunged from her record if she remained on her good behavior for two years, which she did.

Laura Kriho said she could not think of any reason why she would be unable to do justice by the 19-year-old defendant. She believes, to this day, that she was a fair and impartial juror, and that she took seriously her duty to weigh the facts of the case as assessed through the honest filter of her conscience. She was seated.

In the jury room after the trial, 11 jurors—carefully pre-screened to guarantee they were in favor of the War on Drugs—wanted to convict. Laura Kriho disagreed. In the course of their discussions, she allegedly mentioned the likely sentence.

The judge had specifically instructed the jury not to consider the possible sentence. Outraged at not being allowed to quickly convict the defendant and go home, a fellow juror snitched on Laura Kriho by passing a note to the judge.

Outraged himself, District Court Judge Kenneth Barnhill called back the jury, declared a mistrial, and charged juror Kriho with contempt of court, obstruction of justice, and perjury, the last for failing to volunteer facts about her political opposition to the drug war and her own youthful drug offense—even though she was never specifically asked about them.

The trial of juror Laura Kriho was set for Sept. 30, 1996, in a small town near Denver. She faced a jail term exceeding six months and an unlimited fine. It was estimated that even a modest defense would cost $10,000.

• • •

Laura Kriho's defense attorney, Paul Grant: "Voir dire is supposed to guarantee the defendant a fair and neutral jury, but instead [judges and prosecutors] are using it to 'clean up' the juries [and get rid of] those opposed to the court's policies. They don't want an independent jury. They believe it's *their* jury.

"The standard is supposed to be 'a reasonable doubt.' But the way they're using voir dire now starts jurors thinking: 'Is there anything that would make me hesitate to *convict*?' That instruction violates the presumption of innocence. I think it's a very dangerous instruction.

"Juror misconduct, which is what they're charging Laura Kriho with, generally involves bringing in outside influences. On appeal, they generally won't accept an affidavit from a juror who says he misunderstood the instructions and regrets voting guilty. So you can't bring in questions about how the jury deliberated when it weighs on the other side, when it might help the defendant.

"The judge was miffed that Laura didn't follow his instructions. Well, how can he instruct the jury how to deliberate? He told them not to think about the sentence; he told them not to question the wisdom of the law. Why have a jury, if the people on it can't think? If the prosecution of Laura Kriho is successful, we're going to need a law in Colorado that a judge has to warn jurors of their rights, that they can be imprisoned if they deliberate the wrong way.

"If this goes to trial the other jurors will be called as witnesses against a fellow juror. How can Laura get a fair trial when the jurors [weighing the evidence against her] are being instructed that they too can be thrown in jail for not deliberating according to the judge's instructions? They're going to want to read the judge's mind and give him what he wants and not cross him.

"And that's what the judge wants, to do away with the independence of the jurors. So why have a jury at all? I don't see how this case can go forward at all; it essentially destroys the jury system."

• • •

The judges and prosecutors of Gilpin County, Colorado, hell-bent on making an example of Laura Kriho, did indeed face a problem.

How were they going to explain to the jurors at Ms. Kriho's trial (without inviting an indignant rebuff) their contention that jurors should be *jailed* if they allow themselves to be empaneled on a jury even though they have doubts about the Constitutionality of the law or the reasonableness of the decision to prosecute?

How were they going to ask those citizen jurors to confer on the government the heretofore undreamed-of power to jail fellow jurors who—once in the jury room—dare to think for themselves, saying things like, "I'm not going to send this girl away for years on some minor possession charge," after His Holiness has "instructed" them "not to think about or discuss" such matters?

Not surprisingly—given how easily the system can be manipulated if the judge operates as an arm of the prosecution—a solution was indeed found by the time the trial of Laura Kriho began on Oct. 1, 1996, on charges of being a juror who refused to convict.

First, Judicial District Chief Judge Henry Nieto assigned himself to the case. He immediately ruled Ms. Kriho's attorney, Paul Grant, couldn't bring in any evidence—or expert witnesses—dealing with the traditional right of jurors to deliberate without intervention from the government-salaried judge. Then, he ruled Grant and Kriho could not have any additional time to prepare for this first-of-its-kind case, and that prosecutor Jim Stanley—who lost the original drug case thanks to Kriho—could prosecute Ms. Kriho as well. (No potential for vindictiveness there, surely.)

Finally—get this—although the prosecution had originally granted Laura Kriho's request for a jury trial at her Aug. 16 arraignment, Judge Nieto allowed prosecutor Stanley to promise that, in the event the wayward juror was convicted, he would seek jail time of less than six months.

(Although the Constitution specifically states, "In all criminal prosecutions, the accused shall enjoy the right to a speedy and public trial, by an impartial jury," today's courtesan courts have ruled that the Sixth Amendment doesn't really mean that at all. What it really means is the government need grant you the "privilege" of a trial by jury only if you face a sentence of more than six months.)

Laura Kriho didn't get a jury. The little brotherhood known as the Judges of Gilpin County, determined to asphyxiate our traditional jury rights and replace our citizen juries with government lackeys, sworn in advance (under penalty of imprisonment) to convict as instructed, decided they would simply judge and sentence poor Laura Kriho themselves, without allowing any pesky "panel of her peers" to get in the way.

(Another of the handful of Gilpin County judges, Frederic Rodgers, wrote an article for the Summer 1996 issue of the local *Judge's Journal*, explaining to his fellow Philistines how to prosecute "obstructionist" jurors.)

"To deny me a jury trial leaves little doubt about the outcome of the trial," Ms. Kriho told Joe Vigorito of the group Colorado Legal Eagles a week before her appointment with the kangaroo court. "I can't imagine how I can ever get a fair hearing in front of any judge in this district, when they have all probably read Judge Rodgers' article. It looks like they intend to make my case a demonstration case, so they'll be free to prosecute other jurors who want to acquit based on reasonable doubts."

The Crying Jury

We'll return to the ongoing tribulations of Laura Kriho, an unwilling martyr and hero of the burgeoning jury-rights movement, who simply spoke her mind in the jury room.

First, it's important to note that this "crisis" in our justice system—namely, the citizen rebellion against a subversion of our courts that has been gradually turning our juries into little more than trained government dogs, balancing on their hind legs in their tutus and yipping on command—is not being created by bad jurors.

Just the opposite. As with any scheme to subvert the people's natural rights, those running the scam eventually get greedy and take things too far. What's happening is that this century-old con game by a gang of despicable lawyers and judges systematically stripping defendants of the Constitutional safeguard of a speedy trial before a randomly selected jury of their peers is finally starting to fray around the edges.

They took it too far. The police state has grown so huge that practically everyone by now has a friend or relative in stir, and jurors are starting to throw nonsense laws and unnecessary prosecutions back in the faces of these government toadies, even *without* knowing it's their historical right and duty to do so.

When first learning of the jury-rights movement, the initial tendency of many folks is to weigh the advantages versus the disadvantages of allowing juries to bring back an acquittal in the face of the facts of the case, simply because they find the law itself an abomination against the Constitution, against common sense, against human decency.

But we might as well debate whether we should allow soldiers to return the fire of the enemy, whether we will allow birds to fly or beavers to build dams. It is in the nature of the given task. It is what soldiers and birds and beavers are here for. These are their proper roles.

If the defendant has not harmed anyone, a real jury—sound of mind and free of intimidation and willful misdirection—will set him free. A group of people who will agree to the imprisonment or execution of a fellow citizen whom they do not believe has harmed anyone or done anything truly wrong is not a jury. It may be a hand-picked cadre of salaried government stooges or a group of hostages fearful of their own freedom and safety, but it is not the "jury" that the Founders guaranteed us as part of the deal under which we ratified this form of government.

Nor is the exercise of "rediscovering" jury rights, at heart, only intellectual. Those who mince and patter about whether we should allow juries to do this or that don't realize the emotional dynamite they're playing with, the kind of explosion that can result when the peasants finally tire of hearing folks debate whether they should be allowed to rise from the mud before his lordship's coach has passed fully out of sight.

The information necessary to understand why the Founders were so adamant about protecting us against overzealous prosecutions by guaranteeing we would retain our *pre-established* right to have the whole operation reviewed by a randomly selected dozen of our peers—a jury that could meet to deliberate in secret and acquit us for any reason, including its belief that the law itself was ridiculous—is *historical*.

The process by which we analyze this information and come to understand how the trial by jury has been purposely perverted into little more than a kangaroo court, stacked with government stooges sworn in advance to ignore their conscience, never to demand to see the written statute the defendant is accused of violating, to willingly lobotomize themselves until they can dutifully fill out a draft conviction form provided by the government court, and to not even wonder if that's the way things are supposed to work, is *intellectual*.

But the depth and determination of the fully informed jury movement in America today can never be properly understood unless we realize that it has its birth in a trauma, an appalling sense of helplessness and betrayal, which is profoundly *emotional*.

This is the phenomenon of the crying jury.

More and more, in recent years, we have witnessed the appalling spectacle of American juries convicting their fellow citizens, then breaking into tears and hugging the defendants whom they firmly believe have done nothing wrong, begging their forgiveness while explaining that, "Under the judge's instructions, we didn't see that we had any choice but to convict."

Again and again, these jurors will volunteer that, "We thought they had the wrong people on trial. It's those government agents who should really have been on trial for what they did to these people." Yet, handed little "check-off-the-boxes" jury sheets by the judges, these jurors fall into the test-taking mode they remember from their days in the mandatory government schools, dutifully filling in the blanks that lead to the final line ("If you have checked all the boxes above you must now check the box marked 'Guilty'") for all the world the way they dutifully fill in line after line of a tax form that will place them in "voluntary" lifetime penury, because, "That's the way it said to do it, in the instructions."

Such citizen juries operate in pitiful ignorance of the fact that their main task and raison d'etre is to *protect* the defendant against an out-of-control government, that historically it is not only their right, but their *duty*, to bring back an acquittal in the very teeth of the judge's instructions, if that is the only way they believe justice can be done.

The classic case of the crying jury—certainly the first one with which I and many other jury-rights proponents became familiar—was that of Darlene and Jerry Span of Phoenix, Arizona.

'You Have to Let Them Rape You'

On April 7, 1988, the lives of the Span family were ruined.

Two burly men in slacks and shirtsleeves showed up that morning at the home of Bill Span, 74, to show him a photograph of a man they said they were looking for. The 63-year-old fugitive they were seeking was named Mickey Michael. In fact, Bill Span did have a son named Mickey Michael, but he was only 39 years old at the time. He was clearly not the man in the photograph.

The two visitors later testified that the elder Span answered their questions, graciously allowed them to search his home, then gave them directions to the family's place of business, where he said they might find Mickey.

That report doesn't mesh very well with the account of Bill's daughter Alice, who claims she found her 74-year-old dad lying on the kitchen floor that morning, sobbing and bruised with a knot on his head and a swollen eye. He told her he had insisted on seeing a search warrant. Instead, one of the men—his name, it was later learned, was Garry Grotewold—pinned the frail old man against the wall while his partner searched the place.

Bill Span died two months after this beating.

The two visitors then took their search to the recycled building-materials business operated by Bill's wife Virginia and his son and daughter Jerry and Darlene Span, who lived next door to the business.

Speaking to the men in the driveway in front of their home, Darlene and Jerry confirmed that Darlene had a brother named Mickey Michael, but again said the 60-ish man in the picture wasn't Darlene's 39-year-old brother. When Grotewold began threatening Darlene, Jerry asked the two to leave, and he and Darlene then turned their backs on the visitors, to wait on a pair of Virginia's customers.

Jerry later testified it was at this point that Grotewold hit him on the back of the head, kicked him in the back, and knocked him to the ground. Meantime, the other man, David Dains, grabbed Darlene by her hair and slammed her head into a nearby fence, whereupon both fell to the ground.

One customer, later testifying under oath, said Jerry and Darlene "had their backs turned when they [were] blindsided. Darlene and Jerry never knew what hit them."

Jerry and Darlene's brother, Pete Span, had a camera, and began taking pictures of the beatings. Soon, Bill's wife and Darlene's mother, 72-year-old Virginia Span, arrived with a Polaroid. She too began taking pictures, which show the assailants holding both Jerry and Darlene in headlocks, forcing them down onto the hoods and trunks of cars in the driveway in front of the business.

Brother Pete and other witnesses later testified that the second assailant, David Dains, grabbed a roll of film from him and ground it into the dirt with the heel of his boot, crushing the cannister and destroying evidence that might have helped establish how the opening stages of the struggle developed. To save his remaining film, Pete, a marathon runner, fled the scene.

According to witnesses, Dains and Grotewold then turned on 72-year-old Virginia, grabbing her neck, twisting her arm behind her back, and finally throwing her to the ground in an effort to wrest away her Polaroid.

One witness later stated, "I'd have tried to kill them if it had been my mother. All she was doing ... was standing, watching, and occasionally taking a picture."

As they were being assaulted, Darlene kept screaming for her relatives and customers to call the police.

Uniformed Phoenix police finally did arrive and prepared to arrest the trespassers who had attacked the Spans. But then the two assailants identified themselves. They said they were U.S.

Marshals.

Phoenix police were skeptical, asking why the men did not display any badges or other identification. The men said their identification was in the car. As it turned out, it was, proving that they were indeed federal law-enforcement officers.

Phoenix police did finally make several arrests. Based on statements from the marshals that Jerry and Darlene and the elderly Virginia Span had assaulted them while they were in performance of their official duties, the city police arrested the Spans.

(One of Grotewold's claims was that he suffered a puncture wound to his hand when he was bitten by 72-year old Virginia Span. At the time, Virginia Span had no teeth. It later developed that Bill Span's dog may have bitten the man while he and his partner were assaulting the old man at his home earlier that day.)

Jerry and Darlene Span were put on trial.

On Feb. 30, 1990, U.S. Marshal Tomas Lopez wrote to the prosecutor in the Span case, acknowledging that both Dains and Grotewold had reputations for provoking assaults. The judge, however, did not permit the letter to be entered as evidence on behalf of the defendants. Instead, Lopez came under fire for writing the letter. Lopez was reprimanded, but later won a whistle-blower lawsuit.

It later turned out that the federal prosecutor—working in court under her maiden name—was the wife of Dain's and Grotewold's supervisor, and that U.S. District Court Judge Robert C. Broomfield personally purged from the jury panel anyone who wouldn't swear in advance to apply the law exactly as he gave it to them, anyone who admitted having strong religious or moral convictions, anyone who belonged to a group whose "purpose [was] to promote and enhance individual rights," even those with bumper stickers of which he didn't approve.

After the two conflicting versions of the events had been heard, the judge instructed the jury that, even if the federal agents had failed to show their badges or to identify themselves as law officers in any way, "Federal officers engaged in good faith and colorable performance of their duties may not be forcibly resisted, even if the resister turns out to be correct, that the resisted actions should not, in fact, have been taken. The statute requires him to submit peaceably and seek legal redress thereafter."

"The judge told the jury that the law required that they lie there and take the beating," is the way Don Doig, national coordinator of the Fully Informed Jury Association, summarized it.

"Given this instruction," reported staff writer Judy Huston in the account of the Span case that appears in the "Jury Power Information Kit" of the Montana-based Fully Informed Jury Association, "the jury returned verdicts of guilty against both Darlene and Jerry, even though they felt the marshals were the ones who initiated the assault." Witnesses in the courtroom said some of the jurors were in tears, and sought to hug the defendants and ask their forgiveness.

Several later stated that they thought they had no alternative but to convict.

Darlene Span told me in an April 1998 interview, "The jurors knew we were innocent. They came up to us and said they were afraid they would be thrown in jail for contempt of court if they didn't convict us.

"He told them, 'You took an oath.' He must have said that a dozen times. The jurors knew the marshals beat us up, but they felt they had to convict because of what [U.S. District Court Judge Robert C.] Broomfield told them. What the government did is they left off the second half of the paragraph, the part that's supposed to say 'unless the marshals are themselves out of bounds.' The government left it off, and [defense attorney Oscar] Goodman never even objected to the judge leaving off the important part of the instructions.

"I asked one of the jurors, 'What if they wanted to rape me?'

102

and she said, 'You have to let them rape you. The law is wrong and we would like to change the law.' But it turned out the law isn't wrong, it was just misquoted on purpose."

Five jurors, including Sally Osborne, later signed affidavits requesting a new trial, expressing their belief that they had been misled about the choices open to them by Judge Broomfield in his jury instructions.

The 1990 sworn statement of juror Robert Hapip, later signed by four of the other jurors, states: "These actions by Dains and Grotewald were unprovoked. ... The struggling of Jerry and Darlene Span consisted of wiggling and trying to get away and didn't include any excessive, unreasonable, or deadly force. ... I believe Jerry and Darlene Span did nothing wrong and it is unbelievable and inconceivable to me that the law requires them to be convicted based on the facts described herein, but the legal instructions given to the jurors by the Court were such that even if the incident occurred as we believe it did, and as it was described herein, the law would require us to find Jerry and Darlene Span guilty;

"I believe such a law is completely unfair and against everything that the United States stands for; I do not believe Jerry and Darlene Span should have to go to jail for what occurred on April 7, 1988, because I do not believe their actions constitute a crime."

Yet all these jurors voted "guilty," contributing to a years-long legal nightmare which eventually bankrupted the Span family with $350,000 in legal bills and contributed to the deaths of both their parents.

Request for a new trial denied.

• • •

"Assaults by the officers on Jerry, Darlene, and Virginia ... who had to be rushed from jail to the hospital, where she nearly

103

died ... were photographed, witnessed, and attested to by several private citizens—yet the jury delivered guilty verdicts against Jerry and Darlene," comments J. Huston in the FIJA write-up of the case, based on the original story by Michael Lacey appearing in the weekly *Phoenix New Times* of May 16, 1990.

"Why? Had the jurors known that they had the right to judge the law as well as the defendants according to that law, two innocent victims of law-enforcement brutality would not be facing a prison sentence today."

The Spans' first appeal was handled by noted Harvard Law School attorney Alan Dershowitz.

Dershowitz argued that the judge had not given the proper instructions to the jury. The proper instruction, wrote FIJA national coordinator Don Doig in the Summer 1996 edition of the *FIJActivist*, "would have pointed out that citizens under U.S. law have the right to resist the excessive use of force by law-enforcement officers. Excessive use of force by an officer is not considered to be a good-faith performance of duty."

The Ninth Circuit Court of Appeals agreed, but said that since the defense counsel had not formally asked the judge for the correct instruction, they let the conviction stand.

Did we all get that? The defense trial counsel now has to *specifically request* that the judge not lie to the jury, or the judge can give it a try, and any conviction achieved by the government under these false pretenses will stand.

Broke, and still facing up to three years in prison, Darlene Span, a plain-spoken blue-collar gal who had never sought the public limelight, filed another appeal, this time pro per—that is to say, arguing her own case without benefit of counsel, except for a few interested law students.

Her only remaining avenue was to seek a reversal based on the fact that her original defense counsel—well-known Las Vegas wiseguy attorney Oscar Goodman—had been incompetent in not seeking a proper jury instruction, and that her Sixth Amendment right to effective assistance of counsel was thus denied.

Attorney Oscar Goodman "didn't even submit the pictures of my mother bleeding and getting beaten up [into evidence]. The government took us into a little room next to the courtroom and threatened us. They said if we put the witnesses on they'd file felony charges against our entire family. We said, 'We don't care. Put the witnesses on anyway.'"

Incredibly, in 1996, eight years after the Spans' nightmare began, the Ninth Circuit Court of Appeals ruled:

"While we recognize that not every instance of counsel's ineffective handling of the jury instructions requires vacation of the underlying conviction, the egregiousness of the facts and the magnitude of trial counsel's incompetence in this case require that we do so.

"Reversed."

Why did the federals file criminal charges against the Spans at all? The reason for this now-standard pre-emptive tactic became clear when the Spans attempted to file a civil suit against their assailants, Marshals Grotewold and Dains. They promptly lost that suit, after the judge told the jury that it was the Spans who had, after all, been convicted of assault.

How handy for the marshals, who have now filed their own $2 million civil suit against the Spans for that old standby, "knee injuries"!

"My mother died in 1992," Darlene recalls. "She hung on but she never was a person again, she never could go out, she never could drive. She never recuperated; she was just like a vegetable in her wheelchair.

"She never got to see it reversed. She died before we got it reversed, because it took us more than five years. It took us over five hundred thousand. I lost my home and my business. And then they tried to get her estate when she died" (see "Appendix II").

But the history of juries that either allowed themselves to be buffaloed into bringing back convictions against their best judgment or had to dredge up an unusual degree of moral courage to do what the Founders would only have considered their simple duty goes far beyond the cases of Laura Kriho and those who convicted Darlene Span.

Since I started writing a syndicated column in 1993, cases of this kind have cropped up so frequently that I've got to believe they happen literally every day. Here are just a few.

'Not Only Are the Defendants on Trial, But the Laws Are on Trial'

Despite the jury having found all defendants innocent of conspiracy, U.S. District Judge Walter Smith shocked his San Antonio courtroom by handing down one maximum sentence after another to the surviving Waco Branch Davidians on July 17, 1994, declaring: "These defendants engaged in conspiracy to cause the death of federal agents."

Declaring the defendants "unremorseful" for defending their families against the all-out assault by 75 machine-gun toting federal agents in black ski masks, who disobeyed their own orders and fired blindly through the walls and windows of a building housing innocent children, Smith prated, "Not one single defendant apologized or expressed any real sorrow for the dead or injured agents."

If Smith or any other federal agent has apologized for the unprovoked shooting deaths of six Sunday churchgoers that day (the Ninja-suited raiders pouring out of their cattle trailer didn't even have a search warrant in their hands, let alone make any effort to serve it peaceably), or for burning the defendants' children to death without provocation two months later, it has so far gone unreported.

Despite the fact that the jury in San Antonio found the Davidians innocent on all major charges, Smith used the pretext of convictions on minor counts to sentence five of the Waco survivors to maximum 40-year prison terms. Three other defendants received sentences of five, 15, and 20 years—the last meted out to defendant Graeme Craddock on a single guilty plea of possessing a hand grenade that he never used. Smith justified the heavy sentences with the claim that "automatic weapons, the most destructive kind, were involved."

Yet the prosecution never screened videotape that they earlier bragged would show the gun battle commencing with machine gun fire from the church. Nor were they ever able to display any of the medium or heavy machine guns they claimed were present ... because there were none. Half the rifles picked up on the field were revealed under cross-examination to have been left behind by the ATF raiders, and an automatic weapons expert who writes for a leading firearms magazine tells me he advises clients never to allow semi-auto firearms to be sent to Quantico where the FBI tests them for automatic firing, since, "They never get a weapon there that they can't get to fire full-auto after a little tinkering."

• • •

I called Sarah Bain, an English teacher at New Braunfels government High School in Texas and the foreman of the Waco jury, at home to ask how she felt about Judge Smith's sentences.

"They certainly didn't reflect the jury's intention at all. We thought that the weapons charges would be a slap on the wrist, that when we found them guilty of aiding and abetting voluntary manslaughter, the emphasis would be on the 'aiding and abetting,' not the manslaughter."

Based on their deliberations, what would the jury have considered appropriate punishment?

"The time served plus maybe a year, as a slap on the wrist."

Do Bain and other jurors now wish they had acquitted on all charges?

"That's absolutely right," Bain responds. "I wish everyone had just been acquitted on all charges. I've seen some extremely persuasive evidence since the trial—evidence we didn't have access to then—that it was absolutely self-defense. ...

"The federal government was absolutely out of control there. I don't remember that the sheriff's ability to work with Koresh was part of the court testimony. It *was* court testimony that a couple of the ATF agents were invited to come out to Mount Carmel while they were checking the paperwork of one particular gun dealer [who'd had dealings with David Koresh and the Davidians]. Koresh happened to call this dealer while the agents were there. The gun dealer told Koresh the ATF men were asking about him, and Koresh said, 'Well, bring 'em on by,' but they refused to talk to him.

"We spoke in the jury room about the fact that the wrong people were on trial, that it should have been the ones that planned the raid and orchestrated the raid and insisted on carrying out this plan who should have been on trial."

But if the jury felt the wrong side was on trial, why not just acquit the Davidians and issue a general finding that the court should order ATF Director Higgins and his henchmen to appear before a grand jury, explaining why they themselves should not answer charges of conspiracy to murder?

"We saw no way in the paperwork they gave us where we were even able to make any comments or recommendations, any physical place where we were able to do so," answers Bain, who is, after all, a government employee.

"But I've made that comment numerous times that Higgins and [Houston-based ATF field commander Philip J.] Chojnacki need to be called in and asked some questions, to actually be held responsible. ... Apparently we did have that right, in reading some information from the Fully Informed Jury Association."

Didn't the jurors receive mailings from the Fully Informed Jury Association during the trial, which would have informed them of the jury powers, which the Founders meant to preserve with the Bill of Rights?

"Yes, it did reach us, and following the judge's instructions I turned that over unread. He did not tell us we had that power to judge the law as well as the defendants."

I asked Bain how it is voluntary manslaughter to return the fire of one's unprovoked attackers. Isn't that self-defense?

"In the voluntary manslaughter charge there was a phrase about reacting to undue provocation. I can't tell you—we were unable to keep our notes, all the notes that we took during the month-plus were taken away from us. So although there was an instruction on self-defense, I don't know that it was so strong as to say that they could be found innocent on self-defense. There was a page on it [in the 68 pages of instructions], but I couldn't tell you right now whether we were told they could be found innocent based on self-defense. ...

"It was Woodrow Kendricks, one of the defendants acquitted of all charges, who greeted me and three other jurors very warmly and told us we shouldn't feel badly, that we did the best we could with the information we had. He probably lifted my heart more than anything else that happened in this trial. ...

"One thing that I have become aware of since the trial is that not only are the defendants on trial, but the laws are on trial. That has been lost."

'The FDA Underestimated You'

In April 1994, three carloads of gun-waving FDA goons busted vitamin dealer Rodger Sless of Albuquerque, seizing his computer and other records and charging him with 15 counts of conspiring to sell GH3, or Gerovital, a substance that's available over the counter in Nevada, California, and most of Europe.

Just what Gerovital is was part of the debate heard by the New Mexico jury. Lacking the space to diagram a lot of six-sided benzene rings here, suffice it to say the stuff contains a buffered form of the local anaesthetic procaine, which breaks down quickly in the body into an alphabet soup of metabolites such as PABA and DEAE. The defense, headed by lawyer/physician and 1992 Libertarian vice presidential candidate Nancy Lord, argued that these substances are vitamins, the building blocks of such harmless nutrients as folic acid and choline. Gerovital has been used safely, the defense's expert witnesses told the jury, for 40 years. As to whether the stuff is effective in making people feel years younger, only drugs need be proven effective, Lord pointed out. Vitamins need no such official government cachet.

The prosecution made a big deal of the fact that defendant Sless rented post office boxes under assumed names in 1991 and 1992 to receive shipments of the stuff from overseas. Lord responded that the defendant did that to protect himself from an FDA that has become widely known for its Gestapo-like tactics, pulling armed raids to seize vitamins and food supplements without bothering to go through the public hearings required by their own regulations to determine whether such compounds pose any danger.

The prosecution argued the FDA has the power to seize unapproved products in emergencies. But, "When Congress gave them the power to seize a product without making a rule, Congress was not thinking about vitamins," Lord rejoined. "Congress was thinking about food that contained botulism toxin."

To make a long story short, the jury acquitted Rodger Sless on 11 counts on June 17, 1994. The jury hung on the other four counts, with only one juror holding out for convictions, arguing, according to attorney Lord, that, "Anyone who's in business for himself has to be a crook."

The FDA went home empty-handed.

Jurors, spilling into the hallway to warmly greet Sless and his attorneys after the acquittals, "styled the case as an issue of personal choice and government overreaching," Scott Sandlin reported in the daily *Albuquerque Journal.*

One juror, Tania Chavez, told the *Journal* that she buys herbal cough drops and medicinal teas already "plastered with FDA warnings," and that jurors "worried that so much a part of our lives is going to be cut out." An FDA official testified under Lord's cross-examination that capsicum, the active ingredient in chili peppers, is already a prescription drug, and that the FDA could move to control the chili pepper itself as a drug anytime it wished. Juror Chavez said she knows people who patronize *curanderas*, traditional New Mexican folk healers, and feared she might need to use one some day and be prevented by the FDA.

"What really helped," Lord told me following the verdict, "is that the FDA is such a bunch of arrogant bureaucrats. We were able to show there was no warning letter, no notice, no hearing. They had gone through none of their own procedures to show that this was a new unapproved drug."

Lord's closing remarks in Albuquerque make a comprehensive case against this new tyranny. My reconstructed transcript runs to 24 pages, but a few paragraphs convey the flavor:

"This case is about a federal agency that has spun so completely out of control—out of control of the people, out of control

111

of Congress—that they are now no more than a band of armed terrorists," Lord argued. "They want their subjects—we, the people—to obey rules they haven't even made. They want you to endorse this by convicting Rodger Sless, so that they can use him as an example. ...

"The Founders ... wanted to prohibit government from doing certain things. It never occurred to most of them to tell the government it couldn't forbid herbs. ... The idea of government control of medicine occurred to two people—Benjamin Rush, George Washington's personal doctor and signer of the Declaration of Independence, and Thomas Jefferson. Benjamin Rush warned, 'Unless we put medical freedom into the Constitution, the time will come when medicine will organize into an undercover dictatorship. ... To restrict the art of healing to one class of men and deny equal privileges to others will constitute the Bastille of medical science. All such laws are un-American and despotic and have no place in a republic. ... The Constitution of this republic should make special privilege for medical freedom as well as religious freedom.'

"But in spite of Dr. Rush's prophetic warning, the right to freedom in our choice of health care is not part of the Bill of Rights. The Founders never imagined that a trial such as this would ever take place in America. Because they never thought the federal government would even attempt to control what we keep in our medicine cabinets. ...

"In our country today, though not at the turn of the last century, the statutes allow agencies to create regulations that also have the force and effect of law. But in this case, ladies and gentlemen, they [the agency] did not even create a regulation. They never tested this vitamin. They never published notice, never asked for comment, never held hearings, and never gave Mr. Sless any warning. Now they expect Rodger Sless, and others in his position, to have some clairvoyant ability to divine rules that even the

112

FDA has yet to make—or face criminal charges. ...

"The FDA agents moved in against Rodger Sless using deadly force: firearms they were brandishing and apparently willing to use. And they did so without even determining if he was engaged in criminal activity. This is a reckless violation of both individual rights and public safety. If the jury endorses these acts, it will set loose a swarm of armed and dangerous agents to trample on people's rights in every health food store, vitamin distributor, and alternative clinic in the country. ...

"They're hoping that you will have trouble believing that our country now has a government that will trump up a total of 15 dubious charges on one person, and will compromise by finding him guilty of something. The FDA underestimated you. ...

"Justice Byron White said in 1975, 'The purpose of a jury is to guard against the exercise of arbitrary power—to make available the common-sense judgment of the community as a hedge against the overzealous or mistaken prosecutor.' ...

"'When a person sits on a jury,' John Adams said back in 1791, 'It is not only his right, but his duty, to find the verdict according to his best understanding, judgment, and conscience.'"

It's interesting that in today's federal courts, Ms. Lord, as brave as her closing argument is, felt it the better part of valor not to recite the last phrase of Adams' charge to jurors: "... though in direct opposition to the direction of the court."

"Tell the FDA that you want them to leave [defense witness] Dr. Priestley and all of her colleagues in the supplement industry alone," Nancy Lord concluded. "Tell the FDA to go back to Rockville, Maryland. Tell them to take their guns and badges with them. Tell them that the only thing in this trial that isn't safe and effective is the FDA."

And the jury did.

'There Are No Slaves Here'

One factor contributing to the acquittal of vitamin dealer Rodger Sless was the leafletting of the Albuquerque federal courthouse by representatives of the Fully Informed Jury Association. Unbeknownst to the FIJA volunteers, those leaflets also reached jurors hearing the months-long federal case against the Aguirre family of Deming, New Mexico, for supposedly operating a $70 million, 100,000-pound, marijuana conspiracy.

When the Aguirre jury came in July 12 following a six-month $1 million trial, agents of 30 different law-enforcement agencies were "sandwiched into benches awaiting the verdict," as were "a phalanx of federal marshals ready to take the defendants into custody," according to the *Albuquerque Journal*.

Given the supposed popularity of the Drug War—the progressive demonization over a full century of the dreaded "large-scale drug dealer"— those federal agents were about to receive an even bigger shock than the FDA's "vitamin police" received in the Rodger Sless case.

No convictions. None.

Three of the nine Aguirre defendants were completely exonerated. The jury hung on the 20-odd charges against the remaining six, charged with conspiring to operate a multi-state marijuana ring that backpacked the vegetable product across the border from Mexico. At least three jurors voted for acquittal on each charge.

Jury foreperson Mara Taub told the *Journal* she was disturbed the government would spend more than $1 million "on a case that had no victims," when she had to walk past homeless people daily to get to the courthouse.

"All the jurors agreed the government's case, evidence, and informant testimony were sloppy, shoddy, and at the same time repetitious and misleading," Taub told me in a telephone call after the verdict.

"They presented four thousand pieces of paper and over three hundred witnesses, and now they're planning to retry these six people. The message was very clear that we were sent to the jury room to convict them, and six people believed that from the very start. There was one woman who repeatedly said people are guilty till they're proven innocent."

How did the jury agree on the three acquittals, then?

"I think there were a couple of us who had thought about these issues in advance, who had thoughts about the injustice of how prisons function. And we were especially upset because we knew the sentences these defendants would get would be so long, would be up to and including natural life, and that this judge sentenced so harshly."

How did Taub and two other jurors survive the careful screening process that generally removes independent thinkers from today's idiot jury pools, I wondered.

"There's very little voir dire in the federal courts in New Mexico. I've worked with the Coalition for Prisoners Rights. But they never asked me, 'Have you done prison reform work?' They never asked me if I favored the abolition of prisons."

What if they had? Is it justified to lie during the "voir dire" stacking of the jury?

"If we feel that we live under an unjust system, it's very important to think of ways to resist it. I was talking to a Roman Catholic nun, and the way she put it was, 'What if someone comes to your door and asks for sanctuary, and then the next person at the door says, "I'm after the escaped slave; is he here?" The answer is, "There are no slaves here."' That's a true answer. It's a question of what's the larger truth. One of the things I felt during this whole trial is that everyone was lying," especially the two dozen informants who received reduced sentences in exchange for their prosecution testimony, Taub added.

115

"The judge repeatedly lied to us. He told us repeatedly that nothing he'd done during the trial should be interpreted to express any opinion about the case. But in his chambers afterward, he said he would really have thrown the book at the three women defendants; he would have given them maximum sentences. He said they were going to re-indict and add cocaine and tax-evasions charges. He said, 'We are going to get them.' This judge did not seem to understand the difference between the executive and judicial branch of government. ... So in terms of prejudice and lying and lack of open minds and guilty-until-proven innocent, I think that's shocking. ...

"The phrase 'the whole truth' took on a whole new meaning to me. I don't think anyone was telling the whole truth. No one on the jury felt comfortable that they really knew what was going on. These defendants were from Deming, near Las Cruces, and they were being tried in Albuquerque, and there are real cultural and historical and language differences between the border area and northern New Mexico where the jury was from."

The jury consisted of seven Hispanics, two American Indians, and three Anglos, but only one man, Taub says.

"All the lawyers in this case were men. Only three of the defense lawyers were Hispanic and they were treated badly by the judge. None of the prosecuting attorneys were women or Hispanic or people of color in any way. ... Essentially the case was the story of the border. There was an awful lot of going back and forth across the border that was treated as suspicious. There were documents in Spanish entered in evidence that were not translated and were treated as suspicious. The use of different names by the defendants was considered very suspicious, when people who are Hispanic usually have two first names and two last names. ...

"It helped that there was not a strong Anglo man on the jury who went in determined to convict and called for a straw vote right way. There might have been the votes for conviction if we

116

hadn't had the time to sit down and talk it out. We looked at every piece of evidence at least once, four thousand documents, and some more than once. A lot of them were just filler, phone bills they'd subpoenaed of people who weren't even on trial.

"I was told later the prosecution expected us to come back with all convictions within two hours. But we didn't rush and I think that led to a higher-quality decision. In the end, we were out for two months."

First Amendment Is Latest
Casualty of the Mad War on Drugs

The mid-1990s were not happy days for federal prosecutors and federal judges in northern Nevada, either.

In recent years, these federal jailkeepers claimed to have busted multiple international drug conspiracies in the Reno and Lake Tahoe areas. But after all the arrest publicity generated by the usually docile local press, the one thing prosecutors like Nevada U.S. Attorney Kathryn Landreth and Assistant U.S. Attorney Tony White (chief of the Organized Crime Drug Enforcement Task Force in Reno) haven't been able to scare up are major convictions.

Sixteen purported mobsters were put on trial in Reno in 1994 on charges of belonging to a $140 million marijuana-smuggling ring run by wealthy Squaw Valley, Calif., developer Ciro Mancuso.

When that case failed to generate any convictions, federal prosecutors offered sweetheart deals to the wiseguys for their agreements to testify against their own attorney, Patrick Hallinan of San Francisco, whom the feds then dubbed the "actual ringleader."

The six-week trial of Hallinan, long a thorn in the side of the zealous feds, ended in Reno on March 7, 1994. The jury stayed out long enough to eat one free meal on the government, acquitting Hallinan on all charges after six hours.

"Most of the government's witnesses came across as well-scripted during government examination," jury foreman John Tonner told the Associated Press. "During cross-examination, it all fell apart. ... When it came to important points, they were lying."

How frustrated were federal prosecutors? Having lost all their big fish, but desperate not to come up with a totally empty net, they proceeded to spend $30 million on the 11-month trial of 51-year-old Jay Regas and his 31-year-old son, Troy, on cocaine and methamphetamine charges.

(These remaining "drug kingpins" were so big-time that when the federal government seized all the assets of Jay Regas, they added up to $3,000. Yet the court ended up giving him more prison time than Manuel Noriega.)

Meanwhile, wholesale florist Yvonne Regas of Reno, the 50-year-old ex-wife of Jay Regas and mother of Troy Regas, had some "True or False" brochures—produced by the Fully Informed Jury Association—placed under windshield wipers in the courthouse's public parking lot as this last trial was wrapping up.

Eight months later, on Feb. 17, 1995, the federal government charged Yvonne Regas with conspiracy and three counts of jury tampering.

"Jury tampering" means approaching an individual juror and trying to sway his vote in the jury room. Yvonne Regas did not do that.

What was this hideous brochure, so terrifying that federal prosecutors and the FBI are willing to flush the First Amendment, willing to send this grandmother away for years, for merely daring to distribute it in a public parking lot?

"True Or False?" the cover of the little brochure asks. "When you sit on a jury, you have the right to vote your conscience."

Inside, and next to an artist's rendering of blind justice, the Fully Informed Jury folks answer, "True ... But it's extremely unlikely the judge will tell you this, because in most states the law doesn't require that you be fully informed of your rights as a juror.

"Instead, expect the judge to tell you that you may consider 'only the facts' of the case, and may not let your conscience, your opinion of the law, or the defendant's motives affect your decision.

"How can anyone get a fair trial if the jurors are told their sense of justice doesn't count?

"A lot of people *don't* get fair trials. Far too often, jurors actually end up apologizing to the person they've convicted!" the brochure goes on.

Although she says she purposely avoided speaking to any of her son's or ex-husband's jurors, Yvonne Regas says jury tears are precisely what she saw when Jay Regas was sentenced to life in prison, and young Troy Regas to five years, after the jury convicted Troy, for instance, on only two of 38 charges, and the most amorphous charges at that: "conspiracy" and "continuing criminal enterprise" (whatever that is), in a case where prosecutors presented no wiretaps in evidence, no videotape, no money, not even any drugs.

"FIJA [a proposed Fully Informed Jury Act] would require that trial judges resume the former practice of *telling* jurors about their right to judge both law and fact," the dangerous brochure goes on.

What? Resume the "former practice"?

"Yes, it was standard procedure in the early days of our nation and before, in colonial times," the brochure goes on. "America's Founders knew that trials by juries of ordinary people, fully aware of their rights as jurors, would be essential to the preservation of our *freedom*. ... "

Then comes the really scurrilous stuff, as the FIJA brochure quotes such dangerous radicals as Thomas Jefferson and John Adams, our second president, the latter saying of the juror two centuries ago: "It is not only his right, but his duty, to find the verdict according to his own best understanding, judgment, and conscience, though in direct opposition to the direction of the court."

"My son was facing four hundred and fifty years" for delivering a single package as a favor to his stepmother in 1986, says Yvonne Regas. "I thought the jury should vote its conscience. It [distributing the leaflets] wasn't for any other reason."

• • •

By November 1995, when prosecutors realized Yvonne Regas' defense attorney, Nancy Lord, wasn't going to plea-bargain, but had instead lined up top-notch legal scholars to testify about the history of American jury rights and how First Amendment free-speech rights apply outside courthouses, they beat a typically rabbit-like retreat, dropping all charges without even requiring Ms. Regas to plead guilty to federal littering. Yvonne Regas had to agree to a few months of "diversion," which means she had to avoid murdering any federal officials for a few months before her "record" would be expunged.

Although there has since been a 1998 state felony conviction of a particularly colorful FIJA pamphleteer—who pushed the envelope beyond what any national FIJA organizer would endorse, chastising jurors through a bullhorn for their sheepish behavior—no U.S. prosecutor has ever proceeded with a FIJA case when it's become clear he or she would have to hand jurors, as the prime prosecution exhibit, the very FIJA brochure these weasels despise—quoting the likes of John Adams on the right, nay, the duty of juries to do what they think is right.

120

'If You So Find, Then You Have No Choice But To Convict ... '

Central California hemp activists Ron Kiczenski, Douglas Weissmann, and Craig Steffens couldn't get arrested.

The three believe hemp farming should be legal for industrial use. Hemp is the plant that produces marijuana, though its potency as a drug is much reduced when the head-high stalks are grown for their strong rope-like fibers instead.

Thomas Jefferson was a hemp farmer. Growing hemp for war use was considered patriotic in America as late as World War II. Proponents of its renewed cultivation here—though there's little doubt they also have in mind a back-door approach to ending 60 years of marijuana prohibition—peddle numerous conspiracy theories about Depression-era business magnates who wanted hemp banned because the fiber could make a cheaper newsprint than their Canadian pulp factories.

But how to get that case heard? Ron Kiczenski says he started out mailing half-pounds of marijuana to the White House, the FBI, wherever he thought he could attract the most attention. He says he followed up with specific requests that someone arrest him.

"The White House just denied there was any contraband in the package they received. The FBI said they don't arrest people for that; I'd have to go see the DEA."

Finally, Kiczenski and his two buddies came up with a sure-fire strategy. Notifying local newspapers and television crews of their plans, the threesome put up a 20-foot banner made of hemp fabric and announcing "Marijuana Planting Today" along Highway 41 near Coarsegold, Calif.—not far from Fresno—on the Fourth of July 1994. They then proceeded to stage a thoroughly public planting of 20,000 cannabis seeds.

Finally Dirk Kinkel, a Madera County Sheriff's Deputy with

a ponytail as long as Kiczenski's, did what the hemp activists had prayed for. He arrested them. They would have their day in court. Or would they?

First, Superior Court Judge Edward Moffat ruled the defendants could not explain to the jury why hemp should be legal.

"What they're trying to do is to put on evidence as to why marijuana should be legalized and that's something that should be reserved for the political process," explained Deputy District Attorney Michael Keitz in defense of the gag order. "They're trying to turn the courts into a political media [sic] and that's not what they're designed to do."

The trial judge, John De Groot, continued to insist the Constitutionality of the marijuana-cultivation ban could not be argued in his court. The only question was whether the three defendants planted the stuff.

(For the record, this type of judicial holding is pernicious in the extreme. Trials are public not only to guarantee the defendant fair treatment, but also because they are highly instructive to the populace. The prosecution may very well hope the lesson the public takes away is, "Obey the law or you'll go to jail," but that's only one side of the case. The judge, as a nonpartisan arbiter, is supposed to make sure the defense has an equally broad opportunity to argue any case it may choose, *especially* the contention that a law is unjust, unconstitutional, or based on faulty premises. Where else does the judge think the public will ever find vitally interested parties to present such a debate as forcefully as possible—and under penalty of perjury—if not in a court of law? Besides, once a man demonstrates he's actually willing to risk imprisonment for the mere chance to make his case in public, he has surely earned the moral right to speak any defense he pleases.)

Attorney Nancy Lord, representing Craig Steffens of San Luis Obispo, risked contempt citations more than once, grabbing the courtroom flag at one point and declaring, "This flag is made of polyester. But when this country was founded, it would have been made of hemp."

Judge De Groot gaveled her to silence. "The jury was never allowed to learn the true benefits of industrial hemp and the true reason why this demonstration took place," Lord told the local *Fresno Bee*. "They got bits and pieces here and there; frankly we got more in than I thought we would."

Needless to say, the judge did not inform the jurors of their right to judge the law as well as the facts.

"While juries have the right to nullify an unjust law, the judge has no obligation to tell them and attorneys are prohibited from telling them," Lord said while the jury was out. "It used to be, in the early days when this was a great country, that juries were told. ... That's how the fugitive slave laws were overturned, that's how alcohol Prohibition was overturned, because juries just refused to convict."

The jury deliberated for two days. On Aug. 25, they found all three defendants innocent. Although they admonished the defendants in a prepared statement, "We are not sending you on a seed-planting mission, but rather we suggest you pursue your cause through alternative methods," the Madera County jury had, in fact, "nullified" California's marijuana-cultivation law.

"The judge's biggest fear was jury nullification, but the jurors could see there were things he wasn't letting me bring in," Nancy Lord told me after the verdicts were announced. "They could see there was a defense we wanted to present and weren't being allowed to present, so that's exactly what he got: jury nullification. ... The jury just retaliated."

Unfortunately, jury decisions have no power as binding precedents. The act of one jury in "nullifying" a law today cannot stop authorities from arresting, trying, and convicting another poor sap on the same charge tomorrow.

Unless *his* jury acquits, of course, and the next jury after that.

The fact is prosecutor Keitz is wrong when he says the jury room is not a place for political expression. The citizen's vote in the jury room is far more important and powerful than his vote in the election booth, especially now that government has taken over determining which "approved" candidates and referenda can appear on the ballot.

It is only in the jury room that we have a final veto over the tyrannical excesses of the state against our fellow citizens, if we will only find the courage to do what we know is right.

Only when juries start setting defendants free one after another, until no defendant will accept a plea bargain but all demand jury trials and the courts collapse under the very weight of these absurd prohibitions, will we begin to regain the thousand freedoms that have been systematically stripped from us in the past 80 years.

Juror Found Guilty of
Harboring Anti-Government Opinions

And that brings us up to Feb. 10, 1997, when word arrived that District Chief Judge Henry Nieto of Gilpin County, Colo., had found juror Laura Kriho guilty of contempt for failing to stand up during "voir dire" questioning and volunteering that she held opinions about the drug laws that might differ from those of the prosecution.

Judge Nieto took four months to craft a nine-page ruling that he obviously hoped would steer clear of the appearance that Ms. Kriho was being punished for what she said in the jury room ... though, of course, she was.

Judge Nieto found Kriho innocent of perjury, acknowledging that she had never lied in answering a direct question about her opinion of the drug laws, since no such question was ever asked.

This leaves us with the absurd notion that potential jurors commit a crime by failing to stand up and demand to be excused if they have any doubts at all ... *before* hearing the evidence ... that they may be able to bring in a guilty verdict.

I wonder if jurors called in for voir dire questioning could now ask to have a court-appointed lawyer sit and advise them when they must stand up and shout out their opinions even on matters about which they have not been questioned—given that the judges of Colorado now hold one can be fined or jailed for failing to do so.

"By deliberately withholding this information, she obstructed the process of selecting a fair and impartial jury," Judge Nieto rules. "The selection of jurors who have open minds and who have not preconceived the verdict is essential for a fair trial. Ms. Kriho's lack of candor about her experiences and attitudes led to the selection of a jury doomed to mistrial from the start."

That is not true. The original trial judge ended matters the moment a government snitch among the jurors slipped a note to the bailiff that Ms. Kriho was deliberating in a way contrary to his instructions, by discussing how long the original defendant might be jailed if convicted. Had the deliberations been allowed to continue, who knows whether she might have been able to convince the other jurors to unanimously acquit? Then no mistrial would have resulted.

Clearly, Judge Nieto only approaches the matter from the point of view that, in Ms. Kriho's absence, a unanimous conviction must inevitably have resulted—an attitude typical among government judges these days, I'll admit, but hardly the presumption of innocence to which the court still pays lip service.

In fact, the goal of such judges is precisely to *avoid* seating fair and impartial juries, if by that we mean randomly selected juries representing an accurate cross-section of public opinion.

125

The Fourth Circuit Court of Appeals ruled in 1969, in U.S. vs. Moylan, "We recognize, as appellants urge, the undisputed power of the jury to acquit, even if its verdict is contrary to the law as given by the judge and contrary to the evidence. ... If the jury feels that the law under which the defendant is accused is unjust ... or for any reason which appeals to their logic or passion, the jury has the power to acquit, and the courts must abide by their decision."

The neat solution of the judges of Gilpin County? Simply screen out potential jurors who may possess such unwelcome opinions, by holding the threat of jail over any who fail to *volunteer* such opinions in advance.

But thus neutering the juries castrates one of the most vital safeguards against tyranny—those checks and balances they were always droning on about in school—that our Founders put in place.

The Founding Fathers understood tyranny could come from a legislature that progressively grew more distant from the common folk, as easily as from a single monarch. So juries carried a far more important responsibility than merely deciding whether Jim Bob was the first one in the barroom to draw his knife, that fatal night.

The D.C. Court of Appeals held in U.S. vs. Dougherty in 1972: "The pages of history shine on instances of the jury's exercise of its prerogative to disregard uncontradicted evidence and instructions from the judge. Most often commended are the 18th century acquittal of John Peter Zenger of seditious libel [the case that gave Americans our freedom of the press] and the 19th century acquittals in prosecutions under the fugitive slave laws."

Why do we believe, today, that all those Northern ministers caught hiding runaway slaves in their basements were acquitted back in the 1850s? Because the juries believed those fearful, barefoot, black folk found hiding in the basement were really the preacher's brother Jebediah and his family, come to visit from

New Hampshire? I don't think so. There was no question about the facts—by law, the preachers were guilty as sin.

So how could those acquittals have happened, if the judges asked every potential juror in advance whether he was willing to send the parson to prison for breaking that law and summarily dismissed anyone who admitted he would have a problem casting such a vote in the jury room?

The answer, of course, is that there *was* no such questioning. Juries were a random cross-section of the populace, not screened and sifted for their political views at all. And since strong Abolitionist sympathies would be present in at least 25 percent of any Northern jury pool, every jury contained at least two or three Abolitionists, making such prosecutions hopeless.

With randomly selected juries—as guaranteed by the Bill of Rights—no conviction could obtain under any law consistently viewed as unjust or unreasonable by even nine percent of the populace—one juror in 12—and such current nonsense as imprisoning people for consuming "banned" drugs or mere possession of "illegal" weapons would evaporate like a pestilent mist under a bright summer sun.

(Actually, the percentage of the populace that needs to actively oppose a law in order for prosecutions to consistently fail under a *properly functioning* jury system is considerably less than nine percent: See "Appendix I").

That is what black-robes like the "honorable" Henry Nieto—not even-handed arbiters, but mere jumped-up prosecutors still drawing government pay and showing off the loyalties that go with it—are really worried about.

• • •

By February 1997, perhaps thanks in some small measure to my repeated columns on the Laura Kriho case—appearing in the

100,000-circulation *Colorado Springs Gazette*, as well as in a few dozen other papers around the country—a somewhat brighter spotlight began to shine on the mockery that the judges of Gilpin County had set out to make of the once-magnificent safeguard of our liberties known as "trial by jury."

The *Rocky Mountain News*, largest newspaper in Denver, in Colorado, or anywhere thereabouts, editorialized on Feb. 15, 1997, under the headline "Free the Rollinsville One":

"The issue: Should a holdout juror be punished?

"Our view: No. It damages the jury system.

"Fellow jury slaves: There are at least two lessons to be gleaned from the recent finding that juror Laura Kriho of Rollinsville is guilty of contempt because she 'obstructed justice.'

"First, if you're going to hold out in a criminal case, you'd better convince at least one other person to join you. They probably won't string up two or more, but if you stand alone, you'll hang alone.

"Second, as a potential juror you apparently have fewer rights than the defendant. The defendant doesn't have to say anything to anybody; a would-be juror is expected to answer not only direct questions, but to remember, and reply to, questions asked of other people earlier in the day. ...

"What's really at work in this highly unusual case? We hope we're wrong, but it looks like revenge. It's clear that had Kriho joined the other 11 jurors in voting to convict, the state wouldn't have cared one iota what convictions and prejudices she may have failed to disclose.

"Sure, Kriho has been an active hempie—a strange but not uncommon breed in our mountains. But it's not the business of the court to ascertain jurors' political philosophies. When you command their appearance, you should take what you get and be grateful for it.

"After all, jury service is a sort of civilian draft. There's no good reason jurors should have to supply much more than name, rank, Social Security number—and whether or not they have a direct stake or interest in the case, such as knowing the attorneys or principals. ... That's all the law requires. ...

"[Gilpin District Judge Henry] Nieto seems to be creating a new legal duty in which a juror is obliged to confess not only to past deeds but to current thought crimes. In a drug case he'd just as soon reject author William F. Buckley Jr. and Baltimore Mayor Kurt Schmoke as Kriho—since all have questioned the efficacy of the drug laws.

"It goes against the whole concept of the jury to purge it of those who are critical of the government and some of its laws. That's why juries were created in the first place—to be a check on runaway government.

"We hope Kriho's conviction is overturned somewhere along the way, even if it has to go to the U.S. Supreme Court."

But Don't Juries Only 'Try the Facts'?

By October 1996, my syndicated columns on the Laura Kriho case were starting to draw some attention from other quarters, as well.

J.M., a confessed 20-year police veteran of the Drug War witch-hunts, sent me the following e-mail:

"Here's the way a jury is supposed to work, Mr. Suprynowicz, so you'll understand what's going on next time. In a jury trial, the jury is the trier of fact. Their job is to determine whether, based upon the evidence they're allowed to see, the person sitting there in the courtroom did the act which the prosecution is trying to prove. ... The judge is the trier of law. He or she will determine,

129

again based upon the rules, whether the evidence gets admitted, how much the jury gets to hear, and stuff like that. ...

"If a juror can't do their [sic] duty properly, and trust in the system to provide justice, then they should say so at the outset, and get dismissed from the panel. If enough people do this, the courts will be unable to get juries in cases like this, and your problem is solved—without having to resort to lying. And lying is what it is when a person gets on a panel by *not* speaking up. If that's what Kriho did, I've got no sympathy. She should be prosecuted," J.M. continues.

"Incidentally, this business about not discussing the sentence is also appropriate. It's none of the jury's business what the defendant is going to 'get' if he gets convicted. ... "

Ah, the old "jury judges only the facts" chestnut.

Why is it, then, that the Constitution of the state of Maryland—which the Founding Fathers knew intimately—states that the jury shall be the "trier of law and of fact"?

Noah Webster said he was publishing his first American dictionary in large measure to set forth the meaning of words as used by the Founders in the Declaration and Constitution, so those original meanings would not be lost. Webster, a prominent Federalist, defined the jury as the "trier of law and of fact."

Surely the biggest court case in America in the generation before the Founding was that of John Peter Zenger. The New York printer and newspaper publisher was accused in 1735 of printing libels against the king. The judge made it clear to defense attorney Andrew Hamilton and the jury that, under British law, "libel" meant a criticism, whether true or not. Truth was no defense.

Thus, Hamilton told the jury he had no allowable defense to offer, since he and Mr. Zenger had to admit that Mr. Zenger was indeed the publisher.

The judge instructed the jury that the defense had admitted publishing the criticism of the king in question, thus they had no choice but to find the defendant guilty. Yet the jury unanimously let John Peter Zenger walk free with nothing but a token fine of pocket change, establishing American freedom of the press for all time.

Do we today curse the names of these jurors who "violated their oaths"? Of course not. We celebrate their wisdom and their courage.

The Zenger jury did not only try the facts—there was no dispute about the facts. The Zenger jury tried the law. They found the law was a ass, and they acquitted.

The Founders were all well aware of this case, and of the British tradition of juries judging the law as well as the facts— heck, it was only after a jury disobeyed the judge's orders and freed William Penn on charges of preaching an "illegal" Quaker sermon in London that the Penns emigrated to America and founded Pennsylvania, where both the Declaration and Constitution were signed.

Deciding the case of the William Penn jury (the jurors were actually imprisoned for days without food, water, or toilet facilities for acquitting against government orders), John Vaughan, Chief Justice of the Court of Common Pleas—the highest appeals court in England—ruled in 1670, in a summary of the system of English trial by jury that echoes with majesty down the corridors of history: "The jury are perjured if the verdict be against their own judgment, although by directions of the court, for their oath binds them to their own judgment."

Not to "take the law as I give it to you," you latter-day political weasels. "To their own judgment."

If the Founders had wanted to go against that well-understood tradition, it would have been easy enough for them to write the Sixth Amendment to read: "The accused shall enjoy the right to a speedy and public trial, by an impartial jury of the State and district wherein the crime shall have been committed, *which jury*

131

shall judge only the facts and not the law." But they didn't do that, did they? Why not?

And if judges have any power to dictate what can be said or thought in a jury room, why don't they and their armed guards sit in during the jury's deliberations, eh? Ever wondered that? Government agents can watch you and arrest you on sight for breaking the law anywhere they have jurisdiction, can't they? If you're ever seated in a jury room, ask the judge to come *into* the jury room to answer a question. Insist. You will find he will not do it, because he knows he cannot. The jury room is sacred, and the judge is profane, and his judgeship would evaporate like a vampire caught out in the sunlight should he ever so much as set foot in a jury room while 12 jurors are there ensconced.

But how can that be, if he has any power to dictate how the jury shall deliberate? Why would he be given a power but no mechanism to enforce it?

This fabricated nonsense that juries—drawn by random lot since the ninth century—must now be stacked to contain only those who will swear in advance to obey the judge's orders instead of their own conscience, is an outright lie, of course. Dismissing those honest enough to admit they oppose many a new piece of legislated puritanism is a hideous betrayal of our tradition of freedom.

The jury that freed William Penn in 1670 did so precisely because the judge refused to let them read the law Brother William was supposed to have violated. In fact, the judge refused even to read the law to them aloud. Our judges today have reverted to the same high-handed humbug, assuring the quasi-literate varlets and serfs down below that such groundlings would never be able to figure out what their legislators meant—instead, we'll just explain to you, in words of two syllables or less, what the courts have *decided* the law means.

Juries can and should acquit in all cases where the judge refuses to let them carry the lawbook in question into the jury room. If the law can't be understood by a lay jury, how do we expect that it was to have been understood by the "lay" defendant?

No jury can in good conscience convict any fellow-citizen of violating a law they cannot understand, or are not allowed to read for themselves. Our citizen juries have the absolute power to demand a written copy of the statute, a demand that they can enforce by simply acquitting in all cases where such a demand is not met. The government has no appeal of an acquittal, and this is precisely why: because it makes the power of the jury to acquit, *for any reason*, absolute and unchallengeable.

The reason advocates of the current and ever-expanding police state fear the assertion of proper, traditional, jury power is not because juries will go mad and free murderers and rapists who are obviously guilty—we all know they won't—but precisely because these stormtroopers know what will become of their precious Drug War, as well as such tyrannical concepts as "illegal firearms," once modern jurors find out about our proud tradition of jury nullification.

It was this tradition, after all, that led prosecutors to give up any attempt to prosecute those who harbored runaway slaves in the 1850s, or those who made wine in their basements during Prohibition.

Juries would have none of it, and we were quickly rid of such bad laws, passed in fits of political madness. But we are rid of them only *because* juries knew they had the power to ignore the orders of both salaried government prosecutors—the one in the tailored suit in front of the bench, and the other one, in the black robes, behind the bench.

Why else would John Adams, who was to become the second president, have in 1771 made his statement about a juror's duty to follow his conscience, even if it means directly disobeying the judge?

Why else would John Jay, first Chief Justice of the United States Supreme Court, have said in charging the jury in Georgia vs. Brailsford, 1794, "You [the jurors] have, nevertheless, a right to take upon yourselves to judge of both, and to determine the law as well as the fact in controversy"?

Why else would Alexander Hamilton, first Secretary of the Treasury, have written in People vs. Croswell (1804): "That in criminal cases, the law and fact being always blended, the jury, for reasons of a political and peculiar nature, for the security of life and liberty, is intrusted with the power of deciding both law and fact"?

Why else would U.S. Supreme Court Justice Samuel Chase have agreed, also in 1804, that: "The jury has the right to determine both the law and the facts"?

Why else would Theophilus Parsons, Chief Justice of the Massachusetts Supreme Court, have said in 1806: "Let any man be considered as a criminal by the ... government, yet only his fellow citizens can convict him; they are his jury, and if they pronounce him innocent, not all the powers of Congress can hurt him; and innocent they certainly will pronounce him, if the supposed law he resisted was an act of usurpation"?

The court only began to erode the jury's right to judge the law—or more properly, to instruct the lower courts that it was no longer necessary to advise jurors of this right—with Justice Harlan's execrable decision in Sparf and Hansen vs. the United States (1895).

And look today at how peaceful our cities are, compared to the frenzied dance of violent death that characterized the 1890s, back when juries knew they had the power to throw out unpopular laws.

Why, the lone police constable today, on an average Saturday night in Detroit, New York, or Los Angeles, has nothing better to do than drink birch beer while listening to the brass band in the park gazebo, cheerfully returning the occasional wandering child to his mum and pop, does he? Just compare that to the desperate drive-by shootings that terrorized America and kept cops patrolling in full military armor—always in pairs—back when drugs were legal in the 1890s.

Oh, what a wonderfully sober and peaceful society our drug laws have given us, compared to 1895! Oh, what a great job has been done by those who have expanded our lawbooks 20-fold since 1912, until ninja-clad government assassins can invade our homes and ruin our lives (if we survive at all) on the mere suspicion that we may possess harmless plant extracts that were as common as aspirin in grandma's medicine chest in the late 1890s, or that we may be hoarding war souvenirs Uncle Bob brought home from Flanders fields in 1918.

Do well over 90 percent of the populace agree that we should jail or otherwise punish drug users, purveyors of pornographic videotapes, people who chop down trees or build sheds on their own land, or otherwise law-abiding citizens who want to own an M-16 rifle, with or without the stock cut off?

They do not. Thus, if we had the randomly selected juries we were guaranteed—rather than juries purposely stacked by the state—most prosecutions in such cases would fail. Prosecutors would have to stop bringing such cases, just as the brothers Mather gave up prosecuting "witches" in colonial Salem—saving who knows how many innocent lives—after 23 hung juries in a row.

We must remember, of course, that jury "nullification" is a bit of a misnomer. Hung juries or acquittals based on a finding against the law are granted no weight of precedent by courts or prosecutors. These smug and zealous worshippers at the altar of the omnipotent state can and will continue to use the same supposed laws to entrap another sap tomorrow or the day after—they can even re-try the same defendant on the same charge after one hung jury ... or two.

135

But if the second jury acquits, and then the third, politics soon come into play. Prosecutors and judges are both political animals, and to hold their heads high they believe they must keep up a 90 percent record of success. They may not much care that such prosecutions are a waste of taxpayers' money, but once they realize that assertive juries are tarnishing their own precious professional batting average, the police will quietly but firmly get the message that no more such cases are welcome on the docket.

What do you think happened to the statutes against co-habitation by persons unmarried, or the statutes against sodomy? Most are still on the books, you know. Cops and prosecutors will smoothly tell you, "We must enforce all the laws equally." But that's a lie, and they know it. Take them a list of unmarried persons living together within a block of the station house, along with a copy of the never-repealed statute, and ask them to conduct a raid.

Mind you, I'm glad they gave up enforcing such silly laws against private behavior. Now, if police would just begin to add all the other consensual sex and drug and non-violent firearm "crimes" to the list of those to be ignored (as fully informed juries can force them to), that would be enormously to the good. The courts and jails would be cleared of the backlog of victimless crimes that now clog them. Suddenly they'd have plenty of time and resources to promptly lock away truly violent predators—no more endless continuances, no more plea bargains—all without requiring our cowardly lawmakers to take the politically courageous step of repealing half the nonsense they've enacted in the past 80 years.

What this black-robed brotherhood fails to realize is that the guarantee of a trial by a randomly selected panel of our fellow citizens serves the same function in our society as that little weight that jiggles on top of a pressure cooker. It may seem noisy and untidy, but tie it down and soon the whole operation will blow up.

To date, the vast majority of citizens who have a problem with the government have been willing to surrender peacefully to the process of justice, confident they'd eventually have a chance to "tell it to the jury," to convince their neighbors they'd been wronged, no matter what the ever-expanding "letter of the law."

If the Gilpin County judges—and others like them all across America—finally succeed in tying down that safety valve, why wouldn't more and more victims of government taxation and oppression, urged to surrender and get a fair trial, figure, "No chance in that rigged game; I might as well take as many G-men with me as I can"?

If the courts continue down this road, it becomes increasingly likely—however strongly we may advise against such a drastic course—that bodies will eventually hang, kicking, from the light posts in front of every government building in America.

And that many will wear black robes.

• • •

But fortunately, the nonsense of the Sparf case cannot prevail. For the 4th Circuit Court of Appeals held as recently as 1969, in U.S. vs. Moylan, that, "We recognize, as appellants urge, the undisputed power of the jury to acquit, even if its verdict is contrary to the law as given by the judge and contrary to the evidence. ... If the jury feels that the law under which the defendant is accused is unjust, or for any reason which appeals to their logic or passion, the jury has the power to acquit, and the courts must abide by that decision."

Indicted Colorado juror Laura Kriho is an American hero—though I doubt she set out to be one. And her prosecution—by judges who reached into the jury room and are now attempting to censor what can be said there—is a travesty against the rich thousand-year tradition of our liberties (see "Appendix II").

137

And Always Let Your
Conscience Be Your Guide

From time to time a reader writes in, wondering how he can do his duty as a juror, if honestly answering the judge's crooked "voir dire" questions will get him dismissed—leaving the defendant's fate to the tender ministrations of a dozen brain-damaged soap-opera fans and guys in bowling shirts, well-meaning but blissfully ignorant of how they've been misled and manipulated (by judges cheerfully assuring them, "This is the way it's always done") into swearing in advance to "take the law as I give it to you."

Two New Jersey criminal attorneys, writing under pseudonyms in the May 1995 edition of the *New Jersey Libertarian* (see "Appendix II"), offer a somewhat more dramatic recommendation how folks of good conscience can get themselves retained on juries, not to set free violent criminals (Libertarians join with most folk in wishing justice for that kind were prompter and more certain), but to see to it that jurors understand their right to acquit defendants charged under bad laws.

"We recommend dealing with this in the following way: Lie."

Lying, the attorneys argue, "ought to be treated like the use of force." While it's never permissible to initiate the use of force, using force in self-defense "may be the only possible moral response in many circumstances."

Similarly, they write, "The attempted trial and conviction of someone on charges of, for example, drug use, or giving oral sex, and so on, is, in itself, a criminal act. You owe no duty of honesty to such a tribunal, nor to anyone involved in such a farce. A 'drug bust' is nothing more than an armed robbery/kidnapping, which is far worse than one committed by any private party precisely because it is done with the full authority of the law. A trial is the continuation of this travesty. ... "

138

Since the law recognizes the right to defend the defenseless innocent, the New Jersey barristers continue, "We urge Libertarians (and all men of conscience) to engage in the defense of the innocent by intentionally misrepresenting your views regarding unjust, victimless 'crimes' so that you may get on jury panels and nullify the laws in question."

(We've already covered the fact that individual acts of jury nullification are granted no weight of precedent by courts or prosecutors, of course. *Repeated* juries have to do the same thing before the prosecutions will actually stop.)

Even if only eight percent of jurors refuse to convict in such cases, the lawyers point out, that would be enough to "hang" virtually every jury. "And due process (as interpreted by the courts) requires that charges be dropped after three or four such 'mistrials.'

"Abuse of the system? Hardly. This was exactly the outcome intended by the Constitution's framers. The whole document was designed to protect the rights of individuals and minorities. ... Nullification was designed expressly as a mechanism to thwart unjust laws."

This is the reason the right to trial by jury is enshrined in no fewer than three of the first 10 Amendments. And the D.C. Court of Appeals confirmed in 1972 that the jury still has an "... unreviewable and irreversible power ... to acquit in disregard of the instructions on the law given by the trial judge. The pages of history shine upon instances of the jury's exercise of its prerogative to disregard instructions of the judge; for example, acquittals under the fugitive slave law."

At the voting booth, the New Jersey barristers conclude, "the majority calls the tune, as Libertarians are all too painfully aware. But in the jury room, it is the individual who controls the outcome (or, more correctly, can prevent an unjust outcome). As long as this remains true, we urge you to vote your conscience in the jury room."

The Verdict I'd Like To See

Let's say you do manage to get yourself onto a jury.

"Then what?" folks keep asking.

OK: try this.

Once you're safely ensconced in the jury room, perform this simple test. Do you believe the defendant deserves to go to prison, because he harmed someone?

Who?

If you're satisfied the defendant willfully harmed someone without justification, and you can name who that person was, convict the SOB.

If, however, you can't figure out who was harmed, but instead hear your fellow jurors talking about how they "have to convict" because the "judge's instructions are clear" about "what the law says," you now have a chance—perhaps the greatest chance of your life—to strike a blow for freedom.

Have the bailiff ask the judge to send into the jury room an actual statute book that contains the law in question, so you can read it.

If the judge refuses, tell your fellow jurors (not the judge or his henchmen) without equivocation that you cannot vote to convict a fellow citizen of violating a law if you're not allowed to read the law yourself. Your precedent? The acquittal of William Penn, for the "crime" of preaching a Quaker sermon in London. It was in all the papers.

If you *do* get a look at the statute, try to determine when it was enacted. If the law was enacted *after* 1912, ask your fellow jurors why.

Would a state (or territory) have allowed murder to remain legal for years, not getting around to outlawing it until after 1912? How about rape? Kidnapping? Armed robbery? Of course not.

Everything that should be against the law was against the law by 1912. Virtually every enactment since then—from the income tax to the Federal Reserve Board to the drug laws to the National Firearms Act of 1934 to the whole regulatory alphabet soup of the New Deal—has been part of the scaffolding of the welfare-police state.

Refuse to convict any fellow citizen under any law enacted since 1912. If the judge told you you have to convict, remember: This is the government that stole half your family's lifetime income before you even got to see it, forcing both spouses to work their entire lives so you never got to see your kids (if you could even afford kids)—and then used the proceeds to murder women and children at Waco and Ruby Ridge and to put up Red Chinese spies in the Lincoln Bedroom.

You're only likely to get the one chance. They can't take away your home, bank account, or family for voting your conscience in the jury room ... yet.

Go for it.

In fact, if you can easily get your fellow jurors to vote unanimously for acquittal on some bogus drug or gun or tax or sex charge, don't stop there. (This may well be the last jury on which you'll ever be allowed to serve.)

Ask your fellow jurors if they'd *really* like to send the government a message. After all, a "not guilty" verdict still sends a blameless defendant to the poorhouse with hundreds of thousands of dollars in legal fees, while his tormentors collect overtime, vacation pay, and time credited toward their pensions. To partially correct this, propose a verdict in four parts.

"The verdict and finding of this jury is in four parts. Should any part or parts be overruled or held invalid—though we protest no one has that power—the remaining part or parts shall remain true and binding.

"1) On all charges, we the jury find the defendant 'not guilty.'

"2) On all charges, and for all his actions to date, we the jury

141

also find this defendant 'innocent.' Our purpose in this finding is to prevent any government functionary from ever stating, 'The jury only found him "not guilty"; that's not the same as "innocent." That's why we're still free to proceed with our "administrative or regulatory sanctions."' We the jury hereby order—and respectfully request and instruct this court to order, on penalty of summary imprisonment for contempt of court—that the government's agents not attempt to take away any of the defendant's assets or professional licenses or privileges, or to seek to punish or discipline him in any other way, for his actions to date or for any repetition of those actions in future.

"3) We the jury hereby award the defendant all his court costs and attorney fees, which shall be judged reasonable by this court, to be paid by the government, with half those costs being assessed against the budget of the prosecutor's office and/or those prosecutors who have appeared in this court on this case personally; and half to be assessed against the budget of the arresting police agency and/or those police officers who have appeared in this court on this case personally.

"We also award the defendant compensation of $200 per day for each and any day he has been incarcerated, to be paid in greenback dollars or gold coin, whichever he shall prefer, within 24 hours, and to be assessed against the same government agencies and/or personnel just detailed. We also order that any assets seized from the defendant or destroyed or damaged be returned, or—if they cannot be returned in their original condition—that the defendant be compensated for them at their replacement value. This specifically includes (but is not limited to) any contraband, or material or items which the police or prosecutors have held to be 'illegal' or 'controlled.'

"And, if the defendant can demonstrate that he has suffered any interruption of his business, whether that business is legally licensed and sanctioned or not, these same aforementioned government agencies are hereby ordered, instructed, and found liable to recompense this defendant at the rate that would be standard for any major insurance company providing business-interruption coverage in this jurisdiction.

"4) This court is respectfully requested and instructed by this petit jury to place the circumstances of this prosecution before an appropriate grand jury now empaneled in this jurisdiction, or the next such grand jury that shall be empaneled, with a respectful request and instruction that said grand jury consider whether the prosecutors and police agents who have appeared in this courtroom, and other government agents unnamed and presently unknown to this petit jury, should and shall be indicted and charged with the felony crimes of conspiracy to obstruct justice and of violating this defendant's civil rights under color of law, with particular attention to his rights under the First, Second, and Ninth Articles of Amendment to the U.S. Constitution, based on the circumstances and actions reported in the official transcript of the court case, which, with these words, is now concluded.

"Have a nice day."

• • •

When the other side says, "The jury room is not the place to decide political questions," they are wrong. Such an assertion must also raise the objection, "Well, where the heck *are* we allowed to decide political questions?"

Overwhelming 80 percent majorities in Arizona and California voted in 1997 to legalize marijuana in those states for medical use. But the courts and law-enforcement agencies—fearing that such a humanitarian "foot in the door" might eventually collapse their entire apparatus of racial terror (yes, racial—just count the percentage of those jailed for drug offenses who are black and Hispanic) have defied that popular will through every procedural loophole they can find. So, despite all smug and sneering assertions to the contrary, it turns out we have no power to change this repressive police state at the polls, even on the rare occasions when we can actually get such questions onto the ballot.

Instead, our last chance at liberty, short of the kind of "reform of the bureaucracy" practiced ankle-deep in blood in the streets of Paris from 1789 to 1795, is to walk into the jury rooms and see to it that dozens, hundreds, thousands of tax and drug and sex and firearms and "militia" and regulatory defendants in a row walk free, starting today.

But let's not be naive. As the people start to reassert their ancient and honorable jury rights, do we suppose the anal-retentive control freaks in government, and their kept women and peg boys in the courtesan press, with all the power and loot they share under the current welfare/police state, are just going to shrug and allow private citizens to restore their neighbors' ancient rights and freedoms—at first piecemeal, and then en masse?

I don't think so.

First, expect them to choose and publicize a few select cases, which actually have little to do with jury nullification (I doubt, for instance, that the O.J. Simpson jury was suggesting we stop enforcing the laws against murder), ululating and pounding their drums for all the world like African beaters driving game through the underbrush and under the guns of the white sahib, as they rant in mock terror about how "runaway juries" are "setting dangerous felons loose on the streets."

(This will be done with a straight face, in the nation with the highest incarceration rate in the world. This, even when the whole point of the jury-rights movement is to free people accused of victimless "bureaucratic" crimes, in order to free up faster trial dates and more jail space for the *real* violent felons, who are routinely pleaded down or released on parole or probation under the *current* system.)

And what solution will these oily salesmen propose? Why, allow a binding conviction by a jury vote of 10-2, of course, or even 9-3, to block any opportunity for a few "conspiring obstructionists" to "jam the wheels of justice."

Such a margin "is still greater than the two-thirds majority which is necessary for the ratification of a Constitutional Amendment" we will be assured. (It's also greater than the percentage of tricks you need to capture in a game of contract bridge in order to make a bid of four hearts. Care to suggest your own non-sequitur?)

Amazingly—given their self-righteous "liberalism" and tendency to carelessly brand any opponent a "white supremacist"— these slick purveyors of tyranny will then almost certainly play the race card, pointing out that (as they see it) many of the "bad juries" in question are dominated by blacks and Hispanics—the same race as the serial rapists and murderers they're in the process of setting loose on your helpless white wives and daughters!

Meantime, simultaneous with this "reform" proposal, expect a parallel campaign to convince us that—since the average jury today seems to be composed primarily of epsilon-minus semi-morons in bowling shirts who never read anything more challenging than *Soap Opera Digest*—we obviously need an alternative system, providing us with arbiters better able to comprehend and rule on complex arguments involving tax laws, copyright laws, SEC regulations, and the like.

(The degree of chutzpah here is truly astonishing, since—to the extent that our juries today are indeed largely made up of puzzled retirees in T-shirts—this state of affairs is the direct result of the current practice of voir dire, under which both sides and even the judge conspire in advance to remove from our juries virtually anyone wearing a necktie or professional garb, anyone who will admit he or she has ever read or studied the law, anyone who will admit to reading substantive books and newspapers—

let alone writing them—and having firm opinions about the current issues of the day.)

The solution? Clearly, we will be told, we need a cadre of "professional jurors" kept on government retainer to help decide such cases—perhaps some retired men and women of impeccable character.

Don't worry. Such "professional juries" will still be "randomly" selected—attorneys for both sides will get to choose 12 from among 36 who report for work down at the courtroom each trial day.

If the term "professional jurors" doesn't fare well in the focus groups, expect to hear these professional court sycophants, fops, collaborators, courtiers, and cronies called "arbitration panels," or "mediation committees," or whatever else will play well to the peanut gallery.

And, of course, we'll be assured they'll "only be used in complicated civil cases, and only when both parties voluntarily agree."

Yeah, sure. You can plunk down a $50,000 "trial deposit" and wait for your trial date to come around—in eight or nine years—or you can volunteer to go before the "professional government arbitrators" while all your witnesses are still alive and both parties are still in business.

Before long, a trial before an actual jury of housewives and grocers and dentists down at your local courthouse will be about as common as a total eclipse of the sun.

Near the end of *The Godfather*, a failing Vito Corleone advises his son Michael, "Remember, whoever comes to arrange the meeting with Barzini, that's the traitor."

Similarly, though these devils will come clad in a pleasing raiment, speaking honeyed words, remember that the ones who come to you with the proposal to erode the jury system, to eviscerate it, to gut it like a fish are the traitors.

What is this "trial by jury," which the U.S. Constitution neither invents nor defines, but merely guarantees us will remain in effect, as it was in 1787? This is our thousand-year-old tradition and institution that says government ministers may not deprive us of our life, our liberty, or our property unless they attain the *unanimous* approval and conviction of a *randomly selected* panel of 12 of our fellow private citizens, free to judge the law as well as the fact, and to hear any defense we wish to offer, including arguments that the law in question is itself evil, unconstitutional, and based on faulty information and false premises.

This thousand-year tradition has safeguarded the liberties of English-speaking peoples since the time of Alfred the Great, who summarily hanged several of his own judges for the crime of removing jurors who refused to convict and replacing those obstinate honest citizens with more docile souls, amenable to rubber-stamping the prosecution's case.

(Some may wonder whether that would be an appropriate punishment for the judges of Gilpin County, today. Indeed it would be—though I would extend to them a courtesy they deny to others, offering them a trial by jury, first.)

Trial by jury, since the 10th century, has managed to survive Norman conquest, plague, fire, witch-burnings, famine, anarchy, regicide, the War of the Roses, Roundheads, Cavaliers, Ned Ludd, Guy Fox, Civil War, World War, the Battle of Britain, Revolution, Depression, Abraham Lincoln, and Franklin Roosevelt. Yet now we can expect to be told we must join in sweeping aside this lynchpin of our liberties, proven in the furnace of a thousand years, since otherwise the government will find itself unable to successfully prosecute a few thousand more hard-working black and Hispanic lads who choose to party with marijuana on a Saturday night.

147

IV

PUBLIC SCHOOLS
A FRESH LOOK AT AMERICA'S
YOUTH PROPAGANDA CAMPS

---

*Sometimes it is said that man cannot be trusted
with the government of himself. Can he, then, be
trusted with the government of others? Or have
we found angels in the form of kings to govern
him? Let history answer this question.*

— Thomas Jefferson

Pennsylvania Man Charged
With Tutoring His Son

In March 1995, when Pennsylvania woodworker Charles
Hayden met with teachers and guidance counselors at the Harrold
Middle School in Hempfield, near Pittsburgh, he was informed
his 13-year-old son Chris was in danger of failing five subjects
and having to repeat the seventh grade.

The elder Hayden didn't beat around the bush; he took action. Three days a week—34 times over an 11-week period—
Charles Hayden picked up his son from study hall, where the
bureaucrats had taken to parking him between the end of his last
class and the official end of the school day. He drove the young
man to his woodworking shop and tutored the teen at least two

hours a day.

Mr. Hayden told teachers about his tutoring plan and received notes from them each day about the things Chris needed to focus on.

The 110 hours of extra study paid off. Chris Hayden passed all his classes, with an average of 85.8.

One might have expected the officials of the Hempfield Area School District (yes, it's a wonderful name) to award Charles Hayden some kind of little plaque, hoping to motivate other parents to show similar concern.

Instead, administrators charged the elder Hayden with violating the state's compulsory attendance law by illegally taking his son out of school 34 times. At the time the story hit the news wires, Hayden was facing a maximum fine of $22—the penalty is $2 to $5 for each full school day missed—plus court costs.

"It's similar to a student saying, 'Home room is not real valuable, so I'll just sleep in,'" explains Superintendent C. Richard Nichols.

"I'm just kind of dumbfounded," responds Charles Hayden.

It would have been fine by the administrators of the Hempfield Area School District if young Chris Hayden had simply wasted the final hour of every day, reading a magazine or shooting spitballs in study hall.

And, if he had flunked the seventh grade, that would have been all right with them too. Why, who knows, some extra remedial programs might even have been available the next year, for which the school system might have collected some extra money.

But how dare some parent assume that improving the education of a single youth—in a manner that disturbed no one—was more important than the orderly troop management of huge masses of students shuffled about to the sounding of the bells?

The case of Charles and Chris Hayden seems easy to dismiss as just one of those silly things that slightly klutzy bureaucrats do when they blindly apply their blanket rules. But actually it's typical, and it's crucial. The schools claim to promote "education," but education (above all things) is a uniquely individualized event. Who hasn't watched the delight of a child finally figuring out how something works—realizing he or she can now make the same thing happen again and again, that the universe is a little less an unpredictable mystery, a little more subject to human control?

Yet those individual unregulated moments of insight that create a lifelong love of learning are the one thing the government schools can neither produce, nor tolerate.

"Education" is to occur only within the context of orderly obedience to the mandates of the bureaucracy. "I was just realizing how this spider spins its web" is no excuse for being outside your assigned room without a hall pass.

"Education" as an undertaking of unionized government bureaucrats has been systematically redefined as something quantifiable through the memorization of various facts and lists—the kind of thing appropriate to mass lectures and mass testing. Individual intellectual discoveries in defiance of that imposed structure are tolerated with mild embarrassment up to a point. But take it too far, and you'll find yourself labeled at least a "behavior problem"—if not literally headed to court.

How did we come to such a pass? Two landmark 1920s Supreme Court cases (Meyer vs. Nebraska, 1923, and Pierce vs. Society of Sisters, 1925) established the right of parents "to direct the upbringing and education" of their children, and have never actually been overturned. But the courts have been about their usual mischief since, finding one "compelling government interest" after another to justify eroding this simple doctrine.

As early as 1944, Prince vs. Massachusetts found the corrupted Roosevelt court whining that the "rights of parents are not beyond limitation," mentioning such specific areas where state schemes can trump parental rights as "compulsory school attendance" and "mandatory vaccination policies."

But, of course, a right is precisely something a government cannot overrule. Even in Nazi Germany, publishers retained the "right" to print almost anything they wished—engagement notices, furniture ads, sports scores. Who could object if only a few political stories had to be submitted in advance for approval? After all, "The rights of publishers are not beyond limitation."

Fortunately, someone's finally gotten fed up with the kind of Red Brigade thinking that's going on in our government propaganda academies. Conservative author and activist Jeffrey Bell has set his Virginia-based group Of The People to work, promoting a state-by-state campaign aimed at winning adoption of a Parental Rights Amendment (see "Appendix II") to each of the 50 state constitutions.

The Parental Rights Amendment would merely codify the rights of parents long ago established: "1. The right of parents to direct the upbringing and education of their children shall not be infringed. 2. The legislature shall have power to enforce, by appropriate legislation, the provisions of this article."

Sounds straightforward enough. But if so, it shows how far we've strayed from common sense that statist legislators are attempting to sidetrack the amendment in virtually every statehouse where it's been submitted.

Syndicated columnist and Stanford economist Dr. Thomas Sowell probably put the issue best: "If someone came into your yard and ripped up your geraniums, replacing them with daffodils, you wouldn't debate the relative merits of geraniums and daffodils. You would tell them to get out of your yard.

"Once you start debating the relative merits of geraniums and daffodils, you have already given up the central issue: Whose yard is this? Similarly, the issue is not whether schools should teach sexual abstinence or hand out condoms. The issue is: Whose children are these?

'A Despotism Over the Mind, Leading by Natural Tendency to One Over the Body'

In the early years of our republic, when we prized liberty above obedience to the state, the government didn't run public schools.

As New York State Teacher of the Year John Taylor Gatto reports in his slim but estimable little volume *Dumbing Us Down* (see "Appendix II"). "Our form of compulsory schooling is an invention of the State of Massachusetts around 1850. It was resisted—sometimes with guns—by an estimated 80 percent of the Massachusetts population, the last outpost in Barnstable on Cape Cod not surrendering its children until the 1880s, when the area was seized by militia and children marched to school under guard."

The main purpose of Horace Mann and the other founders of the modern American government school was never to teach the "three R's," which they knew children can pick up in a hundred hours from any willing parent or relative (12-year government schools sentence children to 6,400 hours in the care of "education experts," who still often fail to get it done). Rather, their intention was to "socialize" the largely Catholic offspring of our teeming urban immigrants, teaching them a secularized version of the Protestant work ethic and other useful values, presumably in place of whatever Papist or proto-Bolshevik ideas they might otherwise pick up at home.

Wise men and women warned, of course, that government schooling would always have a different goal than what was claimed. "A general state education," wrote Charles Darwin's compatriot, Herbert Spencer, "is a mere contrivance for moulding people to be exactly like one another; ... the mould in which it casts them [being] that which pleases the predominant power of the government."

The "success" of such schools, therefore, is to be measured

not by how well the students remember how to spell or figure sums, Spencer warned, but rather by how well "it establishes a despotism over the mind, leading by natural tendency to one over the body."

"Every politically controlled education system," wrote Isabel Paterson in *The God of the Machine* (1943), "will inculcate the doctrine of state supremacy sooner or later. ... Once that doctrine has been accepted, it becomes an almost superhuman task to break the stranglehold of political power over the life of the citizen. It has had his body, property, and mind in its clutches from infancy. ... A tax-supported, compulsory educational system is the complete model of the totalitarian state."

Schools don't fight violence, drug use, and scorn for achievement, Gatto argues. They teach them. Isolate children from family and community and they never really mature. "Interrupt kids with bells and horns all the time and they will learn that nothing is important; force them to plead for the natural right to the toilet and they will become liars and toadies; ridicule them and they will retreat from human association; shame them and they will find a hundred ways to get even." How? Through exactly the kind of addictive and dependent pathologies we expect from any inmates—drugs, tattoos, violence, random sex.

It was in this context, in the winter of 1995 (and as though to prove all the aforementioned Cassandras right in spades), that I watched lobbyists for the nation's teachers unions promote in our state legislatures a wish list of educational oddities, including another stab at Teachers Full Employment known as "compensated monitoring" (which Gatto, himself chosen as a mentor in New York many years ago, calls "a plan that's pretty well dead on arrival").

A mentor is a veteran teacher who takes a rookie under wing and shows him or her the ropes. But in current practice, most such arrangements work out only if the young teacher is drawn to

154

ask advice from a more experienced colleague spontaneously and in private.

Since the main advice a young teacher needs is how to cut through the bureaucratic double-talk and figure out the real low-down (as opposed to the company line), having the school district assign and pay older teachers to do this job will almost always prevent a young teacher from getting the mentor (or "monitor") he or she would have chosen independently. In fact, the best mentors will never be allowed to take part, since (by definition) they're not viewed by the hierarchy as "team players."

Gatto also complains such a proposal would nearly complete the transition of the neighborhood schools into full-service welfare offices, since teachers would then also be paid to "monitor" a child's success in accessing various non-educational government social services.

In Nevada, this proposal surfaced as Assembly Bill 376, sponsored by Assemblywoman Chris Giunchigliani, authorizing state funding so that "Each school district may establish a program to provide, at various schools in the district, health care and other social services for pupils, family members of pupils or the residents of the district."

The bill proceeds to define "health care" and "social services" to include delivery of hot meals to the homes of the frail elderly, food-stamp assistance, Aid to Families with Dependent Children, assistance to the medically indigent, low-income home weatherization, and on and on. Giunchigliani proposes nothing short of turning the schools of once-Libertarian Nevada into full-service welfare bureaus.

"That's an idea that's about two hundred and forty-five years old," Gatto commented when I called him at home in New York City. "It comes from a series of six volumes written by an insane German named Johann Frank around 1750, called 'The Complete System of Medical Policing.' What Frank said was that

155

the Germans were wasting their time trying to track and control people through their system of police spies and so forth, that the best way to keep track of what people are doing is through their doctors and their health records, that this way you can control people's behavior in a way that the people being controlled would only be aware they're being taken care of. ... When I stumbled on this a couple of years ago I laughed out loud."

My reaction, precisely, to the gargoyle known in Carson City as Assembly Bill 376. At a time when the government schools are having an ever-harder time maintaining the shopworn scam that they can even teach arithmetic and geometry, I honestly thought AB 376, on first glance, was some absurd parody dreamed up by the forces of education liberty. I would have been easily convinced this bill was designed to illustrate just how close our schools have come to abandoning all pretense of education in favor of training our youngsters, as early as possible, in what the state sees as its real proper role: lining up for succor at the breast of the Benign and Therapeutic State.

A Nation Dumbed Down

The gyrations of our current crop of politicians, as they propose one bizarre fix after another for the anti-social behaviors of our youth, rank right up there with the equally goofy—and equally tragic—failures of earlier generations to correctly link cause and effect.

The ancients burned witches and Jews for causing the plague. Rats and fleas were left unscathed to carry the infection further. Generations of doctors killed their patients by draining their life-blood to purge "evil humours."

Instead of acknowledging that teenage boys, in particular, have always (in every culture known to geography and archeology) sought consciousness-altering experiences in their search to understand God, the world, and their manhood—instead of therefore empowering fathers to take those boys out in the woods for a few months with enough mind-altering drugs and survival gear to deal with the biologically necessary change—our mommified culture threatens to jail any father who hands his kid a hallucinogenic mushroom or a hunting weapon, reducing the once-vital civilizing role of "fatherhood" to little more than the bill-paying handyman/stooge so frequently portrayed in today's TV sitcoms.

Virtually all of America's late-19th century "social workers" were women—it's no coincidence that the current welfare culture systematically replaces fathers with government handouts to make adult males superfluous, nor that the most demonized enemy of progress these days is a male who insists on some widely ridiculed out-of-date stereotype of family roles.

Instead, the mommified culture of the welfare state assures us we can safely chemically castrate our adolescent males with various sedative or hypnotic drugs designed to tame their "unruly behaviors" while they sit through 12 endless droning years of government propaganda, taught to spy on and turn in their fathers (yes, in particular, even if the DARE officers carefully use the euphemism "parents") for anything from drugs to guns to "family violence," which now includes threats, loud talk, bullying, and Politically Incorrect views.

Meantime, these pitiful twerps try to banish from sight every possible consciousness-altering substance a youth might lay hands on, from LSD to marijuana, for all the world like the fairy-tale king who tried to ban all needles from his kingdom so Sleeping Beauty could never prick her finger, as foretold in the fairy's curse.

The result? Instead of using marijuana and LSD, which never killed anyone (and as a direct result of these do-gooders misdiag-

157

nosing the problem, when they presume it's "availability of drugs," rather than the biological fact that all teenage boys will seek out consciousness-altering experiences), their kids turn to sniffing glue and paint thinners, which, tragically, *do* kill them.

And now? Now we're promised that the installation of a "v-chip" in our televisions will reduce youth violence. Never mind that youngsters of earlier ages gathered round the campfire to hear the tale of Beowulf and the spear-Danes, or burned candles late into the night reading tales of Genghis Khan and Richard Lionheart splitting their enemies from shoulder to waist with axe or sword. It must be TV.

If it's not TV, it must be guns and drugs—ban them and everything will be fine. This despite the fact that 12-year-olds hunted regularly across America, while opium and marijuana could be bought without prescription at any pharmacy from 1789 to 1915, without spurring any crime waves.

Well then, it must be the lack of prayer in the schools ...

The list of excuses—and ever more bizarre proposed remedies—are all hogwash. The reason our children act like prisoners is that they *are* prisoners.

"Put kids in a class and they will live out their lives in an invisible cage, isolated from their chance at community," writes Gatto in *Dumbing Us Down*, which should become the manifesto for the overthrow of our socialist schools. "Children and old people are penned up and locked away from the business of the world to a degree without precedent; nobody talks to them anymore, and without children and old people mixing in daily life, a community has no future and no past."

Think of what's killing us as a nation, Gatto warns—narcotic sex, the pornography of violence, gambling and alcohol—"all of these are addictions of dependent personalities, and this is what our brand of schooling must inevitably produce."

The brilliant Austrian economist Friedrich Hayek reminded

us, "It is … an old discovery that morals and moral values will grow only in an environment of freedom, and that in general, moral standards of people and classes are high only where they have long enjoyed freedom. … It is only where the individual has choice, and its inherent responsibility, that he has occasion to earn … moral merit."

We Obviously Need Universal Oxygen Generation, Or We'd All Die

Of all the topics I tackle, that of government schooling exposes the most yawning chasm of "refusal to believe." No matter how much evidence is compiled—anecdotal or statistical—that the government schools are evil in their very conception and systematically destructive to the goal of a free and peaceful nation, the answer comes back from the chorus of the faithful:

"All right, if you look hard enough, we acknowledge you can find some areas where the public schools are failing. In any enterprise this vast, that should come as no surprise. But what good can come of being so negative? We obviously need universal public education, or the next generation would be completely illiterate, with a devastating impact on our technology, our culture, and our leadership in the world. So instead of being such a Negative Nellie, such a Cynical Sue, what constructive suggestions do you have to help us reform the public schools and put them back on the right track? Are you willing to pitch in, for instance, and help us win passage of our next proposed bond issue, which we desperately need to buy more books and science-lab equipment? Surely you can't argue there could be anything wrong with buying our children more schoolbooks, lab equipment, and computers? Won't you help us build our children up, instead of always tearing everything down?"

I've given it a lot of thought, and I think the problem here is one of time—time measured not merely in years, but in generations.

Let the government submit that if we abandoned the War on Drugs, the vast majority of the population would soon become incapacitated addicts of heroin and cocaine, the seductiveness of which exceeds any human power of resistance. Factories would fall idle for lack of workers. Gunfire, child and spouse abuse, looting, and chaos would reign. Personal hygiene would disappear. Our skin scabbed and running with open sores, we'd be nodding off among heaps of feces, garbage, flies, and maggots as the mobs rioted for ever more potent fixes. All would be lost.

Steps forward a brave Libertarian dissenter, with the courage to declare that the emperor has no clothes. "Wait a minute," she says. "All these drugs you're talking about were legal up until 1934, and this was the most productive nation on Earth. The factories worked full speed ahead, even though children's cough syrup contained heroin and the worker's lunchtime bottle of Coca-Cola contained twelve grains of cocaine. In fact, there seems to be some evidence that it's *Prohibition* that creates all the problems you're talking about. Chicago and Kansas City were torn apart by corruption, lawlessness, and drive-by Tommygun shootings in the 1920s, but all those problems disappeared overnight when your guy, Franklin Roosevelt, *re*-legalized alcohol in 1933. Why shouldn't we expect the same result from re-legalizing these other drugs?"

This argument wins. It prevents the government Drug Warriors from sticking to their initial argument. Watch them. Whenever this rebuttal is presented in a calm and orderly way, the Fearless Drug Warriors are forced to retreat to the far weaker stance that, "Well, drugs are still bad, and if we legalized them that would send a signal to kids that it's OK to use them, so we have to keep

160

trying."

(So we're shredding the Bill of Rights just to "send a message to the kids"? As Jack Warner once said, "If I wanted to send a message, I'd use Western Union.")

But *why* does this common-sense rebuttal destroy the government's first outrageous claim that legalized drugs would bring the end of civilization? Because when the brave Libertarian stands up to call the government's bluff, a couple of senior citizens in the crowd can generally be counted on to stand up and confirm, "She's right. I remember the 1920s. I remember how you could get a real buzz from a couple of bottles of Coke—we even called it 'dope' when we ordered it at the soda fountain. None of us turned into worthless junkies. And I remember how the violence ended when FDR got rid of alcohol Prohibition, too. She's right about that. Maybe drug prohibition *is* the problem."

Likewise, when the government claims that any repeal of existing gun regulations—including the massively unconstitutional National Firearms Acts of 1934 and 1968—would lead to the slaughter of millions by gangs with machine guns, there are plenty of Americans alive who remember when there *were* no such federal restrictions, and when America was a far more peaceful, polite, and civil nation than it is today.

In each case, the government scheme in question has only been in place for 65 years, and there are still living Americans to laugh out loud at the fantasy that a nation without such federal interventions would be worse off in any substantive way. But Horace Mann and his cohorts started tax-funded government schools in Massachusetts in the 1850s—*one hundred and fifty years ago.* The last holdouts on Cape Cod were marched to the new government schools at bayonet point in the 1880s—*six generations ago.*

After more than 100 years, there's no one left alive to point out that when Alexis de Tocqueville toured this nation in the 1820s, he found the common people to be the most literate, well-read, and well-informed on public issues of any in the world. Not only did wealthy men like Jefferson, Madison, and Washington never attend a government school, neither did Abe Lincoln or Ben Franklin, the kind of poor lads who learned their letters at home and then rose to join the ranks of our most effective and literate leaders, scholars, and inventors, learning as they worked their way through apprenticeships from their early teens, never having set foot in (or even so much as imagined) a school funded by some distant government at taxpayer expense.

I have struggled to come up with an example that would be just as absurd yet hermetic as this presumption that only tax-funded schools stand between us and illiterate chaos. Try the following:

As the federal government allocates more and more money to subsidize "science," those receiving this money are not stupid enough to fail to realize what kind of work is wanted.

The Ph.D.—a concept imported from Germany in the 1840s by the same folks who created our regimented government schools on the Prussian model—essentially recreated American scholarship on the model of a medieval guild. Candidates for permanent university teaching posts earn this necessary credential not by passing some objective test of their subject knowledge, but by proposing a new theory and then doing the research to confirm it—a theory and a body of research that must be approved by three professors who are *already* members of their particular Ph.D. guild.

As a herd of students far in excess of the real talent pool tramples such already well-worn ground as Modern Language and Literature, or the Schools of Education, in search of fresh thesis topics, the idiocy that results these days has been pretty well-documented. Is there any classical or modern literary figure in whose work a Ph.D. candidate has not yet discovered a "hidden gay or lesbian subtext"? Could there be anything more ab-

162

surd than granting a Ph.D. to an "Education" researcher who contends there is some better way than phonics to teach children how to read the English language—a language with a phonetic alphabet?

(Well, actually, there is something more absurd—adopting that theory for use in teaching an entire generation to "look and guess" the meaning of words "from the context," rather than sounding out syllables.)

But the impact of the three-Ph.D. signoff requirement, now combined with federal research funding, has never been so insidious as it reveals itself in the really important disciplines, like economics, history, and hard science.

If a scholar's research leads him to adopt a more and more free-market model to explain developments economic or historical—to follow von Mises and Hayek and Rothbard in arguing the free market solves problems, while government intervention causes them—he is going to have a tough time finding three established (thus, government-funded) Ph.D.s to sign off on his thesis. Either he will revise it to grant some usefulness for government controls and regulations, or he will likely be out of a job when he comes up for tenure after two years, and the administration finds his Ph.D. incomplete.

(Gifted historian David Beito was denied tenure at the University of Nevada-Las Vegas a couple of years back, despite a list of publications as long as your arm, many of which broke useful new ground in revising our standard history of the late 19th and early 20th centuries when it came to the development of such anti-competitive guilds as the American Medical Association. But showing how government meddling had crippled free-market economic solutions did not make young Mr. Beito popular with the socialist sob sisters who comprised much of the rest of the UNLV history department. Beito was sent packing and replaced with a woman—who had not yet completed her Ph.D. and who had a much less impressive list of publications, but whose Politics were much more Correct.)

Just try proposing a thesis that the discretionary wealth created by the free market was already cleaning up pollution before government got involved, that all that was really needed was streamlined access to the courts by individuals who want to sue polluters for infringing their property rights, and that in fact government anti-pollution efforts are now dominated by lobbyists for big corporate campaign donors, who carve out loopholes for their sponsors which actually freeze existing pollution in place at unnecessarily high 1970s levels.

You're going to have problems getting that thesis approved.

Propose that industrialization has had no adverse effect, for example, on "ambient oxygen levels," and you'll be advised to pick a different time frame, to show a set of results more conducive to arguing for more government regulation.

(Are you a moron? Don't you know who *supports* this research?)

Having laid the groundwork for this politically correct "new science," let us now submit that some hungry young grad student takes up that challenge, and writes a paper that takes advantage of the endless volatility of such atmospheric readings to contend that (based on some carefully selected time frame) we now face a growing "oxygen shortage."

Imagine with me that the government response is to fund an "experimental oxygen measurement and generating station," located in and therefore creating more jobs for the district of a powerful congressman.

Initially, such a project might be ridiculed by those of us Hillary Clinton has branded the "extremist right-wing anti-government conspiracy." After all, everyone knows the atmosphere contains zillions of cubic acres of oxygen, that its main sources of replenishment are volumes of plant synthesis and volcanic combustion next to which no manmade generators could ever represent a drop in the bucket.

But the answer comes back that it's better to be safe than sorry, and besides it's all just "experimental." You can't possibly object to "more objective research into the extent of the problem," can you?

After 60 years of proliferating federal oxygen-generating stations, they would become familiar landmarks, dotting the landscape. The plant workers' trade union—the Oxygen Generators Association—would become an electoral constituency not to be trifled with. From time to time, some good publicity would be arranged as the staff at one of the local oxygen plants raced to the aid of some poor old lady collapsed on the sidewalk from an attack of emphysema.

Further, the government might well be prevailed upon to adopt as a method of executing its political dissidents a televised public ceremony in which the culprit is sealed into a glass chamber, from which all the air would then be sucked out, resulting in an agonizing object lesson, as to where we would be if we ever stopped paying the "oxygen tax" that supports the crucial government oxygen-generating stations.

Even after 60 years, there would still be some senior citizens to hoot at such nonsense, insisting everyone could breathe just fine back before the government ever started assessing any oxygen tax.

But after 150 years? Even if the oxygen tax rose till it consumed half of the average worker's paycheck, would we really have the courage to stop paying it and risk having the oxygen generators shut down? After 150 years of being assured that it is only through such unstinting unselfish government efforts that we continue to breathe?

Wouldn't congressmen win re-election by pointing out that the well-meaning challenger is a political novice who never would have had the influence to win budget approval for not one, not two, but *three* new oxygen plants in the district in the past two years, adding no fewer than 500 jobs to the region's employment base?

No no, my friends, now is not the time to change horses in mid-stream. Let's stick with the incumbent party, all the way to President Smedley's visionary goal: oxygen self-sufficiency for all America by the end of this decade!

And wouldn't well-meaning souls be writing in to chide me, "All right, Mr. Suprynowicz, if you look hard enough, I acknowledge you can find some areas where the public oxygen-generating system has grown wasteful and inefficient. In any enterprise this vast, that should come as no surprise. But what good can come of being so negative? We obviously need universal oxygen generation, or we'd all die, clutching our throats in agony like the convicts on TV. So, instead of being such a Negative Nellie, such a Cynical Sue, what constructive suggestions do you have to help us reform the public oxygen-generating system and put it back on the right track?

"Why do you hate the Oxygen Generation workers so much? Don't you know how dedicated they are, how overworked by their ever-increasing quotas, how underpaid for the difficult and thankless job they do, especially now that the scientists have discovered the terrifying new threat of the Asian Sulphur Dioxide Plume? My wife is an oxygen worker, and I'll have you know that even after her grinding six-hour shift at the plant, she comes home and spends up to two hours each evening, generating oxygen at a little portable generator we have here at home. That's how dedicated she is, you ingrate! Don't you believe we owe it to the children to provide them with just as breathable an atmosphere as our parents struggled and starved to provide for us?"

In the past, our ancestors were afraid to sail out of sight of land, lest they fall off the edge of the world. In the past, we were afraid to stop torturing and burning witches, lest Satan take over the earth. Someday, will our descendents say of us, "What a waste. Out of fear of the unknown, they bundled off their own children, when they were only tiny tots, to become brainwashed slaves of the mandatory government youth propaganda camps, because they were too lazy and unimaginative and terrified to try any other way."

Was it Mark Twain or Will Rogers who reminded us that it's not what we don't know that hurts us, but what we think we know that turns out not to be true?

What if the government schools turn out to be not only unnecessary, but totally counterproductive, a complete waste of funds and energies, actively subverting America's heritage of freedom and liberty while actually *reducing* historical literacy levels and financially impoverishing us all, along with the very children we claim to want to help?

Remember, the system that Horace Mann and his pals brought back from Germany and installed in this country as "the public schools" in Massachusetts in the 1850s was, essentially, the Prussian response to that martial nation's ignominious defeat at the hands of Napoleon Bonaparte in the 1790s and early 1800s.

The Prussian elite decided the problem couldn't possibly have been bad generalship on the part of the landed-gentry officer class. Instead, it had to be the common foot soldier who had failed in his duty. And why? A lack of discipline—an unwillingness to march unflinching into enemy fire. In response, they vowed to organize a system of training the peasants—and only the peasants—which would stress regimentation and obedience.

Children would be dragooned from their mother's knee as soon as they were old enough to use a latrine and placed in huge public buildings, grouped together by age—just like recruits into the army. There, along with some rudimentary skills of reading and arithmetic—mind you, it wouldn't do to *over*-educate future

167

soldiers and factory workers in the kind of philosophical disciplines that would only lead them to question the wisdom of their superiors—they would be raised up to be physically strong through exercise and to obey without question.

When the bell rang, they would pick up their books or slates and race en masse to the next classroom or group exercise—sounding off by name and number, doing everything together, even showering—just as in the future they would be expected to march to the next machine in the factory or to execute a military maneuver without hesitation, without question or doubt. None of mommy's blubbering, "Do unto others, only as you would have them" crap. Just as in prison, the pecking order in those shower rooms would always bestow leadership on the strongest and most aggressive. The children would soon learn the real way of things. The state had the power, and the powerful were not to be questioned. It was strict obedience to orders that mattered, no matter how mindless or otherwise pointless the task. An "A" would be awarded to those who colored only within the solid lines, not to those who couldn't learn to march in step. The most loyal toadies would be named "prefects" or "hall monitors" or "honor students," awarded special privileges and badges of rank and expected to keep order even when no "master" was in sight, just as the army draws its sergeants from the same social rank as the recruits. The good of the state would be the good of all.

As we examine each failure and fraud in attempts to "reform" this American school system—all on the dubious premise that it was ever intended to produce well-rounded, well-read, thoughtful participants in a republic that ranks individual liberty above the needs of the machine—keep asking yourself: Which theory better explains what I'm seeing here? The notion that the public schools are good and necessary things that have just gone a little bit astray? Or the premise that this whole set-up is a dangerous and alien imposition of an arrogant Prussian-style bureaucracy on a previously free nation, aimed at nothing less than propagating itself, while reducing us all to a condition of ignorant subservient bondage to the state?

Pursue Excellence ... And Cast It Out

In 1993, the Nevada State Legislature amended the law requiring local school districts to provide special programs for crippled and retarded kids. In accordance with the latest politically correct phraseology, it replaced the term covering such children ("handicapped") with the word "disabled." Then it added an afterthought: "Each school district shall make special provisions as may be necessary for the education of pupils with disabilities *and gifted and talented pupils.*"

That sounded clear enough to Pamela Triplett, mother of 9-year-old Josh Triplett, in the state capital of Carson City. Josh has an IQ in the 160-180 range. At age 9, he read at the college level and demonstrated math, science, and computer skills more typical of high-school students.

Pam Triplett approached her local school district that year (1993), asking whether it would be possible for Josh to remain with his third-grade classmates for sports and extracurricular activities, while taking advanced classes or tutorials in selected subjects.

The district refused. The least disruptive thing would be for Pam to put Josh in a private school or home-school him, they said.

Josh spent 1993 at home, being tutored by his mom, while the Tripletts went through the district's appeal procedure. An impartial arbiter ruled for young Josh. "So the school board got rid of that arbiter and appointed another one," says Bill Hanlon, an outspoken member of the State Board of Education and himself a math teacher. In an attempt at "compromise" in the summer of 1994, the Carson City board even suggested that—given that Josh has a slight speech problem—it might be possible to put him in a "special" class after all: one for the handicapped.

Pam Triplett declined that offer. Appointed to advise the Carson City school board throughout all this, Hanlon says, was Nevada Deputy Attorney General Melanie Meehan Crossley.

In that summer of 1994, the dispute reached the state Board of Education. Hanlon favored a preemptive ruling on young Josh's behalf. But Hanlon was outvoted and the board opted to seek a ruling from the office of the attorney general. In a curious opinion, the attorney general's office ruled that although one state law requires special programs for the gifted "as may be necessary," a separate statute only requires custom-tailored individual programs for "pupils with disabilities." And the statute that makes the *lesser* requirement on the state outweighs that which requires the state to do more, the AG's office ruled.

So Josh Triplett stayed home again in 1994.

The assistant attorney general assigned to write that opinion? The Carson City School Board's legal advisor, Melanie Meehan Crossley.

While millions are spent on those whose disabilities make it unlikely they will ever excel, the Triplett case is a typical example of "the way the gifted and the talented get screwed," Hanlon says.

And not by accident. Pulitzer Prize-winning culture critic William A. Henry III died of a heart attack at the age of 44, also in the summer of 1994. But his book, *In Defense of Elitism*, was issued posthumously that year by Doubleday. Coming as it did from a baby boomer, registered Democrat, and card-carrying member of the ACLU, Henry's analysis of what's going on in the nation's schools is devastating.

"The same quixotic liberalism that led to the 'deinstitutionalization' of genuine lunatics, who now stand on street corners swaying and talking to themselves, has taken hold of public education," Henry reports. "Egalitarians have proclaimed that the self-esteem and limited learning opportunities of the disabled are more important than the advancement of the fit."

Teachers and administrators are "guided to this misplaced indulgence" by a number of factors, in Henry's view. "One is the new place of schools as social worker and national nanny, providing everything from free hot lunches for the indigent to counseling and physical protection for the abused. This breeds in teachers a sense that their primary mission is to succor the young rather than instruct and assess them. ... School administrators and counselors now see their institutions ... as rehabilitation centers obliged to make up for the social and psychological deficiencies of some parents, the ignorance or bone idleness of others, the economic privations of others still, and the myriad unkindnesses of nature. ... "

The U.S. Department of Education reports that only two cents out of every hundred dollars spent on K-12 education support special programs for the talented; they're also among the first programs to be sacrificed at budget-cutting time.

"American egalitarians continue to believe Marxian romantic twaddle about the invariable blamelessness of the unaccomplished," Henry marvels. "They argue that talent is distributed absolutely evenly along class and educational lines, in defiance of everything we know about eugenics. Consequently, they insist that differences in attainment are explained entirely by social injustice."

This has led to the move to eliminate "ability tracking," based "on the theory that bright children ought to be helping slow ones, rather than maximizing their own achievements and pulling ahead.

"I'm not making this up," Henry insists. "This is actually popular, if not prevailing, educational theory. Not far below the surface, this attitude embodies a Marxian belief that the smart pupils' intelligence is not theirs to allocate and command, but is instead a communal asset to be deployed for the whole class's good."

171

Or simply to be sent home to mom, apparently, if the kid is bright enough to present teacher with a puzzling square peg, when her guild training hasn't provided her with anything but round holes.

All the Wealth of Midas

The next time someone tells you the educrats could fix our mandatory youth propaganda camps if we just gave them a little more money:

In June 1995, the Supreme Court decided the case of Missouri vs. Jenkins, ending what the Separation of School & State Alliance calls "one of the most spectacular failures of government control of schools.

"In 1985, a single judge took control of the school district in Kansas City, Missouri. Spending $1.5 billion over the normal budget, the judge created state-of-the-art school facilities with greenhouses, athletic arenas, a planetarium, radio and TV studios, and computers in every classroom.

"The result: *no measurable improvement* in academic achievement, a fallen attendance rate, and a dropout rate that remains at 60 percent for high-school students."

National History Standards: Bad Results of a Bad Idea

As they divert more and more time and energy into social-engineering schemes, our government schools stray further from what is now disparagingly referred to as the "core academic curriculum."

Couple this with feel-good grading schemes designed to make sure no child suffers damage to his or her self-esteem—no matter how far they are from mastering the material—and you have a recipe for the widespread collapse of our technology in the early 21st century. (As self-esteem replaces competence, kids who would once have flunked will now find work as architects, elevator installers, and pilots.)

Today, not one high-school graduate in 100 could meet the college admission requirements of just 60 or 70 years ago. Latin? German? Locke and Hegel? Not a clue.

But for a real measure of the damage the government schools have done, merely note that the McDonald's chain a few years back made the kind of decision we would once have expected only in the Third World: that the only way they could trust typical inner-city kids to ring up a cheeseburger was to teach them to push the button with the picture of the cheeseburger on it. Our 18-year-olds can no longer even count change—a basic commercial skill once taught in the second or third grade.

When the National Endowment for the Humanities finally released its report in 1987 revealing that two-thirds of high-school seniors could not identify the half-century in which the Civil War had been fought, the problem could be ignored no longer.

Meeting in Charlottesville, Va., in 1989, George Bush and the nation's governors agreed, unanimously, that national standards should be set in five subjects, including history.

Lynne V. Cheney, then chairwoman of NEH, championed the project. The National Center for History in the Schools at UCLA was put in charge.

The volumes that resulted—issued in late 1994—lay out a series of broad educational goals. The recommended classroom projects include a mock trial of industrialist John D. Rockefeller.

By October, the battle was joined.

Cheney herself denounced the about-to-be-released standard—particularly those for U.S. history. Writing in the *Wall Street Journal*, she complained that Paul Revere merited not a single mention, while Harriet Tubman got six. If the standards are adopted, she warned, "Much that is significant in our past will begin to disappear from our schools."

In January 1995, in a nonbinding vote, the U.S. Senate denounced the standards, 99-1.

There are two separate problems here. The standards do cast a bright spotlight, at last, on the prevailing belief among many of today's educators that our European-based culture, built on a foundation of capitalism and property rights, is an evil one. Our savior, in this view, has been FDR-style big government, castrating the evil capitalists while enforcing racial and gender equality.

The anti-statist opposition wants our children taught that our political and economic traditions are admirable and worth passing along. They object to a fanciful rewriting of history to pretend that Molly Pitcher had as much to do with winning the Revolution as Washington or Franklin.

The traditionalists argue that notions like personal liberty, religious tolerance, political pluralism, and the sanctity of property rights developed in Europe, and were spread around the world by people who happened to be mostly white—though their champions today can be of any color.

They're right. True, the days have passed when our schools could get away with portraying the conquest of the Indians as an unalloyed triumph. Good riddance to such smugness. Let the kids read *Bury My Heart at Wounded Knee*, by all means. The underlying values of our culture will not be shaken by acknowledging the many times those values have been abandoned or betrayed—especially by the tyrants of the Potomac.

But the Political Correctness of the schools has gone way beyond some useful debunking of myths about cherry trees and happy colored folk singing folk songs down on the plantation.

174

Now our education colleges dismiss *any* insistence on demonstrable historical truth as a mere cultural prejudice favoring Caucasian men—such "ice people" simply don't understand that women and "sun people" think differently, and deserve equal tolerance for their more "intuitive" and less rigorously logical way of "arriving at the truth," you see. Such truths can be validated as "emotional truth," which an ice person with his charts and graphs and rigorous so-called "logic" would never understand.

When all these kinds of "truth" have equal standing, who will dare debunk a black scholar who insists the ancient Egyptians developed electricity and flying machines (as he can see depicted in their wall paintings, once he looks hard enough)— discoveries that obviously must have been wrested away from them and destroyed by invading white folk, depriving the black Africans who ruled Egypt of their proper historical credit?

No amount of archaeological evidence can defeat such twaddle, once it's made clear that such teachings are good because they make black children feel good about themselves—a higher "truth" in itself than the interpretation of some endlessly debatable details about dried-up pot shards.

An insistence on "right answers" and even on "truth" itself— to this way of thinking—is a racist plot.

(And we wondered why liar Bill Clinton's popularity remained so high in the black community, doubtless much to the chagrin of hard-working, moral, black Americans who had believed their culture of honor and truth-telling was the same as everyone else's.)

Once this rewriting of history to make us all feel better got underway, there was no end. Where previously those of Indian or Latin descent had been made to feel shame that their distant ancestors had been backward blood-soaked autocrats, practicing human sacrifice in pre-Columbian Mexico, now it could simply be asserted that the Aztecs were running free-love communes where everyone had an equal share in the groats and buckwheat, until the nasty Europeans arrived to torture everyone to death.

Put John D. Rockefeller on trial? When Rockefeller and his ilk were done, kerosene and many other commodities were far cheaper for the common man than they had ever been before, improving the standard of living for all. Besides, since when are people "put on trial" in a free and proudly capitalist country for creating wealth and jobs?

The history standards—and particularly the proposed classroom exercises—should indeed be dumped.

But the second and bigger problem was the assumption that the flaws in our education system (largely caused by increasing centralization) could be cured by retaining more bureaucrats—*California* bureaucrats!—to further centralize the lesson plans.

Experimentation and freshness, challenge and discourse, can never be nourished by one-size-fits-all mandates handed down by the stifling fist of authority in a distant imperial capital, no matter how many times the bureaucrats whine that all their guidelines are "optional."

Lobotomized By the Government

Appalled at the hordes of arrogant antisocial illiterates being poured forth on a society that paid in good faith for something very different, Americans for 40 years now have attempted to restore some "accountability" to the government schools through political means, usually by demanding that their elected representatives require mandatory competency testing, either of the government school teachers themselves, or of their students.

Unfortunately, the efficacy of such schemes relies on the of-

176

ten unstated assumption that, once a pattern of inadequacy is detected, hard and firm changes will quickly be imposed.

Fewer than 70 percent of a given class has mastered the required subject matter after a year?

Since 70 percent mastery (a C-minus grade) has long been considered the absolute minimum evidence that the basic subject matter has been absorbed, unless it can be demonstrated that said class contains a statistically abnormal percentage of congenital morons, it's naturally assumed that the teacher will be fired and blackballed from any further labors in any other government school. Why else would we have bothered instituting the competency tests?

More than two or three teachers in a given school system turn out to have been hired and retained despite the fact they can't spell or solve simple algebraic equations? Not only is it naturally assumed those charlatans will be promptly dismissed, but also that everyone in the administrative chain of command who had anything to do with hiring and retaining them will similarly find themselves out on the sidewalks within 30 days.

That's the way such a testing program would bring quick results in the private sector, after all. Heads would roll. Get us a quality product and a good return on investment within six months or you're all fired and we'll start again.

Naturally, the naive voters and taxpayers assume that once some basic inventory and quality-control systems have similarly identified and isolated the problems in the schools, all those administrators will get busy and ream out the bottleneck.

But do such testing requirements really bring any such results when applied to the government schools?

In Clark County (Las Vegas), Nevada, standards in effect in the spring of 1996 called for students, by the end of third grade, to be able to "read orally with proper projection, enunciation, expression, phrasing, and fluency."

177

But the proposed *new* third-grade goals submitted for adoption as of 1997 specifed: "In some cases, children will work from a wordless picture book, but increasingly, they will read written text, with animation, for others." Students were also to be taught "a variety of strategies to derive meaning from print."

I know one good strategy for "deriving meaning from print." That would be to sound out ("read") the words. What are some others?

What this double-talk means is that kids who still can't read by the end of the third grade will be urged to look at the pictures and "guess" what the words say; then they will be promoted to the fourth grade based on "a good try."

In 10 or 15 years, these functional illiterates will be our co-workers, employees, or attendants, trying to figure out what "caustic compound" means as they refill the cafeteria juice dispensers, or wheeling your hospital gurney past the Greek-to-them sign that reads: "Urgent warning: no elevator car in this shaft."

Too bad there weren't any pictures.

A series of investigative reports in the *Las Vegas Review-Journal* in April 1996 revealed that, while as recently as 1992 Nevada students were expected to master simple addition, subtraction, multiplication and division before exiting the third grade, those goals were replaced in Clark County in 1992 with an "assessment for mathematics" that discourages teachers from relying too heavily on "paper and pencil" activities and "testing to assign grades."

"You can call it dumbed down, watered down, diluted, lowered ... whatever you want," says Bill Hanlon, director of the Clark County School District's math institute and an elected member of the state Board of Education. "It's right there, staring us in the face. Why should anyone be surprised when our low test scores match our low standards?"

Even worse, Hanlon says, is the fact that vocational students

178

are now allowed to count courses such as drafting and carpentry toward their high-school "math" requirements.

A real educator like Hanlon is clearly the odd man out in this den of malarkey.

"This is the 1990s," responds Yvonne Shaw, who astonishingly is allowed to represent Reno on the Board of Education despite the fact she's president of the Washoe County teachers union, one of the main enforcers of mediocrity in Nevada's government schools. "It's not the 1950s. Bill lives in the 1950s, when kids studied just to get smart. Unfortunately, that's no longer the reality."

Yep, Mr. Hanlon is just lost in the past.

Forget 1950: Nevada now spends six times the $991 per pupil per year that it spent in *1970*—twice as much per pupil even when we correct for inflation. Yet despite all this new treasure—taxes so high a second spouse usually has to work outside the home just to cover the increased burden—it turns out we're merely nostalgic codgers to expect our schools to even *encourage* kids to "study to get smart," let alone demand it.

At Las Vegas High School, senior English teacher Dorothy Powell says she's changed some of her teaching strategies over the years. There are still vocabulary quizzes, but not much homework, because many of her students have jobs.

"I work within their world, within their reality," Powell says, sounding like nothing so much as a counselor of the insane.

Ms. Powell's students now read Amy Tan's *Joy Luck Club* instead of Shakespeare's *Macbeth,* because they can better connect with the characters, she says.

So are we now prepared to set loose upon the world a generation convinced they're "educated," who will likely assume it was Homer Simpson who first called life "a poor player that struts and frets his hour upon the stage ... a tale told by an idiot, full of sound and fury, signifying nothing"?

How many of our kids now graduate high school having taken biology, chemistry, and physics? How dare we pretend we're going to continue competing in the global marketplace when we offer foreign languages only as after-hours "club" activities, while many of our European and Japanese competitors expect their graduates to demonstrate a conversational mastery of *two* foreign languages—and flunk them if they don't?

The question is no longer whether our schools have been dumbed down. The real question is whether the current system can any longer be reformed.

In-house reform has been going on for two generations now—since the Russians sent a shudder through our complacent notions of technical superiority by launching Sputnik in 1957. Yet test scores continue to plummet, even after they're "re-normed" to hide the erosion.

Frankly, I doubt the entrenched political and educational bureaucracies will ever "get it." But one thing is for sure: Reform will never come until failure means loss of funds, and thus fewer underlings, smaller offices, and falling salaries. The government schools will reform themselves only as fast as, and only to the extent that, parents (or grandparents, or the next-door neighbor) have their school taxes reduced by the amount they spend on private schools, home-schooling, or new community tutoring arrangements not subject to government control or oversight. Today, we reward failure by increasing school allocations—the worst schools get the biggest raises. But if you subsidize failure, you will only get more failure.

Just as cheap zippy little Japanese autos that could go thousands of miles without major repairs forced American automakers to change fast or die, so is competition the only answer for American education.

But make no mistake: Detroit would never have changed if the law required each buyer of a Japanese car to first pay $10,000 in damages to the Big Three. And that's exactly what we're doing if we continue to force everyone to pay more and more for this glorified baby-sitting service that no one wants.

Teacher Testing: Farce or Fraud?

We've seen how counterproductive it can be to allow the educrats to institute new "standards" for our young scholars. But what about testing the teachers themselves? Surely they couldn't find a way to convert *that* into another costly and useless boondoggle. Could they?

As Nevadans sent their kids off for another year of school in late August 1998, many parents doubtless took comfort in the knowledge that, for most of the past decade, new teachers entering the Nevada public schools have been required to take a battery of tests designed to measure their general academic knowledge, their knowledge of the educational methods now taught in the education colleges ("pedagogy"), and their specialized knowledge of the subject area in which they plan to teach.

It turned out those parents might have been somewhat less comfortable, however, if they knew the number of prospective Nevada teachers who are told, "Sorry. You've failed your tests. I'm afraid you don't get that teaching job after all."

That number would appear to be: zero.

No one is ever denied an entry-level teaching job because he or she failed the teacher competency tests.

In fact, up to 55 percent of Nevada's new public school teachers enter the classroom without having passed their basic competency tests. An entire new layer of expensive state bureaucracy has been added to supposedly guarantee "accountability," but in the end fewer than one percent of teachers are ever pulled out of the classroom for failure to pass such tests (after those subject to the tests are given three years to try).

And to further dilute any real-world impact, both the selection of tests and the establishment of a passing grade are left up to committees of teachers who are instructed to set those "cut levels" not according to any absolute standard of subject mastery, but at a level low enough to guarantee the school district can fill its "demand" out of the current applicant "supply."

Mary B. Snow, Ph.D., a full-time "evaluations consultant" with the state Department of Education in Carson City, writes up the department's reports on how the Nevada Competency Testing Program is working out. I asked Ms. Snow for the number of prospective teachers who are rejected for failing their tests. At first she replied by explaining that the department's bookkeeping systems are not set up to track such persons—she studies only how long it takes teachers who have failed those tests on their first try, to subsequently pass the tests and get those restrictions ("provisions") removed from their teacher licenses, after they are hired.

But do *any* applicants take the test and then get turned down, I asked her again.

"Well, they already have a job, in most cases," she replied.

So by the time they take these tests, prospective Nevada teachers have actually been hired? And then, even if they fail the tests, they still get their licenses and get put into classrooms?

"They get the license to teach for a certain period of time," Ms. Snow responds. At that point, though already working in the classroom, the teachers have three years—it used to be two—to pass the tests, which they can keep taking again and again. The teachers can also get a waiver of the most basic academic test, the "Pre-Professional Skills Assessment," if they take certain specified university courses, passing those courses with a grade of "B" or better.

In addition, new hires are granted automatic waivers of the

182

Pre-Professional Skills Test if they have been awarded a Masters degree, or if they have three years of teaching under their belts and a license from another state, or if they received a pitifully low 420 Verbal score (460 in math) out of a possible 800 on the Graduate Record Exam (the SAT for graduate-school admission) and maintained a 3.0 grade point average during their undergraduate studies.

Applicants with out-of-state teacher licenses and three years' experience also get a bye on the pedagogy section of the tests. Few if any waivers are allowed for the 91 percent of teachers for whose specific classroom disciplines a "specialty area test" has been adopted.

From Sept. 1, 1990, to Sept. 15, 1992, Ms. Snow tracked the 55 percent of Nevada teachers who received conditional licenses—teachers who were placed in the classroom despite the fact they had not passed their competency tests. She determined that, depending on the test still needed, 85 percent to 93 percent of those provisional teachers "either took the test or tests one time or supplied evidence of qualification for an exemption after their licenses were issued. Only a small percentage took the same test multiple times."

But 26 to 28 percent spent up to two full years working in a public-school classroom before completing their requirements, and "3.8 percent of the cohort studied failed to remove their competency testing provisions" (pass their tests at all) "by the Sept. 11, 1994 deadline."

At which point they were fired?

Well, no. "The Commission [on Professional Standards in Education] was prevented from enforcing the competency testing regulations by a court-ordered injunction issued in Clark County," Ms. Snow reports.

In the 1994 case Morris et al. vs. Peterson et al., District Court Judge Don Chairez eventually ruled against the 27 Clark County licensed personnel due to be removed from Clark County classrooms (down from 66 when the suit was originally filed—the "class" for the class action suit kept getting reduced as more teachers got their scores filed, or won waivers) on their contention that the testing program was "capricious and arbitrary." The court found the state had every right to test its teachers for competence, and that the nationally standardized exams being used were appropriate.

However, in a second section of his ruling, the judge held that teachers failing the tests should be allowed to take university courses as a substitute.

"The thing that bothered me was that it was unfair," Judge Chairez told me in August of '98. "They had different standards for different people. Teachers who were there before January of 1991 were grandfathered in. Their licenses would come up for renewal after five years and they were evaluated on their performance in the classroom; they didn't have to take any tests, whereas new people had to take the tests. Well, why couldn't the new people be evaluated on their performance in the classroom? It should be the same for everyone."

Eventually, a negotiated settlement was reached out of court, which provides for the classroom alternative to the basic academic-skills segment of the test (but not the other two portions), and which does allow the removal of teachers from classrooms if they fail after two (now three) years to meet those requirements.

And then?

In 1997-98, of the 18,396 teachers working in Nevada's public-school classrooms—out of the approximately 3,000 who enter the system each year and thus had reached their testing completion deadline—28 teachers "were removed from the classroom" because their time limit had expired without their presenting evidence they had passed their teacher competency tests, according to Keith Rheault, deputy superintendent for instructional research and evaluative services at the state Department of Education in Carson City.

Finally a number: 28 teachers. And after being given half an hour to pack their personal belongings in a box, those 28 are no longer welcome in any Nevada classroom?

"We don't know that for sure," says Ms. Snow. "If they've failed the basic-skills part, then they can substitute a university course, and that often happens. And when they take care of their remaining requirements, they're reinstated; they don't have to start from scratch. People have left because of that, but we have not up to this point had the mechanism to follow people and find out exactly what's happened, because our licensing bookkeeping wasn't automated to track by Social Security number; it didn't allow us to do that. Now we have a new system that hopefully will."

• • •

What about Nevada's largest city, Las Vegas? George Ann Rice, assistant superintendent of human resources for the Clark County School District, says she has no idea how many teachers are "grandfathered in" where testing is concerned—no count is kept of teachers still teaching despite never having taken the competency tests, since they were in the system prior to 1990.

However, of the 11,510 teachers now working in the Clark County public schools, "We show 2,039 who still have time on their license to take the test. They are within the time limit of taking the test." In other words, nearly one in five new Clark County teachers is running a classroom, without having demonstrated basic competency.

Over the four-year period since 1995, Ms. Rice reports that approximately 4,200 new people have been hired as Clark County classroom teachers. The three-year limits of those hired with provisional ("non-renewable") licenses in 1995 are now at hand, and "as the date approaches, if we find that person has not passed the exam, we terminate them. … Thus far, from the time this went

185

into effect in 1995 to the present, we have actually terminated eighty-six people."

And after they're "terminated"? A colorful new hat and uniform at Wendy's? The first bus out of town?

"You may apply to be a substitute or a support staff worker," Ms. Rice explains. "If you then pass the test and those provisions are removed, you may come back and re-apply, but they are counted as brand new applicants and they have no seniority with us."

Except that—keep your eye on the little ball, now—"If re-hired within eleven years they do regain their seniority, under our board policies and regulations."

And when failed teachers re-test? Do they confront a new examination each time, or can they end up re-taking tests that contain the very same questions they've seen before?

"I don't know," responds the head of personnel for the Clark County school district. "We're not allowed to see the test or samples of the test."

Still, Ms. Rice insists none of this should be any concern, since, "This is just one area that is used to look at competence." Before teachers are hired and subjected to these tests, "We of course have their transcripts; we have their application; we have an interview with an experienced administrator; and one of the more important things we have are three confidential evaluations written by someone who has actually seen them in a classroom.

"Then they are on probation at least their first year. During that probationary period, their administrator is required by law to give them three written formal evaluations, and each of those evaluations is based on several classroom observations."

• • •

Ms. Snow's authoritative 1995 report on "The Nevada Competency Testing Program for Educational Personnel" (an updated version is due shortly) reports, "Since September, 1989, all persons seeking an initial license in Nevada have been required to take basic skills, professional knowledge, and specialty area tests unless certain exemptions applied."

Note the use of the verb "take"—not "pass."

Then we learn that the first 16 months of the testing program—from 1989 to early 1991—were "no fault," so that those in charge could determine where the scores were falling on these national tests (provided by the Educational Testing Service of Princeton, N.J.—the SAT people), before setting Nevada's passing score on each test.

To this day, whenever a new ETS "Praxis" test is adopted in Nevada, the first year of testing is "no fault"—conducted mainly to provide a track record of scores, which are then used by panels made up entirely of Nevada schoolteachers and administrators to set a "cut score," allowing a chosen percentage of applicants to pass.

For comparison, imagine the U.S. Navy needs aviators who can land a plane in 600 feet. All applicants are tested to see in what distance they can land planes—the results ranging from 500 feet to 1,000 feet. In order to allow 50 percent of applicants to pass—the percentage required to fill all the available cockpits—the panel decides that any applicant who can land a plane in 750 feet will be accepted. True, the Navy would be losing planes off the far end of their 600-foot carrier landing decks like turkeys cashing it in at Thanksgiving time—especially if those who *failed* to pass even the 750-foot landing test were allowed to fly for three years while they kept trying to figure it all out—but the recruiters would sure as heck be filling their quotas.

Ms. Snow's history describes how the state Board of Education back in 1985 directed the state Department of Education to convene panels of Nevada educators to decide which tests to adopt and what the passing scores on those tests should be. Among the considerations that those panels were allowed to consider when establishing the passing scores? "Scores attained by Nevada examinees during the no-fault period," and "supply/demand considerations."

"When we're putting in a new test that we haven't done before, we do a year of no-fault to see where the test scores are coming in," Ms. Snow explains. "We look at the results. ... At the very beginning I'm sure you can understand that the committee was nervous; they'd never done this before, and they just wanted to make sure that nothing bizarre was going to happen. There's that possibility that something could look weird, and that's never happened."

And what would "look weird"? If 50 percent failed a test?

"We would certainly investigate that," Ms. Snow confirms.

Should Massachusetts change its standards, then, since 59 percent of new teacher applicants there famously failed that state's first exam in 1998 ... exhibiting particular difficulty understanding passages from "The Federalist Papers"?

"Not necessarily; there might be something inherently wrong with the test," Ms. Snow replies.

• • •

Does this "Everyone Passes Go, Everyone Collects $200" testing system smell suspiciously like something the teachers unions themselves might have dreamed up, if given the chance to impose their own interpretation on "competency testing"? It should come as no surprise to learn that, once again, we do indeed find the inmates almost completely in charge of the asylum.

By an act of the 1987 Nevada Legislature, the advisory Commission on Professional Standards in Education was "replaced with a permanent autonomous commission," of whose nine members only four were supposed to be teachers—a provision that

188

sounds an awful lot like a political safeguard against having the process completely dominated by the very henhouse residents who were supposed to be under examination.

Yet, oddly, the president of the Nevada State Education Association (the teachers union) testified in favor of that 1987 bill, preening, "In order to provide our children with the best possible education, it is time to make educators responsible for setting standards for their own profession."

Which is it? Are teachers in the minority in setting these standards (as the "four-out-of-nine" provisions of Senate Bill 467 would seem to intend), or do they run the show, top to bottom?

Reading from a list of the nine members of the commission at the time Ms. Snow filed her 1995 report, state Board of Education member Mr. Hanlon responds to the seventh name, Frank Follmer, with "There's your first non-teacher."

And the special panels convened to decide which Specialty Area Tests are adopted, along with what the passing or "cut" score shall be for each? They turn out to be even *more* heavily dominated by unionized school personnel.

"There's at least one university representative, but they are all teachers, certainly," confirms Ms. Snow.

"Then we have a competency testing review committee made up of ten people, and they represent all the various educational associations in the state—the teachers association, the administrators association, the principals association, et cetera, and their job is to study the results that came in from those teacher panels and then to consider some other factors, such as the standard error of measurement, and then they look at the passing scores used in other states," Ms. Snow further explains.

And they're allowed to consider supply and demand?

"That factors into it," confirms Mr. Rheault. "In areas like Special Ed, advanced science, and math, we're real short this year. You could go to a real high cut score, but then you could be eliminating seventy percent of eligible applicants."

But if parents are under the impression that prospective teachers have to meet some fixed standard, doesn't that constitute a kind of fraud?

"No," responds Mr. Rheault. "They never look and say, 'Oh, we're short this year. Let's lower the standard.' That's never happened. Last year we ended up raising the bar on three of them."

In fact, a list of Nevada's passing test scores as of January 1998 shows the state generally in the middle of the pack. Nevada's cut score for the Pre-Professional Skills test was 172, compared to 170 in Arkansas, 172 in Florida, and a national high of 178 in Virginia. In one of the mathematics specialty tests, Nevada sets a cut score of 135, identical to Hawaii's and five points below Oregon's 140.

The question is—if other states are using the same supply-and-demand criteria to choose the level to which they will float their passing scores, and then trading information so no one chooses a way-out-of-line score that would make everyone else "look bad"—so what? If you started systematically busing in thousands of retards from the state farms for the feeble-minded to take these tests, the current system would quickly re-norm the passing grade to allow you to hire the best 70 percent. Nowhere in this carefully crafted system is anyone given the responsibility to say, "Wait a minute, these applicants are all morons. I don't want a single *one* of them in our classrooms."

State Board of Education member Hanlon also teachers the course Mathematics 123 at the University of Nevada, Las Vegas—one of the make-up courses in which teachers can enroll to get around their PPST basic academic test requirement. And from what he sees, he doubts if that process is really doing much good.

"The teachers who are being caught up in this are Special Ed teachers, foreign language teachers. I am not finding people who are actually regular classroom teachers. For Math 123, it's a very non-white classroom, let me tell you. The people that we're catching—I think we had three teachers last year from the special school—they're actually teaching kids to get the food from their spoon to their mouth, and I mean that literally. But what I wasn't getting was typically regular classroom teachers. It's scooping people, but I'm not sure that I want to scoop those people."

Hanlon also worries about the heavy emphasis in the teacher competency tests on the pedagogical section, the so-called Principles of Learning and Teaching Test, which measures knowledge not of academic subject matter, but rather the latest trends and theories taught in the education colleges.

This requirement has the effect of keeping out professionals who might otherwise be brought in to the schools through alternative licensure, Hanlon fears. "We take people who are not trained in the college of education and keep them out of the system. ...

"I teach math teachers how to teach," says Hanlon, who runs the Clark County School District's Math and Science Institute. "I sell videotapes [designed to help math teachers and home-school teachers] all over the country. But when I learned math, we 'borrowed.' Now, you're supposed to 'group in sets.' So when it comes to today's pedagogical terminology, I don't know if *I* could pass that kind of test. ...

"What drives me crazy is that we have a shortage of qualified math teachers; the university is letting go instructors [who haven't completed their doctorates], and we're not able to grab them up," Hanlon complains. He attributes this to an exam section that tends to ask not how to parse a sentence or solve an equation, but "Describe how you would identify a learning disability," "Name three ways to motivate children to complete a lesson," or "What factors most heavily influence a child's reading behavior?"

• • •

191

In the nation's capital, Jeanne Allen, president of the non-profit research and advocacy group Center for Education Reform (who provided the three examples of typical pedagogical questions above), agrees many states have allowed the teachers unions and their allies in the education colleges to institute tests designed to validate current hiring practices, while shutting out those who haven't learned the code talk of the nation's schools of education.

For instance, Ms. Allen thinks the recent state-generated teacher competency test in Massachusetts, which produced a shocking 59 percent failure rate, was a huge step in the right direction.

"It's sad, but also it's a great step. For the first time in Massachusetts history there was a check and balance on aspiring teachers. There had never before been an entrance exam, and that was only considered to be at the ninth-grade level in terms of difficulty ...

"This was a test in which ninety-nine percent was devoted to content. It assessed, in a very fair way, general knowledge. It was a test that every teacher should have passed with flying colors. And fifty-nine percent failed. So imagine the repercussions, now that the public is aware of that. ... There should be a much higher-level entrance exam to get into the profession."

But if the current level of applicant can't even pass the *current* tests, who would fill the gap?

"There is no shortage of qualified applicants," responds Ms. Allen, "there is only a shortage of *certified* teachers. And what we should be talking about, anyway, is opening up the teaching profession to qualified professionals, professors, scientists, allowing people into the classroom who have an interest in returning something to the community. ...

"There is a serious disagreement between the people who run the teachers colleges and the vast majority of rank-and-file teachers who have been in the classroom more than a few years," Ms. Allen continues. "The teachers college fans and the unions want everyone to believe the only thing you have to know about teaching is how to teach; they don't believe in content. And even a cursory glance at the statistics of American student achievement completely disproves that theory. ...

"There has to be more strenuous testing," Ms. Allen continues. Several states have attempted to require, at the least, that incoming teachers pass the same tests required of graduating high-school seniors. But the teachers unions have shot down that proposal on every occasion, she says.

"The Praxis exam [trade name for all the New Jersey-based tests used in Nevada] is still a very low basic competency test; it basically tests functional literacy. People have basically pegged it between the eighth- and tenth-grade level. And I don't think anyone wants to settle for teachers who can just pass a basic functional literacy test. ...

"The Massachusetts test was just a shot across the bow. States like Nevada have to start asking what it is that they are asking prospective teachers to know."

And a higher failure rate—one that actually threatened to create a crisis of empty classrooms—would be a good thing?

"Oh, absolutely," Ms. Allen replied. "Because it would open up the field to applicants other than certified teachers."

• • •

Postscript: In late August 1998, the state of Massachusetts dealt with the fact that 59 percent of entering teachers had failed the state's first-ever teacher competency test—by lowering the passing grade to 60, so that thousands of incoming teachers who had previously failed the test are now considered to have "passed" with the equivalent of a grade of D. No one had to sit for another exam.

Those thousands of incompetent teachers are now in the government classrooms of Massachusetts. Parents there have no way to know which ones they are.

'The System Causes Ninety-Nine Percent of All Learning Disabilities'

A typical posting on the Separation of School and State Internet talk group (sepschool@SepSchool.org) warns, "The schools will destroy your child; can you afford to leave him in the classroom?" And a typical rebuttal comes from one D.B. of Los Angeles:

"A bit apocalyptic, wouldn't you say? I know lots of families living in nice suburbs whose children are getting a decent education in public schools. ... They haven't been 'destroyed.'"

While it's true a minority of American youth still leave our government-run schools with an adequate education—or at least the intellectual tools necessary to get one elsewhere—I remain unconvinced this outcome is the *product* of the government propaganda camps.

If I kidnap your six-year-olds for seven hours a day and make them eat dirt, and they not only survive but actually grow (albeit at a slower rate than if I didn't feed them dirt), have I thus proven the nutritional value of dirt?

Or have I just proven that the young homo sapien is a remarkably resilient critter, providing there's still someone at home willing to feed him or her something *other* than dirt the other 17 hours of the day?

The great myth of compulsory uniform government schooling is that, given enough money, the educrats can produce the desired product out of virtually any raw material.

Yet, put to the test, they inevitably whimper, "What do you expect? Look at the material you give us to work with. These kids come from single-parent welfare-project homes, rife with crime and drug abuse. Some of them are dirty, hungry, sick, or deranged. So of course we couldn't teach them to read in only ten years. It would be different if you'd sent us to one of those nice suburban schools!"

This is like charging a high price on the contention that you can teach any animal to pee on fireplugs, and then only succeeding with the dogs.

Beyond the elementary grades, what our overpriced educrats are mostly doing is taking credit for "found" learning that would happen faster if they simply let the kids spend their time in a decent library, with occasional breaks to watch The History Channel.

("Oh, I suppose you think they could just learn Spanish without any formal classroom instruction?" the defenders of the current system inquire. Heck, I'll go further than that. Not only is it *easier* to learn Spanish through simple immersion among native speakers (something best done far away from any structured government program), I would argue that it is virtually *impossible* to teach conversational skill in any foreign language through the absurdly fragmented, mass repetition, grammar-and-vocabulary-list methods employed in the typical American government-school classroom.)

As for the newly discovered epidemic of "learning disabilities," Robyn Miller, formerly a government school teacher in both rural Montana and suburban Denver, was getting tired of being told not to correct spelling errors lest she damage her charges' self-esteem.

But what finally turned Ms. Miller—profiled by Brandon Dutcher in the February 1996 edition of *The Education Liberator* (see "Appendix II")—into a home-schooler was the "Special Education" scam. Miller estimates 80 percent of those inmates have "normal sight, hearing and intelligence," but simply cannot read "because of ineffective teaching methods."

"Sentencing" such kids to learning-disability classes creates in them "a pattern of failure for so many years to come," Ms. Miller worries.

195

"When I was a public school teacher, I used to think the system caused seventy-five percent of all learning disabilities," Miller says. "Now I think it's about ninety-nine percent."

Home-Schoolers Say, 'The Public Education System Has Failed Us'

Those who claim we have no choice but to continue funding the government schools through taxes pretend there are no proven alternatives.

In fact, private schools—religious and otherwise—have a well-established reputation for turning out better results at less than half the cost. (Not so hard to do, once you realize that at least 70 percent of the money now spent on government education goes to administrative overhead and duplicitous paper-shuffling.)

But in order to meet state requirements that they provide an educational setting that "looks like" a public school, trackable by "school year" and "grade level," few private schools really explore vastly accelerated learning or learning environments of vastly different structure.

That's been left to the home-schoolers.

• • •

A dozen years ago, most folks would have dismissed home-schooling—if they'd heard of it at all—as a fringe activity practiced by a few extremists either of the libertarian left (who believe that public schools teach kids herd-like obedience to arbitrary government authority, marching them around to the sound of bells and indoctrinating them to turn in their own parents for marijuana use) or of the religious right (who believe that public schools have "evicted God" and prayer, school nurses hand out condoms to the kids, and—yes—it's all a plot to breed support for the Godless welfare state).

They would have been largely correct.

For Nevada's 1984-85 school year, only 43 students were registered with the Clark County (Las Vegas) School District for the home-school exemption from mandatory attendance. By 1986-87, although that number had doubled, it was still an insignificant 90.

And Marge Comeau—who has since 1989 been the sole person accepting those "Notifications of Intent to Provide Home Instruction" in her tiny office amidst the jumble of institutional-yellow portable classrooms that form the county's "Alternative Education" nerve center on East St. Louis Avenue—agrees. "When I first started this job, it was mostly for religious reasons."

No more. The number of home-schooled students in Clark County surged from 671 to 1,040 in the autumn of 1993, and to 1,466 in the fall of 1995. Today, Clark County parents home-school more than 1,700 students—nearly half of the officially registered 4,000 home-school students in Nevada.

And today, "It's mostly because of the violence," Comeau reports. "They come in and say the schools are so violent, the gangs, my kids are afraid. That and—with the gifted students—they say their kids are just not being challenged."

The boom in Nevada home-schooling only tracks a national trend. Although other sources estimate the number of American kids being home schooled at 500,000 to 750,000, the National Home Education Research Institute (NHERI), headed by Ed. Dr. Brian D. Ray in Salem, Ore., from 1994 to 1996 conducted a massive survey of more than 5,000 home-school students (and their major curriculum distributors) and concluded 1.2 million American students are now schooled at home. That's more students than attend public schools in Hawaii, Montana, Rhode Is-

197

land, South Dakota, Alaska, North Dakota, Delaware, Vermont and Wyoming—combined.

And those numbers are beginning to translate into political power. In 1996, when a proposal surfaced in Congress to require home-school parents to obtain teaching certificates, home-schoolers swamped Capitol Hill switchboards. The measure failed, 424-to-1.

Testing Requirement Dropped

What is home-schooling? The U.S. Department of Education, speaking plain English for once, defines the practice as "education of school-aged children at home rather than at school." The modern movement is generally traced to the research of professional educators Raymond and Dorothy Moore, who in their 1980s' books *Home Grown Kids* and *Home-Spun Schools* attributed such development problems as hyperactivity, nearsightedness, and dyslexia to prematurely taxing a child's nervous system and mind with continuous academic tasks, like reading and writing. Their research convinced the Moores that formal schooling should be delayed until age 8 or 10, or even as late as 12.

In its 1997 report, "Strengths of Their Own: Home Schoolers Across America," Dr. Ray's NHERI ranked Nevada as one of the 14 most highly regulated states when it comes to state supervision of home-school parents. These 14 states "require parents to send notification of achievement test scores and/or professional evaluation, plus other requirements (e.g. curriculum approval by the state ...)." By comparison, the eight "low-regulation" states— including Idaho, Texas, Illinois, and Michigan—have "no state requirement for parents to initiate any contact with the state."

Nevada's ranking may well have to be changed, however, after the state Board of Education voted in the fall of 1997 to

198

eliminate all testing requirements for home-schooled children.

Carri Benson, president of Southern Nevada's Home School Advisory Council, says such a step only made sense, since the NHERI research shows that home-schoolers in "low-regulation" states score, on average, in the 86th percentile on nationally standardized academic achievement tests, while in those states with the strictest regulation, home-school students score ... in the 86th percentile.

"So the state supervision makes no difference at all."

(Given the overwhelming majority of schoolkids still attending government-run schools, the average test performance of students there falls, obviously, right at the 50th percentile.)

"We were seen as an agency that was supposed to monitor home-schooling, and the fact is that we weren't and we can't," says Bill Hanlon.

"My personal feeling is they ought to be held to the same standard [as kids in public schools]; if we're going to test some we should test them all," says Hanlon, who ended up voting with the 6-4 majority to drop the testing requirement. "But the home-schoolers didn't feel that should be the case. So we asked [Deputy Attorney General] Melanie Meehan-Crossley for an AG's opinion, and basically she said that we can't enforce the testing. The law said 'options for showing improvement,' but it did not stipulate it had to be done through testing. So if we're ... not going to get into the business of overseeing home-schools, let's not have a farce."

The Ninth Graders Return

The age of students being home-schooled in Clark County forms a nearly perfect bell curve. While only 75 first-graders are home-schooled, that number climbs to 151 in third grade, and

160 in the fifth. The numbers peak at more than 200 students each in the sixth, seventh, and eighth grades—the middle school years where students may encounter gangs and violence for the first time.

But then the number drops again, sharply, to 145 10th graders, 118 high-school juniors, and only 17 high-school seniors.

The low number for 12th-year students is in part because home-school students are allowed to take GED exams—and earn the equivalent of a high-school diploma—at age 17. By the time they turn 18, most home-schoolers are either in the work force or pursuing post-secondary education.

But the sharp drop in home-schooling at the ninth-grade level has at least three other explanations.

First, many students by that age are anxious to participate in team sports, choir and band, or other extracurricular activities that are harder to duplicate outside a large school system. Science students may also have trouble gaining access to the kind of chemistry labs available in the public schools.

The second most frequently stated reason why more than 50 percent of ninth-grade home-schoolers return to the public schools is that parents may feel "out of their depth" when it comes to teaching their own children calculus, or chemistry and physics—though the home-school support groups do provide a network for locating tutors or specialized video materials.

Finally, there is the fact that a home-school student who does not return by ninth grade cannot possibly earn the 22 credits required to receive a Nevada public high-school diploma. That means home-schoolers seeking college admission must depend on either the GED and a personalized portfolio of their work or an alternative diploma from one of the approved correspondence courses—courses that can cost $400 to $1,200 per year.

"As a worst-case example," Hanlon of the state school board recalls, "we had a young lady who was home-schooled through tenth grade, so she came into the eleventh and twelfth grade at, I think, Clark High School. ... For the next two years she was a straight A student, but she could not graduate high school; she didn't have enough credits. And because of that she couldn't be named valedictorian and so forth. And that's a damned shame. She couldn't qualify for the valedictorian scholarship, the Top Ten scholarship, et cetera. They need those twenty-two credits. In my opinion, that was a real sad case."

Eliminating Racial and Income Disparities

In general, as the government schools demand more and more tax money, while offering only an endless list of excuses for their collapsing academic and social results, home-schooling seems to be a trend whose time has come. In a January 7, 1998, policy paper for the Washington-based Cato Institute, Isabel Lyman, a longtime home-schooling parent and co-director of the Harkness Road High School of Amherst, Mass., concludes homeschooling has "snowballed into a grassroots revolution" now growing at a rate of 15 to 40 percent per year.

The rats are escaping.

The victory of homeschooled 13-year-old Rebecca Sealfon in the 1997 National Spelling Bee brought national attention to a movement that has also produced 15-year-old country singer LeAnn Rimes, Army Specialist Michael New (the decorated U.S. Army medic who was recently court-martialed for refusing to don a United Nations uniform as a matter of principle), and Barnaby Marsh, who after being home-schooled in the Alaskan wilderness went on to graduate Cornell University and become one of the 32 Rhodes Scholars selected in 1996.

The *Orlando Sentinel* was prompted to run a major feature

on home-schooling this winter when home-schooled Orlando 17-year-old Erin Toelcke scored a perfect 1600 on her SATs. The *Sentinel* reports that Florida home-schoolers have grown by 83 percent in the past five years, to 25,900.

Dr. Ray's research indicates that home-schooling produces test scores averaging in the 80th to 90th percentiles regardless of factors that can affect performance in the public schools. While math achievement of public-school students falls from the 63rd percentile for the children of college graduates to the 40th percentile for the children of high-school graduates and all the way down to the miserable 28th percentile for the children of parents who never completed high school, that slippage is reduced, among home-schoolers, to a mere five points: Home-schoolers whose parents completed college score in the 88th percentile, while those whose parents never finished high school still score in the 83rd percentile.

(This result is doubly amazing, given that in the government schools, students of all backgrounds presumably share the same professional teacher with a degree in education, while in home-schooling, the high-school dropout in question generally *is* the teacher.)

Similarly, white and minority home-schoolers score in the same 87th percentile in reading, while in the public schools minority students are allowed to slip to the 49th percentile, while white students' average performance places them in the 61st percentile.

With one exception, the biggest differences Dr. Ray's study could find between public-schooled and home-schooled children (other than those test results) lie in the areas of computer use—83 percent of home-schooled students use a computer at home, as opposed to only 26 percent of all American families—and television viewing.

While the most common remaining criticism of home-schooling is a failure to "socialize" children, only six percent of home-schooled children watch television or videotapes three or more hours a day. By comparison, among public school students, Dr. Ray found a whopping 62 percent watch television or videotapes more than three hours a day—despite the fact they're supposedly so much better socialized to group and team activities.

The single largest difference between home-schooling and public schooling? The public schools turn out an average 50th percentile student at an average cost of $5,325 per student per year, *excluding* the capital costs of bonding and building the schools themselves, according to U.S. Department of Education statistics for the 1993-94 school year. Average annual cost to produce an average 85th percentile *home-schooled* student? $546—plus the sacrifice of a potential second income, of course, by a family that is still taxed to support government schools it does not use.

'Values' Education

"Usually the biggest beef is their social skills, which is a joke," says Carri Benson of the Home School Advisory Council, who home-schools her own children—Jeremy, 15; Logan, 14; and Candice, 12—in a modest white house set amidst the horse properties in the far north of the Las Vegas Valley. "These kids are very much into scouting, church, gymnastics, and they have home-schooling friends. There's nothing socially inept about them.

"In our home-school group, we'd get together every week, and it was very interesting to watch our older kids interacting with the five- and six-year-olds and the eight-year-olds. There was no age gap. The age gap is created *in* the schools, not outside. You've got brothers and sisters who can't associate because one is in fifth grade and one is in third grade. Does that make sense? When you go to work, you don't work with all twenty-year-olds or all sixty-year-olds.

"If you can get along at home with your own family, you can get along with anyone in the world. ... If my boys fail, I'm going to have my kids living with me in my golden years. So it's going to behoove me to see that they achieve. Nobody is going to care more for my children than I am. And if I fail it's not only going to reflect on me, but I will pay the price. If the public school fails my child, my child doesn't go to live with that teacher who failed him."

The Bensons' children (Carri's husband works for a local home-builder) had completed kindergarten, second, and third grades, respectively, when she pulled them out of the Nevada public schools seven years ago, after spending a year researching the home-schooling movement.

Benson read John Holt's book *How Children Fail* and remembers thinking, "No, that can't be happening with the curriculum in *my* school. But I went down and made an appointment with the principal and she showed me the curriculum and it was all there. They [require the students to] keep a journal, which is unconstitutional. Any journal has to be private; they can't be made to read out of it to the class. But every day the teacher would ask a question about their home life, and then they'd write their feelings in their journal. 'How did you feel the last time you were punished?' Well, I don't know any kids who felt ecstatic the last time they were punished. But I did not send my kids to school to have my parenting skills questioned. ...

"Go into the schools today. You won't see individual desks, they're all in groups. So if there's one who's achieving they all ride on his coattails, and they all look better. Well, I want my kids to be self-sufficient."

"The biggest complaint today is this values teaching, 'How do you feel?' Stuff other than the three R's," agrees Bill Hanlon.

"She's in her twenties now, but my daughter came home from the third or fourth grade and said if I spanked her that was child abuse and she'd call the police. I laugh now, but I'll tell you, I didn't think it was funny at the time. I was pretty well irked."

Carri Benson remembers testifying before a state Senate committee in Carson City, "and this state senator said home-schooling should be illegal, that it's like living in a cave, the kids don't get any socialization. I said show me the cave, I'll move in, because I'd like to cut my kids' socialization about in half.

"I drive Jeremy to the [Latter-Day Saints] seminary in the afternoon, right through the milling throng of kids getting out of school. What you see is all black clothing, purple hair standing up at all angles, earrings, nose rings, every other thing pierced. The other day I said, 'Jeremy, do you want to go back? I'd be glad to send you back.' He said 'No thanks, Mom.'"

For his doctoral dissertation at the University of Florida in 1992, Larry Shyers videotaped 8- to 10-year-old children at play, and then had their behavior observed by trained counselors who did not know which children went to regular schools and which were home-schooled.

"The study found no big difference between the two groups of children in self-concept or assertiveness," reports Isabel Lyman in her Cato Institute report. "But the videotapes showed that youngsters who were taught at home by their parents had consistently fewer behavior problems."

Successes and Failures

The home-school success stories are plentiful. Lyman cites the example of Joyce Swann of Anthony, N.M., who, "armed only with a high-school diploma, decided to home-school her five-year-old daughter Alexandra, by using the Calvert School's elementary school correspondence program."

At age 16, Alexandra had earned her master's degree from California State University. At age 18 she was teaching U.S. history at El Paso Community College. Today, seven of Alexandra's nine home-schooled siblings also hold master's degrees.

The Colfax family of Boonville, Calif., famously saw three of their four home-schooled sons accepted by Harvard. Christopher Shea, in the Feb. 2, 1996, edition of the *Chronicle of Higher Education*, actually reported a boom in homeschooled students winning admission to selective colleges.

Bill Hanlon presents the other side of the equation.

"As home-schooling grows, initially most home-schooling parents were extremely hard-working people, and I'm sure they still are. But you might have five percent of those people using the kids as baby-sitters.

"Since my office at the Math Institute is just a stone's throw from Marge [Comeau's] Homeschool office, sometimes Marge will send someone who she thinks is out to lunch down to talk to me about their math program. One guy whose daughter was probably at the seventh-grade level told Marge the kid was already through algebra. Well, I asked the young lady a couple of questions on algebra and she didn't have a clue, so I went down to basic math and she didn't have a clue.

"So I asked the young lady, 'What is your typical day like?' She said she got up about ten, watched TV, spent time with her friends when they got out of school, did some schoolwork from five to seven p.m., and then watched TV and went to bed. So I told the dad, you're screwing it up for people who are trying to do a good job.

"So you do have those examples where they're screwing it up. I wouldn't want to see many middle school kids left to their own discretion, but this guy was off working from seven to three, and those are the things that really bother me. By not interfering or knowing what's going on, I think that's child abuse and neglect. That particular man made me so damned mad, he was believing what his daughter was telling him. She was telling him she was all the way through algebra, and he was just accepting it at face value."

But, I asked Hanlon, wouldn't that argue in favor of just the kind of mandatory testing that the state school board just eliminated?

"We're talking single digits, those who are abusing the system," he replied. "And I don't want to be in the job of trying to catch them. The attorney general ruled against the testing. But they do have to present their curriculum every year, and they do have to show some level of performance ... so if we have to get involved, [that gives us] an ability to check and see.

"But my perception is, by and large the people who are doing home-schooling are doing a damned good job. ... "

'The Cure is Freedom'

When I write about the government youth propaganda camps, the emotional tone of the e-mail is consistent. Not angry so much as pathetic and desperate, with some of the sluggish puzzlement of a deer caught in your headlights. Most of my Internet correspondents argue that the government can't possibly give up requiring *some* degree of government-approved education.

After all, "Our growing jails and welfare lines are undeniable evidence of irresponsible parenting," one recent correspondent wrote. These parents, left to their own devices, "are very likely to put their kids to work pumping gas or pushing drugs or prostituting themselves." Since "education is vital, if we stop requiring it, we risk dropping back to Third World status."

Well, since McDonald's clerks who are required by law to have completed 10 years of government schooling now ring up a cheeseburger by pushing the button with the picture of the cheeseburger on it, at least in our urban centers I'd argue we've already "dropped to Third World status." But I guess it's all worthwhile, given how well the "socialization" part is working out.

I've used this example before. Lest anyone shrug it off, let's be more specific. In the autumn of 1998, in Las Vegas, Nevada, I entered a McDonald's restaurant to buy a fast-food breakfast for $2.17.

For generations, while muscular young men might be given a start in the stockroom, the classic entry-level position for a young female high-school student in American industry was that of part-time cash-register attendant, using skills traditionally taught all children at the age of 9, in the third grade.

For centuries, these young women (yes, and some men) wrote down or punched in the prices of the items purchased, keeping separate track of which items might be subject to a local sales tax. As the kids' ability to figure a three percent sales tax faltered, at some point a handy chart was introduced, telling them the rounded-off tax to charge on the taxable sum. If the total announced to the customer was $2.17, and he proferred a $5 bill, change was counted: "Two-eighteen, two-nineteen, twenty, twenty-five, three dollars, four, and five dollars."

Nowadays, the prices are entered by scanning bar codes or pushing colored buttons bearing cartoon pictures of specific food items. The machine figures in any tax. Handed a five-dollar bill, my helpmate on this occasion entered $5, and was instructed by her machine to hand me $2.83, which (if counted at all) is now counted "Two, two seventy-five, eighty, and three cents."

However, on this occasion, just after she had punched "$5 paid in," I said, "Wait a minute, I've got the seventeen," and laid down exactly seventeen cents on the counter.

The degree of palpable alarm and utter confusion this caused would be hilarious, were not an entire technological civilization at risk. I was reminded of H.G. Wells' science fiction novel, *The Time Machine*, in which the lovely but mindless Eloi use the surviving relics of their ancestors' technology as toys, but have no idea of their origin or how anything actually works.

The young woman literally had no idea how to proceed. Attempting to help, I explained that she could now simply give me the even number of dollars. She hesitantly handed me two dollars ... not three. Finally, an older manager appeared to complete the transaction in a flash. I sincerely doubt the young woman got it, even then.

The pitiful whining and denial goes on and on. Government schooling can't be part of some big conspiracy to enslave us, I'm told, because we get to vote for or against the fellow citizens to sit on the school boards, which run everything.

Oh really? Ask a member of your local school board whether they could transfer the entire Special Education budget to fund more German teachers next year, if they decided to. To send the German students for two weeks in Germany, perhaps. Ask them if they could transfer a single penny, for any purpose whatever.

The federal recommendations and guidelines may supposedly be "advisory" and "optional." But a strict obedience to these national edicts provides the only relative safety from an endless purgatory of special-interest litigation, aided and abetted by the schools' own professional union staff (who—it's a poorly kept secret—write most of the guidelines, anyway).

For that matter, let me know the last time you had a chance to vote for the option "No more government schools; auction them off and give me back all my money." Was it the first lever or the second?

A student council deciding the color of crepe paper with which to decorate the gym for the big school dance at least has a better appreciation of the true limits of its power.

We've seen the way the gleeful gremlins of the pedagocracy run circles around the most modest and sensible attempts to institute student-achievement standards and teacher-competency testing. Weren't those little snark hunts strenuous enough for you? Care to bet a month's salary you can come up with a proposed "reform" that they can't soon reduce to a meaningless slogan and an excuse to hire two more assistant superintendents in charge of filing the compliance papers?

Government schools today must be excused their failures, comes further extemporizing, because they faced an historically unique challenge due to the unprecedented number of non-English-speaking Asian and Hispanic immigrants pouring in. This argument comes, of course, from know-nothings who forget that many East Coast urban teachers in 1912 faced a clear majority of young students who not only spoke no language but German, Italian, Croatian, Serbian, or Polish, but who had only recently seen their first light bulb and their first flush toilet. (A number of *those* kids grew up to run the Manhattan Project.)

The excuses never cease. But all these wild-goose chases only serve to disguise one fundamental underlying premise of the monopoly government-school advocate: that the kind of people who manage to have children are not suitable to teach and raise children. The loudest argument, the final trump card in favor of mandatory government schools always seem to come down to the argument that most parents neither can nor will educate their own children; they simply will not make the personal or financial sacrifices necessary to *get* them a good education, unless forced to do so, at gunpoint, by the state.

Of course, those who make this argument never include *themselves*, or their parents, or even "their own kind." In their smugness, they clearly mean "the other kind." What they mean—pardon me, ladies, while I gingerly lift the hems of your little white-hooded robes—is that black parents, and Mexican parents, and white-trash parents don't love their children enough to do right by them, or simply wouldn't know how.

Now listen. I decline to argue from "religious authority." None of this "The Good Book teaches us … " stuff here. Whatever the form of Nature's God, He or She gave us our intellect and the tools of rational inquiry and discourse to convince one another of what's right *without* thumping on some holy book and implying all those who disagree with us are bound for hell.

But I don't believe that restricts us from occasionally arguing a point from moral conviction. So listen up, sisters:

That these children should be entrusted to the care and upbringing of these parents who have born them was decided before you came into the picture. It was decided by a Higher Authority. Do you get my drift? If the Nuremberg trials decided anything, it is that social engineering that goes so far as to strip children from their parents reaches the point where it is inherently evil, and that men of good will, who cherish freedom, must and will risk and even sacrifice their lives to destroy it.

You cannot have these children to dispose of as you will. You shall not have them. This is one of the tyrannies against which a fair number of us, taking our lead from Mr. Jefferson, have sworn eternal hostility on the altar of God.

If in your insufferable smugness you believe you have a superior wisdom that allows you to decide from which mothers' breasts the babes in arms may be ripped away and sent for 12 years to be doped up on Ritalin or Prozac and thence turned into Zombies of the State, then you'd better go to whatever holy book has been handed down to you in your culture and look up what happens to those who think their plans are better than the Creator's.

You will find reference there to fire and brimstone, to flood,

211

to plagues upon the land, to the deaths of the first-born, and to pillars of salt. Now go, and contemplate on these things.

You might also want to go back a mere 150 years in our history and read the eerily similar utterances of another related clan that contended we could not afford to turn responsibility for their children's education over to a certain class of natural parents because they were not "ready." Yes, yours is precisely the argument used in the 19th century to explain why black slaves could not be freed. Why? Because they had no experience of living in freedom.

To this the great British abolitionist Thomas Macaulay answered as follows: "There is only one cure for evils which newly acquired freedom produces, and that cure is freedom. When a prisoner first leaves his cell, he cannot bear the light of day, he is unable to discriminate colors, or recognize faces. The remedy is to accustom him to the rays of the sun.

"The blaze of truth and liberty may at first dazzle and bewilder nations which have become half blind in the house of bondage. But let them gaze on, and they will soon be able to bear it. ...

"Many politicians of our time are in the habit of laying it down as a self-evident proposition, that no people ought to be free till they are fit to use their freedom. The maxim is worthy of the fool in the old story, who resolved not to go into the water till he had learned to swim. If men are to wait for liberty till they become wise and good in slavery, they may indeed wait forever."

Too Important for Freedom

A.W. from Tennessee writes: "If we do not now provide for education at the reading and writing level, a member of society could not function as a contributing member. What is the proper structure for providing that educational base, and the proper mechanism for funding? I submit that government is a reasonable system for that kind of collective effort. I am not opposed to the exploration of alternatives. ... It's just that education is too critical to leave totally to individuals."

Here we go again. De Tocqueville found Americans to have the highest literacy rate he had ever seen—yes, even among the working classes—in the 1820s, long before the first tax-funded primary or secondary government school had ever been established on these shores. Yet after 150 years, here again is this unquestioning adherence to the pathetic notion that without the government running education, Americans would be unable to read a stop sign, *in spite* of the fact that kids educated without government meddling—in home-schools or private schools—score above the 80th percentile.

"Too critical to leave totally to individuals." To how many of their endeavors have the collectivists now applied this velvet rationale for the mailed fist?

What's so odd about seeing it here, though, is that learning is a process so *ill*-adapted to collectivism.

How on earth can a society "collectively" educate a child? When you come right down to it, one student learns from one teacher. Surely most of us have watched a child "get it" while sounding out her first strange printed word, watching steam condense, or realizing the glass cracked because the water expanded when it froze.

This learning process happens naturally, and nearly constantly. For government to take credit for the fact that learning continues to transpire under its supervision (though at a far slower rate than otherwise) is a fraud only slightly less brazen than collecting a huge oxygen tax on the threat that we'd soon be unable to breathe if the state didn't keep manufacturing new oxygen, at secret factories, which of course we're never allowed to see for security reasons.

To assume that you could line up 100 kids on a parade ground, arranged by height and age, and require that they all experience the revelation of "getting" something at the same scheduled moment is patently absurd. Yet we keep trying.

Walk into the average 10th-grade classroom today (not some specially selected class for the gifted) and you'll see the result: While the young scholars will likely guess that John Locke and Thomas Paine might be NFL place-kickers, your main feedback will be a sneering demonstrative insolence, expressed in clothing, self-mutilation, posture, and voice. Smug mockery of the Dead White "Founding Fathers." A heartfelt avowal to never crack another book "once I get out of this place."

To the extent that the transaction of "education" is effected by shanghaiing the subject to a place he doesn't want to be (boys are far more severely damaged than girls, as was first seen with captive Indians), and then funding the enterprise with money looted from the unwilling, of course the little prisoners will become increasingly resistant, progressing from spitballs and pigtail-dipping to firearms and cocaine.

As more and more resources are diverted into security and discipline, it's the wardens more than the inmates who will come to shudder at a mention of the "old-fashioned academic core curriculum," since parents could easily recognize how far behind the little charges were slipping if they were allowed to directly compare today's progress against how far mom had gone in the same book in 1973, or grandma in 1946.

So, the curriculum has to be tarted up and changed enough to become unrecognizable every generation, throwing out the good with the bad until eventually the trendy equivalents of bright shiny objects (AIDS, recycling, turning in your parents for drug use) supplant any studies that could be objectively measured.

Every experiment needs a "control." The control group here are the home-schoolers. If only a government ant farm bigger than the Manhattan Project can educate children, why do home-schoolers taught by "amateur" housewives consistently place two to three years ahead of the government-kidnapped cohort by the seventh grade, totally regardless of parental race, income, or even educational level?

The assertion that we "dare not get rid of the Department of Education, because education is so important," will someday sound as absurd as some sweating Russian bureaucrat wiping his brow and ululating, "We dare not get rid of the Ministry of Vegetables, because food production is too critical to leave totally to individuals."

There is (I sincerely hope) no longer any Soviet Ministry of Vegetables. No central government authority (at least, none that can enforce its absurd pronouncements) any longer checks to make sure the "right quantity" of cantaloupe is planted each year across the vast Russian steppe.

As a result of which, for the first time in 70 years, there are now sufficient melons in Moscow.

Why the Schools Fear Freedom

S.N., a second-grade teacher in Phoenix, writes in response to my columns on unqualified teachers in the classroom.

"I am a teacher. I do not belong to NEA or AFT. I must say I'm a very good teacher. I have a Master's degree plus 30 hours. I continually spend my own time and money to increase my knowledge and my skills. ...

"I am not unusual. What about all of those of us who are doing a good job of educating your children? What about those many teachers ... who have slaved and sweated to learn the very best methods of educating your children? ...

215

"I am well aware that there are problems with the education system. I more than welcome the idea of more local control, more parents involved in textbook selection, curriculum design, teacher hiring, and classroom participation.

"What disturbs me is the idea that we need to throw out the whole system and that these new, no-government-involvement, parent-directed solutions will make the perfect system for our children. It won't happen. Yes, we need changes. We also need to be careful what we change and to what we are changing. ... "

I responded:

Dear S.—Thanks for your thoughtful missive.

I have nothing against "those many teachers ... who have slaved and sweated to learn the very best methods." Not only was my father the first in his family to attend college, he was also the first to earn an M.S., and then a Ph.D, and then to become ... a teacher. My pride in his accomplishments—coming from a background in which the last of 12 children of immigrant parents was never expected to undertake a career any more intellectually challenging than tobacco picker or at best a blue-collar artisan—knows few bounds.

But why this fear that, in a free economy, without government seizing the wherewithal at gunpoint, good teachers wouldn't do just fine? Surely 99 percent of parents—allowed to keep the income now seized by a government monopoly with an "overhead" as high as 75 percent—would immediately arrange for their own kids' education. The hiring market for truly dedicated and able tutors and instructors—working in private homes, in community schools, in any number of arrangements we can't even foresee—would be huge.

Why not assume the best of them would be rewarded with higher pay and more respect, as has been the result in every other field where competition has been allowed?

Whenever we can, Jeanne and I love to attend the arts-and-crafts fairs organized twice a year by the Mill Avenue Merchants Association in the college town of Tempe, Arizona.

Part of the fun is the food.

Not to imply there's anything haute about it ... or even overly healthful. But the variety of Indian fry bread, vegetable tempura, teriyaki beef sticks, grilled shrimp, fresh corn-on-the-cob, home-made potato chips fried before your eyes ... it's a phantasmagory of dyspeptic delight.

One year, there was a single Cajun food booth. The next year, word had been carried home about the success of that enterprise and there were three *competing* Cajun booths, vying with each other for variety, spiciness, and portion size. It was so good, we literally couldn't sample everything.

This year, we were told that the annual arts-and-crafts fair operated as a charity for the city hospital in Boulder City, near Las Vegas, was equally good. We decided to check it out.

Although the show was smaller, enjoyed less urban energy, and was more focused on the graphic arts, it was indeed nice to see the exhibitors (many of the same folks we see in Arizona) in a grassy park under the trees, rather than on the hot sidewalks of Tempe. The big difference, however, was the food.

We found the "food court" in Boulder City and walked up to one of the tents. The menu offered hot dogs, pizza slices, ready-made ham sandwiches, and Pepsi. No Coke.

Hardly inspiring. We decided to check out the next tent, which we could see across the way. The menu there consisted of ... hot dogs, pizza slices, and ready-made ham sandwiches. No Coke; Pepsi.

Rather than allowing private vendors to descend on the place with all their chaotic variety and competition, the folks who orga-nize the Boulder City Arts Festival—a branch of the city govern-ment—had simply contracted with one purveyor, who had sub-contracted to one soda-pop provider.

A "varied menu" had been ordered up. But it was all the

same varied menu at each tent. A government monopoly.

I'm afraid the public-school monopoly has gotten us all used to settling for a pizza slice and a Pepsi. "Reform" might offer us a cold slice of pepperoni, in addition to plain cheese. But this can only be a pale imitation of real innovation, like the puzzled Soviets of the '70s finally "allowing" their people some limited selection of knock-off blue jeans and Western music, always a decade behind the times.

Would you be happy to get your groceries by going to your assigned grocery store, only to be handed a brown bag containing your assigned menu for the week—breaded veal cutlets every Tuesday whether you liked it or not—and then sent to the checkout counter to pay an average of three times what you're paying today; no questions asked or you'd be threatened with arrest? (Yes, well-grounded, Christian, home-schooling parents have been arrested for violating the truancy laws in this country within recent memory—I hear from some of them.)

Of course not. But this is the way we "buy" education for our children today. And if we dare propose a wide-open system in which each parent could go to an education supermarket and custom tailor an education menu for each child—stopping by a specialty store to pick up a music lesson or a gunsmithing apprenticeship on the way home—we're told, "What disturbs me is the idea that we need to throw out the whole system and that these new, no-government-involvement, parent-directed solutions will make the perfect system for our children. It won't happen. ... "

The underlying problem is not just the lack of the kind of vigor that would otherwise be injected by competition, but the fact that no one within the monopoly can *imagine* what such a vigorous competitive system would look like ... just as Russian tourists used to think it must be a put-up job when they visited an American supermarket and were told the common folk shopped amidst such eye-popping plenty ... just as the locals who told

218

Jeanne and me in good faith that we'd love the Boulder City Arts Festival had no idea how wanting we'd find it, since they know nothing better.

"Yes, we need changes," writes S.N. from Phoenix. But, "We also need to be careful what we change and to what we are changing."

But who is "we"? The collective, of course. And it's here I'm afraid we're destined to disagree.

I look at the social pathologies—the gangs, the violence, the self-mutilation— and I don't see a collective, state-run institution in need of "more parents involved in textbook selection, curriculum design, and classroom participation" (which generally translates to: Thanks for loaning us the cosmetic appearance of your involvement. Now you yokels go hold a bake sale and raise some money for soccer uniforms; us experts will take care of the rest. ... ")

No, I see something new, something that didn't exist in the far more civil America of a century ago, something *created by the government school monopoly.*

How many times have I heard schoolteachers (now allowed to double-dip by holding seats in the state Legislature, in my state as in many) whine, "The schools only reflect the problems the kids bring in from the outside world."

Nonsense. As recently as 1950, fewer than half of American youths completed high school. It wasn't because they were street thugs. They had to leave school to marry the gal who was going to have their kids, to help out on the farm or with dad's business, or else to enter the armed forces.

This was not considered any kind of national tragedy. It was well-understood that only a minority had the interest, the intellectual acuity, the money, or the leisure to go to college.

Fast-forward to today. The wet dreams of the education bureaucrats have finally come fully and hideously true. Tax-funded state education lasts from age 4 to age 22, and if the kid goes home in the afternoon he finds nothing but an echoing empty sub-division. Long gone is grandpa, along with his unsanitary pipes, his coin and gun collection, and his stamp album (all of which taught geography and history in ways a sterile classroom can never replicate), replaced by endless repetitive pre-literate tank-gunner-training videos, disguised as "games."

Where 50 years ago mom and grandma might have been found preparing supper, asking the kids to pitch in and learn something about gardening, nutrition, cooking, and self-sufficiency, today mom is out working full time just to pay the taxes on dad's pay-check (effective combined tax rates on the middle class are now literally 10 times higher than they were in 1953, up from five percent till they're pushing 50—mostly to pay for the temples to full-service social work that the public schools have now become). And grandma's vegetating in some rest home, convinced she has nothing useful left to teach anyone.

Education and socialization are now, finally, fully in the hands of the government bureaucrats with their ed-school graduate de-grees. And what has been the result of this dream come true? Two generations of functionally illiterate sociopaths.

Today's kids of 17 and 18 are still having kids, just as they were on the farms in the 1930s and '40s. One could almost con-clude this seems to be part of the plan of Nature's God. But in-stead of leaving school, taking honest work, renting an apartment, and starting to save for a house, the unemployed and thus self-hating young fathers simply send the mother of their children down to the welfare office to arrange for subsidized housing, food stamps, AFDC—the whole cornucopia of socialist debilitation. The only restriction is the young dad *can't* marry or live with her.

With socialist minimum-wage laws having banned the entry-level jobs that might once have made use of their muscles and their boundless energy until they caught the eye of an employer in search of a dedicated and hungry young fellow, these young men are left to hang out hopelessly on street corners, objects of fear and scorn, cadging quarters, dealing drugs, or dreaming of more lucrative crimes.

O, the socialist paradise!

Their parents? Working three jobs between them just to pay the welfare-state taxes required to prop up this whole massively dysfunctional scheme.

Thus, the "outside world" these teachers complain about isn't in any way natural. It's entirely an artificial creation of the welfare state, of which the government-run, tax-funded, mandatory, welfare schools are an integral part.

In fact, far from urging kids to do the right thing—take a job and marry the mom of their kids, in the case of the majority who have no aptitude for studying philosophy and ancient Greek—one of the main businesses of the schools these days is to *discourage* that kind of "dead-end irresponsible behavior," instead teaching the kids how better to access the various goodies of the welfare state, all available if they'll only postpone reproduction (or, failing that, marriage and commitment) beyond their most fertile years, to stay in school.

What does "stay in school" mean to a 17-year-old who gave up learning to read anything more complicated than a soup can when he was 10—whose inclination or aptitude for Latin or calculus and for discoursing on the contrasting worldviews of Locke and Hegel—the stuff any *real* high-school graduate could do in 1938—is now nil?

Couldn't a cynic easily understand this desperate insistence on staying in school to mean "not go looking for a job, which will only balloon the official unemployment rate up much closer to the *real* unemployment rate, defeating our ongoing efforts to hide how much private-sector job destruction the welfare state has already caused"?

I worked one summer on a dairy farm. Occasionally, we'd

hear a cow bellowing in pain, off in the field. Two of us lads would trot out to the poor beast. We would place our shoulders to her haunch, and give a shove. To regain her balance, she would shift the hoof with which she had been stepping on her own tit. The pain suddenly relieved, she would then go meandering off, in the eternal way of cows, without so much as a look of thanks or realization.

At this point, they've finally dumbed down the diploma till the most "developmentally challenged" can earn it with his eyes closed. As the Prussians first envisioned, the diploma rewards not real learning and intellectual fertility, but simply the willingness to keep showing up and following orders, even as bored 13-year-olds sit circling all the pictures of objects that start with the letter "B."

The whole system is so inflated that no one bats an eye when college freshmen must take remedial reading *en masse*. Some day, one of these "social promotions" will be hired to repair the elevator on which your life depends. Good luck.

The government schools are nearing the end of their rope. They stand bellowing in pain, demanding endlessly more money and even harsher penalties for those who resist their tender ministrations.

They never realize that their problems are of their own making, the inevitable result of force, fraud, and coercion.

It's time for someone to put a shoulder to their haunch and give a good shove.

Robbing the Industrious of Their Rewards, Socialism Is the Ultimate Perversion

I've been writing about these subjects nearly every week since 1993. Yet in the summer of 1998, "Teacher in Texas" emailed:

"I noticed you're quick to point out what's wrong with the educational system, but offered no solutions. Any ideas, or just blowing off some steam?"

Does anyone else get the feeling that we've come almost full circle here?

I replied:

I thought I'd been making it pretty clear: If you're talking about how we can reform the current government-run, socialist/ redistributionist, public-employee-union-dominated, school system to make it "work better," then there are no "solutions"—because you are seeking an answer to the wrong question.

The Constitution grants no authority for the federal government to be involved in education. Therefore, freedom from government interference in education is an individual right, under the Ninth Amendment. Under the Fourteenth Amendment, it became illegal for any state to deprive any United States citizen of such a constitutional right. Therefore, all government interference in education (federal *or* state) is unconstitutional, as well as extremely dangerous to our other freedoms (since it exposes our children to 12 years of pro-big-government propaganda in some of their most crucial formative years).

If you doubt this, find me a public-school classroom where equal time is given to the theory (I would argue it's an easily established fact) that Franklin Roosevelt was a dangerously unprincipled opportunist who thoughtlessly embraced state socialism, thus violating his oath to defend the Constitution. Show me a public-school classroom where a common exercise is to stage a mock trial of Mr. Roosevelt, in which the children decide whether he should have been impeached and hanged as a usurping tyrant.

The very unthinkableness of such a lesson being taught in today's government schools (while mock trials of John D. Rockefeller, for the "crime" of unrestrained capitalism, are seriously recommended in the proposed new National History Standards) reveals just how "objective" they are on any subject that bears on the legitimacy of the bureaucracy.

The "solution" is obvious: a complete separation of school and state, similar to the wise and beneficial separation of church and state that has long been an American ideal.

Existing school facilities should be auctioned off to the highest bidders—which, in many cases, would turn out to be new private-school companies, offering free-market education.

Based on what's happened when other government-monopoly "services" have been privatized, I estimate tuition costs would eventually drop to one-third of what the government collects and allocates per student—meaning that parents would actually pay less in school tuition than they now pay in school taxes, *despite* the fact that parents of school-aged children today are "helped" by the unwilling "contributions" of the half of the population who send no children to the government schools.

In these new private schools, violent troublemakers would be expelled immediately. The ban on government interference means any parent suing (based on the notion that his or her child's violence and failure to allow others to learn constitutes a "disability") would be told to take a hike. The right of private contract and association would return to primacy.

Persistent, "Texas Teacher" wrote back a few days later:

"Very interesting take. Much of what you said made sense and I think I better understand your position."

My correspondent then posed two more questions:

"1) Under the de Tocqueville model, do impoverished children receive the same caliber of education as the wealthy, or just the best they can afford?

"2) Do you attribute all literacy problems to federal and state mandated programs, or do you also consider other paradigm shifts? Don't forget that mentally retarded children and other "different" kids (i.e. autistic, ADD, learning disabled) were not sent to school

224

in 1820, but were hidden away at home. Also, children with brain injuries often died, but with increased numbers of traumatic brain injury centers, they're living ... and attending schools. Could these factors influence literacy rates in public schools?"

I replied:

Yes, I'm sure more severely disabled kids are surviving these days. But I do think provisions for their care are a separate (primarily medical) question for the socialism-vs.-free enterprise debate.

In fact, one of the big *problems* with the schools today is that they've become more or less full-service social-service agencies. This facilitates what I think is a pretty intellectually dishonest trick to sidestep inquiries into the quality of education being provided: "We have to feed the hungry; care for the abused; counsel the psychologically traumatized; build self-esteem. How do you expect us to accomplish much in the far more minor areas of teaching science and history when we spend so much time on these far more important matters?"

As I've said before, this is tantamount to demanding a huge sum on the promise you can teach all the animals to pee on fireplugs and then only succeeding with the dogs.

Sorry; the taxpayers thought they were funding *schools*, on the promise all you Ph.D.s could educate *all comers*. Of course, the school can be used as a field hospital for trauma victims during an *emergency*. But to pile all these functions into one building, do them all badly, all the time, and then use the fact that you've sidetracked into all kinds of ancillary do-goodisms as an excuse for failure to accomplish the main mandated purpose starts to resemble a bad comedy act in which all three of the Stooges point the finger of blame at someone else.

Of course, a compassionate and wealthy nation (but please note that only free economies produce wealth; socialist nations in the end help no one because all they can really do is spread impoverishment) can and should help the severely disabled, when possible. But the shift in emphasis onto helping the afflicted, at the cost of allowing the gifted to reach *their* maximum potential, has gone much too far.

Anyway, I sincerely doubt the severely retarded are taking the same tests and thus being included in the sample from which we draw our comparison measurements of literacy ... don't you?

But as to your most serious questions:

I think it would be disingenuous to deny that, in a free-market economy, free from state interference in education, the wealthy can and would continue to be able to afford better education than the poor.

The same way the vast majority of elected officials and even public-school administrators would continue to send their kids to the best *private* schools they can afford—not to the zombie academies they run for us.

One of the main incentives for studying hard, working hard, prospering, and accumulating wealth is that one can then afford to provide for one's family better food, better clothing, better housing, better medical care, and (yes) better education than someone who goofs off, fritters away his or her life indulging in drugs and alcohol, makes bad life decisions, fails to postpone instant gratification in order to accumulate savings, and generally just slinks along in short-term jobs.

This is a law of nature. Marx and Lenin thought they could repeal that law. Despite 80 years of terror on a scale unimaginable, they failed.

• • •

The well-meaning socialist says, "Why punish the child for the sins of the parents? This is unfair to the child of the shiftless fellow. Let us lift just a few dollars from the paycheck of the hard-working souls to fund a school for the children of the poor.

They will hardly notice this tiny levy. It's for the chillldren."

There are three or four problems with this attractive-sounding recipe:

1) Donate all you want of your own earnings to fund scholarships for the poor at private schools, but don't tell me the conveyance of stolen funds enriches either your soul or those of the fellows from whom you have stolen. This is not true "charity."

2) The government schools are failing most markedly with the children of the poor, so the squawk that private schools for the poor would be less fancy is a sheer red herring.

We have seen how, in 1985, a single judge took control of the school district in Kansas City, Mo., and spent $1.5 billion over the normal budget, creating state-of-the-art school facilities with greenhouses, athletic arenas, a planetarium, radio and TV studios, and computers in every classroom.

The result? After a full decade, no measurable improvement in academic achievement, a falling attendance rate, and a high-school dropout rate that remained at 60 percent. *No* amount of money spent on the government schools will solve their problems. On the other hand, Marva Collins' private West Side Prep in inner-city Chicago does a splendid job with "disadvantaged" children, despite its modest means.

3) But these excuses that "We can't succeed with kids who are starving and in rags" (describing, for the most part, fat boys in $100 Adidas sneakers, stopping after school for a quart of Coke and a two-dollar bag of Doritos) in turn lead to the obvious corollary: The tax-funded "welfare school" cannot exist in isolation. We are soon informed that we cannot supply "equal education" for the poor unless we also institute food stamps (income redistribution to equalize nutrition), Section 8 housing subsidies, Medicaid and other piecemeal agglomerations of socialized medicine (income redistribution to equalize health care), etc. About the only

thing we haven't gotten around to yet are "state stores" for redeeming "clothing coupons," though I'm sure they'll think of it soon.

In short, "partial socialism" doesn't stay partial for long. Once we have accepted the *premise* that we have the right to loot the paychecks of the productive to succor the "unfortunate," why should we stop until we have communism, out of whole cloth? There's always one more perceived "social inequity" to blame for preventing our *existing* redistributionist schemes from working properly. Ask the Democrat, the bureaucrat, or the public-employees' union member to name one benefit that they would *not* extend to the poor, via tax funding.

I doubt they can think of any.

4) Finally, of course, our "tiny levies" on the wealthy, the hard-working, and the prosperous must come down to "We leave them what they require to live." This is already happening. When the IRS rules you owe back taxes (no court judgment is required), they sit down and assign you a budget on which you are expected to live. The government takes the rest (it's called "garnishment"), before you even see your paycheck. There is no "maximum percentage" beyond which they will seize no more.

Look at Eastern Europe. Combined tax rates now exceed 100 percent, so no one has any choice but to hire gangsters to either intimidate or murder the government tax men. There *is* no readily detectable wealth, except among the criminal class. The currency is a joke, so everything is barter—again frustrating the tax collectors, in turn leaving even such "basic" government services as trolley cars, police, and the courts decrepit, unreliable, and often available only to those who can pay the biggest bribes.

Yet Bill Clinton goes to Moscow and lectures the Russians that they must "pay their taxes, even though it may seem hard"!

Any Russian who had wealth and didn't want to become an armed gangster fled by 1921, was killed for his wealth long ago, or has it hidden away where no one can find it. The state "guarantees" everyone the made-up "rights" of free food, free housing, free medical care, and a fine free education, and delivers *none* of these things. Socialism doesn't *work*. And this is the very road down which we started when we enacted your first tiny well-meaning "school tax."

• • •

The best hope for education for the poor is to hope like heck that a free market economy allows *everyone* to get richer—as certainly happened in this nation from 1787 to 1911, during which time the standard of living of "the poor" increased many times over.

By the way, the only reason we still *have* "poor people" in this country any more is that we keep raising the bar. My newspaper last year ran a classic break-page photo of a "poor woman" complaining that the city housing authority had not yet repaired cracks and water stains in the ceiling of her virtually free tax-subsidized apartment. In the photo, this well-nourished woman points angrily at the damage with the *antenna of her cellular phone*. Behind her her three boys—one obviously older than 16—sit lounging on the couch, watching daytime programs on the color TV. Tell me another nation on earth where you could with a straight face identify this woman as "poor," "disadvantaged," or the victim of any kind of "neglect."

Yet was she pushing her children into their bedrooms to hit the books in order to better their condition, or out the door to go find work? Was she even offering that her sons would do the repairs if the city merely supplied the materials? No. She was yelling in self-righteous fury that the taxpayers were not doing enough for her, and they'd better hop to it!

This notion that even taxpayers with no children gain something from supporting the government schools—because kids kept busy in school at least won't be beating and robbing the neighbors—peels down to some mighty thinly disguised blackmail. Do you really mean to tell me if I don't subsidize your kids' day care you'll send them over here to beat and rob me? Or that—lacking a tax-funded education—you have no intention of teaching them to fend for themselves in the world and that I deserve to have them leeching off me later, if I decline to subsidize your discretionary breeding habits today?

How far does that principle extend? Am I obliged to fund the education of the children of China, lest I "deserve" to have them invade this country and seize my wealth later on?

In fact, school socialism teaches kids precisely the lesson you claim to be rejecting—that if enough lazy people demand to be fed by the productive classes, their victims will have to pay up or else.

On the other hand, absent burgeoning socialism, as the rich grow richer through their labors and their wise habits, they are free to—they have demonstrated that they will—fund scholarships for the poor. Even the modest middle class has demonstrated that they have no objection to paying private school tuitions 11 or 12 percent higher than they would otherwise pay, so that 10 percent of each class can be made up of gifted poor children—chosen by competitive examination—on *full* scholarships. In fact, I know of hardly any private schools that don't do this.

But the collectivists don't want charity, do they? That would be "demeaning." They prefer to steal outright.

Go Ahead. Steal From
Your Neighbors. It's Legal.

Forget the desperate Drug War hypocrites, frantically pantomiming their "compassion for the children" by promising to airdrop the 82nd Airborne into Topeka to shoot all the dope smokers.

Forget your uncle crossing his fingers for that defense contract to get renewed down at the plant, or the federal guarantees that hold down the interest rate on your mortgage or your niece's college loan.

Where most of us first sell out to the blandishments of the "progressive" welfare state (and darned cheap, at that) is in the local school bond.

All taxation is theft, right? If the "contributions" were voluntary, it wouldn't be a tax. There's always a fat guy with a gun in the background, somewhere, threatening to pile the furniture on the sidewalk outside the yellow police tape and auction off the house if we don't pay up.

If it's unacceptable to loot the paycheck of Citizen A to fund services you contend A "needs"—fire engines, roads—isn't it doubly evil to loot Citizen A to fund the education of the kids of B?

And for a real triple-header of evil, how about taxing A to pay the *interest* on the money you're borrowing to build your brick government propaganda camp for the indoctrination of little Sean and Tabitha B?

Still, we're assured, dare to turn down the school bond and Junior and Sis could be forced into double sessions.

That's the rationale I found being offered by the proponents of the latest $642 million Clark County (Las Vegas) school bond in 1996.

Las Vegas has a better excuse than most. Surely the administrators can't be blamed for the explosive growth of the fastest-growing school district in the nation—a side effect of the nation-wide gambling craze to which they can only react.

(Why gamble? Because taxes and inflation melt away savings like a warm rain on snow—savings scooped up by the government if we try to leave them to our kids, anyway. Might as well risk it all on a turn of the wheel, hoping to earn enough to

231

hire the kind of financial advisor who knows how to get the loot to Switzerland, where the banks won't turn over your entire worldly wealth to Uncle Sam and bounce all your checks upon receipt of the first "Notice of Intent to Levy.")

So what if past bond issues have never quite built as many schools as promised, if despite all the tax hikes there are still English classes serving 150 kids with 47 textbooks?

True, borrowing this amount of money—and that's what a school district really does when it issues bonds—means taxpayers will cough up an additional $530 million in interest over the next 20 years, shouldering an obligation of more than $1 billion in all, requiring taxes to be raised by at least $38 per year on each $100,000 home. (Raised, you understand. This bond issue is merely being piggy-backed onto all the others which have gone before.) But what else can be done?

Starve the behemoth to death, of course.

Obviously, few counties or states in America lack the wherewithal to guarantee every child who has the wit and the will the chance to pursue an education just because of poverty. In effect, the taxpayers donate full-tuition scholarships for such kids, right now. There's little doubt the citizenry would continue to do so, regardless of the mechanism.

But, that said, what's "fair" about assessing those who choose to have no children, or who struggle to fund their own kids' educations at private schools? What's "fair" about forcing them to subsidize the decisions of those who choose to have kids but fail to allocate enough for their schooling?

Many a middle-class American whose pride would be insulted if you knocked on her door with a bag of rice and beans, implying she needed "charity" groceries, today accepts "charity" schooling without blinking an eye, and then has the nerve to complain about the quality of the handouts she's given.

America's leftist elite used to sneer that those who opposed "progressivism" were foolishly "hunting for socialists under the bed." No need to look there. If you have ever voted in favor of a school bond—taking money from your neighbor on the threat of the government seizure of his or her house, in order to school your own kids—then you are a socialist. And as with alcoholism, you are not going to get cured until you admit it.

Public schooling suffers from a yawning schizophrenia. Our educators now acknowledge parental involvement is the single most important determinant of academic success. Yet the very underlying premise of our current system is that only "professional educators" are qualified to take our little darlings in charge from the age of five, after which incompetent "amateur" parents seeking any meaningful curricular involvement usually find themselves relegated to organizing bake sales to buy band uniforms.

Just as visitors from countries where food distribution was handled by the government used to stare in disbelief at the bounteous variety of our supermarkets, so might we be shocked at the proliferation of high-quality, affordable, educational options that would spring up were we to return to the system that was universal in this country before the 1850s, with parents given complete control of the "tuitions" they now pay as taxes.

But if we haven't established anything else by now, surely it's clear that the kind of vested interests who now fatten at the trough of "public education" will run us in gleeful circles and never allow us to get there through any "gradual transition." The rule of nature and of history is that the new seeds sprout in the sun only after the old tree has finally toppled in ruin.

So: Why prop up this rotting hulk any longer?

Why?

V

WHY PEOPLE HATE
THE GOVERNMENT

'When You Send Your Collector,
Have That Woman Send Her Waco Killers'

Elmer Wade, 61, has lived on the same 80-acre, 250-animal, hog farm in Cedar Creek, N.C., with his wife Lois and his four sons for more than 30 years.

With his sons growing and hoping to branch out, Wade decided to accept a 1985 invitation from the U.S. government to bid on a total-confinement, 250-sow, hog farm in neighboring Bladen County.

Wade's bid of $185,000 was accepted and the U.S. Farmers Home Administration agreed to finance 90 percent of the purchase.

Things went fine for nearly a decade. The Wades were making their annual payment of $21,770, no problem. Then, in 1993, according to Mickey Cochran, director of agricultural credit for the FmHA, now called the U.S. Farm Service Agency, several spills of hog and chicken waste—none of them involving Wade's properties—fouled coastal streams in North Carolina.

In 1995, the federal Environmental Protection Agency responded by increasing the number of acres of adjacent grass required for each pig. (After hog sewage has steeped awhile in sewage lagoons, modern pig farmers get rid of the liquefied manure by spreading it over adjacent grasslands as fertilizer, thus keeping sewage levels under control in their lagoons.)

Wade figured that would be no problem. The 88-acre Bladen County farm has 14 acres covered with buildings and 13 acres in grass, which still leaves 61 acres in woods. He'd simply clear another 26 acres of woods to meet the new grassland standards that the EPA said would be required after 1997.

"I was sent to the Soil Conservation Service to get help to plan the compliance process," Wade says in an open letter to "the President of the United States and all of you people in Washington, D.C. that run the government"—a letter he mailed to many major newspapers around the country.

The Soil Conservation Service agreed Wade would have to clear the additional 26 acres of woodland and plant it in grass. However, "Before I could clear the woods, I would have to have a Wetland Determination made," Wade writes.

You guessed it. Although the federal government participated in clearing the woods for the hog farm for the first owner circa 1981, the wetlands folks at the EPA informed Wade that the definition of "wetlands" had now changed, and that no more woods could be cleared.

"I went to the FmHA and informed them that the government sold me a farm and made rules that made it impossible for me to farm," Wade writes. "If I couldn't farm it I couldn't pay for it and would have to give it back to them. They said I couldn't give it back, but if I didn't pay for it they would take it. Then they would sell it and make me pay the difference.

"They repossessed and sold it. It sold for only $30,000 because it is worthless as a hog farm. In Raleigh, N.C., Federal Judge Fox said I would have to pay for it, and gave the federal government a judgment against me for $153,000."

Mickey Cochran of the Farm Service Agency confirmed for Estes Thompson, an Associated Press writer out of Raleigh, that the FSA indeed would not let Wade give the farm back.

Why? In bureaucrat Cochran's words, because, "The animal-waste regulations did make it uneconomical" for anyone else to operate as a hog farm, of course.

Mind you, there's no critical pork shortage in America. Why the federal government has been flushing your tax dollars down this kind of manure lagoon is a separate question—and a good one. "The first guy ran it for four years; I figure he left owing 'em about half a million dollars," Wade says. "And they just let him walk because he didn't have nothin'."

Thompson of the AP reported in December 1995 that, "Wade has a small sandbag bunker near a stand of bamboo outside his house, shotguns in the corner of his dining room, and a pistol under his easy chair.

Wade fears the government means to go through with its threat to seize his original homestead to make up the extra $153,000 it says he owes on his original loan for the now-useless government-built facility over in Bladen County.

"I'm within two steps of a gun all the time," Wade told Thompson. "They won't take it from me. They might take it from my estate. I've never gone back on my word."

In his open letter, farmer Wade warns the people in Washington, "I am writing this letter so you won't have any surprises. Through no fault of mine I am being put upon. I've had all I can stand from you in the front, and I do not plan to roll over. So when you send your collector, have That Woman send your WACO KILLERS with them. They will need them. Living is not very much fun with you standing on my neck. If you do it right, dying will be one hell of a party."

I called Wade, who lives near Fayetteville, in January 1996. The wooded area they will now not let him clear "is the same kind of land that was originally cleared for the farm," he says in his slow drawl. "Do you know what it does to a farmer when the federal government takes away your credit, has a judgment against you? They effectively put us on a weekly cash flow."

His son John had been running the Bladen County farm with two employees, Wade says. Two more for the unemployment rolls. "We may lose this one, too," he told me, referring to his original, 80-acre, Cedar Creek spread. "They've just taken everything we worked all our lives for.

"I have no quarrel with the waste-management rules," Wade says, "and I have no quarrel with the wetlands regulations. But it seemed to me if they make it so I can't run the farm anymore, you ought to be able to give it back to them. ... Those fellows are doing more harm to good fellows than people know. I would like to officiate over their demise."

Next time Bill Clinton or Dick Gephardt accuses those who oppose the current enforcement of our water and wetlands laws of being greedy industrialists out to "poison our waters for profit," we'll all know who they're talking about. Elmer Wade.

Four Months In Chains

Sissy Harrington-McGill, 60-year-old proprietor of Solid Gold Pet Foods in El Cajon, Calif., opened her all-natural animal-feed company in 1974, eventually developing 30 products for dogs, cats, and horses, sold nationally in animal-supply and health-food stores.

Although Solid Gold's animal-feed license was issued by the Department of Agriculture, it's the FDA that has harassed Harrington-McGill over her claims for all-natural animal foods. Among other things, she's been told it's unlawful to use endorsements or testimonials to sell a product, or to state, "Your pet will live a longer and healthier life with natural, vitamin-enriched, pet food."

At one point, she says she was threatened with fines and other legal action for failure to list the preservatives in her foods. She replied that her pet foods contain no preservatives. In that case, she was told, a citation and other action would be forthcoming against her for failure to include preservatives, which everyone knows are necessary to stabilize the animal fats in pet foods. She replied that her foods contain no animal fats.

Said Harrington-McGill: "They made me change my labels eight times in nine years. They won't give you an OK in writing, they do it all by phone. You get the OK, you make the change, get everything printed up, and then they make you change it again. So it drains the company of money, and that's the purpose."

In March 1990, the FDA turned up the heat, notifying Harrington-McGill her stores would be closed.

Harrington-McGill appeared on July 10, 1990, before U.S. District Court Judge Gordon Thompson in San Diego. Harrington-McGill says she asked FDA attorney Colleen Martin to cite the statute she was supposed to have broken. "They said 'We don't have to tell you.'"

Harrington-McGill contends that the judge told her to plead guilty anyway, promising to assess a minimal $500 fine. If Harrington-McGill made trouble by insisting on a trial, however, she was warned that she would do time in the maximum-security federal pen.

Harrington-McGill demanded a jury trial. Judge Thompson refused to grant her one and on July 12, 1990, he found Harrington-McGill guilty and told her to come back in six weeks for sentencing.

Harrington-McGill now believes the timing was significant. The U.S. House passed a new Health Claims Bill on July 30, 1990. The Senate was expected to pass the bill quickly, but did not. "They convicted me of violating a law that hadn't been passed yet. [The judge] told me he was going to make an example of me and put me in chains for being 'arrogant.'"

Harrington-McGill's feet were shackled. A chain was strung around her waist and her hands were cuffed. She was hauled off to the maximum-security federal lockup in San Diego, sentenced to 179 days in chains and a $10,000 fine. (The United States Supreme Court has ruled, in its infinite and creative wisdom, that while the Sixth Amendment clearly says we have a right to a jury trial "in all criminal prosecutions," what it really means is "in all criminal prosecutions that can result in a sentence of at least six months—180 days.")

At age 57, Harrington-McGill was the oldest inmate in the penitentiary. She had a stroke while in prison and was chained to a bed in San Diego's Mercy Hospital.

The Senate finally passed a version of the Health Claims Bill that October, but it wasn't what the FDA had wanted. Instead, it asserted that vitamins, minerals, and herbs are foods, not drugs, and that store owners should inform their customers of what the products did. George Bush signed the bill on Nov. 4, 1990. Shortly thereafter, citing the holiday season, Judge Thompson ordered a "compassionate release" of Harrington-McGill, who had served 114 days.

I sought some explanation for Harrington-McGill's bizarre experience. Prosecutor Greg Vega in San Diego remembers there was such a case, but says he played a small role and can't remember anything about it. A dozen calls over a two-week period to the FDA press office in Rockville, Md., failed to turn up anyone willing to comment on the Solid Gold case.

Judge Gordon Thompson's clerk in San Diego, Jeff Benz, said, "The judge would not be at liberty to discuss this case or any past or future case."

You'd almost think our brave federal crime-fighters aren't proud of what they did to Sissy Harrington-McGill.

(By the way, if you're wondering about the Congressional

authorization for the federal Food and Drug Administration to regulate the content and labeling of pet and animal feeds, there is none. Turns out that's the job of the Department of Agriculture ... the folks who licensed Ms. McGill to start producing animal feeds in the first place. But Bill Clinton and his ilk still can't figure out why some people "love their country but hate their government.")

The Political Trials Begin

On April 16, 1990, Scott Scarborough came home from work in rural Davisburg, Mich., picked up his wife Karen, and drove the 33 miles to the post office at Royal Oak, a suburb of Detroit. This was the second year they planned to join the tax protesters there (the 15th had fallen on a Sunday that year.) They picked up a friend, Peter Hendrickson, on the way. All were members of the Libertarian Party of Michigan.

Karen would later tell the grand jury she was feeling ill—the beginnings of what turned out to be the rejection of a transplanted kidney—and that she stayed in the car, lying on the back seat. She testified that Hendrickson remained in the car with her while Scott got out to visit with the eight or 10 picketers. Scott says he heard sirens almost the moment he emerged from the car, and figured there had been an accident.

At about the same time, an eyewitness saw a man drop a manila envelope into one of the mailboxes that the post office had designated for last-minute tax returns—now believed to have been the envelope containing a phosphorus smoke device. Government experts have testified the device had no timer, but bore a fuse that had to be lit with an open flame, at which point ignition occurred within 90 seconds.

The eyewitness described a man who did not match Peter

Hendrickson. The eyewitness later viewed Peter Hendrickson in a photo lineup, but picked out a postal employee instead. She was unable to identify Hendrickson in a "live" lineup, either. No one even bothered to put Scott Scarborough in a lineup. "[The eyewitness] described someone clean-shaven, and Scott's always had a mustache. They were talking about someone with different colored hair, about five inches shorter," says Ralph Musilli, Scott Scarborough's attorney.

The smoke device ignited. Postal worker Thomas Berlucchi received slight burns to his hands and legs in the course of removing the smoking device from the bin, burns that later healed without causing any scarring or permanent disability.

That was the extent of the damage caused by the great Michigan post office bombing of 1990. But it was only the beginning of the nightmare of Scott and Karen Scarborough.

• • •

"These people are clean as pins," says Musilli of the Scarboroughs, never before accused of a crime, married seven years with a 20-year-old daughter (Scott's stepdaughter) now in cosmetology school. "They go to work every day and pay their taxes and make their mortgage payments and visit with their family. The most radical thing they ever did was write an article for the Libertarian newspaper.

"There were all kinds of people protesting at the post office that day," says Musilli, "but they grabbed right at the Libertarians. Those are the only ones they were interested in. They took them all before the grand jury."

Why?

After all, the Libertarians, who call for the end of the income tax and the War on Drugs, are the only national party that requires every new national member to pledge: "I do not believe in the use of force to achieve political and social goals."

Yet a federal prosecutor would later warn the Scarboroughs' jury: "You're going to hear some Libertarian views, some of which you may find strange or even offensive."

Lawyer Musilli has a theory. "We [went] from a Constitutional Republic in this country to a democracy, probably in the 1930s," says Musilli, who's 50 and has been practicing law in Michigan since 1969. "Then we have gone in my lifetime from a democracy to what I would call a bureaucratic aristocracy, and the next step will be a dictatorship."

No one suspected Scott and Karen Scarborough of setting the smoke device. But in the course of checking out the Libertarians who had been at the scene, federal prosecutors stumbled on the Scarboroughs' young friends, Peter Hendrickson and Doreen Wright. Although Doreen was out of the country at the time of the tax protest, she worked as a high-school science teacher, where she had access to red phosphorus, the substance used in the device. And Hendrickson and Wright had failed to file federal income tax returns for the two previous years.

The Scarboroughs were granted immunity to testify before the grand jury, where prosecutors hoped they would tell of attending meetings where Hendrickson had proposed committing the crime. Instead, Karen told of the government's prime suspect sitting in the car with her the whole time the smoke-bomb incident was in progress.

The attorney for Hendrickson and Wright volunteered to bring his clients in for an arraignment if required. Instead, 15 armed agent staged a massive raid two days later, seizing the young couple from their home at 7 a.m.

Doreen Wright was breast-feeding her seven-month-old baby, Katie, at the time of the raid. The officers pulled the infant from her breast and turned it over to a state social worker they'd brought along as they hauled the couple away in handcuffs. Wright telephoned her ex-husband, who often baby-sat for the couple, and who agreed to come take charge of the child that day, but the postal inspectors in charge of the scene refused to allow that, according to Musilli.

Wright's mother was given custody of the child that evening, but it took a day or two—accounts vary—for Hendrickson and Wright to regain custody. A lawyer had to be retained, since "abandonment" charges had been filed.

Yes, the postal inspectors had pulled a nursing baby from the mother's arms and hauled the mother away in chains—and then charged the couple with "abandoning" their baby because it was left alone in the house.

It's a type of thinking that takes some getting used to.

"You've got all kinds of these paramilitary organizations in the U.S. government now," says lawyer Musilli. "The FBI, the ATF, the DEA, the postal inspectors, the list goes on and on. They've all got their own stormtroopers and they love to do this stuff. We've got one in Michigan called DRANO, the Down River Area Narcotics Organization, and there's one called COMET, I forget what that stands for, all armed, multi-jurisdictional, task forces anxious to go use the fancy equipment, and they're all running around like Keystone Kops."

• • •

Peter Hendrickson eventually pleaded guilty to the two unrelated charges of failure to file federal income-tax returns, plus one count of the "lesser" charge of possession of an incendiary device. The Scarboroughs theorize he did this in return for a promise that Doreen Wright would not be charged, and that they could keep custody of their child.

But any expectation Hendrickson may have had of a soft sentence was shattered when the judge handed down an order for 27 months' incarceration.

Federal prosecutors said they couldn't do anything for Hendrickson unless he could give them some higher-ups in the Michigan Libertarian Party on the smoke bomb charge. Hendrickson offered them the Scarboroughs. Musilli says the prosecutors were dubious, since the Scarboroughs had never been suspected, and asked Hendrickson to take a polygraph test. He flunked.

Desperate, Hendrickson now embarked on the scheme in which prosecutors would consistently insist they were unaware and uninvolved—though for some reason, Hendrickson's date to report and start serving his sentence kept getting delayed during precisely this time period, due to the representation of prosecutors to the court that Hendrickson was "cooperating" with them.

Wiring Doreen Wright for sound with an amateur tape recorder and microphone beneath her sweater—a far cry from the kind of high-tech equipment a government agency might be expected to use—more than two years after the great 1990 smoke bombing, Hendrickson took Doreen Wright to pay a series of social calls on the Scarboroughs, two at their home and one at a nearby Red Lobster restaurant, hoping to tape statements that might be construed as admissions of their complicity in the post office "bombing."

Six-and-a-half hours of tapes resulted. But there was one hitch. "I listened to all six-and-a-half hours, and you can't understand a thing," Musilli says. The cheap microphone and the heavy sweater had proved a disastrous combination. "It's really grim."

The Scarboroughs were arrested and brought to trial anyway. Again, their attorneys offered to bring them in peaceably for arraignment. Again, a couple with long-standing ties to the community were subjected to dramatic and unannounced raids featuring large numbers of armed postal inspectors. Scott was led away in irons from his job at Ford Motors; Karen was hauled out in front of the neighbors at home.

There was a problem with Karen Scarborough, however. Although she appears active and vivacious, Karen Scarborough has had diabetes since the age of nine. Legally blind, she has undergone three kidney transplants and depends on insulin and anti-rejection drugs, both of which were confiscated at the time of her arrest. She was due for her first post-operative examination following cataract surgery the day of her arrest.

"I have arthritis in my arms as well, and they kept trying to handcuff me behind my back even though I was in tears and pleading with them not to. Finally they just couldn't get my arms to bend that far so they cuffed me in front.

Again, as with Hendrickson, the Scarboroughs were not actually charged with bombing the post office. They couldn't be charged with that—they'd been granted immunity in return for going before the grand jury, back when Hendrickson was the main suspect. So they were charged with conspiracy to obstruct justice by lying to the grand jury.

What lies? "They told the grand jury they had no knowledge about the placement of the incendiary device. They also said Peter Hendrickson could not have been involved because he was with them at the time the device went off," Berg summarizes. And Hendrickson, of course, had subsequently broken and pleaded guilty.

• • •

Hendrickson said he had prepared the smoke device and given it to Scott Scarborough, who had actually dropped it in the mailbox. Asked why the handwriting on the envelope didn't match his own, he said he had written left-handed to disguise his script. Told the ingredients of the bomb, he reconstructed for the jury how he had put it together. Told a tea bag had been found at the site, he said he had placed it in the envelope to commemorate the Boston Tea Party.

"Unfortunately, the government's own forensic expert said the tea bag couldn't have been in the envelope, or it would have been loaded with phosphorus," Musilli laughs. "Their own expert said it must have been on the ground nearby for some time and been swept up with all the other debris."

"Their own experts said Pete's story about how he built the bomb was impossible," recalls Scott Scarborough. "They listed the ingredients and he tried to make up a story to match and they said it was nonsense."

Then, on the witness stand, Hendrickson blurted out that he had been subjected to a lie-detector test when he had first implicated the Scarboroughs, and that he had flunked.

Surely that was a welcome opening for Musilli to pursue?

"I was admonished not to go into the polygraph matter," Musilli explains. "The judge said if I did she would declare a mistrial, which would have cost me my license. The prosecution figured I put Hendrickson up to it."

The state's main witness?

"Right."

For his help, Hendrickson finally served one year of his 27-month sentence, 51 days of that in an actual jail. The last 10 months of his time were served in a halfway house, under an arrangement that allowed him to return home to work during the day.

"He got a reduction on the basis of his cooperation," confirms prosecutor Berg.

The defense called the eyewitness, who repeated the description that matched neither Hendrickson nor Scarborough.

Incredibly, though, with both the eyewitness and Scarborough present in the same courtroom in front of the jury, neither attorney asked her whether Scarborough was the man she had seen.

On cross examination, "I did not ask her if Scott Scarborough was the man," says Deputy U.S. Attorney Berg. "That was because I didn't know what she'd say. I didn't want to—you don't want to be suggestive by showing her a picture or anything. So I just figured if she recognized him she might say it, but as a strategy matter you don't generally ask a witness something if you don't know what the answer will be."

"I don't know why my attorney didn't ask the eyewitness if it was me," says Scott Scarborough. "The tactics among attorneys are strange."

• • •

Finally, that left only the tapes.

"They had no warrant to tape in these people's home, to tape conversations between social friends. Besides which, you can't understand a thing. So I filed an objection to the tapes, but the judge overruled me and admitted them," Musilli explains.

"Then they took six hours of tapes and edited them down to about five minutes. They pieced together parts of various conversations. Some of the sections end in the middle of a sentence, to make them come out saying what they wanted them to say. But since you still couldn't understand them, the prosecution prepared transcripts of what they thought the tapes said.

"I objected, and the judge compromised. She said she'd let the jury have the transcripts in the jury box, to read along with what the state contended the tapes were saying, but she'd inform the jury that the transcripts weren't in evidence, only the tapes."

On the tapes, Doreen Wright spends most of her time suggesting that, since Scott Scarborough had been granted immunity and could not be charged with the post office bombing, he should admit to some related misdemeanor in order to take the heat off Hendrickson.

The transcripts contain no admissions of complicity by the

Scarboroughs. Presumably their very willingness to tolerate such discussions counted against them with the jury, as Karen Scarborough's repeated statements that Scott was reluctant to "cooperate with the government" may have. However, even in excerpts carefully selected by the government, Karen Scarborough at one point states: "We have to keep in mind that Scott didn't do it."

"He told us he pleaded guilty to something he didn't do, and I thought that's what they wanted me to do," Scott Scarborough says of the conversations, all initiated by Hendrickson and Wright. "There was a point later in the conversation where I said I couldn't do that because I was innocent, but that part of the tape got thrown away."

"It's accurate to say our excerpts did not contain all the statements on the tapes," responds prosecutor Berg. "The excerpts the government played were evidence the government felt showed the Scarboroughs had not told the truth. It's not the government's responsibility to put in portions that we don't think were relevant. We had a factual finding from the judge that the transcripts were accurate word for word … for the parts we played. The defense had several opportunities to play portions or submit transcripts of portions that they thought were exculpatory. Tom Wilhelm [Karen Scarborough's attorney] tried to play a portion of a tape, but either he couldn't find it or he couldn't get it to play the way he wanted it to."

"So when the jury went to deliberate, they didn't have the transcripts, only the tapes," Musilli recalls. "And after two hours they sent a message to the judge that they wanted the transcripts, so she asked, 'Does anyone have any objection to my giving them the transcripts?'

"I said, 'Of course I object, your honor. The transcripts aren't in evidence, and they're not allowed to have anything in the jury room that's not in evidence. This obviously proves my original contention, that they can't understand the tapes. Otherwise they wouldn't be asking for the transcripts.'

"And the judge says, 'Well, I let them have them in the jury box, so I'm going to let them have the transcripts in the jury room. I don't see that it makes any difference.' "

Federal District Court Judge Nancy Edmunds, a Bush appointee, had been on the bench about 18 months at that time. This was her first judicial appointment. As a private attorney, her specialty was commercial litigation.

The jury convicted the next morning, although Karen Scarborough says at least one juror was in tears as the verdict was read. The prosecution recommended prison sentences of 18 to 24 months.

For testifying that a friend sat in a car with Karen one day in April of 1990.

Why?

"We think they wanted us to incriminate a fellow Libertarian," Karen says. "He didn't have anything to do with the bombing either, but we knew who they wanted. They wanted us to roll over on him."

"I've lost my job over this. We're taking out a second mortgage to pay the legal fees, which are over $30,000," says Karen Scarborough.

And the local Libertarians?

"I was the vice chairman of the party last year. All the major events, including the reception for the presidential candidate, were held at our house. So they knew if they took care of us, it'd shut down the party in the state.

"This has effectively removed our protest now. Nobody goes down to the post office any more on tax day to protest the IRS."

A Scarborough Postscript

The Scarboroughs' dedication to one another, their insistence on their innocence, and their perpetually stymied efforts to obtain a copy of the "jury wheel" from which their Michigan jury had been selected—to check into courthouse rumors that the judge systematically purged from the jury duty pool any prospective juror who might have been politically or philosophically predisposed to sympathize with the Scarboroughs—have never wavered.

After serving their time, the Scarboroughs moved to Virginia. Scott found work for a small automobile-parts testing laboratory, and Karen—despite continuing health problems—eventually started up a business handling commercial printing and business services.

End of story?

Well, as it turns out, even a quarterly newsletter of a Libertarian Party affiliate in a small desert state does not long escape the attention of the federal prosecutors and their dutiful informants.

Shortly after the above account of the Scarborough frame-up appeared in the *Arizona Libertarian*, assistant federal persecutor Terence Berg took the trouble to write a formal letter on his official government letterhead from distant Michigan to my employers, the editors and publishers of the 160,000-circulation daily *Las Vegas Review-Journal*, informing them that he had spoken to me on the telephone about the Scarborough case only because I had represented myself under false pretenses, as an employee of the *Review-Journal* working on a story for the *Review-Journal*.

The fact that the account had finally appeared in an "official organ" of a Libertarian Party affiliate obviously proved I was some kind of subversive political operative, who had infiltrated a legitimate newspaper under false colors, which was why I should be disciplined or fired, Mr. Berg urged.

Interestingly, the vengeance-seeking prosecutor never bothered to allege that I had misreported a single fact in the case, or "misquoted him," or "taken him out of context" (an old favorite), even once.

The "Oh-this-couldn't-possibly-be-true" instincts of America's ladpdog press (the same instinct that kept our most esteemed dailies from reporting the Jewish Holocaust from 1938 to 1945, as they systematically discarded, rewrote, or buried the dispatches of their own European correspondents; the same instinct that prompted them to report the fantastic government hokum about a "mass suicide by fire" in Waco, Texas) had effectively shielded Mr. Berg and his superiors from exposure in any major newspaper or magazine. Heck, one would have thought he'd be satisfied that "the system" was working just fine.

For that matter, since I did keep calling back to make sure I had his response to each of the Scarboroughs' points, this somewhat over-the-top effort to discredit me in the eyes of my employers could even lead one to wonder what it was about my story that prosecutor Berg didn't like. Unless, once again, we have here a federal prosecutor who isn't proud to have his methods and accomplishments fully aired.

Fortunately, everyone to whom prosecutor Berg decided to vent his ire was well-aware that I had first submitted the Scarborough piece for publication in the *Review-Journal*, and obtained permission to submit the work elsewhere after the *R-J* declined to publish. Also fortunately, the editors of the *Review-Journal* have plenty of experience dealing with the threats, tizzies, and foot-stomping hissy fits of petty bureaucratic toads who can't believe anyone would have the gall to criticize them.

So as it turns out, the federals haven't managed to get me fired. Yet.

'An Overall Strategy To Overthrow
the Government of the United States'

In the summer of 1995, 39-year-old electronics engineer Jim Bell of Vancouver, Wash. (coincidentally the scene of the climactic battle between militia and central government forces in Ian Slater's potboiler paperback, *Showdown: U.S.A. vs. Militia*), penned an intriguing and controversial essay called "Assassination Politics," which has since been kicking around various Internet discussion groups, triggering responses from delight to outrage.

The following section from Mr. Bell's introduction gives the gist.

"A few months ago, I had a truly and quite literally 'revolutionary' idea, and I jokingly called it 'Assassination Politics': I speculated on the question of whether an organization could be set up to legally announce that it would be awarding a cash prize to somebody who correctly 'predicted' the death of one of a list of violators of rights, usually either government employees, officeholders, or appointees. It could ask for anonymous contributions from the public, and individuals would be able to send those contributions using digital cash.

"I also speculated that using modern methods of public-key encryption and anonymous 'digital cash,' it would be possible to make such awards in such a way so that nobody knows who is getting awarded the money, only that the award is being given. Even the organization itself would have no information that could help the authorities find the person responsible for the prediction, let alone the one who caused the death. ...

"Obviously, the problem with the general case is that the victim may be totally innocent under libertarian principles, which would make the killing a crime, leading to the question of whether the person offering the money was himself guilty.

"(But) my speculation assumed that the 'victim' is a government employee, presumably one who is not merely taking a paycheck of stolen tax dollars, but also is guilty of extra violations of rights beyond this. (Government agents responsible for the Ruby Ridge incident and Waco come to mind.) In receiving such money and in his various acts, he violates the 'Non-aggression Principle' (NAP) and thus, presumably, any acts against him are not the initiation of force under libertarian principles.

"The organization set up to manage such a system could, presumably, make up a list of people who had seriously violated the NAP, but who would not see justice in our courts due to the fact that their actions were done at the behest of the government. ... "

In a follow-up essay titled "Fishing Expedition Swims Against the Tide," published in the May 14 edition of the daily *Portland Oregonian*, Bell wrote, in part:

" ... I've been openly debating the idea on the Internet since then with anyone who will listen. My essay surprises many and shocks more than a few, but I am pleased that such a truly revolutionary concept has been so well-received. ...

"The only 'threat' in the essay is to the jobs of the people who have been parasites on the rest of us for decades, as well as to the future of tyrannies around the world. But that's why, on April 1, 20 federal agents burst in and took my computer, told the news media I was 'armed and dangerous,' and began engaging in a fishing expedition including harassing people simply for knowing me. (No arrest or charges so far.) ..."

The charges were forthcoming.

Jim Bell was arrested on May 16, 1997, and was thereafter held without bond in the Pierce County Jail in Tacoma, Wash., on a federal complaint alleging:

"Beginning at a time unknown, and continuing to the present, ... JAMES DALTON BELL did corruptly obstruct and impede ... the due administration of the internal revenue laws, among other things, by collecting the names and home addresses of agents and employees of the Internal Revenue Service ('IRS') in order to intimidate them in the performance of their official functions; by soliciting others to join in a scheme known as 'Assassination Politics' whereby those who killed IRS employees would be rewarded; by using social security account numbers that were not assigned to him to hide his assets and thereby impede the IRS's ability to collect his unpaid taxes, and by contaminating the area outside of the office of the IRS in Vancouver, Washington, with mercaptan, a chemical that causes a powerful odor." Nor does the complaint stop short with an alleged "stink-bomb" floor mat, proceeding to allege that Mr. Bell has at times discussed poisoning water supplies, sabotaging government computers, and, well … "overthrowing the Government of the United States."

The question here would appear to be whether Mr. Bell has actually taken substantive steps, as alleged, to "implement" the theory in his speculative Internet essay, or whether it is the IRS—which began on Feb. 20, 1997, seizing the theretofore non-violent Mr. Bell's car, wages, and bank accounts—who are doing the "threatening and intimidating" in an attempt to send a message to anyone who dares speculate about how justice might ever be obtained against federal agents, given that they are rarely if ever indicted, even for the willful murder of children, as at Waco and Ruby Ridge.

If the defendant Bell has indeed taken substantive steps to set in motion the murder of any specific government agent, that of course is a crime, for which he should expect to face the consequences.

On the other hand, if writings of the "What if someone … " variety have now become a felony so serious that one can be seized and held without bond, most of America's adventure and science-fiction writers—who up till now have felt safe spinning thinly veiled yarns about near-future government coups and such—had better watch their backsides.

Mr. Bell's attorney, Peter Avenia of the Public Defenders Office in Tacoma, told me shortly after Bell's arrest that he fully expected Mr. Bell to be indicted by a federal grand jury within a few weeks.

I asked Mr. Avenia if he believed the case will present substantive First Amendment questions.

"It certainly does concern me."

Is the IRS making an example of Mr. Bell, to chill any further discussions on the Internet of how justice can ever be had in the case of uniformed killers who apparently need no longer fear being indicted or brought to trial in this country?

"It's certainly a possibility. In the context of the Oklahoma City bombing, it's certainly a hostile atmosphere for any such defendant. I think we can ask whether the government is trying to send a message to people who pen inflammatory writings."

In the end, later in the summer of 1997, having turned down at least one offer of free, expert, legal help in preparing court briefs based on the First Amendment, Mr. Avenia accepted a Draconian deal on behalf of Mr. Bell, who was sent away to prison for years without ever being released on bond, or ever speaking to the press.

Those who assume this treatment had nothing to do with his writings, and thus implies no threat to our First Amendment freedom of the press, might want to look at the subsequent 1998 California arrest of author Peter McWilliams, an AIDS patient who smokes marijuana to ease the nausea caused by the chemotherapy that he believes keeps him alive, or the arrest in early 1999 of California marijuana activist and recent gubernatorial candidate Steve Kubby, another recovering cancer patient who smoked marijuana for medical purposes.

Personal use of marijuana for medical purposes was OK'd by an overwhelming majority of California voters in 1996, of course. The drug is from time to time passed out in free co-ops in

San Francisco. Yet Mr. McWilliams, and subsequently Mr. Kubby and his wife, were held without bail for weeks, while being denied their vital medications, for the "crime" of growing a few (now confiscated) plants for personal use.

This couldn't have anything to do with Mr. McWilliams's high-profile authorship of such in-your-face libertarian hardcover tomes as *Ain't Nobody's Business If You Do: The Absurdity of Consensual Crimes in a Free Society* (Prelude Press, 1993), or Mr. Kubby's publication of *The Politics of Consciousness* (Loompanics Unlimited, 1998), could it?

Naw—singling out people for selective prosecution because of what they write couldn't happen in America.

Make Way For The 'Officers'

In August 1996, the interim State Records Committee of the out-of-session Nevada Legislature, drafting new language for the state's Open Records Law, had before it the draft of a good bill.

The preamble of the updated legislation stated that citizens "are entitled to know and be informed fully about the conduct and activities of their government."

Maybe they should now take out the word "fully."

The information originally to be available to the public was to include not only the salaries paid public servants, but also their performance evaluations and information on their accumulated sick leave and vacation time.

But the public employees' unions objected to the annual performance evaluations of its members being made available to those who pay their salaries—even though the original bill called for an (unnecessary) delay of three years before such documents were to become public.

So, on Aug. 21, the committee obligingly removed those stipulations.

At this point, as open-government advocate and former director of the Nevada Press Association Ande Engleman notes, "This closes down more than is presently available."

While it may indeed sound a bit intrusive for members of the public to be sifting, out of idle curiosity, through the records of some poor courthouse janitor to see how many times he's called in sick, it's vital to see this battle in the context of how our government bureaucrats today use the loophole of "confidential personnel matters."

Recently, a guard at the Clark County jail in Las Vegas was dismissed after an incident in which he beat up an inmate who was trying to warn jail personnel that she had a blood-sugar problem and was about to have a seizure.

This was not a matter of the guard being a little rough. The inmate, already ill, had her face repeatedly pounded into a concrete floor, and patches of her hair torn out, in front of witnesses, including other jail employees.

Long after the incident, jailhouse authorities contended the name of the guard, and any details of the incident, were none of the public's business. Why? It was "a personnel matter," of course.

Perhaps we were all wrong at Nuremberg. Should we have let the German civil service deal with Goering, Bormann, Hess, and the rest, do you think? Their episodes of unfortunate overzealousness were, after all, just "internal German government personnel matters," weren't they?

Nevada's Chief Deputy Secretary of State Dale Erquiaga, who sits on the Records Committee and who voted against the new restrictions, says, "Public employees work for the taxpayers. The people who pay our salaries have a right to see how we perform." Mr. Erquiaga says his office may propose further amendments to the Legislature.

I hope so. In the most revealing admission of the Aug. 21 debate, Bob Gagnier, executive director of the State of Nevada Employees Association (the union), said his members now object to being called "public servants." He convinced the committee to instead refer to them as "officers and employees."

"Public servants [is] an older term," Mr. Gagnier simpered. "It is not used much any more except by people when they are running for office."

So now it's "officer." As in: "Yes, officer, with my hands on the roof of the car and my feet spread like this?" Or: "Yes, officer, here are my guns and my children; do you need my bank book, too?"

Apparently, a tiny minority of our imperial rulers are still forced to go through the demeaning ritual of pretending to be our "servants" for a few months every other fall. But the vast majority, who aspire to control every detail of our waking lives without having to subject themselves to any such indignity, now want their immunity from such dated rituals to be formalized, even in the wording of our laws.

If they don't want to be "public servants," serving the masters who pay their salaries, bending to our will, subject to our oversight and scrutiny, these swarms of tax-bloated functionaries should go seek other work.

Or, perhaps, they'd prefer to go and become "officers" under some other system of government, where they can wear crisper uniforms, with big hats and shiny boots, and where the cowering mob will doff their cheap cloth caps and show proper deference as their masters walk by with their billy clubs, their leashed dogs, and their machine pistols.

Make way for the "officer"!

Even Everyday People Hate the Government

From the *Houston Chronicle* of May 27, 1997, comes this bylined account of another costly failure on the part of that armed federal protection racket against unwanted competition for the nation's billion-dollar pharmaceutical giants we proudly call "the FDA."

"A Houston cancer researcher who once faced 75 federal charges stemming from the interstate shipment of his experimental cancer-treatment drug was acquitted Tuesday of the lone remaining count," reports staff writer Deborah Tedford.

"A federal court jury found Dr. Stanislaw Burzynski not guilty of violating a 1983 court order prohibiting the interstate sale of the drug, which Burzynski developed. The verdict ended, without a single conviction, a 14-year effort by federal authorities to make a criminal case against the Polish-born physician.

"Patients and their families who packed the courtroom in a show of support wept and shouted when the verdict was read after about three hours of jury deliberation.

"Burzynski, too, was elated.

"'It's the end of fourteen years of war. It's the beginning of the end of the war on cancer,' he said.

"He predicted that the verdict would put his class of experimental drugs, known as antineoplastons, on the fast track for approval by the U.S. Food and Drug Administration."

(Don't bet on it. When it comes to a contest between the welfare of dying patients and getting back at someone who's embarrassed a federal bureaucrat, it's a forgone conclusion who wins and who loses.)

"'I found the government's behavior offensive,' said juror Stephenie Shapiro, a Houston attorney. 'A lot of people felt it was. This was a Big Brother issue.'

"'From the beginning, this has been about patients' rights to choose their own treatment,' said Steve Siegel, president of the

260

Burzynski patient group.

"'It's been nothing but a witch-hunt," Siegel said of the prosecution, which dropped 40 of 41 original charges, leaving the jury to decide on only a lone remaining "contempt" charge, after dogging Burzynski for 14 years.

Your FDA, in Peace and War.

• • •

Meantime, 900 miles to the northwest, staff writer Angela Cortez reports in the *Denver Post* of June 8, 1997:

"Carole Ward, who won a $325,000 judgment against the Internal Revenue Service in a Denver federal court this week, had more—much more—to say against the federal government Friday.

"'Based on my fifteen minutes of fame, I would've expected a greater loss of life and property of the federal government by now,' Ward said to shocked hosts on KOA's morning radio talk program Friday. 'There is a conspicuous absence of violence against the government.'"

Ward's family business was raided by armed IRS agents in 1993, four weeks after she insulted an agent, telling her (according to court documents): "Honey, from what I can see of your accounting skills, the country would be better served if you were dishing up chicken-fried steak on some interstate in West Texas, with all the clunky jewelry and big hair."

Government looters padlocked all three Kids Avenue clothing stores in Colorado Springs and posted notices that some customers interpreted as evidence that Ward was a drug smuggler.

David Jay Johnston, writing in the June 9 *New York Times*, reports Judge William Downes of the U.S. District Court in Denver, in a harshly worded 17-page opinion, found that one of the IRS agents, James Dolan, was "grossly negligent," acted with "reckless disregard" for the law, and made three false statements in a sworn declaration.

(We'll be waiting for those forthcoming perjury indictments, Judge Downes.)

Downes also criticized Gerald Swanson, an IRS district director, and an aide, Patricia Callahan. Three months after the raid, as guests on a Colorado Springs radio talk show, they said that Ms. Ward still owed $324,000 for six years of back taxes, even though they knew the bill had been settled the week before for little more than one percent of that amount—$3,485.

Ms. Ward was still seething June 6, according to Angela Cortez of the *Post*, "telling the talk show audience that while she was not about to grab a weapon, she could see why some people would make bombs or take up arms against the government.

"'What about the high-risk group, which is young white males without college that don't have the communication skills I do?' Ward said. 'They might be saying, "I'm going to get a gun. I'm going to make a bomb."'

"KOA talk show hosts, taken aback, implied Ward was making a tough statement, given the Oklahoma City bombing trial of recent weeks.

"'I don't know if it's a tough thing to bring up at all,' she responded. It's a natural consequence of abuse by government. … I knew how to gain support. I knew how to get the word out. What about the ones at risk? [They] are the ones you're going to have trouble with.'

"I have dreams of taking a machine gun to a room of people," Ward said later, from her new home in Albuquerque. "I could never do that. But if I feel like that, could you imagine what someone else might do?"

VI

THE COURTESAN PRESS
EAGER LAPDOGS TO TYRANNY

The Ministry of Truth

About the time the syndicated Warner Bros. science-fiction TV show entered its fourth season in early 1997, I became a belated adherent of J. Michael Straczynski's "Babylon 5."

For 30 years, the benchmarks of televised sci-fi have been the spinoffs of the late Gene Roddenberry's "Star Trek," the best of which was "Star Trek: The Next Generation."

But inevitably, a universe concocted for us during the administration of Lyndon Johnson must betray its socialist/utopian roots.

In all four "Star Trek" series, the good guys represent the shadowy "United Federation of Planets," headquartered in San Francisco (historical birthplace of the U.N.), to which aspiring cultures have to "apply for admission." These cultures must have "matured" to the point where, so far as I can determine, no more than one government is tolerated per planet. Furthermore, from what we can tell, all have agreed to forswear money, salaries, arms dealing, or eating meat, in favor of the fair and equal sharing of the reconstituted soy protein that pours forth in endless profusion from the omnipresent "replicators."

Now, this ivory-tower future does seem to be breaking down a bit in the last two spinoffs, where folks wager "replicator rations" (rations?) at the D'abo tables and some smuggling (what?

a lingering demand for commerce?) is occasionally acknowledged. But only rarely does the slightest qualm arise over the fact that, to be "admitted to the Federation," the planet Bajor will apparently be expected to "integrate its militia into Star Fleet."

Compare such status-quo worship of centralized authority to the Hugo Award-winning "Babylon 5," where the commanders end up seceding from Earth after the home planet's takeover by a totalitarian regime, providing us with a set of heroes routinely referred to by the Earth government as "seditious traitors."

But even if I realized "Babylon 5" was making political progress, nothing prepared me for episode 408, "The Illusion of Truth," written (like most) by creator Joe Straczynski, and directed for the first time by a cast member (Stephen Furst).

In the episode in question, a TV news crew from Earth arrives unannounced on the station, seeking to film a report that will "get your side of things" across to the viewers back on Earth.

Despite initial skepticism, the commanders of the breakaway station agree to be interviewed. Afterwards, awaiting the broadcast, they reassure each other, "We kept anything we said down to short, declarative sentences to make it harder to quote us out of context. ... What can they do to us?"

Tuning in to Interstellar Network News, they find out—in spades.

In a virtually perfect simulacrum of one of our contemporary newscasts, the smug, oh-so-sincere newscasters (Jeff Griggs and Diana Morgan, the latter near-android in her lockjawed perfection) bring us political prisoners confessing to their anti-government activities on cue, and advise the citizenry of the latest Martian War developments:

"President Clark announced today that Earthforce troops have now reclaimed seventy-five percent of the colony, which broke away in an act of sedition two hundred and fifty-nine days ago. ... To celebrate this latest victory against the tyranny of a fanatical few who have endangered the lives of our citizens, Clark proclaimed today a planetary holiday. Curfew has been extended a full two hours, until nine p.m. EST, so go out and enjoy!"

Next up, it's the turn of the Babylon 5 crew to be eviscerated, complete with re-shot footage of their interviewer asking different questions to give completely new meaning to their answers, and even a ready-made white-haired medical expert, who modestly demurs from his office at Harvard Medical School, "I don't like to make long-distance diagnoses," whereupon he proceeds to do just that, explaining that war hero and Babylon 5 commander John Sheriden (Bruce Boxleitner) obviously remains mentally ill from his time as an interstellar POW, suffering a new version of the old sympathy-for-your-kidnappers phenomenon, which the good doctor has dubbed for the occasion "Minbari War Syndrome."

The flawless precision of this little exercise left me pacing like a caged cat. The "Illusion of Truth" episode of "Babylon 5" should be required viewing by every college class studying the ethics of journalism (if the subject hasn't already been deleted in favor of "Negotiating Your Network Contract"), as well as by every convention of professional journalists, Libertarians, and other interested parties who can lay hands on a tape.

(No, you can't get one from Warner TV, at least not until the series is released to home video. I asked.)

I tracked down series creator J. Michael Straczynski at his production office in an abandoned warehouse in southern California's Sun Valley. I asked if he'd just dreamed up this carefully coiffed nightmare vision of propaganda passed off as "news," or if he sees our own major broadcast media heading irrevocably down this same road.

"On the political side, what we've tried to do over the last couple of years is show the process by which a democracy, however flawed, can fight against totalitarianism," Straczynski explained.

"Usually you come into a fascist science-fiction series with the fascists already in place. We want to show the slippery slope. … We've tracked it from the assassination of President Santiago in the very first season to the establishment of Night Watch, the establishment of the Ministry of Truth, the takeover of the media, the establishment of a fascist state.

"When they see this going on, what is the role of the citizen, of the soldier? That's the kind of question we're examining. For an army to work you have to follow orders; there has to be a chain of command. But what do you do if the order is immoral? When Sheriden secedes from Earth, he is in effect committing an act of treason. So the question is, when is that justified?

"Before what was in essence a totalitarian takeover, the media had some bias, but nowhere near as bad as we see now. We wanted to show how easily they can manipulate facts and data to make things appear the way they want them to."

A temptation to present the government-endorsed angle to which our own news media increasingly succumb?

"There have been some charges that the media misuses quotes to throw candidates in a bad light. But the charges come from both sides, that Rush Limbaugh takes things out of context to make the liberals look bad, too. So it's a matter of degree."

I asked Straczynski why the "Babylon 5" universe seems so much more anti-authoritarian than that of the "Star Trek" clones.

"The Star Trek universe as it is portrayed currently is bereft of human flaws and frailties; they seem to have leached out the qualities that give us all our more independent nature. The cohesiveness of the characters—it seems like they're all just pumped out by the same machine. To the extent that they have pursuits or interests, it's all perfectly safe and incidental; they drink Earl Grey tea or they listen to Shakespeare.

"In 'Babylon 5,' of course, the characters are just plain nuts. They're fractured; they're flawed. Our goal is to show the power

266

of the individual to change the world ... and beyond that.

"We're all taught from a very early age that you can't fight city hall, that you can't change things. Well, in fact, the world is being changed every day. In this show, the themes are choices, consequences, and responsibility. That you can and must make choices in your life, and then taking the responsibility for those consequences.

"We have been called on occasion a moral show, and in fact we ain't. What we is, is an ethical show. My job isn't to make a point for or against corporations, individual rights, religion. Our job isn't to tell you what to think, but to honestly portray both sides of an issue—political questions, social questions, religious questions. ...

"We got to the death penalty once or twice in the course of the show. They have substituted the death of personality: They wipe your memory clean and then they reprogram you to serve society, so you will believe you want to serve the community you harmed. So the first question is, is that better politically or morally than the death penalty? Here's a Catholic priest who's been doing good works, helping people, but then he begins to remember, discovers that he used to be someone else, that he was a mass murderer whose memory was wiped. ... "

"That was an excellent episode," I told him. "It starred the treacherous mentat from 'Dune'—"

"Yes, that's Brad Dourif, a fine actor.

"So the question there was, where does forgiveness end or begin? How does he repent his sins if he doesn't know what they were? These are the kinds of questions television doesn't often get into.

"The problem with television overall—I'll be killed for saying this—is it has too many trivial answers and not near enough damn good questions. The question always is, will they defuse the bomb in time? The answer is: It's always the green wire, never the blue wire.

"The real questions are: Who are we, where are we, how did we get here, and where are we going?" Because it deals with such sterner stuff, Straczynski figures, "'Babylon 5' appeals to a very wide political landscape, conservatives, liberals, Libertarians.

"We've lost the sense that we were going somewhere. Remember a time in this country when there were 'kitchens of the future'? We wanted to know where we were going and when we were going to get there. But we stumbled with the Kennedy assassination and we stumbled with Vietnam, and if you stumble too many times you take your eyes off the horizon and look at your feet. Science fiction's job is to take people's eyes and put them back on the horizon. We need to look to our ancestors, who say to us, 'Make it so our lives had meaning,' and then we need to look to our descendents and build for the future.

"Don't 'just say no.' Just say yes: Say yes to creating something."

Peruse the darkest programming recesses of your local cable system. Set your VCR if necessary, but locate "Babylon 5." If you find the conventions of science fiction infantile, pretend the guys with the spots on their heads are Chinese, or Palestinian … or Branch Davidian.

Whether J. Michael Straczynski's "Babylon 5" prospers or succumbs may have wider significance than even he realizes.

For the alternative is, I fear … the Interstellar Network News.

• • •

A few days after the above essay went out to subscribers, I received an e-mail from a K.W., somewhere on the Internet, for which I'm grateful, since it ended up providing the catalyst for this chapter.

Mr. Suprynowicz:

My wife and two teenage daughters watch "Babylon 5" regularly. The episode you speak of in your column brought constant knowing nods and comments from all of us concerning the methods of the news team on the show. ...

What is amazing is how our press today responds to the cultural pressures placed on it by the societal elite and their political and moral views. There is no need of government strong-arming where the thought processes have been disengaged. This does leave itself open for the government to easily use the press to promote the views of the elitists in power.

One might be tempted to think the show goes a little overboard, unless one has seen the same tactics used against businesses or other groups and individuals to destroy their reputations.

I replied:

Thanks for your thoughtful response.

Having worked in the newspaper business for 25 years, I'm often at pains to explain to folks that the pro-big-government slant of the news media (though very real) is not a "conspiracy" in the simplistic sense. That is to say, I've never known an editor to wear a hole in his carpet, pacing the floor as he waits for the phone call from the Tri-Lateral Commission (or whomever) to "instruct" him which stories to feature and how to interpret them.

What goes on is much subtler than that, as you have correctly surmised. Unprepared young reporters are generally assigned to cover complex government agencies, whose meetings are full of indecipherable "code-talk" about bond ratings, amortization of tax-exempt debt, RFBs ("Requests For Bids")—a whole arcane sub-language.

In over their heads, smart young reporters will ask a helpful government bureaucrat or "Public Information Officer" to sit down and explain it all. PIOs *love* to do this. Soon, the reporter feels very important, and far more secure, as he or she carries around not only the government spokesman's office phone number, but also his/her home phone, cellular phone, and even pager number. Occasionally, "exclusive" interviews can be arranged with even more important figures.

What's more, those on the city desk are happy to be receiving copy from a reporter who seems to be a "quick study" at the complex science of squeezing revenues out of the taxpayers and building up the size and power of government, all the while making it sound as if what's being done follows the most sensible and unimpeachable rules of economic science.

The reporter isn't actually bribed (though a few free dinners and "junkets" may come his or her way). Rather, he or she feels happy to have been inducted into the inner circles of the cognoscenti, those who "know what's what," and to have quick and easy access to the powerful "decision-makers." The reporter's career advances as the politicians and flacks he or she met at city hall move up over time to offices at the state—or even the U.S.—Capitol. The TV stations start inviting the new press "expert" to appear on talking-head shows. Soon the reporter is buying tailored clothes from the same stores as the bureaucrats and officials he or she covers.

The reporter—only two generations ago a role usually filled by a guy in a crewcut more likely to play cards and drink beer down at the firehouse—now starts to move in the *social* circles of the governing elite. And, of course, the reporter wouldn't stay at it if he or she hadn't been convinced by years of academic indoctrination—unchallenged by any real-world experience, say, trying to operate a business in the face of some arrogant and arbitrary bureaucracy—that government is generally beneficent, forcing racial harmony on the benighted racists, stopping greedy industrialists from polluting the air and water, and so forth.

270

(I've been challenged on this reference to "no real-world work experience," and can only reply that I've been working full-time in the American newspaper business, east and west, north and south, for 25 years, and must report from experience that newspapering is a lot like the Army. You've got to start young and fresh out of school, because the miserably long hours and low pay scales forbid a mid-level career change *into* newspapering. With the exception of some "guest star" columnists, virtually no modern newspaper reporter or editor has ever done anything else.)

Now, imagine someone approaching that reporter with a "story" about how the government agencies he or she covers every day are systematically bleeding the citizenry of both their prosperity and their rights. It becomes second nature to dismiss such a critic as a "wacko conspiracy nut."

Reporters are rewarded for learning the *language* of the bureaucrats they cover. They come to speak a patois that naturally refers to stifling tax hikes as "modest revenue enhancements."

Reporters don't *have* to be subverted by any secret "news management" conspiracies. A little laziness, a hunger for the "glamour" of rubbing elbows with the rich and powerful, and most of all the lack of the "troublemaker's" willingness to question and ridicule authority—a trait that *defined* the profession of Mark Twain and H.L. Mencken—are usually all that's required.

To a Fish, Explain 'Wet'

Explaining the nature of the nearly uniform bias in America's media is one of the toughest things I try to do. Uniformity tends to imply organization. Thus, you don't have to be a very dedicated conspiracy theorist to wonder how hundreds of individual newspapers and TV stations could come to parrot precisely the

271

same kind of pro-big-government propaganda purely by coincidence. If there were a hailstorm in your hay field and the hail precisely spelled out the word "Hello," would you figure it was just a coincidence?

But then again, just because all zebras have stripes doesn't mean someone has been out painting them. Sometimes results tend to be the same because causes tend to be the same.

The apparent contradictions do take a little patience. Consider these three statements:

1) The vast majority of American reporters are honestly convinced that they and all of their cohorts are objective and politically neutral.

2) People from the political right, and especially Libertarians and constitutionalists, are convinced that 98 percent of the American media are handmaidens to the oppressive, collectivist state, puking forth little but undigested, unquestioned, manipulative, pro-government propaganda.

3) Both of the above statements are true.

The problem involves definitions and paradigms, like one of those old picture-book puzzles where it appears impossible to connect all the dots by drawing only three straight lines, but the answer is that you're free to extend the lines "outside the box."

Talking to most reporters about their political prejudice is like trying to explain to a fish the word "wet." The fish has no idea what "wet" is, because it's never experienced anything else.

Reporters think "bias" is when you're accepting cash in plain brown envelopes to keep a corporate chemical spill out of the paper, or writing only nice things about a political candidate because you're shacking up with him/her in the guest cabin on the weekends. If they're not involved in such stuff—if they cover their press conferences and rewrite the government press releases the way they've been taught—they take great offense at any accusation of "bias," and respond with ridicule or a counterattack.

272

But drilled in a pro-big-government, collectivist outlook by unionized, Roosevelt-worshipping wardens in the government youth propaganda camps since they were ripped from their mommies' apron-strings at the age of five or six, these young reporters can no more help describing things in the clichés of collectivism than a French child can help putting her adjectives after her nouns.

You can see it every day. Watch the evening news on a Saturday—slowest news day of the week. Listen to the happy talk. Some file footage from NASA shows a bunch of shuttle astronauts getting in each other's way up in space, and the Pretty Young Things hired to read us the "news" smile, bite their lower lips, or scrunch up their noses at each other as they agree, "Yes, some very important work being done up there, Marque."

No, there isn't. Today's space program is a pointless multibillion-dollar boondoggle to create jobs and contracts—in other words, to prevent massive layoffs—in the bribe-paying aerospace industry.

Yet imagine how shocked Handsome Marque would be if Gayle of the Golden Helmet smiled when the footage was done airing and said, "Actually, Marque, I got on the phone to NASA this afternoon while you were having your hair done and asked why they need five astronauts up there doing nothing but measuring each other's respiration and urine production and baby-sitting an automated telescope that could take much better pictures at a tenth the price if we didn't have five overpriced human chimps bouncing around causing a lot of extra vibration. And you know what? No one could tell me."

The next news segment will usually be some public-relations scam—the Red Cross staging a disaster drill out at the airport, with "victims" doused in ketchup being loaded into waiting ambulances.

These stories originate when the Red Cross people call the

273

station and ask what would be the best day to stage their drill. The TV news director knows he'll be short of "footage" on Saturday (no government meetings) and says Saturday morning would be great. An opportunity is created for some amateurish "suspense" when the segment starts with the "disaster footage," whereupon Gayle and Marque quickly allow the shocked viewers to breathe a sigh of relief as they chuckle, "But it was only a drill, conducted as a readiness exercise by the Red Cross today at the municipal airport."

And how did the "drill" work out? Inevitably, we're solemnly assured by the trainee weekend minority reporter with the bad diction, "live" on tape from the airport, that the drill has "proven the local Red Cross is ready for any emergency."

Really?

The folks at the Red Cross are fine people, of course, with the best of intentions, and it would be considered in bad taste to criticize their little publicity charade. But reporters are supposed to be skeptics, not cheerleaders. What good is an "emergency drill" that's scheduled days in advance?

Real disasters have the darndest habit of happening at the worst possible times, like during driving rainstorms and floods, late on a Saturday night. Try to call out the ambulances at that point—smug in the assurance that you've hammered it all out to a fine state of readiness in your "drill"—and what's likely to happen? First, you discover half the phone lines are down. Didn't "drill" for that, did you?

Then, what if it turns out that some fool forgot to gas up the ambulances last night, and the only guy with the key to the gas pump is on a hunting trip in Alaska?

Those are the kinds of problems you might want to simulate in a drill intended to determine how your people would *really* respond to the unexpected. But what the TV station wants is ketchup on the corpses at 10 a.m.—and that's what they get.

OK, it's a minor fib. But what we're talking about here is attitude—taking a career that used to involve snooping around and exposing the corruption and hypocrisy of the powerful and turning it into a remorselessly hollow exercise in junior-high-school Babbitry.

As ye train, so shall ye perform in the crunch. And our weekend reporter is being trained to pronounce what's on his script in precisely 15 seconds, not to ask any embarrassing questions that might cause his segment to "go long."

Bill Clinton is shown shaking hands in some union hall, and Gayle intones from her pre-packaged script, "The president vowed today to stand by his pledge to raise the minimum wage, boosting the income of America's poorest workers."

After 12 years in the government schools, that's the only way our neatly coiffed airheads are going to describe the ongoing, incremental enactment of one of the major planks of the 1932 platform of the Socialist Workers Party. They can't hear the "political prejudice" in such a summary, because it's the only way they can *imagine* covering something as wonderful as a hike in the minimum wage.

Everyone wants a raise, don't they?

But hand the newscasters a script that says, "The president today vowed to raise the minimum wage, outlawing the jobs of many of our poorest workers, thus throwing at least seven percent of America's neediest part-time laborers completely out of work, depriving them forever of the dignity of a paying job," and they'll quickly say, "I don't know; this sounds kind of *political.*"

Yet Dr. Lowell Taylor of Carnegie Mellon University examined California's retail employment after that state raised its minimum wage in 1988, and found that every 10 percent increase in the average retail wage (the goal of all minimum wage hikes) reduces employment by seven percent, with the most marginal workers usually taking the fall.

Try it yourself, at your own place of work. Assume your company operates at a 10 percent profit, at an average wage of $10 per hour. Imagine that a government regulator arrived tomorrow and said the minimum wage was now $20 an hour. Do you really think everyone would still be working there next month, taking home twice the pay for the same work? Or would nearly half the staff be laid off immediately, while the owners tried to figure out whether to double their prices, move the operation overseas, or shut down completely?

That's reality ... and then there's television.

Disarming the Fundamentalists

How did our TV networks and major newspapers change from watchdogs over the government to a "softening-up" brigade for the forces of repression?

Over the years, entire newsrooms have developed a version of the Stockholm Syndrome, coming to empathize with the manly struggles of the very bureaucrats they're supposed to expose, much like hostages coming to sympathize with their captors.

Gradually, a "corporate culture" develops, which views a willingness to whittle away at the First, Second, and Tenth Amendments as "sensible moderation." In turn, those who believe, say, that it's treason to require any law-abiding American to apply for government permission to own a firearm have been branded "dangerous, anti-government extremists." Rooting out and exposing such extremists is now one of the highest callings of the journalistic fraternity.

This consensus has been formalized. Read the rules by which "investigative series" are judged for various journalism awards. Special credit is usually granted if the applicant can show that

276

some government action followed close on the heels of the "exposé." Please attach tearsheets.

At that point, the problem of timing becomes critical. Investigative reports that air in a calendar year generally have to be submitted for awards the following January. But federal investigations move so slowly that a spring exposé would almost never result in a gratifying series of arrests by December. Unless ...

What if federal agents were to tell their favorite reporters about an investigation already under way, likely to result in arrests or a highly publicized consent decree in just a month or two?

Once a newsroom has accepted such a paint-by-numbers kit, its reporters would have to be stupid or crazy to get the story "wrong." The scheduled raid provides the series with its natural climax. Photo opportunities of brave marshals in white hats are pre-arranged.

That's why, when the network and syndicated magazine shows decided to take an interest in a fundamentalist Montana outfit called the Church Universal and Triumphant back in the spring of 1994—adopting the familiar attitude that "This would be funny if it weren't so dangerous; these people are *heavily armed*; they even have *jeeps* and *trucks* hidden in hillside bunkers!"—I doubted we'd have long to wait.

Imagine my lack of surprise when *The New York Times* reported in early June that "a religious group has agreed to stop storing weapons on its remote ranch near Yellowstone National Park in exchange for the restoration of its tax-exempt status."

With the fearful precedent of Waco to hold over the church members' heads, the federal strategy was quite simple: By retroactively revoking the Montana church's tax-exempt status, the government could claim the group owed $2.6 million in back taxes. The government, according to the AP, also "accused" the church of "amassing military-style weapons, including semiautomatic rifles, armored personnel carriers, and thousands of rounds of ammunition." (These are not crimes, of course. Were they also "accused" of prayer?)

Under terms of the agreement, the government agreed to restore the church's tax-exempt status and drop the $2.6 million extortion demand, while the church in turn agreed to sell off the weapons in its bomb shelters.

Mind you, there was never an allegation that church members had used their weapons to harm anyone. No, all the government really seems to fear is that peaceful groups thousands of miles from Washington might, even in theory, possess the wherewithal to resist federal authority.

And the press dutifully played along with the government script, softening up the public to accept the forced disarmament of the peaceful followers of Elizabeth Clare Prophet on their 28,000-acre ranch in remote Montana.

What a fine "public service." Do we all feel safer now?

Wait a Minute ... These Are All the Choices?

The Gannett Sunday supplement *USA Weekend* now claims to reach 39.1 million readers.

On April 14, 1996, we find a political quiz by Victor Kamber and Bradley O'Leary, offering readers the chance to "pinpoint yourself politically," on a scale that ranked Jesse Jackson at the left with 40 points, Bill Clinton and Colin Powell in the "center" at 25 and 20, and Rush Limbaugh and Jesse Helms at the right with the lowest ratings (of course): five and zero.

The problem with this discredited left-to-right spectrum, of course, is that all these characters have essentially the same view on the crucial political question of our time: whether a large and meddlesome bureaucracy should run our lives, or whether people have natural, inalienable rights that pre-date government and (in fact) government must protect and defend, lest it find itself with no legitimate excuse for existing.

Sure, Messrs. Helms and Limbaugh would argue for slightly less regulation and taxation of business enterprises, while the likes of Jesse Jackson might argue for government to stay out of a few token areas of personal choice, like abortion and sexual preference.

But these are only minor tactical disputes about which "problems" an ever-growing bureaucracy should "solve" first.

Will any of these characters espouse the instant end of the form of slavery known as the income tax? A reduction in government to 10 percent of its current size? The restoration of the right of any law-abiding American to carry a military-style firearm without applying for a "permit"? My Ninth Amendment "retained right" to buy and sell cocaine and morphine by the ton, without any government "license," just as my great-grandfather could?

Of course not.

Where on this one-dimensional scale would we find Russell Means, Milton Friedman, L. Neil Smith, Ayn Rand, Bumper Hornberger, or Dr. Thomas Szasz? Nowhere. No surprise, then, that the *USA Weekend* "political quiz" allows room for only statist opinion.

Let's examine a few of the questions, to illustrate the point:

—Which would we prefer, the quizmasters ask, a more activist government with "higher taxes" or a less activist government that "taxes less"?

Where's the space to indicate "All taxation is slavery"?

—Would we support "national legislation [to] ban the sale of handguns other than to the military and police"?

Where's the box that lets me note that any legislator who voted for such "legislation" would be violating his oath to defend the Second Amendment, and should thus be tried and hanged?

279

—A flat tax or a graduated tax?

Where's the box to call for "taxation only in proportion to the census," as specified by the Founders?

—Who should have the greater voice in deciding what books children read in school: teachers or parents?

But by choosing either answer, don't I endorse a role for the state? How do I indicate that all government involvement in schooling must be banned? If teachers were hired directly by parents, how could this be an issue?

—"Should tests for HIV, the virus that causes AIDS, be mandatory for professional athletes in contact sports?"

HIV does not cause AIDS, as amply demonstrated by Dr. Peter Duesberg in his mighty book, *Inventing the AIDS Virus.* Is *USA Weekend* a "news" organization, or one of the propaganda branches of the Centers for Disease Control?

—"Which level of government is better able to administer key welfare programs such as Medicaid?"

Since all mandatory income-transfer schemes are immoral, unconstitutional, and counterproductive, what's "key" about them?

—"Should you be allowed to carry a concealed handgun to protect yourself?"

Gee, I don't know. Should I be "allowed" to write books, or pray, or breathe through my nose? Who on earth is doing the "allowing"? Listen up, bub: "We hold these truths to be self-evident, that all Men ... are endowed by their Creator with certain unalienable rights. ... "

Not too much of a presumption here that our omnipotent central government can "allow" or deny permission for any darned thing it wishes, is there?

And so it goes. Providing such limited choices—forcing Libertarians or anyone with the slightest grasp of economics or history to toss such paltry subjects aside in disgust—it should come as no surprise that such transparent "let's-back-the-government" cheerleading as this "poll" will self-select only respondents who have memorized their government-school, pro-government-extremist catechism. Such a poll couldn't help but produce results like the reported 90 percent support—in a call-in following a March 10 story—for the proposed "mandatory testing of all pregnant women for HIV," identified once again, without attribution, as "the virus that causes AIDS."

Whereupon we would do what, pray tell? Put the symptomless mothers on AZT, a toxic chemotherapy described by many European medical critics as "AIDS by prescription"? Would we tie them down if they resisted?

Precise language facilitates clear thought. But the traditional, murky theory of the "left-to-right" spectrum, as we've seen, awards "more points" to self-declared "moderate" socialists who favor various income redistribution schemes "on the left" (Jesse Jackson), but then leaves unanswered the question of why we should reject both the "extremes" of right and left represented by the "opposites" of Hitler and Stalin, who both favored government management of the economy and puzzlingly both called themselves "socialists."

Didn't such ruthless characters merely carry the bureaucrats-know-best politics of Jesse Jackson and Charles Schumer and Derek Shearer to their natural conclusions, with some minor differences as to whether the ancient czarist or Junker families should still be allowed to keep title to (and some of the profits from) their arms factories?

How are these "opposites"?

Setting up a vertical scale to measure support for individual rights like medical freedom (including drug use) and liberty of religious and sexual choice, and a horizontal scale to measure support for economic rights including property rights and freedom from taxation and government regulation, this improved "Nolan Chart" reveals that Hitler and Stalin weren't really at the "opposite extremes" of "left and right" as we're taught in our government schools. In fact, they fall together at the low end of both freedom scales (see "Appendix II").

For the Real News, Look Elsewhere

Not within the memory of any American under 65 has a tidal wave of political change swept in unnoticed by such a huge number of those who represent themselves as, variously, "informing" the public and "interpreting" the events of the day.

The last time such a massive "disconnect" prevailed was probably during the period 1936-1941, when the American East Coast intelligentsia found themselves so devoted to the cause of "peace at any price" that it seemed only a minor smudging of the facts to report that Hitler, Mussolini, and Stalin weren't bad Joes, just economic reformers intent on restoring some sensible central planning.

Today's equivalent? Check out this mystery quote:

"The international press treats the disgruntled classes as cretins, unenlightened about the glories of the interventionist state. In fact, they are all too educated in what a hustle it is.

"Notice too how the Left, defender of the old order, increasingly speaks in elitist terms. When it loses a political battle, it says the people just don't know what's good for them."

Who penned this emperor-has-no-clothes analysis? Readers aren't likely to find it in a month's worth of *Washington Posts* or network talking-head shows. These passages come from an essay by Llewellyn Rockwell in the November issue of *The Free Market*, the monthly newsletter of the Ludwig von Mises Institute at Auburn University (see "Appendix II").

"Notice the Left's hatred of talk radio," Rockwell continues.

"It can't stand any challenge to ruling-class power. ... The Left fears and hates the groundswell of opposition to statism, which has only become dominant in the last two years. ... This popular shift has coincided with increasing government authoritarianism. The less support the state has, the more desperately it attempts to crush its opponents. That is why state enforcers think nothing of trespassing on rights that were considered inviolate only a few years ago. ...

"It's the Left that cheers an expansive federal police power, whether in Waco, Ruby Ridge, Vidor, Ovett, Oklahoma City, Berkeley, or Wedowee. At last we are allowed to see the real face of modern liberalism: what Isabel Paterson called the humanitarian with a guillotine."

As for the aforementioned lies being relentlessly perpetuated about AIDS—surely the most dangerous public misinformation campaign since "radium clinics" promised to cure any known malady through exposure to the miracle of radioactivity 90 years ago—here's another summary of recent developments on an issue of enormous public concern, not a word of which is likely to turn up in the *Baltimore Sun* or the *L.A. Times*:

"Despite over 10 years and 22 billion dollars spent on research in the USA alone, no one can answer the basic question—how does HIV cause 'AIDS'? ...

"The scientific standard that is used to prove a microbe's causal role are three classical laws called 'Koch's Postulates.' The first of these laws states that the microbe must be present in all cases of the disease and in sufficient amount to cause disease. ... Despite this, it has long been known that a proportion of people with AIDS have no HIV. HIV-free cases of AIDS have been reported in the scientific literature since 1986 and there are now over 4,500 documented cases of HIV-free AIDS. ... HIV, then, spectacularly fails Koch's first Postulate.

"The second states that the microbe must not be found in

any other disease, but HIV is supposedly responsible for almost 29 different diseases, some as unrelated as wasting and cervical cancer.

"The last of Koch's Postulates states that the microbe must be isolated [and] cultured, and then induce the same disease on re-inoculation. This is usually done on animals and over the last 10 years more than 150 chimps have been experimentally inoculated with HIV. All produced antibodies to HIV, just like humans, and none have developed any AIDS-like symptoms.

"Thus, HIV fails all of Koch's Postulates and cannot legitimately be said to cause AIDS. ... "

These were the introductory remarks of Wayne Moore, co-chairman of the British alternative health group Positively Healthy (see "Appendix II"), at the British McCarrison Society Conference, Sept. 23-25, 1994.

" AIDS also fails against other classical criteria of infectious diseases, because unlike them AIDS is almost exclusively and non-randomly restricted to men in America and Europe, although no AIDS disease is male specific," Moore continued. "Thus, there is no reason to believe that AIDS is an infectious disease. ...

"Sexual transmission of HIV is extremely inefficient and studies have shown that it depends on 1,000 heterosexual contacts and anything between 100 and 10,000 gay sexual contacts with antibody-positive people. ... Any virus depending on these kinds of contact rates would soon die out. ...

"As if all these health risks weren't enough, the HIV/AIDS hypothesis itself can be life threatening in many ways. Foremost of these is the AIDS treatment drug AZT, which is also prescribed as AIDS prophylaxis for healthy HIV positive people. ... AZT kills non-selectively all cells it comes across. ... It has, quite rightly, been called 'AIDS by prescription' and has caused, and been implicated in, an unknown number of deaths which are universally ascribed to HIV. Not surprisingly, the benefits of AZT treatment are negligible. ... "

Here, surely, is a well-researched refutation of modern medical orthodoxy as earth-shattering as anything Martin Luther ever nailed to a chapel door. But you'll look in vain for any mention of it in the *Boston Globe*, in *USA Today*, or the in *New England Journal of Medicine*.

And Now, Live, From Oklahoma City: the Government Line

Turning on the TV on April 19, 1996, I was pleasantly surprised to hear the sound of an orchestral chorale filling the house with stirring music.

Half-asleep, I wondered for a moment whether what was obviously a memorial service was being televised to commemorate the sacrifice of the American patriots who fell resisting a government attempt to seize their unregistered military-style weapons in Lexington, Mass., on April 19, 1775, or the sacrifice of the desperate Jews who faced the final assault of Nazi storm troopers furious at the unthinkable resistance of an illegally armed "subhuman" rabble in what was left of the Warsaw ghetto on April 19, 1943, or the sacrifice of the Branch Davidian Christians—many of them black or Asian, dozens of them women or children under 12—who were burned to death by government forces intent on seizing their perfectly legal military-style weapons in Waco, Texas, on April 19, 1993.

None of the above, of course. In America today, we doff our hats in respect only for the tax-bloated G-men—living off money pilfered from my paycheck without my permission, providing "services" never authorized in the Constitution—whose careers were cut short by a clumsy and stupid bombing in Oklahoma City on April 19, 1995.

Has President Clinton promised to find the perpetrators of the murders in Waco and "seek the death penalty" against them? Of course not. All the perpetrators have received medals and promotions, just like the Nazi murderers of April 1943. Do F-16s fly "missing-man" formations above the ruins of Mount Carmel in Texas? Did any of the "independent" major network news shows choose to broadcast remote from Waco on April 19?

No. Only Oklahoma City was "memorialized."

So much for the notion that we have three or four "independent" television news sources, whose main job is to criticize the official government line.

The bureaucrats who truly govern us behind the scenes—unchanging no matter who does this year's ribbon-cuttings—are not just immune from criticism. The nobility of their goals is never questioned. And any opposition to the endless growth of their empires is dubbed "anti-government extremism"!

I don't believe I heard a single mention during that April week of the fact that the Murrah Building—the one that got blown up— was the site of the BATF office where the raid on Waco was planned. I guess the American people have no "need" to be reminded of that. Better to let them think the target was randomly chosen, the better to terrorize them with warnings about "right-wing hate groups," a phrase I believe Dan Rather must have used 10 times during his half-hour of pro-government propaganda, which now passes for a "newscast," on Thursday evening, April 18, 1996.

Mind you, as I've said before, whoever blew up the Murrah Building managed to be stupid, incompetent, and criminal. Even if killing children were not always immoral—which it is—it's enormously bad public relations. (Though I can't help noting that federal agents killed children both at Ruby Ridge and at Waco without repercussion. I also haven't noticed Mr. Clinton cutting off foreign aid to Israel after Israeli shells killed scores of children in a Lebanese civilian refugee camp, also on April 18, 1996, with then Prime Minister Shimon Peres promptly announcing it was the fault of Hezbollah for being nearby.)

The Oklahoma City bombing was not only criminal, it didn't even accomplish what I assume was its primary goal—it killed not a single BATF agent.

But does that justify the media's purposely and repeatedly linking the Oklahoma City bombing in the public mind with "right-wing militias," when none of those charged were militia members? (In fact, the perpetrators were actually kicked out of the only such outfit they ever tried to join, when members of the legitimate Michigan militia immediately spotted them as violence-prone kooks.)

And why are there only "right-wing hate groups"? Why aren't those who organize to strip us of our Second Amendment rights or who make no secret of the fact that they would ban all ranching, mining, and lumbering in the West if they had their way, referred to on television as "left-wing hate groups"?

Just as Leni Riefenstahl gladly took on the technical challenge of editing "documentaries" with the main goal of promoting Adolf Hitler's political vision, so do our network newscasts today gladly assume the duty of interpreting the official government line in story and song. Just watch these clumsy shills busily plug for a new billion-dollar "anti-terrorism" bill with dire feature stories warning of all the dangerous hypothetical things rogue "terrorists" might someday do via the Internet, unless government steps in now with a strong regulatory hand—like kids in school who get to the end of the chapter and find the "workshop" assignment: "Imagine three examples of bad things that could happen if we didn't have a strong FBI and BATF with new tanks and helicopters. Write them down and discuss."

Then give them a gold star, I guess.

287

The United States vs. Gomer Pyle

On May 19 and 21, 1996, CBS aired the mini-series "Ruby Ridge: An American Tragedy," based on the book *Every Knee Shall Bow* by Jess Walter, who covered the siege at Ruby Ridge for the *Spokane Statesman-Review*.

As everyone who has not been in deep hibernation must know, former Iowa factory worker Randy Weaver moved with his wife and young children to a ridge in isolated north Idaho in the 1980s, to home-school his children and escape what he and his wife Vicki saw as a corrupted world below.

Hoping to turn him into a snitch against the members of a nearby white separatist church which he had attended once or twice, federal BATF agents set up Randy Weaver in 1990, using an undercover agent provocateur to convince him that good money could be made smithing sawed-off shotguns.

But after he was entrapped, Weaver wouldn't cooperate by agreeing to "wear a wire" and record his neighbors in their homes and in their church, in exchange for a promise of "lenience" for his government-created "crime." So, frustrated and outraged, government agents, determined to teach Weaver the price of "refusing to cooperate," issued fugitive warrants. After Weaver failed to come into town for 18 months, a team of U.S. deputy marshals—in full Vietnam-style camouflage, with night-vision goggles and full-auto M-16 machine guns—was sent to "reconnoiter" the cabin.

"The program focuses on the growing conflict between the United States government and citizens who view the government system as illegitimate and tyrannical," says producer Edgar Scherick, in a prepared statement. "This is true now in Montana, it was true in Waco, and it was certainly true at Ruby Ridge."

The mini-series divides neatly in half. The second half does a masterful job of portraying the tragic lies, blunders, incompetence, and bureaucratic overkill that finally arrayed hundreds of govern-ment agents—equipped with enough helicopters and armored personnel carriers to conquer a small nation—against one couple and their young children, who made the mistake of believing it was still OK to go live in the woods and own firearms in America.

But the first installment of the drama is, I'm convinced, the filmmakers' conscious attempt to say: "Don't get us wrong. The Weavers were no heroes. We don't like them, and you shouldn't, either. They were bad. Bad bad bad. True, an unarmed mother with a nursing baby in her arms didn't deserve to be murdered by the government, but don't confuse *us* with these weird, Old-Testa-ment-spouting, religious fanatics."

Start with the casting. Laura Dern as Vicki Weaver does bril-liant work, forming the riveting emotional center of the piece.

But why was Randy Quaid cast as Randy Weaver?

"He was the one they wanted the most," a spokesman for the producer told me Friday. "He is much bigger than Randy Weaver, who's five-foot-eight; he's a full head taller. But they wanted him because he has played so often the sort of laid-back character; he's played a lot of country kinds of roles."

He's played a lot of semi-retarded dorks, I responded. You're telling me Quaid wasn't chosen precisely to avoid a handsome leading man who might appear too sympathetic? Randy Weaver may well be a racist, but those who know him say he's a real charmer. Quaid gives us Gomer Pyle on quaaludes.

"I think that that's true," came the refreshingly honest re-sponse, "but mainly he's just a country-type person."

To see my point, try this exercise: Gary Graham, who since 1989 has starred in the off-and-on Fox TV series "Alien Nation," appears in the small role of Deputy Marshal Hunt, who led the first federal team onto Ruby Ridge. Watch this guy. Graham has charisma when he just stands there. As you're watching, imagine the handsome, likeable Gary Graham cast as Randy Weaver, and

Randy Quaid playing a knuckle-dragging, trip-over-his-own-feet, deputy marshal. Tell me the whole impact of this presentation wouldn't undergo a tectonic shift.

The mini-series leaves the impression that Randy Weaver—a benighted soul who teaches his kids racial epithets and builds a "menstrual shed" where the womenfolk can be locked up "when they're unclean"—never worked a day in his life after he moved to Idaho, sustaining his family mainly by stealing irrigation pipe.

In fact, those who know him say that when he could find work, he worked hard at construction or wood-cutting. Those (perfectly legal) deer rifles that family members carried didn't arrive as prizes in a Cracker Jack box.

Finally, the filmmakers betray their true sympathies with the oddest omission of all: In a docu-drama that names all the other major characters, the FBI sniper who shoots and wounds Weaver and Harris and blows off half of Vicki Weaver's head, though properly played by an Asian-American, is never named.

"The sniper who shot Vicki Weaver is now under federal protection due to threats against his life," says the closing title-crawl.

That sniper's name is Lon Horiuchi, and helping to "protect" him is the final admission of the political prejudice of the piece. Of course, no one should do to him what he did to Vicky Weaver. He and his entire gang—up to and including disgraced Assistant FBI Director Larry Potts—should, by any reading of Idaho law, be indicted and tried for murder or manslaughter, a trial at which they would be perfectly free to offer the defense that they were "just following orders."

(In fact, the local Boundary County prosecutor finally indicted Horiuchi for manslaughter in late 1997, just before the statute of limitations was due to toll. The federals immediately got the trial transferred to federal court, where it was promptly dismissed, without dead-eye Lon even having to report back to Idaho. Now there will never be any trial. Blowing the heads off defenseless mommies is now "in the line of duty" for FBI agents, it turns out. Just in case you thought we'd won that revolution, all those many years ago, against the sovereign who "quarters large bodies of armed troops among us, and protects them, by a mock Trial, from Punishment for any Murders which they should commit on the Inhabitants of these States.")

Author Jess Walter says in his book: "Ruby Ridge resonates in the minds of people who have no trouble imagining themselves in the besieged cabin. ... The Weaver case is not proof of broad government oppression and tyranny, but of human fallibility and inhuman bureaucracy, of competitive law-enforcement agencies and blind stubbornness."

He's half-right.

Ruby Ridge did display an inhuman bureaucracy at work. But the Weaver case—and especially the fact that the FBI murderers never faced any punishment for their killings—*is* proof of broad government oppression.

Are we to believe that the BATF agents who set up Randy Weaver lost their jobs? That the Bureau of Alcohol, Tobacco and Firearms is not better armed, better funded, more active in the same entrapment and persecution of harmless gun owners today than it was in 1990?

Didn't BATF agents pull an armed raid on a gun store in Taft, Calif., in the autumn of 1998, supposedly seeking to arrest the owner for selling "illegal guns" (there are no such things—only a transfer tax was in question), during which armed assault the suspect allegedly shot himself in the mouth with his own gun ... whereupon the G-men plugged his corpse with half a dozen more rounds, "just to make sure"?

And weren't the federal marshals who trespassed on Randy Weaver's property in the dead of night—with no intention of serving a warrant or making an arrest—and who killed his harmless dog and shot a fleeing 14-year-old boy in the back in the spring of

1996 given the highest award for valor offered by the U.S. Marshals' service?

"Valor."

Is that supposed to convince us this could never happen again?

The Soviet cinema used to be laughably transparent in its propagandized casting. Even in the works of the great Sergei Eisenstein, czarist agents would always be greasy, corpulent mustache-twirlers, while the heroic workingmen were always tall, blond, clean-cut, and handsome. No room for subtlety when the punishment for failure to convey the proper message— in terms simple enough to be understood on a bad day by an anti-intellectual dwarf like Comrade Stalin—was to be hauled out and shot.

In the West, a little more subtlety—even some occasional "casting against type"—used to be allowed.

Butch Cassidy and Clyde Barrow were killers. They were played by Paul Newman and Warren Beatty.

Randy Weaver never shot anyone. Why would it now be impossible, here in America, to portray him as anything but a cud-chewing cross-burning Gomer Pyle?

'Vile Hateful ... Trash'

None of the 20-odd newspapers that publish my syndicated column call to beg for it; I send out samples from time to time to editors who might be interested.

A few subscribe. A disappointing number—particularly in the Northeast—check off the box on the reply card that reads, "We're still trying to convince our readers that Big Government is good for them; leave us alone."

(No, I am not kidding. I provide the box; they check it off.)

Of course, no one is obliged to buy. Freedom of the press has to mean the freedom *not* to publish, as well. Does it get frustrating? Sure. It was Voltaire who said, "It is difficult to free fools from the chains they revere."

But in May 1995 I got a response to my sample column on the Oklahoma City bombing to which I felt obliged to respond. For one thing, the letter-writer, an editorial-page editor at a small coaldust daily, forwarded a copy of his missive to my boss with a hand-written note, urging him to fire me.

So, since the editor decided to take this discussion beyond the realm of private correspondence, herewith is our complete correspondence, starting with his letter of May 9:

> Mr. Suprynowicz:
>
> This is in response to your recent submission of several column samples. I was so disgusted by your writing that I felt the need to personally respond, rather than simply throw the columns in the trash, where they belong.
>
> Have you no shame? No decency? How dare you publish a column that went beyond even obliquely suggesting that the explosion of the federal building in Oklahoma City was deserved retribution. You stated as fact that the feds, and supposedly their children, got what they deserved.
>
> Let me quote your own craven words: 'Did these bullies-with-badges really believe they would forever be able to choose the time and place of their battles, that no one would ever counterattack when they least expected it, at a place where the federals' children—rather than the citizens—were at risk?' And then: 'The Oklahoma City bombing occurred because the ATF attempted to seize the arms of law-abiding Americans in Texas in 1993.'
>
> Forget for now the questions about how 'law-abiding' the Waco cult members were. Forget the mistakes

that obviously occurred in the handling of that situation, mistakes that should be, and will be, punished. It is irresponsible in the extreme to suggest that the Oklahoma City bombing was in any way a justified response to even criminal action by some members of the federal government.

The 166 people who died in the blast were not responsible for Waco, and their deaths are in no way valid retribution for what happened there.

I have some sympathy for the Libertarian philosophy. But the Libertarians I'm familiar with want government to leave them alone, and are trying to achieve that end by electing members of their party to power. In the United States of America, ballots, not bombs, are how legitimate movements achieve change.

I noticed that you had a column merely three days before the bombing vilifying the Bureau of Alcohol, Tobacco and Firearms. How proud you must have been when Timothy McVeigh, or whoever is ultimately found to be responsible, struck a blow against the 'baby-killers of Waco' by killing more babies.

You nauseate me. In this nation, we have the right of free speech. And I will defend even such vile speech as yours. But I will never support your hateful venom by printing it on my page.

On May 19, I answered my correspondent:

Greetings.

And thanks for taking the time to pen a personal response, on May 9, to the sample columns I sent you. You will remember that I did so because you told me last Oct. 10, in answer to some earlier samples, "I read them and they look pretty good. ... Send us more from time to time."

I judge from your response of May 9 that you found my sub-

294

missions easy to understand and thought-provoking. A columnist can rarely ask for more. I am puzzled, however, by your comment, "I was so disgusted by your writing that I felt [like ... throwing them] in the trash, where they belong."

The column to which you apparently take most exception is my piece on the Oklahoma City bombing, "Go Ahead, Turn *This* Into an Excuse to Expand Federal Power." Your main objection seems to be: "You stated as fact that the feds, and supposedly their children, got what they deserved."

I don't think so. I believe I said, "No sensible soul could endorse or justify this bombing. I've written many times against vigilante justice." What I did say—and you quoted it accurately— is that outfits like the DEA and ATF, which had headquarters in the Murrah Building, have been waging a one-sided, violent, deadly, unconstitutional war (they even call it that) against the American public for more than 20 years. I thus find it curious that they could be at all surprised, after waking up literally hundreds of Americans at dawn by shoving loaded machine guns in their noses, that someone finally decided to counterattack, choosing the time and place of a violent confrontation for themselves instead of waiting for the knock on the door.

Given that the ATF and DEA go armed all the time and describe themselves as being at "war" with selected citizens of America, doesn't it strike you as odd that they would house a children's day-care center in their armed compound in Oklahoma City? Would we have set up day-care centers in any military headquarters building or artillery firebase in a medium-sized provincial capital in South Vietnam in 1970? I don't think so.

You say there are "questions about how 'law-abiding' the Waco cult members were," although you are willing to "forget them for now." No, let's not forget them. Although I notice your prejudicial use of the word "cult" (the ATF is a cult; I'm not sure Christian churches are), please explain to me what "questions"

295

exist about how "law-abiding" the following victims of the government murders at Waco were: Cyrus Howell, age 8; Joseph Martinez, age 7; Starr Howell, age 5; Serenity Sea Jones, Isaiah Martinez, Dayland Lord Gent, and Mayanah Schnider, all age 3; Paiges Gent, Bobie Lane Koresh, and Hollywood Sylvia, all age 2; Chanel Andrade, Chica and Little One Jones, twins, and Startle Summers, all age 1, and newborn Gyarfas, too young to have been christened and named.

As to their parents, we now know the bogus charges of "child abuse" had been thoroughly investigated by the appropriate Texas authorities and ruled groundless. When did the ATF receive authorization to enforce local child-abuse laws within the several states, anyway? All the Davidians had always cooperated with previous requests to examine their fully legal weapons, which were returned to them by the local authorities after their legality was determined. The ATF search warrant called for them to knock peacefully, and ATF agents testified in San Antonio that if their fire was returned, their standing orders were to withdraw and not fire blindly into a building containing women and children.

In fact, there are no "questions" about who broke the law at Waco. The ATF broke the law.

You call such government murders "mistakes." You say these mistakes "should be and will be punished." How and when, I wonder. Are you privy to news of some indictments none of the rest of us know about? No government agent involved in Waco was ever indicted. The two leaders of the raid were reinstated with full back pay just last Christmas. Mr. Potts, who OK'd the "rules of engagement" at both Waco and Ruby Ridge, has just been promoted to the number-two spot at the FBI, even as our letters have passed in the mail. Perhaps these actions were taken to lull them into complacency while their "punishments" are readied.

I have spoken at length, in person, with Sarah Bain, the forewoman of the jury that tried the Davidian survivors. She told me the jury acquitted on all capital and major charges, and convicted only a few defendants on the most minor charges, based on the instructions of the judge that they had no choice but to do so, based on admission in the defendants' own testimony that they fired in self-defense.

Incredibly, she says the judge's lengthy instructions contained no option to find the defendants innocent on all charges based on self-defense. Nonetheless, she says the jury's intention was that the defendants receive "a slap on the wrist" for these minor violations and that the jurors were stunned at the inappropriate massive sentences meted out. She wrote the judge, expressing her shock, and shared that letter with me.

Perhaps Ms. Bain told you a different story, in your lengthy personal discussions with her. Or perhaps you believe you have a superior knowledge of the case to hers, from your all-seeing perch in the coaldust mountains.

"The people who died at the Murrah Building were not responsible for Waco," you say. This may be technically true if, as it appears, no ATF agents on the ninth floor were killed. True but misleading. The Waco raid was planned at the Murrah Building. It was led by agents from the Murrah Building. Some of those same agents were at work in the Murrah Building on the day of the blast—including agents returned to duty with full back pay last Christmas.

When the United States Air Force bombed Iraqi Air Force headquarters at the start of the Gulf War—when Norman Schwartzkopf showed the "smart bomb" hitting and sides of building blowing out on videotape, and we all smiled along with him—could we know for certain that the building did not contain a few innocent washerwomen, who had had no role in planning the invasion of Kuwait? If you knew for certain that a few innocent janitors had been killed, would you now favor indicting Norman Schwarzkopf for murder?

297

Yes, I said, "The Oklahoma City bombing occurred because the ATF attempted to seize the arms of law-abiding Americans in Texas in 1993." That's true, and no amount of squealing on behalf of the jackbooted government fascists you so adore is going to change it. What do you think—the perpetrators meant to strike back on the anniversary of the sinking of the Lusitania and just got the date wrong?

If you wish to dismiss armed assaults on churches, or the sniper murder of Vicki Weaver in Idaho, in your pages as mere "mistakes" of noble and selfless government heroes, that is your right. But if you believe that anyone who takes an opposing view should not be published, because any questioning of the sanctity and rectitude of heroes like the ATF constitutes "vile, hateful ... trash," then I wonder how successful readers who disagree with you on these issues are at getting their letters printed in your pages.

Do you, in common with many editors in the Northeast, simply throw away the hundreds of letters you receive each year protesting the absence of any due process in atrocities like Waco and Ruby Ridge? If you do, then you have contributed to the frustration of those who wrongly decide that their pleas and protests can never be heard on such matters through regular channels, and who tragically decide that some kind of violent vigilante action is their only remaining option to draw some attention to these massive injustices.

Such actions are wrong. They are bad and evil. And editors like you, who refuse to let such matters be discussed in your pages, are directly responsible for them.

I hope you are proud of the desperate acts to which men like Timothy McVeigh, or whoever is ultimately found to be responsible, have been driven by your dereliction of your First Amendment duty.

I wonder if the one-sidedness of your editorial pages (and your promotion of economically paralyzing statism in your own state and city) also has something to do with the fact that the circulation of your once-proud paper has slipped 2.7 percent in the past five years, while that of my own has increased 25 percent.

Sincerely,

Vin Suprynowicz.

Oh—I sent a copy to his boss, too.

VII

ALL GOD'S CHILDREN GOT GUNS

'If It Saves Just a Single Life'

Philip Russell Coleman, 42, worked the night shift at a liquor store in Shreveport, Louisiana. He knew the evening shift, which included closing up around 1 p.m., was dangerous. So on Aug. 3, 1996, he went to see Jim Roberts at the USA Pawn Shop, where he was a regular customer, about buying a handgun for self-defense.

Coleman's choice—a chrome-plated .380 caliber Lorcin semi-automatic, would not have been mine. The .380 is a low-power cartridge without much stopping power.

But then, armed robbers in steamy Louisiana presumably don't tend to wear heavy wool or leather coats, which can defeat the little .380 cartridge. And the Lorcin will set you back less than half the cost of a .357 magnum police trade-in revolver—the smallest round that will reliably refocus the attention of an assailant (.40, .44, and .45 are all better). Probably Philip Coleman hadn't yet saved up enough for anything more persuasive. And at least the Lorcin is light and easy to slip in your belt.

Coleman put a down payment on the pistol and filled out the application form required by the federal Brady Law, which asks whether the applicant for permission to buy a handgun has ever been dishonorably discharged from the armed forces, whether he is a wanted fugitive, has ever been convicted of a felony, has ever been committed to a mental institution, has ever pleaded guilty to spouse abuse, smokes marijuana or consumes other illegal drugs (though it cares not a whit whether he's a perpetual drunkard, of course, nor whether he's perpetually doped up on legally prescribed medications), et cetera, et cetera.

Under the Brady Law, local police have up to three days to approve or deny permission for the handgun purchase, after the forms are filled out and the dealer calls in to local police headquarters for a background check, an official intrusion that the buyer himself is required to finance (just as the estates of witches in the Middle Ages were billed for the cost of their own inquisitions). All that having been accomplished, Coleman returned to the pawn shop on Friday, hoping to pick up his handgun.

But although he had answered all the questions on the form in the manner generally preferred, and although Coleman knew full well his answers had been truthful, the folks at USA Pawn had to tell Philip Coleman that the Caddo Parish Sheriff's Office had rejected his application for permission to exercise his Second Amendment rights.

Coleman firmly insisted to pawn shop employees the rejection had to be a mistake on the part of the sheriff's office; he was neither a felon nor a former mental patient.

"He said he needed the gun for his own protection because he worked late hours at a liquor store and he felt it was dangerous," pawn shop owner Roberts later told staff writer Dunstan Prial of the daily *Shreveport Times*. "I told him to go down and straighten it out with the sheriff's office, and I guess he did."

But Coleman didn't return to the pawn shop that day. There wasn't time. Instead, he went directly to work without his gun— and was shot to death just as his shift ended, around 1 a.m. Saturday.

The sheriff's office notified Roberts by fax on the following

Tuesday that Coleman's application had been reconsidered and approved. That approval was received "three days after Coleman was shot to death in a liquor store holdup," reported Prial in the *Times*, under the headline "Murdered Clerk Had Sought Handgun for Protection."

"This is one case where the Brady Bill cost someone their life," said Jim Roberts. "It took away his opportunity to protect himself."

Bill Clinton and others have the habit of tossing around exaggerated statistics about the number of dangerous felons who have been prevented from buying handguns by the Brady Law. More than one pro-Bill-of-Rights reporter trying to document a claim of "100,000 felons" or "69,000 felons" has been blithely told by a White House press spokesman the next day, "Oh, the president misspoke when he gave that number."

But more to the point, victim-disarmament advocates throwing around such figures make no attempt to independently verify how many prospective gun buyers rejected under the Brady Law are *really* dangerous felons. They simply take the number of reported initial rejections—including customers whose applications are later approved on review—and blithely *presume* they were all Mafia button men who stupidly forgot they were supposed to buy their weapons out of the car trunk of some guy named Vinnie and instead walked into a licensed gun store and volunteered to give police their real names and home addresses, signing application forms with their real names, under penalty of perjury.

Up till now, it's rarely been possible to attach a name to any of those statistical "dangerous felons" over whom the hermetic perfection of the Brady Law has held sway. But at least now we know the name of one of them:

Philip Russell Coleman.

The Press Goes AWOL

The death of Philip Russell Coleman didn't get much coverage in the national press.

Neither did the House Judiciary Committee's crime subcommittee hearings one year earlier, on March 31, 1995, at which the congressmen heard from citizens who had used firearms—including since-banned firearms—to defend themselves.

One witness who testified that day was Travis Dean Neel, a Korean War veteran who happened to be traveling to a shooting range near Houston with two nine-millimeter pistols in his car on Jan. 21, 1994. Neel was driving directly behind Harris County Deputy Sheriff Frank Flores when Deputy Flores swerved his car to block the road to an oncoming vehicle containing three armed men.

One of these three escaping thieves—which is what they proved to be—hid in the stolen vehicle while Deputy Flores attempted to place the other two under arrest. The third thief then ambushed the deputy, repeatedly shooting him in the back, shoulder, and upper chest.

"I heard five bullets hit him as he fell from my view, apparently mortally wounded," Neel testified. No other law enforcement personnel were at hand. So, Neel says, "I selected my CZ-75 pistol with three fifteen-round magazines. As I had done at Heartbreak Ridge over four decades ago, I wanted to have as much ammunition as I could carry. Running forward, I ... divided my shots between the three men, firing as fast as my finger would work, changing magazines every fifteen rounds."

Those whose exposure to handgun battles has been primarily through television Westerns might expect dead bodies to have littered the highway at this point. In fact, we do well to recall that the high ratio of casualties in the Gunfight at the OK Corral—three out of eight participants—was primarily due to the fact Doc

304

Holliday and one of the Earp brothers carried shotguns. In order to keep most of their hits on a man-sized target, even experienced target shooters usually practice with handguns at ranges of no more than 20 yards. Add the adrenaline of close-quarters combat, the fact that both shooter and target are generally on the move and seeking cover, and (as I've mentioned before) the seriously overrated stopping power of the 9mm parabellum cartridge, and it should be considered no embarrassment to combat veteran Neel that the net result of his unexpected assault was that the three culprits, in the face of his overwhelming fire, abandoned their vehicle and high-tailed it down the embankment and into a nearby housing project, where they were soon rounded up.

After the three assailants ran off, "I then released at least thirty cars in the intersection and went to examine the Texas peace officer. I was shocked to see him alive."

The Harris County Deputy Sheriff's Union named Travis Dean Neel their Citizen of the Year, 1994, for saving Deputy Flores' life, and for the "heroic actions" that led to all three armed thieves being arrested and charged with attempted capital murder of a peace officer.

"Having those firearms—and those magazines—in my car that day saved my life and that of Deputy Flores," Neel told the subcommittee, while the media turned their faces away. "Those who want to ban guns and the magazines that go with them tell you that only a criminal needs access to such 'large-capacity' magazines. But at the scene of that shoot-out, it was the good people—the deputy and I—who had 'large-capacity' magazines. I fired thirty-nine shots that day. The criminal, the would-be assassin, had a six-shot revolver. ... Far from being a threat to law enforcement and the general public, I—with my pistols and my fifteen-round magazines—was an asset that day. But if the gun and magazine ban had been in effect a few years earlier, things might have turned out differently."

305

Also testifying that day in Washington was Brian Rigsby of Newnan, Ga., who told of the evening he and his friend, Tom Styer, were accosted by two would-be robbers bearing 12-gauge shotguns while camping in the Oconee National Forest on Nov. 24, 1990.

The two assailants first entered the nighttime camp of Rigsby and Styer openly, striking up a rather stilted conversation as they apparently scoped out what the two campers had that might be worth taking. The visitors drove away in their own truck, but when the campers heard the visitors' truck stop and park only a short distance down the road, they sensed trouble.

As the robbers returned on foot—evidently not as silently as they intended—Rigsby grabbed his target-shooting rifle, a Ruger Mini-14 with a 30-round magazine.

One of the armed men came into the light of the camp, wielding a double-barreled shotgun. When Tom Styer asked why he had returned with a gun, the shotgun-toting interloper said, "I'm going to kill you," and opened fire.

Rigsby centered his sights on the assailant's chest and fired two rounds, then fired another six or seven rounds at the muzzle flash of their second assailant, farther back in the bush.

"The would-be murderer that had shot Tom was hit twice, and died at the scene. His accomplice was also hit twice, but survived," Rigsby testified. Although both of their assailants had carried 12-gauge shotguns loaded with magnum buckshot, "in the time it took me to fire nine rounds, the gun battle was over."

The "ugly assault-weapons ban," Rigsby testified, "has driven prices on most semi-autos, even those not on the list, through the roof. I could not afford to buy my rifle at today's prices."

Six other American testified that day in Congress, including a Korean businessman from Los Angeles who protected his business during the Rodney King riots by firing more than 200 rounds from a Beretta 92F pistol and Colt AR-15 Sporter rifle.

Both weapons are now banned from further import or manufacture for civilians in their original high-capacity configuration, pointed out David Joo, although, "That's exactly the kind of firepower we needed." Joo killed no one that day, but "When it was all over, the police came back and arrested Korean business owners for illegal possession of firearms, and disarmed them. I feel that's an injustice. The police couldn't protect us. For whatever reason, they weren't there when we needed them the most. ...

"When law and order breaks down, citizens have a right to protect themselves," Joo said. "It's our most basic right, and I think it's the most important freedom we have as Americans."

• • •

Our national news media—literally hundreds of reporters and cameramen are paid handsome salaries to cover newsworthy developments in the nation's capital—showed their disapproval of such arguments by staying away from those 1995 congressional hearings, though they routinely race to cover tearful ghetto moms whose 17-year-old "little babies" have died in gun battles over drug sales territories.

The latter should be covered, of course. Maybe Americans will someday respond by asking why beer distributors stopped shooting each other up in 1933. But whatever happened to the media's self-righteous crowing about how they "just present the facts; it's up to the readers and viewers to decide"?

The behavior of the American press in presenting the vital public debate over gun control—particularly that of the major TV networks and the leading daily papers on each coast—verges on the criminal.

A strong word, but criminality may be deduced when through willful deception, or the willful failure to take those steps that a normal person of good character would take, the culprit allows a situation to develop that can reasonably be expected to end in an unnecessary death.

In their rigging of the so-called "gun-control" debate, the behavior of these media is not accidental but willful—they actively believe in and advocate victim disarmament. Today, our police forces increasingly turn to rehearsing massive helicopter-borne paramilitary Special Weapons And Tactics raids on urban neighborhoods, and Congress even in the middle of the "Monicagate" scandals in the fall of 1998 continued to debate new Drug War legislation to authorized the permanent stationing of uniformed soldiers with machine guns in every American coastal city and at every airport. Why? It's not some turban-headed Middle Eastern goatherd they're afraid of; it's us.

A lot of folks have obviously come to realize that the frustration of those with a deep and abiding commitment to the keystone human right to bear arms—frustration at their inability to get their case fairly laid before the public—must inevitably boil over in our lifetimes into a massive and bloody civil war. (When the tyrant comes for your guns, after all, you have only one more chance to use them.)

For this civil war, our current dominant press organs will be largely to blame, through their abject and willful failure to truthfully inform.

Our media make a lot of noise about "diversity." Few would have the nerve, these days, to claim an all-white staff could adequately cover the concerns of the black or Hispanic community, just because a few of them had read *Uncle Tom's Cabin*.

But ask your local newspaper editor how many members of his or her editorial board own guns and believe every law-abiding adult has a right to keep a machine gun at home.

How can they possibly know whether the concerns of millions of American gun owners are being accurately portrayed in their pages if every single member of their decision-making team is a gun-banner? What good is a cosmetic diversity in skin color or gender if there is no diversity on one of the most important and divisive political issues of our time?

• • •

Watch your newspaper and television commentaries for the phrase "gun-control extremist." You will find this phrase does not exist. It is only gun-rights activists who are judged capable of "extremism." And to merit that label, they don't even have to call for the repeal of any existing victim-disarmament laws—it's enough for them merely to suggest that the 20,000 existing gun-control laws should be sufficient!

But what does it mean to speak soothingly of "reasonable" gun control if there is no level of proposed gun control that will earn the designation "unreasonable"?

Try it. Ask any gun-grabbing politician or pro-gun-control TV talking head to name a currently proposed gun-control law that he or she would oppose as unreasonable. You'll get a lot of blather about only wanting to ban guns that are unsafe, about preventing tragic accidents involving children and protecting legitimate sporting use. But you will *not* get them to name a single proposed infringement on the Constitutionally guaranteed Right to Keep and Bear Arms that they're willing to condemn as unreasonable!

The pretense of a debate presented by these media would have you believe that on one side we have virtually every sane, rational, civilized person and government in the world. These proponents of "moderate common-sense gun control" understand that guns have no purpose but to cause death, that if they were necessary 200 years ago when this was a lawless land and settlers had to defend themselves against wolves, bears, and heathens, those days are long gone. Obviously, if guns were prohibited to everyone but the police today, crime would vanish or at least be limited to a few non-life-threatening cat burglaries and car thefts. Who could fail to see this?

Still, a problem remains: How to explain to the nodding stupefied public the stubborn persistence of a noticeably large group who, inexplicably, seem to disagree?

Here is the explanation, perhaps never specified in full by media mantra, but clearly implied.

In rural backwaters far from where you, the sensible modern reader, live and work, there still exists a small remnant of drooling, buck-toothed, in-bred Neanderthals—very much like the hillbillies who stalked Jon Voigt in *Deliverance*, or the grown siblings who continued to get grossly malformed children on their own crippled mother in that particularly creepy episode of "The X-Files."

Understandably insecure about their manhood, these yahoos yearn for the simpler certainties of earlier ages, when the largest, most primitive males dominated the world by brute force. These strange holdovers still cling to their guns as surrogate penises, in a last symbolic attempt to validate their right to dominate and intimidate women, intellectuals, progressives, and so on. Predominately snake-handling white Christian fundamentalists, these gunnuts also tend (naturally enough) to be anti-Semitic and anti-black. Given free rein, they would use their beloved weapons to commit genocide against all intellectuals, city dwellers, and inferior races, as outlined in their favorite book, *The Turner Diaries*.

Thus, the right to bear arms—and to kill wild animals, slitting their throats and achieving a sexual climax by thrusting one's hands into their hot sticky entrails—falls into the same barbaric category as the right to burn widows to death on their husbands' funeral pyres, the right to mutilate the genitals of Third World girls, etc. Significantly, all are similarly justified as being "the way our grandfathers did it," oblivious to how appallingly backward such pursuits appear to modern eyes.

Then, magnifying the problem in typical capitalist fashion, ruthless gun manufacturers proceed to prey on the insecurities of these inbred morons, selling them weapons of ever greater (and more pragmatically useless) power, merely to swell their own bank accounts.

• • •

Do Katie Couric, Jane Pauley, and their ilk really believe all this? I believe they do (not that it really matters, so long as they keep selling it). But the fact that they're capable of continuing in this belief demonstrates that they have never done the first thing a *real* rookie reporter would do: Go spend a week with some legitimate, articulate, gun collectors and Second Amendment advocates—including well-educated former Army officers and Marines—with the simplest of requests: "Show me. Teach me to see through your eyes. Why do you believe guns are important? Why are they good?"

Instead, to legitimize the above stereotype via a masquerade of even-handed analysis, lengthy diatribes from Handgun Control (the nation's second largest gun-control organization)—facilitated by helpful sympathetic questions of the "And isn't it also true ..." variety—are "balanced" against brief sputterings (set up with sarcastic questions of the "But you can't really believe ..." variety) from the National Rifle Association, the nation's *largest* gun-control organization.

The NRA—a quasi-government agency founded by retired Union officers that still possesses a government-issued monopoly over the shooting competitions that qualify citizens to buy surplus military rifles at cost—helped write the first National Handgun Control Act, in the 1930s. The NRA endorsed and actively

311

campaigned for the 1968 Gun Control Act ("reasonable, responsible," etc.). The NRA today favors the Brady instant-check national gun registration system—which was expanded to include the national registration of long gun sales starting on Dec. 1, 1998.

Incoming NRA president Charlton Heston, who also actively campaigned for the 1968 GCA, has said repeatedly, "The private possession of AK-47s is entirely inappropriate." The NRA believes those who wish to carry handguns should be forced to apply for government permits, and the group opposes any reduction of training requirements for such permits, lest the permits of "easy" states not be accepted in "harder" states. (In fact, the honoring of such permits across state lines is spotty, at best.)

Just imagine the ACLU endorsing a federal "permit application" system for those wishing to found churches or enter the book or magazine publishing business.

Yet not only is the NRA the sole group that the press will allow to pose as spokesman for all Second Amendment activists, it is then actually reviled for its gun-rights extremism!

Not only will the national press never allow equal time for an articulate response from such *legitimate*, principled, gun-rights outfits as Aaron Zelman's Milwaukee-based Jews for the Preservation of Firearms Ownership or Larry Pratt's Virginia-based Gun Owners of America, they don't even inform their readers and viewers that such organizations *exist*.

I learned this first-hand. In May 1995, I agreed in print with G. Gordon Liddy (though I doubt we agree on much else) that it's fully appropriate for citizens to shoot and kill unidentified Ninja-clad assailants who break down our doors and invade our homes at night with guns ablaze. (Some readers may wish to note this is considerably different from saying it's all right to resist, harm, or interfere with a properly identified police officer who knocks on your door, displays his or her badge, hands you a valid search warrant signed by a judge, specifying the place to be searched and the specific things or persons to be seized, and then allows you a reasonable time to read this document before you agree to let him enter.)

Anyway, because I wrote that it's all right to shoot back at strangers who are firing at one's children, my column was summarily canceled by one of my subscriber papers, the *Mesa Tribune*, a medium-sized Cox daily in Arizona. (I'm not whining; no one can force a newspaper to run what it does not want to run. Anyway, I'm used to it.)

However, prior to this cancellation, the Mesa paper ran an earlier column in which I made a favorable mention of the group Jews for the Preservation of Firearms Ownership. The paper then received a letter from a Jewish reader, accusing me of anti-Semitism, under the theory that I must have meant to ridicule all Jews when I invented out of thin air such an obviously farcical and impossible entity as the JPFO.

Tribune Editorial Page Editor Bob Schuster wrote back to this benighted reader, half-heartedly expressing the opinion that he doubted Mr. Suprynowicz was anti-Semitic. But it became quickly obvious from the editor's rather limp denial that even Mr. *Schuster* wasn't sure the JPFO existed. He finally forwarded the ongoing bundled correspondence to me, asking me to take over my own defense. Whereupon I sent both fellows not only a number of JPFO's fine newsletters and publications, but also photocopies of my own membership card.

At the *Las Vegas Review-Journal*, we strive to present both sides of issues like the gun-control debate on our Op-ed pages, taking special care to provide room for the well-researched work of folks like John Lott of the University of Chicago (see "Private Firearms 'Almost Certainly' Save 400,000 Lives Per Year,' a few pages ahead).

But it's a running joke in the editorial room when I ask whether any pro-gun-rights editorial cartoons have come in recently, for use in illustrating such a piece.

With the sole exception of Mike Shelton at the *Orange County Register*, every syndicated cartoonist available to us—and we subscribe to dozens—parrots the anti-freedom pro-big-government stereotype of the gun owner as a chinless slope-browed moron in camouflage fatigues, either incinerating a tiny fawn with a rocket-propelled grenade or blowing smoke from his muzzle and proudly proclaiming his gun rights as he wades knee-deep through newly slaughtered schoolchildren.

(Do I really need to point out that most gun owners would favor hanging such an offender 12 hours after a fair trial of two days' duration, while it's the hand-wringing leftist gun-banners who would be far more likely to put him away for a few years on a funny farm—after two years of legal shenanigans—based on the defense that he ate too much sugar? Shall we also surmise what would happen to an editorial cartoonist who inaccurately caricatured the physical appearance of any other political group—representing the ACLU, for instance, as a hook-nosed fellow in a yarmulke, or the NAACP as a barefoot sharecropper eating watermelon, or the leaders of Planned Parenthood as cannibals with bones through their noses and necklaces made from the severed ears of little babies? Why is it that gun owners are the *last* group in America who can be thus rendered "sub-human" with impunity?)

The purpose of this chapter—drawn from some of the columns I've written on the subject from 1993 to 1998—is not to present the definitive and complete case for gun rights. I have neither room nor reason to reiterate the fine historical Second Amendment scholarship of Stephen Halbrook in *That Every Man Be Armed*; the evidence that gun control springs from racism and leads to genocide, as developed by the JPFO in such volumes as *Lethal Laws*; nor the emotional firehose of John Ross'

314

novel of the long-suffering gun community, *Unintended Conse-quences.*

My goal is more modest. I simply hope to demonstrate that there *is* a legitimate, logical, life-affirming case for the unrestricted individual right to bear military-style arms, including machine guns.

Mind you, if I could merely establish that the individual right to bear military arms is a fundamental and undergirding principle of our Republic—that without such a guarantee the Constitution would never have been ratified, and that therefore upon its re-moval the entire national government would become an illegiti-mate tyranny—that would be sufficient, even if we could *not* show that the private ownership of powerful arms was any longer of any pragmatic value.

However, as it turns out, we can demonstrate not only the first (sufficient) premise, but also that the possession of such arms, in vast numbers and in private hands, *is* pragmatic and necessary, both for self-defense against freelance criminals and as the *only* sufficient safeguard against systemic government tyranny—the defense of a *free* state for which the Founders told us we must all retain our militia weapons.

If those who believe otherwise still adhere to their histori-cally aberrant views after reading a sampling of real cases for gun rights, that is their right.

However, if they turn away and refuse to read it, then we have reason to ask just which side it is that clings with quasi-religious fervor to outmoded, superstitious, received beliefs—unsupportable both logically and historically—about a thing never examined first-hand. For just as anti-Semites rarely sit down to dine with Jews, lest they be robbed of their cherished and absurd prejudices, so do gun-haters rarely learn to safely handle firearms, lest their own phobias evaporate in the pro-cess.

315

Tourists Are Easy: They're Disarmed

Most of us can still remember the fall of 1993, when the national press seized on the murders of nine foreign tourists in Florida as an excuse to push for full civilian disarmament.

"Florida has been on a homicidal binge since six years ago, when its legislature gave everyone the right to tote a gun," wrote former congressman Lionel Van Deerlin, in the *San Diego Union Tribune*, that autumn.

So loud was the hoopla that to this day many foreigners still believe Florida is full or murderers, a place particularly to be avoided if you're a tourist from abroad.

In fact, what the Florida Legislature did in 1987 was to supersede a patchwork quilt of 400 local gun ordinances. Under the old system, some counties had issued up to 10,000 permits allowing (mostly white) law-abiding citizens to carry concealed weapons, while others "had very high non-refundable application fees, $450 and $500," explained Marion Hammer of the United Sportsmen of Florida, a gun-rights lobbying group, when I called her in Florida that year to get the real low-down. (Ms. Hammer has since been elected to head up the National Rifle Association, in Washington.) "So basically only the politically powerful, the wealthy, and the elite were able to qualify" for carry permits in those recalcitrant counties, Ms. Hammer explained.

No matter. Editorial writers around the nation felt no need to check out the facts before joining in the braying:

"Why is Florida full of gun thugs?" asked an editorial writer at the tiny *Charleston* (West Virginia) *Gazette*. "Because there's no way to prevent deadly parasites from getting all the pistols and ammunition they want, and stalking decent people. The all-powerful gun lobby's ... only solution is to let tourist families carry pistols so they can shoot back."

"I find that out of touch with reality," responded Ms. Hammer, when I read it to her. "Did they comment on the two University of Florida women who were brutally stabbed two weeks ago?"

Richard Anthony Meissner, 27, has been charged with murdering Gina Marie Langevin, whom he may have believed would testify against him in a pending arson case. The attack occurred Sept. 18, 1993, in the Gainesville apartment Langevin shared with Jena Hull, 24, who was also stabbed.

However, "When he stopped stabbing [Hull] was when she got to her night table and pulled out a small gun, and that gun probably saved her life," Alachua County Sheriff Steve Oelrich told the local League of Women Voters a few days after the incident.

Professor Gary Kleck of the Florida State University criminology department estimates more than 1.6 million people use firearms each year to stave off criminal attacks, Hammer says.

"Murder rates in Florida had been dropping steadily since 1989," says Hammer. "Criminals who commit violent crimes are aware that many more people are now licensed to carry weapons and will use those weapons to defend themselves."

The Wright-Rossi survey of incarcerated felons, conducted in that same year of 1993 by the tax-funded National Institute for Justice, concluded felons overwhelmingly fear armed citizens more than police, and increasingly decide not to commit some crimes when they fear a home or business owner might shoot them. But the felons said they had no concern that any gun law would prevent them from acquiring a weapon themselves, usually within 15 minutes of leaving jail.

Could it be, then, that Florida's felons merely shifted their attacks onto tourists—the last group almost certain to be unarmed?

Does that mean the sarcastic editorial writer from West Virginia is right? The only solution is to hand the tourists guns?

"Keeping these violent offenders in jail once we have them there is the first intelligent thing to do," Ms. Hammer responded. "Patsy Jones had been in custody for carrying a concealed weapon

317

without a license, robbing a store with a firearm in her possession, and assaulting the officer who was attempting to apprehend her. But the Broward County state's attorney's office dismissed all those charges and told her to get lost. A week later she shot a tourist. We've been saying for years you've got to lock violent predators up."

Rather than disarming their victims? What a radical notion.

As it turned out, ending the "Florida tourist murder rampage" proved even easier than that—though you may search in vain for the sheepish follow-up stories in any of the same media that were using the mini-trend to beat the drum for gun control.

It turns out the criminals, afraid to point a gun at any native Florida driver (since so many of them now go peacefully armed), simply started jacking the drivers of cars with those big day-glo rental-car logos on their mirrors or bumpers. The vast majority of rental cars in Florida are rented at airports. So, thanks to federal air-passenger disarmament laws, it's a virtual sure thing that any tourist who just got off an airplane and rented a set of wheels will be unarmed.

As soon as the rental car firms removed the tell-tale stickers from their vehicles, the "Florida tourist murder rampage" dried up overnight and has never been heard of again.

Private Firearms 'Almost Certainly' Save 400,000 Lives Per Year

"Allowing citizens without criminal records or histories of significant mental illness to carry concealed handguns deters violent crimes. ... If the rest of the country had adopted right-to-carry concealed handgun provisions in 1992, at least 1,570 murders and over 4,177 rapes would have been avoided."

As well as 60,000 aggravated assaults.

That's the conclusion of the most sophisticated study yet undertaken of "Crime, Deterrence, and Right-to-Carry Concealed Handguns," the title of a 45-page report released Aug. 15, 1996, by John R. Lott, Jr. of the School of Law, and David B. Mustard of the Department of Economics, University of Chicago.

The Chicago study did discover a downside. Although criminals prove noticeably less willing to attack strangers when the chances of their victims being armed are increased by even a few percentage points, it does not appear this leads them to entirely give up their chosen line of work. Instead "property crimes involving stealth"—burglaries and the like—increase when the citizenry is better armed.

Still, the financial gain to the economy from allowing the legal concealed carry of handguns by everyone but felons and the raving insane, the authors conclude, "is at least $6.214 billion," while some 400,000 law-abiding citizens per year report that their use of a gun—usually without discharging the weapon—"almost certainly" saved a life.

The gun-grabbers love to weep over their 18- and 19-year-old "child gunshot victims," even in cases like the one in Las Vegas in the autumn of '96, where it turned out the poor child had been busted for gang-related crimes many times and was finally shot down in the act of stealing someone's tires.

Yes, every death of a young person is tragic. But now let's place in the balance the estimated 400,000 law-abiding American citizens whose lives are saved each year because they or a family member had a gun. And that's before we even allow for the sensible argument of Aaron Zelman of the Milwaukee-based Jews for the Preservation of Firearms Ownership that government genocides occur only in countries where the citizenry has been disarmed.

Once disarmed, how many lives would the ensuing "North American genocide" likely cost us?

The Lott and Mustard report cites and tends to confirm—though it doesn't depend on—the work of Gary Kleck and Marc Gertz of Florida, whose surveys for the journal *Criminal Law and Criminology* found 764,000 to 3.6 million defensive uses of guns per year.

This number completely debunks gun-control myths about how gun owners are more likely to injure themselves or their loved ones than to scare off a criminal, since those gun-grabber statistics count only gunshot incidents written up by police (including suicides and gun owners shot with firearms not their own), not the far more numerous occasions when merely displaying a weapon sends a potential assailant heading in the opposite direction in a hurry.

Crimes committed by those with permits? Florida issued 221,443 firearms licenses between Oct. 1, 1987, and April 30, 1994. Only 18 of those licensees were ever charged with crimes.

Meantime, Lott and Mustard reveal, "Police accidentally killed 330 innocent individuals in 1993, compared to the mere 30 innocent people accidentally killed by private citizens who mistakenly believed the victim was an intruder."

Curiously, I have yet to hear any gun-control advocate calling for a ban on these dangerous police officers carrying firearms.

And this statistic of 330 "accidental" police killings wouldn't even include the police murders of Vicki Weaver, millionaire recluse Donald Scott, or several dozen innocent women and children in Waco, Texas.

Why is concealed carry better? "By the very nature of these guns being concealed, criminals are unable to tell whether the victim is armed before they strike, thus raising criminals' expected costs," the authors report. In other words, this policy tends to help protect even those who choose *not* to go armed.

Even the headlines of the newspaper stories cited by Lott and Mustard read like a catalogue of "Stories Handgun Control Hopes

320

You'll Never Hear," one of my favorites being the *New York Times'* entry of Sept. 7, 1995: "Burglar Puts 92-year-old in the Gun Closet and is Shot."

The good news, in short, is that the number of states requiring authorities to issue, without discretion, concealed-weapons permits to "qualified applicants" has increased from nine to 31 just since 1986, and violent crime has dropped consistently in those very states.

Of course, this begs the question of why anyone should be required to apply for a permit to carry a firearm, under a form of government that Americans agreed to ratify only upon the guarantee that "the right of the people to keep and bear Arms shall not be infringed."

Doesn't it?

Gun Control's Racist Roots

In his book *The Saturday Night Special*, Robert Sherrill tells the real-life tale of the ATF raid on Maryland resident Ken Ballew back in 1971. The federal disarmament police had received a tip that Ballew owned several live hand grenades. (It wasn't true—apparently someone had merely seen one of those novelty items that displays a disarmed empty grenade body affixed to a plaque with a legend reading: "Complaint Department, pull pin and wait your turn.") Did the BATF simply send Ballew a letter, asking whether he might have neglected to pay the proper tax on a "destructive device"? No. Instead, plainclothes ATF agents displaying guns—but no badges or insignia—burst into Ballew's apartment in the evening while he was in the bathtub and his wife, clad only in panties, was in the bedroom. Seeing the armed scruffy-looking men, she screamed for her husband to get his gun. Emerg-

321

ing from the bathroom, Ballew grabbed his antique Civil-War-era cap-and-ball pistol. As he emerged into the living room, Ken Ballew was shot in the head. Today, 28 years later, he remains partially paralyzed and incapable of speech.

"I want to tell you about what they did after the raid was concluded," Congressman John Dingell of Michigan said on the floor of Congress during a debate on BATF funding on Feb. 8, 1995. "They went outside, still dressed as hippies with beards and in scruffy clothes, at which time they first put on their ATF armbands to show that they ... had given proper warning to the individual of their authority, which, in fact, they had not."

Robert Sherrill's book reports Chicago police were never able to develop any evidence that a young man named Craig Davis was the "man named Craig" whom ATF informants said had purchased a sawed-off shotgun. But don't worry, Craig Davis won't be suing the ATF.

If you think white folks have a rough time with the ATF, you haven't spent enough time in this country being black. Young Mr. Davis, you see, was of the Negro persuasion. Mr. Sherill's book reports that agents left him dead with a bullet in the head in 1989, ruling the death an "accidental homicide."

Most of our current gun-control laws had their roots in racism. In the South, all blacks, including freed slaves, were barred from carrying arms before the Civil War. Needless to say, when the occupying Northerners in 1865 instructed the conquered white south that blacks—including Civil War veterans who had returned bearing their military arms—were now to be allowed to vote, and to enforce that right they were also being permitting to retain their arms, the Democratic bigots were not happy.

In answer to state laws extending the ban on black ownership of firearms, Congress ratified the 14th Amendment, barring the states from interfering with the rights guaranteed federal citizens under the Bill of Rights—specifically, the rights of black citizens to keep and bear arms.

At that point, the bigots got more sophisticated. Poll taxes were designed to make it prohibitively expensive for poor black sharecroppers to vote. A similar strategy was then developed to require that those wishing to own or carry a handgun obtain a "permit," to be issued at the discretion of the sheriff. Since all the sheriffs were white, how many pistol permits do you think were issued to black folk? Thus, any black man caught with a handgun could be shot or jailed as a presumptive criminal—a "gun-control" tradition that continues to this day, with campaigns (still pushed primarily by the racist Democratic Party) to remove from the market "cheap Saturday Night Specials," an only slightly bowdlerized version of the old racist phrase, "Niggertown Saturday Night."

(There are reporters still alive today who can recall landing their first low-paying newspaper job south of the Mason-Dixon line. Excited to learn of a multiple shooting and homicide over a card game, more than one naive and Yankee-born cub reporter has started pounding out what he assumed would be a front-page bylined story, only to be told in a bored tone by a senior desk editor, "What was that address again, kid? Make it four paragraphs on page 12; that's in Darktown." To this day, any murder of more than two white people can be enough to put a police manhunt on the front pages for days, while two or three young African-Americans shot dead in what is now euphemistically called "this city's traditionally black neighborhood" still tend to be dismissed within hours as "just another Niggertown Saturday Night"—whether anyone still calls it that or not. While it's Politically Correct to decry this as racist, the "where" question remains one of the reporter's crucial four w's for a reason: 200 dead of cholera in Bangladesh is not as important a story as 200 dead in the next town over, because the fact that the Bangladeshi water source is unsafe is not likely to directly affect our own kids. Likewise, many

American moms—regardless of race—are unnecessarily terrified their own kids may be gunned down during a drive-by shooting, due almost entirely to our TV stations' fear of being picketed as racists were they to include one otherwise crucial sentence in their nightly crime reports: "This crime occurred among the welfare housing projects and crack dens of the inner city—police say the risk of such crime spreading into middle-class neighborhoods even a mile or two away remains minimal.")

Another rationale that proved to dovetail neatly with this scheme to leave racial minorities disarmed and thus politically powerless was the "no legitimate sporting use" gambit. Obviously, wealthy white men would never be harassed about owning "legitimate" shotguns for bird hunting or "legitimate" deer rifles. But the inexpensive concealable weapon required by a poor and often urban black person for self-defense—in a country where the white police were not exactly known for their breakneck speed in responding to calls from Darktown—was by obvious implication "illegitimate," since it had no "sporting use."

So helpful did the American concept of "legitimate sporting use" prove that the Germans borrowed the phrase to disarm their Jews (and most other poor urban minorities), starting in 1928.

And we all know what finally happened to them.

Just How Far Back *Does* Gun Control Date?

Henry St. George Tucker is quoted in Blackstone's 1768 *Commentaries on the Laws of England*—Abe Lincoln's lawbook— warning, "The right of self-defense is the first law of nature; in most governments it has been the study of rulers to confine this right within the narrowest limits possible. Wherever standing armies are kept up, and when the right of the people to keep and

324

bear arms is, under any color or pretext whatsoever, prohibited, liberty, if not already annihilated, is on the brink of destruction."

What largely kept the Dark Ages "dark," we have to recall, was the seamless teamwork of both church and state, instructing the peasant class that things had always been this way and would always be this way. Wealthy men inherited their fathers' horses, arms, and armor—the necessary tools for success on the 13th century battlefield—and no mere peasant could ever hope to raise enough capital to arm himself equivalently. Everyone was therefore best off just sticking to his father's trade—and paying his taxes at sword-point, the way his father had.

But technological innovation—and the liberty it must always bring for the common man—couldn't be halted.

In ancient Rome, a foreign-born tribesman could become a Roman citizen—qualified to vote, own property, and carry his sword in the streets of Rome—after 20 years loyal service in the legions.

But by the 13th century, the Magna Carta was guaranteeing legal rights only to nobles. At that point no one else counted, since no one else could back up their claim to any "rights" on the battlefield.

The re-emergence of the notion that a commoner could have legal rights, that he couldn't be killed and his wife and flocks seized by his feudal master at a mere whim, paralleled the re-emergence of the commoner—or a mass of commoners—as a powerful force on the field of battle.

Crecy and Agincourt were foreshadowings of doom for the monopoly on armed force and political power enjoyed for a thousand years by the armored aristocrat. Literally thousands of French noble knights died at Agincourt, many of them drowning in the mud under the weight of their downed horses and their own armor—after bands of mere commoners engaged them with the Welsh longbow at ranges of up to 300 yards.

325

British casualties: 16.

(The French found this trend so appalling and ungodly that they threatened to cut off the middle and index finger of any Welsh archer they caught. The archers responded by waving those two fingers in the air in defiance—or sometimes just one of them.)

The arrival of the firearm completed this process, allowing bands of mere commoners to overthrow and behead the king of England in 1649 and the king of France in 1793. In between those exemplary examples of thoroughness, the American colonists, incredibly, overthrew the world's greatest military power—with the help of the French fleet, of course, but primarily on the strength of an historical coincidence of enormous consequence—that the average American farmer and backwoodsman had a better military weapon, in the form of the German-made or domestic Pennsylvania rifle, than the British soldier had in his smoothbore Brown Bess musket.

What was shocking about the American Revolution was not so much that the colonial landed aristocracy might seek local autonomy (that had precedent enough), but the far more dangerous theory set forward in Mr. Jefferson's Declaration, that the mere common people had a God-given *right* to toss aside whatever government they found in place over them and to force the creation of a new form of government more to their liking at the point of a gun!

Cynics assumed George Washington—descended from the British royal lineage—would allow himself to be crowned King of America when it was all over, and would even execute a few of his more radical pamphleteers, like Tom Paine, to set things back to rights. Indeed, his suppression of the Whisky Rebellion went part way toward satisfying that prophesy.

But the Europeans failed to grasp a basic new reality. This new notion of the rights of the common man *grew out of the fact* that the common man was now armed, in a militarily effective way. Thus, his "equal rights" were not a thing to be granted or taken away by any "higher authority." He had bought them, "lock, stock, and barrel." He was a "free man" because anyone who said otherwise would quickly find a quarter-ounce of lead puncturing his gut, even out to ranges of 800 yards. This is why the debates over ratifying the U.S. Constitution are full of patriots like Patrick Henry insisting, "The main thing is that every man be armed, that every man who is able be allowed to retain his private arms."

Not for hunting. For shooting tyrants.

The average American commoner remains well-armed to this day, to the continued great consternation and frustration of the European (and New England) moneyed elites, who still consider it a damnably anarchic precedent and example.

Nowadays, our government schools do not teach our children how to shoot, how to love the firearm as the "eye tooth of liberty," how to celebrate the birth of freedom in the spilled blood of the ruling classes. No, they emphasize "stability," and teach our children how to hate and ostracize—even to make an anonymous phone call and turn in—any neighbor prepared to defend his freedoms.

What these moneyed elites want are disarmed multitudes—far easier to track, number, fingerprint, tax, and control. Sure, these members of the tweed-and-corduroy set own guns—usually some $5,000 engraved fowling piece—and present themselves as "responsible hunters," gulling us into thinking they're on our side, that it's for our own good that they urge us to "put up with the minor inconvenience of filling out of just a few forms, in the interest of safety."

The shoguns of Japan never required such subtlety. The shogun Toyotomi Hideyoshi (1536-1598) simply ordered on the 8th day of the seventh month, Tensho 16: "The people of the various provinces are strictly forbidden to have in their possession any swords, short swords, bows, spears, firearms, or other types of

327

arms. The possession of unnecessary implements makes difficult the collection of taxes and dues, and tends to foment uprisings."

Which is why Japan, to this day, is an ants' nest of disarmed slaves.

The Genocide of April 24

Of course, once a minority is disarmed, its members can quickly discover that the taxman is the least of their problems.

In the early years of the 20th century, as members of a religious minority (Christians), Armenians held a role in Turkish society similar to that of Jews in central Europe. They were successful in commerce and the professions, but were generally forbidden the ownership of firearms.

Even though armed Armenians helped the so-called Young Turks depose the sultan Abdul-Hamid and take power in the spring of 1909, by the next year they found themselves again the object of a national campaign of gun control, according to the book *Lethal Laws* by Jay Simkin, Aaron Zelman, and Alan M. Rice of the Milwaukee-based group Jews for the Preservation of Firearms Ownership (see "Appendix II").

On Nov. 24, 1910, the Turkish government banned the unauthorized manufacture, importation, and carrying of weapons— just as our politicians today have banned the importation and manufacture of most firearms, except those they deem to be primarily for sporting use.

By December 1914, Turkey was fully involved in World War I and found herself launching a winter offensive against Russia through the snowy Caucasus. The campaign was a disaster. By early January, out of 190,000 Turkish troops, 90,000 were dead and 12,000 had been taken prisoner.

Someone had to be blamed, and since Armenian volunteers had been spotted fighting alongside the Russian army, they became easy scapegoats. Rumors were spread that Armenian bakers were poisoning food. Historian Yves Ternon reports that, starting in February 1915, "The authorities disarmed Armenian soldiers and police, who were organized into battalions of 50 to 100 men and put to work on road maintenance. ... It became known shortly afterwards that several of these work gangs had been exterminated. At the same time, Armenians in government were dismissed and internal passports authorizing Armenians to move around the country canceled."

(Modern Americans now have "internal passports," too. They're called "drivers licenses." Think they're only to prove you know how to drive? Try boarding a commercial aircraft without showing one. You weren't planning to *fly* the aircraft, were you?)

On April 24, 1915, Turkish authorities rounded up and deported or killed 600 Armenian leaders, writers, and professionals in Constantinople. The same day, 5,000 of the city's poorest Armenians were butchered in their homes, according to the Knights of Vartan Armenian Research Center at the University of Michigan, Dearborn.

Finally came the official proclamation of June 26 (June 13 of the old calendar): "For a few years our Armenian compatriots have been, with foreign instructions, injuring the tranquility and peacefulness of the Ottoman Empire. [Therefore] our government ... is obliged to deport the Armenian population into the interior provinces."

There follow lengthy instructions about the making of portable goods into bales, which would be kept by the government "and given back, just as they are, to the owners on their return."

Armenians who resisted would be "arrested dead," the proclamation warned. "Likewise, those who refuse to depart, disobeying the government's decision and hiding themselves here and there, and those persons who hide them in their houses or feed them to help them hide, will also be sent to Court Martial to be condemned to death."

Armenians were ordered to surrender all arms. Of course, it was never intended that any Armenians would return to reclaim their neatly wrapped bundles. Disarmed men in labor battalions were worked until they collapsed, then shot. Old men, women, and children were sent on forced marches, escorted by Ottoman troops, but without provisions. Those who did not die of hunger, thirst, or exhaustion, once they were too weak to resist, were bayoneted or shot.

"There were few, if any, concentration camps in Turkey," Yves Ternon reports. "There were no reception camps because the deportees were not supposed to arrive."

At least one million Armenians living under Ottoman domination were killed by their own duly established government in the years 1915-1917. But in at least four documented cases—and this is highly significant, especially in the face of today's dispiriting claims that holding onto our military-style arms is "hopeless"—Armenians kept their arms and fought back. In southern Aleppo province (now Syria), armed Armenians took to the hills in July 1915 and stood off 15,000 Ottoman troops, inflicting huge losses. In early September French and British ships picked up 4,000 Armenian survivors from Jebel Musa and delivered them to freedom in Port Said.

As in every other major genocide of this century, the authors of *Lethal Laws* point out, civilian gun control, justified as an "anti-crime" measure, was the precursor. Only where the targeted group resisted confiscation did substantial numbers survive.

"Government officials, not common criminals or hate-group members, committed these genocides," writes Jay Simkin of JPFO. "In every case, gun-control laws were in force before the genocide began. In five genocides [in the 20th century] the lethal law—

330

the gun control law—was in force before the 'genocide regime' took power. ... Every government can become genocidal. Your best life preserver is personal ownership of a military-type semi-automatic rifle."

But can rag-tag bands of civilians really defeat modern armies?

"Afghanistan had no gun control before the Soviet invasion" of 1979, Simkin points out. "In 1989, the war-weary Soviets withdrew their 115,000 troops. The Afghans are a shining example of how armed civilians without heavy weapons can wreck armies. The Afghans undoubtedly saved themselves from genocide."

Though it in no way lessens the horror of the Jewish Holocaust, the fact is there have been a half-dozen genocides in this century. Stalin's Soviet Union, Mao's China, and Pol Pot's Cambodia each slew one million to 20 million souls in their turn between 1930 and 1980.

Are there similarities to the way the groundwork was laid for all these genocides? Yes. So why don't our schools teach today's youth to recognize the government actions that inevitably presage genocide?

Gee, I can't imagine. Who's *running* those schools, anyway?

Jews With Guns

In 1994, World War II had been over almost 50 years. Ronald Reagan laid a wreath at the German war cemetery at Bitburg, where members of the Waffen SS lay interred. To many old warriors, and to generations for whom Stalingrad and Auschwitz and Bastogne are little more than signposts in grainy newsreels, it was time to move on.

Not to Reuben "Red" Hafter. Red Hafter remembers.

Reuben Hafter's father came to the United States from Germany in 1905, his mother from Poland in 1920. Both were Jews. After the war, Hafter, now of Scottsdale, Arizona, journeyed to Israel to examine the rolls of the Holocaust dead, counting the number of Hafters and Oliphants (his mother's maiden name) lost to Hitler's "final solution."

"There were more than two hundred. If the last name was Hafter, they were related. We've been able to establish a link to all the Hafters except the ones in Switzerland, who are Catholic," Hafter says.

Two hundred. Doctors. Lawyers. Mothers. Infants. An entire family ... gone. Hafter was able to track three European Hafters who survived the war in England and then settled in Paris, and "a handful, four or five, who made it to Palestine." With three children and 11 grandchildren of his own, Reuben Hafter, by himself, is responsible for more Hafters than the Nazis left alive in all of Europe.

But don't expect Red Hafter to say, "We didn't know," or "There was nothing we could do." America's Jews did know, he says; they knew about Kristalnacht, the Night of the Broken Glass, when stormtroopers shattered the windows of all the Jewish shops and synagogues of Berlin in 1938. And he says the American military and civilian government knew about the concentration camps long before war's end.

"They've forgotten that Franklin Roosevelt turned his back on them. Later, Secretary of the Treasury Morgenthau was able to save several hundred thousand at the end of the war, but they could have saved a lot more if they'd started earlier. When I was in the military I asked how come we don't bomb the concentration camps, and we knew about them, believe me. I was told we didn't bomb them because there were civilians there. I said 'They're dying there.'"

Red Hafter didn't wait for someone else to do his fighting.

He lied about his age to get into the Army Air Corps, where he was assigned to the top turret of a Ninth Air Force B-25, using twin 50-calibers to tear up anything that moved in daylight against the flanks of George Patton's advancing Third Army. "We did it very effectively. I know that I was personally responsible for turning two hundred seventy-five to three hundred Germans into Good Germans.

"As far as I'm concerned, having been stationed there at Bitburg Air Force Base during the time they were putting up the Berlin Wall, Germany is still Nazi Germany. What scares me is the skinheads and neo-Nazis. While I was there I listened to an interview with their equivalent of our attorney general on German TV. I could understand a lot of German at the time. They asked this fellow, who had resisted Hitler, whether what happened in the 1930s could happen again, and he said, 'Under the right conditions, with drums beating and night gatherings with torches, I'm sure you could get the German people to do it all again.'"

Red Hafter kept going. He became a fighter pilot in P-47s and P-51s, losing a kneecap to small-arms fire flying close air support in Korea. ("You get a bunch of crap thrown at you you just wouldn't believe.") He flew F-86s as well, retired a colonel and went to work for Grumman as an aeronautical engineer and test pilot after he saw the kind of ground rules that were going to be imposed on pilots in Vietnam. ("You couldn't shoot a MiG on the ground; you had to wait for it to take off. They could shoot surface-to-air missiles at us but we weren't allowed to attack the mobile batteries on the ground, at least not at that time. You had to wait for a tanker to pump its oil into a tank at the dock, and then you could attack the oil tank, but not the ship. I could see where that was going, and I got out.")

At Grumman, Hafter rose to assistant vice president, eventually directing the checkout and testing of Lunar Module 3—the first to carry men on the moon. ("So I went from props to jets to the moon landing.") He kept his hand in as a marksman, too, winning a silver and three bronze medals in 1988 World Cup matches and setting U.S. pistol marksmanship records as recently as 1990 at the age of 61.

Red Hafter was a man with a mission in 1944. He remains a man with a mission today.

"I just cannot imagine what Jews who are in favor of gun control are thinking of. Our federal Firearms Act of 1968 is modeled directly on the Nazi firearm act of 1938. Aaron Zelman of Jews for the Preservation of Firearms Ownership wrote a book that compares them item to item [*Gun Control: Gateway to Tyranny*, by Jay Simkin and Aaron Zelman—see "Appendix II"].

"I begin to wonder whether people like [New York Congressman Charles] Schumer and [Ohio Senator Howard] Metzenbaum are really Jewish. The big problem is the majority of the Jewish population is so liberal, they don't understand that Israel was only founded because of firearms. They've had it so relatively good for a period of time. I remember what happened during World War II right here in this country, how anti-Semitic it was. I remember signs on lawns where I was stationed in Biloxi, Mississippi, that said 'Dogs, soldiers, and Jews stay off.' I remember hotels with signs that said, 'No Jews allowed.'"

Hafter says recent historical scholarship shows that the First United States Congress rejected Roger Sherman's original draft of the Second Amendment precisely because it was not strong enough in guaranteeing the *individual* right to bear arms. Yet, he says, newspapers like the supposedly conservative *Arizona Republic* decline to publish his letters pointing this out, when he tries to respond to members of the American Bar Association asserting in their pages the patent absurdity that all the Framers meant to guarantee was the right of *government soldiers* to bear arms.

"I've actually talked to a person who survived the Holocaust,"

334

Hafter recalls. "This guy was speaking against guns like I couldn't believe my ears, and this guy had hidden in an attic like Anne Frank. I asked him, 'If you'd had the chance, wouldn't you have killed if you'd had a gun?' I didn't get an answer.

"You can check with the Simon Wiesenthal Center [for Holocaust Studies] in Los Angeles. Anti-Semitism in this country is getting worse, not better. I think Louis Farrakhan's message is going to become more dangerous. I think before long we're gonna see some Jewish people getting killed. So I don't understand where these people are coming from where they don't want to be in a position to defend themselves."

Even in Arizona, where open carrying of firearms is still legal, "a concealed permit is now going to cost fifty dollars, plus two hundred dollars for the [mandatory] training. I'm a certified NRA trainer, but it looks like I have to go through the course just like a beginner. And I still hold one of the Olympic [shooting] event records for the United States."

Hafter was writing to his U.S. senator, Vietnam veteran John McCain, to complain about the "Gestapo-like tactics" of the Bureau of Alcohol, Tobacco, and Firearms in the Vicki Weaver murder in Idaho and other incidents even before the Waco infant-fry of 1993.

"I could see a pattern taking place; I complained about this eight-hundred number you can use to call the ATF and turn in your neighbors if you think they have an illegal gun, and based on that call they can get a search warrant. It's just the way the Gestapo used to work."

McCain's office turned Hafter's letter over to the ATF, which promptly scheduled Hafter for the first audit of his Federal Firearms License in 20 years.

"I had incidents when I was stationed in Mississippi in World War II, where because I had a gun, people left me alone. You let them see you with it when you're going out to the range to shoot and word gets around. I remember a guy named Barry Farber, who ran for mayor of New York City a couple of times, and later had a TV show there in the early days of television. He came from the Deep South.

"One night I'm watching his talk show and he has various people on there debating gun control, and at the close of the broadcast he explained why he thought gun control was stupid. Growing up in the South, on Friday nights he used to watch the KKK members drinking their courage down at the local bar, and they would go down the list to see who they were gonna hit that night, and when they would hit the names of the Farbers they would say, 'No, no, the old man has a rifle, and the kids know how to shoot, too.'"

Night riders of all stripes "go after people who can't or won't defend themselves. That's what really bugs me about my brethren."

So there's no kind of gun control that would meet with the approval of 50-year warrior Red Hafter?

"Shooting five hundred eighty-nine out of six hundred, when the ten-ring is the size of a dime. That's what I call gun control."

'You Cowards, You Gun Haters, You Don't Deserve to Live in America'

Red Hafter is not alone.

Aaron Zelman, founder of the Milwaukee-based Jews for the Preservation of Firearms Ownership, interviews Dachau concentration camp survivor Theodore Haas.

Q: How did you end up at Dachau? How old were you?

A: November 9th, 1938, was Kristalnacht—The Night of the Broken Glass, the night synagogues were ransacked and burned,

Jewish-owned shops destroyed. ... I was arrested Nov. 10, "for my own personal security."

I was 21 years old. My parents were arrested and ultimately died in a concentration camp in France. I was released from Dachau in 1941, under the condition that I leave Germany immediately. This was common practice before the "Final Solution. ...."

Q: You mentioned you were shot and stabbed several times. Were these experiments, punishment, or torture?

A: They were punishment. I very often, in a fit of temper, acted "while the brain was not in gear." The sorry results were two 9mm bullets in my knees. Fortunately, one of the prisoners had a fingernail file and was able to dig the slugs out. ...

Q: What was the routine like at Dachau?

A: Three times a day, we were counted. We had to carry the dead to the square. Each time, we had to stand at attention in all kinds of weather. We stood wearing next to nothing, had weak bladders, while our tormentors had sheepskin coats and felt boots. The bastards really enjoyed watching us suffer. I remember how the guards had a good laugh when one of them "accidentally" let loose with a machine gun, killing about 30 prisoners.

Q: Did the camp inmates ever bring up the topic, "If only we were armed before, we would not be here now"?

A: Many, many times. Before Adolf Hitler came to power, there was a black market in firearms, but the German people had been so conditioned to be law abiding that they would never consider buying an unregistered gun. The German people really believed that only hoodlums owned such guns. What fools we were.

It truly frightens me to see how the government, the media, and some police groups in America are pushing for the same mindset. In my opinion, the people of America had better start asking and demanding answers to some hard questions about firearms ownership, especially, "If the government does not trust me to own firearms, why or how can the people be expected to trust the government?"

There is no doubt in my mind that millions of lives could have been saved if the people were not "brainwashed" about gun ownership and had been well-armed. Hitler's thugs and goons were not very brave when confronted by a gun. Gun haters always want to forget the Warsaw Ghetto uprising, which is a perfect example of how a rag-tag half-starved group of Jews took up ten handguns and made asses out of the Nazis.

Q: Do you think American society has enough stability that Jews and other minorities are safe from severe persecution?

A: No. I think there is more anti-Semitism in America, some of it caused by leftist Jewish politicians who promote gun control schemes, than there was in Germany. ...

I perceive America as a very unstable society, due to social tinkering of the Kennedy-Metzenbaum politicians. When I first came to this wonderful country after World War II, America was a vibrant, dynamic, and promising society. There really was an American dream, attainable by those who wanted to work. Now, due to the curse of liberalism, America is in a period of moral decline. ...

Q: What message do you have for ultra-liberal organizations and individuals who want America disarmed?

A: Their ignorance is pitiful—their lives have been too easy. Had they experienced Dachau, they would have a better idea of how precious freedom is. These leftists should leave America. These Sarah Brady types must be educated to understand that it is because we have an armed citizenry that a dictatorship has not yet happened in America. These anti-gun fools are more dangerous to liberty than street criminals or foreign spies.

Q: Some concentration camp survivors are opposed to gun ownership. What message would you like to share with them?

A: I would like to say, "You cowards, you gun haters, you don't deserve to live in America. Go live in the Soviet Union, if you love gun control so damned much." It was the stupidity of these naive fools that aided and abetted Hitler's goons. Anti-gun-ownership Holocaust survivors insult the memories of all those who needlessly perished for lack of being able to adequately defend themselves. ... Every Jew should be armed to the teeth, as should every American. ...

Aaron Zelman's interview with Theodore Haas goes on at considerably more length, but we'll end our excerpt there. You get the idea.

As a matter of fact, let's forget the goofy "Pledge of Allegiance," written by a 19th century flag salesman. I'll know this is a free country again when schoolchildren in America start each day by placing their hands over their hearts and reciting from memory:

"You cowards, you gun haters, you don't deserve to live in America. Go live in the Soviet Union, if you love gun control so damned much. A well-regulated Militia being necessary to the security of a free state, the right of the people to keep and bear Arms shall not be infringed"—and then head cheerfully down to the range to take their morning target practice, at 300 yards.

They're Melting Down the Guns

I grew up in the Connecticut River Valley, as did my dad.

As late as 1918, the area proudly dubbed itself the Arsenal of Freedom.

No one surpassed the machinists and inventors of Connecticut and western Massachusetts when it came to improving the affordability and usefulness of firearms, which George Washington called "the eye teeth of liberty." And the machine tools they developed to perfect the Springfield musket and then the Springfield rifle—the arms of Chicopee and Whitneyville and New Ha-ven—eventually revolutionized the American manufacture of everything from cotton gins to furniture to motorcars, kick-start-ing the American Industrial Revolution.

I went home to Connecticut to see my folks in the fall of 1996. The Wadsworth Atheneum—the castle-like art museum in Hartford—was staging a show on the Colt family, including Sam Colt's Hartford factory and guns.

But many in New England these days are ashamed of their heritage as the Arsenal of Freedom. Art critic Jayne Keedle in the weekly *Hartford Advocate*—the often-collectivist sob-sister rag that provided my own first writing job, though I hope she was a tad less predictably pious when we founded her—wrote on Oct. 17: "Curators at the Wadsworth Atheneum knew that the exhibit 'Sam and Elizabeth: The Legend and Legacy of Colt's Empire' would be controversial. ... Sam Colt built his empire on guns. As the inventor of the first reliable repeat-firing revolver, he is the father of modern-day munitions. Which means that, along with the public art, libraries, and churches created all over the city by his philanthropically inclined wife, the violence caused by guns is also part of Colt's legacy. ...

"The Atheneum decided to respond to current concerns about gun violence with a contemporary art installation. When 'The Manhole Cover Project: A Gun Legacy' opens this week on the sidewalk outside the museum, visitors will hear chilling stories told by people in Hartford whose lives have been irrevocably changed by a bullet."

"Sculptor" Brad McCallum came up with the idea for this piece of tape-recorded anti-gun propaganda in early 1995, Keedle relates, when he learned that guns confiscated by Connecticut state police are melted down by a foundry in Massachusetts and made into manhole covers.

"He decided to commission 228 manhole covers from the

340

foundry, weighing a total of 39,216 pounds. It is the exact weight of the 11,194 guns confiscated by troopers since 1992, which is when Gov. Lowell Weicker first ordered that they be destroyed rather than sold at auctions," Ms. Keedle explains.

I look at the black-and-white photo of the artist and his chunky bearded assistant kneeling with their pile of manhole covers outside the Atheneum, and my eyes still well up. Is it in *Shoah* or *Schindler's List* that the camera moves slowly across a Nazi highway—the road to one of the death camps, as I recall—paved with gravestones uprooted from a nearby Jewish cemetery?

Taking the sacred symbols of a culture's freedom, of its unique contributions to the progress of mankind, and purposely degrading them into paving material, suitable for oil spills and horse droppings, the Nazis did have a perverse propaganda genius, as do the gun-grabbers.

Ms. Keedle doesn't disturb our reverie with any report of how much government funding "for the arts" went into "sculptor" McCallum's purchase of 20 tons of finely machined instruments of freedom, melted down into useless 172-pound slabs.

"As visitors stand in the otherwise cold outdoor space," Ms. Keedle wheedles on, "they will listen to the [tape-recorded] voices of mothers talking about how it feels to lose their sons to violence, to trauma center nurses and doctors talking about the futility of trying to heal the damage done by bullets," blah, blah, blah.

But not a word, I daresay, from any survivors of the Holocaust, about how *their* families died wholesale after they'd surrendered their private arms to the German gun-confiscation law in good faith.

"In Hartford, gunshot wounds are the leading cause of death for teenagers 15 to 19 years old," the art review-turned propaganda piece drones on.

What an interesting statistic, carefully crafted to convey an image of innocent schoolchildren mowed down by stray bullets as they dart fearfully home from school.

But bullets can't discern a "victim's" age. Why then aren't bullets the leading cause of death among 14-year-olds, or 13-year-olds? At what age, I wonder, do black and Puerto Rican youths in North Hartford voluntarily choose to become gun-wielding members of cocaine-distribution gangs these days? How many of these gunshot "children" were in fact drug gangsters shooting each other over distribution turf?

Yes, that's still tragic. But the political purpose of both the manhole cover "exhibition" and Ms. Keedle's uncritical apologia is to convince suburban soccer moms that their kids are equally at risk—which they're not.

How many fellow 19-year-olds did Billy the Kid shoot to death in New Mexico in 1878, I wonder? Would we really dub those fellow-desperados "child gunshot victims"?

Also left unmentioned is the fact that more gunshot wounds were survivable just a few years back, when the street weapon of choice was a cheap .25 or .32. The gun control gang banned most of those little "Saturday Night Specials," of course, forcing the street gangster to upgrade his firepower to a .357.

America had more guns per capita in 1934, and hardly any "gun deaths." Congress had just put our last set of violent street gangs out of business without firing a shot, by ending Prohibition.

We wouldn't want to do that again, I suppose?

As I viewed the manhole cover exhibit, I was tempted to wish aloud that when Connecticut is conquered by a hostile invading army—an event that grows yearly more likely, given this lemming-like race toward victim disarmament—the invaders might gather together all the government propagandists who have ever accepted extorted tax money for these little exercises in Politically Correct "installation art" and patiently explain, "See these manhole covers? These were once the finely crafted firearms you could have used to defend your families and your freedom. Instead, you chose to melt them down into these inert lumps."

Then, the laughing invaders would use the 172-pound steel discs to slowly crush their defenseless skulls.

But, as the holiday season was upon us, I decided not to wish that aloud.

Mr. Darwin already had it covered, anyway.

No, No, They're Not 'Individual' Rights

Richard Slotkin is a popular professor of American Studies at Wesleyan University, in Middletown, Connecticut. He has written many books, including *Gunfighter Nation*, which trace not so much the history of American firearms—I would not call Prof. Slotkin a historian of engineering—as the way guns are viewed as talismans in our popular culture.

At the drop of a hat, he will quote Shane, "A gun is just a tool, Marian, like an axe or a plow. It's only as good as the man who uses it."

But Prof. Slotkin does not buy into the myth of the Equalizer, of which he says the most popular expression is, "God may have made men, but Samuel Colt made them equal."

Speaking to a receptive crowd of 50 doyens of the Wadsworth Atheneum of an early autumn evening in October 1996, Prof. Slotkin was quick to assert that this resilient myth "has little to do with the real utility of the handgun. The long gun really won the West."

Prof. Slotkin at least acknowledges that such esteemed historians as Daniel Boorstin of the Smithsonian Institution praise the affordable and reliable handgun for giving "men of all classes equal access to the use of armed force of compulsion." But he clearly rejects such notions.

343

The Second Amendment "does not vest the right to bear arms in individuals, but only in the people as a social collectivity," Prof. Slotkin said, on the occasion of being asked to address the museum's donors in connection with the ongoing exhibit memorializing the legacy of one of the founders of Hartford's industrial prosperity, revolver-maker Samuel Colt.

Modern vigilantism, Prof. Slotkin asserted, "has two forms: ethnic gangs and the so-called 'right-wing militias.'"

But these "are not the true militias, which can only be formed by the whole citizenry through legal channels," asserts the good professor, whose vitae brags that he is frequently called upon as an "expert" on firearms and the Second Amendment by virtually every TV network you can name.

Instead, these modern "right-wing militias" only seek to "terrorize people with their automatic weapons," seeking little more than special personal "exemptions to laws requiring school integration, and banning spouse abuse."

(For those not used to the phrasings of college professors, Professor Slotkin means to say that self-described "militia activists" have no real intention of ever using their guns to defend their families or their communities against tyranny or invasion— they own guns merely to terrorize local police officers out of enforcing local school-integration orders or out of arresting the self-styled "militiamen" for beating their wives.)

The ample ladies of Hartford nodded in eager agreement with these undocumented calumnies.

Imagine for the moment that the good professor had asserted that the First Amendment "does not vest the right to freedom of religion in individuals, but only in the people as a social collectivity," that pastors of dissident churches and synagogues not chartered by the government are therefore only seeking personal "exemptions to laws forbidding sodomy, devil-worship, and infanticide."

One suspects at least one timid questioner might have asked if the professor had any evidence that members of competing religious denominations not licensed by the government in fact practice ritual child sacrifice and systematic buggery of the altar boys, perhaps even getting around to inquiring what in the name of God he means by a "right of the people" that can only be exercised "by the whole citizenry through legal channels."

How would the public respond if this character said that we are free to take a majority vote on which newspaper shall be the official state organ, but thereafter the presses of any other broadsheets can be safely smashed by the police without infringing in any way on the First Amendment, since that document "does not vest the right of press freedom in individual writers or publishers, but only in the people as a social collectivity"?

When George Washington and George Mason formed their Fairfax County Militia to oppose the edicts of both the crown and his agent, the governor of Virginia, through what "proper legal channels" did they gain permission?

The tone of the Colt exhibit in Hartford, throughout, was one of shamefacedness and unctuous attempts to placate anyone who might take offense at the nature of Sam Colt's products and even at his gaudy financial success.

"A system which encourages the unlimited accumulation of wealth ... cannot be expected to produce social or economic equality," said Prof. Slotkin, in disparagement of the unregulated capitalism practiced by Colt and the other founders of American industrialism—the very engine that made ours the wealthiest and freest nation in the world.

This constitutes a problem, of course, only if you believe that armed government should enforce "social and economic equality" of outcome, instead of allowing the free market to produce liberty and equality of *opportunity*—a different thing entirely.

My sojourn home to Connecticut was bittersweet. I saw skilled defense-industry artisans keeping busy doing furniture refinishing and working part-time at auction houses. The solution would be to set these skilled machinists to work churning out M-14s for export to Chechnya, there to help the insurgents win their freedom while (as a useful side-effect) keeping the Russian bear distracted from setting its hungry gaze again upon the Baltics and freedom-loving Poland.

But no, the citizens of Connecticut are today instructed that their heritage as the Arsenal of Freedom is a shameful thing, that guns are best melted down into manhole covers, and that it is no longer true (if it ever was) that—a well-practiced Militia being necessary to the security of a free state—the right of the people to keep and bear Arms shall not be infringed.

• • •

Some months after the publication of the essay above, William Hosley, curator of the Colt Collection at the Wadsworth, was nice enough to send me a letter in response:

"I don't suppose it makes good reading to dwell on the complexities of the more moderate arguments I tried to make in the exhibition, book, and accompanying CPTV documentary. Your description of our efforts as 'shamefacedness' and 'unctuous attempts to placate anyone who might take offense' is not quite fair. You have no idea how much flak I took for mounting an exhibition involving guns in an art museum in the '90s. Unlike the Enola Gay debacle [at the Smithsonian Institution], we did not paint Sam and Elizabeth as villains. Actually, I could overwhelm you with the quantity of the public text that valorized two people I admire in many ways.

"I wholly concur with your point about the 'bittersweet' spectacle of ingratitude and amnesia as a State built on Defense contracts repudiates the source of its affluence. It isn't about guns. It is about 'skilled defense industry artisans,' and a brilliant heritage of precision manufacturing, 200 years in the making, being washed away in a generation. I think I'd faint if I woke up with allies, like you, willing to roll up their sleeves and help us bellow this message from the mountain tops. The arms industry of the Connecticut Valley changed the world of work and made possible the whole mechanism of precision manufacturing. Big story rarely told.

"It is ironic that the firearms community fails to support the efforts of a moderate activist in getting the message out to the mainstream. That some may feel we've diluted the power of the traditional firearms message is not to say that what we've done isn't precisely what must be done to restore balance, neutrality, and open-mindedness about the role of firearms in American life."

Phobia: A Persistent, Abnormal, or Illogical Fear of a Specific Thing

An assault rifle is what modern infantrymen carry into combat. It is relatively short-barreled for easy handling and fires a relatively small round like the .223, designed to wound because a wounded man takes two stretcher-bearers out of action (small-caliber cartridges are also lighter, allowing a larger supply to be carried by a foot soldier in the field). Most characteristically, the modern assault rifle has a selective-fire switch, allowing the soldier to switch from automatic spraying fire to the more sensible ammo conservation of single aimed rounds.

The American M-16, the Eastern bloc AK-47, and the Israeli Galil are assault rifles. All are now, already, for all practical purposes, banned to civilians in America. Apply for a license, get fingerprinted, pay hundreds of dollars in fees, wait six months to

347

get checked out, and you *might* be allowed to buy one at 10 times the market price (due to artificially limited supplies—no more are allowed to be imported)—after which you will be sharing your mailbox and your workbench with the ATF forever.

So, since Colt Firearms is effectively banned from selling civilians the M-16, the weapon with which Americans fought the Vietnam War, it sells a one-shot-at-a-time lookalike called the AR-15 Sporter.

How much do people like Bill Clinton and Charles Schumer and Howard Metzenbaum hate these finely engineered machines? So much that they lie, call the AR-15 an "assault rifle," and attempt to ban it.

Shrieking with near-hysteria, such fellow travelers as the *Washington Post* and American Bar Association join in the ululation, crying that the "assault rifle ban" cannot be repealed if all their various "crime bills" are to have any impact on crime.

This despite the fact that lookalikes like the AR-15 are used in an average of three murders per year. Three. Bowling balls kill more people than AR-15s. Lightning strikes kill more people than AR-15s. Bolt-action hunting rifles kill far more people than AR-15s. Yet the gun-banners still insist hunting rifles are OK, because they have a legitimate sporting use.

This is not rational. These people apparently shudder in revulsion at the sight of a military-appearing rifle, the same way certain other folks do when confronted with even a benign snake or spider. Their test would appear to be: If a teenage boy might be likely to say, "Wow, awesome," upon viewing a particular weapon in an Arnold Schwarzenegger film, that specific weapon must be banned.

I'll tell you how frighteningly compulsive this behavior can become. Bill Clinton is required by law—like any executive-department employee—to guard the assets of the United States from wanton destruction. Until recently, he also professed to be attempt-

348

ing to raise revenues to close a budget deficit. And, of course, in any war America has ever entered, history tells us that combat rifles were found to be in short supply (especially given the materiel losses in initial defeats and surrenders, like that on Corregidor), so that production had to be immediately shifted over to a wasteful emergency wartime footing to get the fighting men even a fraction of what they needed to hold their own.

Yet *Guns & Ammo* magazine reported in 1996 that since Bill Clinton took office, the U.S. government has resumed for the first time in 15 years the destruction by shredding of "obsolete" firearms, including 110,000 45-caliber pistols and 30,000 M1 Garands—the magnificent semi-automatic battle rifle that defeated Adolf Hitler.

Destruction of the weapons—some valued by collectors at up to $6,000 each, "continues at a rate of about 3,000 guns per day. ... Even assuming an unrealistically low value of $200 per gun, more than $60 million worth of historic collectibles has been reduced to worthless scrap." Yet there would probably be a louder outcry if Bill Clinton ordered the extermination of the rattlesnakes of Arkansas.

Meantime, one problem you won't hear much about in the mainstream media is that individual National Guardsmen tend to buy weapons like the AR-15 (at $1,500 apiece, hardly the weapon of choice of your average stickup artist), because they handle enough like M-16s to be of use in honing the marksmanship skills on which we regularly call in time of war.

"A number of us feel this is an issue of military readiness," Douglas R. Leland, a captain with the 158th Cavalry of the Maryland National Guard, told a reporter for Newhouse Newspapers, the same week that *Guns & Ammo* reported the wanton destruction of the fine, historic pieces of 1940s engineering.

"It's very practical for somebody to go out [to a civilian firing range] and work on his individual shooting skills," said Leland.

"Firing a weapon is a little different than riding a bicycle, and with all the other training requirements we have, people feel the need to utilize this other avenue to improve their efficiency."

The 410,000-strong peacetime National Guard, which upon call-up provides more than half the Army's immediately available combat forces, can't provide enough ammunition or target-range time for Guarsdmen to meet their annual marksmanship proficiency tests, say soldiers like Leland. They have to do that with weapons and ammo they buy themselves.

But surely Clinton's Crime Bill granted an exemption for Guardsmen and police officers?

Nope. So far as can be told, the ban applies to Guardsmen. And, "The truth is the so-called 'police exemption' for law enforcement does not cover officers' off-duty weapons, nor does it apply to retired officers," adds the Law Enforcement Alliance of America, which came out firm against the Crime Bill just before its temporary procedural defeat on Aug. 11, 1996. "It will adversely affect every department in the country where officers purchase their own weapons."

But what do the legitimate needs of police—or even of the National Guardsmen who defend America—matter in the face of the desperate need of the bed-wetting lawyers of Washington to scrunch up their faces and wish ever so hard for the bad bad guns to go away?

'As Long as a Man Has Another Cartridge or Hand Weapon to Use, He Does Not Yield'

Those who advocate abandoning the greatest safeguard of liberty—the right of the individual citizen to keep and bear military-style arms—aren't real strong on consistency.

Aiming to gradually erode the quality of arms we have "permission" to bear—back to the level of the muzzle-loading flintlock, if not further—they have been disingenuously mewing for 60 years that they have no objection to arms "for which there is a legitimate sporting use."

Of course, the Constitution says nothing about hunting or skeet shooting. Rather, it says we must be allowed to keep our arms—no "infringement" whatsoever, no tax, no registration, no "application for permit"—because the citizens constitute the militia, the most powerful armed force in any free state.

The gun-grabbers sneer that this is an out-of-date notion, that a bunch of farmers with deer rifles could hardly stand up to the 82nd Airborne ... let alone a Chinese invasion.

But the logical conclusion of that argument is surely that we should encourage law-abiding citizens to keep machine guns and rocket-launchers in the closet ... not ban AK-47s, with or without pistol grips and bayonet lugs.

The victim-disarmament extremists (those who would disarm law-abiding rape victims, but not their assailants, who ignore all such laws) ridicule this as the sheerest homicidal macho fantasy—no modern nation has ever thrown out a tyrant by the simple expedient of the common folk rising up with their personal rifles, nor does any civilized nation today allow its citizens to keep machine guns at home.

Wrong and wrong. Try placing a long-distance call to the American military governor of Vietnam or the Soviet military governor of Afghanistan, to ask them how easy it was to suppress a nation of armed peasants.

And as to the advisability of "allowing" citizen militias to keep modern military arms with them at home—yes, Virginia, the kind designed for no purpose but to kill large numbers of people—we turn to Virginia attorney and Second Amendment expert Stephen P. Halbrook, author of the 1998 book *Target Swit-*

zerland: Swiss Armed Neutrality in World War II, from Sarpedon Press.

Writing in the January 1998 edition of the excellent magazine *Chronicles*, Mr. Halbrook points out, "Since the origins of the Swiss Confederation in 1291, it has been the duty of every male Swiss citizen to be armed and to serve in the militia. Today, that arm is an 'assault rifle,' which is issued to every Swiss male and which must be kept in the home. During Germany's Third Reich (1933-1945), that arm was a bolt-action repeating rifle, which was highly effective in the hands of Switzerland's many sharpshooters.

"Americans of the wartime generation were familiar with the fact that brave and armed little Switzerland stood up to Hitler and made him blink. As a map of Europe in 1942 shows, the Nazis had swallowed up most of everything on the continent but this tiny speck that Hitler called 'a pimple on the face of Europe.' The Fuhrer boasted that he would be 'the butcher of the Swiss,' but the Wehrmacht was dissuaded by a fully armed populace in the Alpine terrain. ...

"The Swiss federal shooting festival, which remains the largest rifle competition in the world, was held in Luzern in June 1939. Hitler's takeover of Austria and Czechoslovakia was complete, both countries having been surrendered by tiny political elites who guaranteed that there would be no resistance. Swiss President Philipp Etter spoke at the festival, stressing that something far more serious than sport was the purpose of their activity. His comments demonstrated the connection between national defense and the armed citizen:

"'There is probably no other country that, like Switzerland, gives the soldier his weapon to keep in the home. The Swiss always has his rifle at hand. It belongs to the furnishings of his home. ... That corresponds to ancient Swiss tradition. As the citizen with his sword steps into the ring in the cantons which have the Landsgemeinde [government by public meeting], so the Swiss soldier lives in constant companionship with his rifle. He knows what that means. With this rifle, he is liable every hour, if the country calls, to defend his hearth, his home, his family, his birthplace. The weapon is to him a pledge and sign of honor and freedom. The Swiss does not part with his rifle."

Mr. Halbrook continues: "On September 1, 1939, Hitler launched World War II by attacking Poland. Within a day or two, Switzerland had about half a million militiamen mobilized out of a population of just over four million. General Henri Cuisan, commander in chief of the Swiss militia, responded with Operations Order No. 2:

"'At the border and between the border and army position, the border troops and advance guard persistently delay the advance of the enemy. The garrisons at the border and between the border and the works and positions making up the defensive front continue resistance up to the last cartridge, even if they find themselves completely alone.'

"This astonishing order was the opposite of the policies of the other European countries, which either surrendered to Hitler without a fight or surrendered after a brief resistance. For example, in April 1940, Denmark's king surrendered the country after a meeting with the Nazis and instructed his forces not to resist. Norway resisted, although 'unlike Switzerland' it had no armed populace and was ill-prepared for combat.

"In response to the invasions of small neutral countries, Switzerland issued its 'directions concerning the conduct of the soldiers not under arms in event of attack.' Intended as a warning to Germany, it was pasted on walls all over the country. It prescribed the reaction against surprise attack and against the fifth column as follows:

"'All soldiers and those with them are to attack with ruthlessness parachutists, airborne infantry and saboteurs. Where no officers and noncommissioned officers are present, each soldier acts under exertion of all powers of his own initiative.'

"This command for the individual to act on his own initiative was an ancient Swiss tradition, which reflected the political and military leadership's staunch confidence in the ordinary man. This command was possible, of course, only in a society where every man had his rifle at home.

"'Under no condition,' the order continued, 'would any surrender be forthcoming, and any pretense of a surrender must be ignored: If by radio, leaflets or other media any information is transmitted doubting the will of the Federal Council or of the Army High Command to resist an attacker, this information must be regarded as the lies of enemy propaganda. Our country will resist aggression with all means in its power and to the death.' ...

"France collapsed in June 1940 after only a few weeks of fighting. Paris was taken without a shot being fired. The Nazis promptly proclaimed the death penalty for possession of firearms in France and other occupied countries.

"In contrast, Cuisan recalled the high duty of the soldier to resist:

"'Everywhere, where the order is to hold, it is the duty of conscience of each fighter, even if he depends on himself alone, to fight at his assigned position. The riflemen, if overtaken or surrounded, fight in their position until no more ammunition exists. Then cold steel is next. ... The machine gunners, the cannoneers of heavy weapons, the artillerymen, if in the bunker or on the field, do not abandon or destroy their weapons, or allow the enemy to seize them. Then the crews fight further like riflemen. As long as a man has another cartridge or hand weapons to use, he does not yield. ...'"

Even old men and children were issued armbands, identifying them as Ortswehren (local defense), so that even if captured they could not be shot as plainclothes partisans under international law, after the time came for them to shoot any invader they saw.

Hitler never invaded Switzerland. Would you have?

Nor has any dictator—military or otherwise—ever attempted to rule the Swiss cantons by "executive order" ... like the one Bill Clinton haughtily signed to outlaw the import of AK-47 variants, which his own ATF had found to be in full compliance with current law.

"There was no holocaust on Swiss soil," Mr. Halbrook concludes. "Swiss Jews served in the militia side by side with their fellow citizens, and kept rifles in their homes just like everyone else. It is hard to believe that there could have been a holocaust had the Jews of Germany, Poland, and France had the same privilege."

Folks ask me: "I'm just one person. What can I do?"

Buy an M1-A, or an AR-10, at $1,100. These are better weapons than are currently standard issue in the U.S. Army. If you can't afford those, buy a surplus M-1 Garand at $500, or even a 1917 Enfield, at $250. For the women and teens, a surplus M-1 carbine apiece, at about $350. Six magazines for each rifle and a couple thousand rounds of surplus ammunition (in bulk) may set you back $900.

Now that licensed gun shops participate in national gun registration, you may want to buy privately at a gun show or via the classified ads in your local paper—until those "loopholes" are closed, too.

But only if you want America to remain a free country, of course.

Freedom is always optional.

But You Don't Mean the Unalienable
Right Is, Well, Unalienable? Do You?

Ernie Hancock and the boys at the Second Amendment Is
For Everyone (SAFE—see "Appendix II") down in Phoenix maintain a web page, presenting information about the right to bear
arms under the slogan: "No compromise; the only way to remain
armed & SAFE!"

A fellow I'll call R.B., a self-described hunter from northern
California, seems to have stumbled on the site recently and responded with the kind of spontaneous outpouring of spleen that
netsters call a "flame."

Here's a representative excerpt:

"This site is appalling. You think that some sick person with
a criminal record should be able to obtain a submachine gun with
no permits, *no* nothing and not even a waiting period to check
their record, take it into a park and blast the *shit* out of innocent
little children. You think that anyone should be able to obtain a
sniper rifle, hide a mile away from a populated urban area, and
pick off people who never did anything to them, totally undetec-
ted. You think people should be able to carry a shotgun through a
populated park. What the hell are you going to do with it? There
is no way law enforcement will let you shoot anything in an area
filled with little children, and anyone with *any* sense (which you
apparently aren't) wouldn't anyway!"

The gentleman goes on at some length, but you get the idea.

Mr. Hancock forwarded the post to me for comment. I responded:

I, for one, have had my mind changed. Let's go to Lexington
and Concord in Massachusetts and pull down those bronze stat-
ues of the Minutemen. Do you realize they took their highly inac-
curate rifles and muskets to the town green in broad daylight,
while frightened little children cowered behind the paper-thin walls

356

of the houses that *completely surrounded* that little town park, and discharged their weapons at government officials doing their assigned duty, in blatant violation of the law, putting every one of those tiny tots at risk?

And why? Because those officials wanted to collect a perfectly legal modest little tax of only 1 or 2 percent—less than one twentieth of what we now know to be normal and reasonable—for use in enforcing perfectly sensible gun control and anti-smuggling ordinances that were favored by a majority of the populace.

Heck, let's posthumously try, convict, and execute those wacko gun nuts in effigy. The perverts! Had a single one of them even submitted himself to a background check to test his mental stability?

Look at the facts: These people were home-schoolers. They didn't trust the government, and they were teaching their children the same dangerous doctrines. They frequented practitioners who prescribed opium and marijuana without any government license. No urine tests for them! They'd piled up huge arsenals of military-style weapons and ammunition, which were not needed for hunting and could serve no possible purpose but crime and mayhem. By every known definition, they were a sexist anti-government tax-resisting white-supremacist drug-addled street-gang militia, sporting their colors.

Now on the other hand, with today's current reasonable and sensible gun controls, sophisticated computer background checks, six-month waits to receive a federal license for a modern military weapon like an M-16, after the modern citizen is fingerprinted and so on, what has happened in terms of mass murders of school-children?

Whereas the crime was completely unheard of prior to 1934, today, it happens with an approximate frequency of ... um, no, wait a minute. That can't be right. ...

"The whole world should be like Canada," R.B. concludes. "You can only buy a hunting rifle, with thorough checking of your records. ... Only private detectives, police officers, licensed private security officers, and people known to be in danger can purchase a handgun of any kind."

Well, bless our mostly peaceful neighbors to the north. But doesn't that sound a lot like the "final status quo" that the gun-grabbers said they'd settle for in Australia ... right up to the time the current massive gun confiscations began?

And doesn't it also describe the balance between armed government agents and disarmed civilians that prevailed in Mao's China, in Stalin's USSR, in Hitler's Germany, and in Pol Pot's Cambodia?

Why doesn't the gentleman mention how well victim disarmament worked out for the peons in those far more prominent recent experiments?

By the way, if gun control works, then surely all those who are even presumptively unstable or criminally inclined must surely be disarmed by now, after 65 years and 20,000 overlapping gun-control laws.

So why is it R.B. the hunter would still allow cops to carry firearms in public parks, or drive around with shotguns or sniper rifles in their vehicles? So that they can "blast the shit out of innocent little children"? So they can "target shoot in an area filled with little kids"? Or is there some other reason he believes a law-abiding police officer might want or need to go armed, that he's not willing to tell us about?

The Bill of Rights Will Be
Violated With Impunity No Longer

Why is there a Second Amendment?

There is a Second Amendment because back in 1787 there was widespread and well-deserved suspicion of the proposed

Constitution for a new consolidated government being offered up to the 13 sovereign states. The states had enjoyed six years of successful independence under the Articles of Confederation, and many of their delegates to the convention in Philadelphia were under specific instruction to consider only modest reforms to the Confederation—not some rustic local version of that "cesspit of corruption" previously known as the British Houses of Parliament.

Today's government-approved history texts laugh off those ancient fears of a central government able to usurp any powers it desired, explaining that a strong central government was necessary to keep seaboard states from charging high tariffs on goods moving through their ports to the landlocked states—despite the fact the first landlocked state, Vermont, hadn't even been admitted to the union in 1787.

What today's schoolkids are not taught is that the Constitution proposed by Madison, Hamilton, and the Manifest Destiny crowd (after Jefferson was safely out of the way in Paris) was in deep trouble. Patrick Henry rose in the Virginia Ratifying convention on June 5, 1788, to protest, "The great objection to this Government is, that it does not leave us the means of defending our rights; or, of waging war against tyrants. ... Have we the means of resisting disciplined armies, when our only defense, the militia, is put into the hands of Congress? ... Of what service would militia be to you, when most probably you will not have a single musket in the State; for as arms are to be provided by Congress, they may or may not furnish them."

Such objections were answered by the promise to add a Bill of Rights, including the Second Amendment. The Constitution was ratified *only* because of the promise to add a Bill of Rights, including the Second Amendment. The Second Amendment was drafted to answer precisely such objections as Patrick Henry's— to guarantee that no act of Congress could ever infringe the right of individual Americans to keep and bear their own weapons, not to hunt deer or defend themselves against less organized banditti, but so that they would constitute a militia that would always outnumber any disciplined army that could be fielded by Congress, and would always retain the ability and the types of arms necessary to "wage war against tyrants."

The words are all there in the Constitutional ratification debates. You can look them up.

This is why Americans who know some history grow a tad irate when smug unread snivelliberals who would throw away the very liberties our fathers and uncles fought and died for argue, "The Second Amendment doesn't grant individuals the right to bear arms."

It's bad enough that these characters think plain English can be made to mean whatever they wish it to mean. What's worse is what they actually *want* it to mean—that we should all be the disarmed slaves of a thoroughly armed and dangerous government.

This is why thousands of American patriots, fed up with endless promises that the latest of the 20,000 laws that now infringe our right to bear arms will be "the last one, honest," are giving up on such temporizing gun-control go-alongs as the NRA and turning to outfits like the Libertarian Second Amendment Caucus, founded by Colorado novelist L. Neil Smith, author of *Henry Martyn*, *The Probability Broach*, and the current and highly recommended *Pallas*, just out in paperback from Tor Books.

Neil Smith drew a standing ovation as the dinner speaker at the 1995 Arizona Libertarian Convention for essentially reiterating the statement of principles of the LSAC, as first formulated by him at WeaponsCon I in Atlanta in November 1987:

"Every man, woman, and responsible child has a natural, fundamental, and inalienable human, individual, civil, and Constitutional right to obtain, own, and carry, openly or concealed, any weapon—handgun, shotgun, rifle, machine gun, anything—any time, anywhere, without asking anyone's permission."

From that starting point, the LSAC straightforwardly proposes that, "given the political power, (it) will:

1) repeal more than 20,000 victim-disarmament laws already on the books ... and abolish all agencies, at every level of government, responsible for enforcing them; 2) decriminalize concealed weapons carry and the act of self-defense; 3) pardon and provide restitution to anyone ever harmed or even inconvenienced by victim-disarmament laws; 4) arrest, convict, fine, and imprison any public official who ever enacted or enforced victim-disarmament laws; and 5) where a violation of individual or Constitutional rights has resulted in fatality, impose the maximum penalty on all such public officials."

The "general resolution" of the LSAC explains the fourth and fifth principles in more detail:

"Be it further resolved that any elected or appointed official who advocates, introduces, sponsors, or votes for such laws—or has done so in the past—be removed from office as the 14th Amendment provides and prosecuted under felony statutes for violating his or her oath to uphold and defend the Constitution. ..."

This—not the cowardly toe-dipping of a frightened and temporary Republican majority that might, perhaps, partially, roll back the "assault weapons ban"—is the new standard for real civil libertarians in this country, since no other civil right will long be safe if we ever lose the right to enforce the others at the point of a gun ... leveled in calm and serious warning at precisely the tyrants Patrick Henry most feared.

Why Can't You Be Reasonable?

I'm repeatedly asked, by doubtless well-meaning souls, why I have to be such a "purist" or "extremist." Why can't I endorse just a teensy-weensy little gun-safety education requirement before people are allowed to buy and own firearms?

The problem, of course, lies not with the gun-safety course—offer them and promote them to your heart's content—but with that word "requirement."

History shows all government license and permit programs start out as "just routine; sign here and we'll mail in the form; everyone gets approved."

Then, how many years will it be before they start yanking the permits or licenses of anyone who's ever been found guilty of spouse abuse, child abuse, or late return of a library book?

You laugh? The first two-thirds of the above list was enacted for handgun owners in 1997, retroactively, snagging thousands of men who years earlier had been charged after a minor domestic spat. Many of those men took their attorneys' well-intentioned advice: "Be a man; get your wife off the hook and put this behind you," pleading guilty to some reduced charge after both husband and wife were threatened with prosecution. (This despite the fact that retroactive laws are specifically banned by the Constitution—Article I, Section 9, paragraph 3.)

At that point, try going to court and suing the government for depriving you of your right to keep and bear arms. The courts will say—the courts *always* say—"Oh no, whether you did or did not at some point have such a right, you waived it when you voluntarily entered into this permitting scheme, acknowledging through your voluntary act of application that government had and has the power to grant, deny or withdraw this new privilege at any time."

This is how the federal government outlawed drugs. Under a 1902 Supreme Court decision that allows the federal government to regulate anything it taxes, doctors, pharmacists, and manufacturers were told starting in 1914 to sign up and get heroin and cocaine and marijuana licenses ... "just so we can check dosage and purity, you understand, nothing to be concerned about. The

362

licensing process would *never* be used to shut down the trade completely, under the guise of the taxing authority."

Can anyone doubt that the gun-grabbers drool over the prospect of demonizing gun possession as thoroughly as they have managed to demonize the possession of once-legal heroin?

Look at the provisions of the 1968 Gun Control Act. Intent on closing the barn door after the horses had run, the government said its goal was to stop the mail-order purchase of guns like the bolt-action WW II-surplus Italian Carcano with which, we were earnestly assured, Lee Harvey Oswald hit John Connally once and John Kennedy three times—once from the front—in less than five seconds, from 100 yards away, through the leafy trees of Dealey Plaza.

To accomplish this, the law now requires that virtually all weapons shipments be channeled through a government-licensed gun store (a holder of an FFL, or Federal Firearms License). The way it works these days is this. Say, for example, you want your gun repaired by an out-of-state gunsmith. You trundle your gun down to a local gun store, which mails it off to an FFL-holder in the receiving state. Everyone along the way copies down all the serial numbers on forms that the government can inspect at any time, duly noting where the gun went and came from, as well as collecting a $15 handling fee, at which point the recipient gun store finally calls your gunsmith to advise him to pick up the firearm, at which point the whole process then waits to be re-initiated in reverse.

Kind of like trying to buy a pound of rice at a Soviet department store.

When hunters and gun collectors and target shooters—remember my old friend Red Hafter?—objected to this rigmarole back in '68, they were told not to worry, virtually any non-felon would be allowed to apply for and receive an FFL.

And that turned out to be true ... at first. Plenty of guys acquired FFLs even though they only bought or sold a few guns out of their basement workshops, just for the convenience of the mailing privilege, knowing that they could pick up the phone and order a rare gun through the mail if they saw it show up in a catalog or auction listing without all the cumbersome middlemen.

Of course, they were required to keep their own records of serial numbers, which the ATF was empowered to come inspect at any time. But they figured, "What the heck, I'm a law-abiding citizen, and this is the government of the U.S. of A. If this is the way they say it has to be to fight crime, I'm willing to compromise and accept a little inconvenience."

Fast forward 25 years. In the mid-1990s, the ATF launches a campaign to take away FFLs from "those who are not legitimate gun dealers." The press eagerly runs unanswered the ATF propaganda that many current FFL holders had acquired those licenses "under false pretenses," that they "were not full-time gun dealers at all."

Why, "some of these people sell guns out of their basements, trailer homes, or car trunks!" the media shrieked in a tone of investigative outrage ... this from reporters who would never admit to any race or class prejudice, of course.

It was simply too great a burden to try and regulate such a large number of license holders, the ATF said, implying that it was through such licensed but now somehow "illegitimate" dealers that guns were slipping through to street gangs and other criminals (as though anyone intent on selling stolen guns to street gangs would bother registering himself with the federal government).

So, a purposeful campaign was launched to jack up the annual FFL fee and to require FFL holders to prove they had a permanent place of business, a fixed address, at which the main activity was "commercial gun store." By the end of 1997, the federals had quickly succeeded in trimming the number of American FFL holders by two-thirds.

Remember, the government initially promised that any non-felon who applied for such a license would get one. Also, the ATF is a division of the Treasury Department—their only congressional mandate (itself a violation of the Second Amendment, needless to say) is to collect taxes and fees from folks who manufacture and deal in machine guns and the like.

When was the last time you heard of a revenue agency complaining that too many people were paying their fees? Also, now that the ATF's "regulatory burden" has been reduced by two-thirds (soon to become 95 percent), has their budget been trimmed by two-thirds? Ha!

In Australia, this same trend has now proceeded to the point where gun stores are losing their licenses if they cannot demonstrate they have *two* on-premises alarm systems directly wired to police headquarters, *and* that they have poured a two-foot-thick solid concrete roof or ceiling above their shops to prevent hypothetical burglars from tunneling down from above to steal their wares.

Needless to say, medium-sized towns are lucky to have one gun store still in business (shotguns and bolt-actions only—the modern semi-autos like the 1938 M-1 Garand are long gone), while many smaller towns no longer have any, at all. ...

Which is just the way the gun-grabbers want it, of course. Step-by-step prohibition masquerading as modest sensible regulation. And then they ask us why we have to be so extreme, how we can possibly object to just a little *more* modest sensible regulation?

(Gee, what's wrong, didn't the gun laws you passed in 1934, or in 1968, or in 1986, or in 1994 *work?*)

Even semi-automatic *shotguns* like my 1905 Browning are now banned in Australia. Owners had to turn them in and watch them being crushed into scrap. (Imagine how you would feel if the government said you could keep a few paperbacks, but ordered you to turn in all your hardcover books and watch them being burned, even if they compensated you at the original cover price.)

And all because these pitiful trusting souls started out figuring, "Hey, I want to be law-abiding. I want to demonstrate I have no objections to meeting a few *reasonable* requirements for gun ownership. I don't want to be one of those people the newspaper editorials keep calling extremists because they won't tolerate the twenty-thousand-and-first *reasonable* piece of gun-control legislation. After all, no right is *absolute*. I don't want to look like the kind of *extremist* who argues teenage girls should be able to buy belt-fed machine guns over the counter at Home Depot without filling out any forms or showing any damned government-issued ID. ..."

Try to point out how these screws are gradually tightened and you'll be ridiculed by the same newspapers and TV commentators as some kind of "extremist nut" who's unwilling to accept even modest reasonable regulations and safeguards, which after all are worth trying if they save the life of even a single child.

Medical malpractice and the known adverse effects of prescription medicines kill thousands of children every year. Do we ban doctors? Cars kill thousands of kids a year, but no one talks about banning cars.

Ah, but cars have a "legitimate purpose" other than killing people, we're assured, while guns are designed "to do nothing but kill people."

Explaining the pleasure of collecting excellent-condition examples of the astonishing engineering feats that are the firearms of the 19th and early 20th centuries—each with a story to tell, many having miraculously survived actual combat—to the gun-hater would be like trying to explain the pleasure of accumulating a complete set of autographed first editions of your favorite author ... to an illiterate savage, incapable of viewing their pages as anything but toilet paper or kindling.

But the fact is, in 98 percent of the civilian cases where a gun proves "useful," it accomplishes its purpose without being fired. The felon surrenders to the armed policeman; the would-be rapist or robber beats a hasty retreat from the sight of the cocked weapon. Those weapons have indeed been used as intended, without even being fired, let along killing anyone.

But let's go ahead and acknowledge, so as not to seem evasive, that the end purpose of the design of the firearm is to kill what it's aimed at—sometimes even a human being.

So what? Don't some people need killing? Would you condemn our fathers and grandfathers for taking their M-1 Garands and BARs and .50-caliber M2 machine guns and setting forth to kill just as many Japanese and Germans as they could, from 1942 to 1945?

"Oh, that's different. They were doing the will of the government," we'll be told.

But George Washington and young Jim Madison weren't serving their government in 1776 and 1777. They were *killing* agents of their duly empowered government, just as the Jews killed uniformed police officers and soldiers in the Warsaw ghetto in 1943. Shall we condemn them, as well, for acquiring and using guns?

"Other times, other places!" the exasperated statists will stomp. This is America, a free country. No government troops would ever set fire to and level with tanks a residential structure in *this* country, firing indiscriminately with automatic machine pistols into a house of worship full of innocent women and children. The massacre at Wounded Knee? An overzealous officer. The MOVE fire-bombing by police in Philadelphia? A clumsy miscalculation. The murder of Vicki and Sammy Weaver at Ruby Ridge, Idaho? Racist anti-government nuts living with someone who had been ordered to appear in court for a non-violent "firearms violation." The Waco massacre? Must have been some kind of suicide cult; Ephrem Zimbalist and Robert Stack would never have done *that*.

Yes, guns kill people. Sometimes, to preserve our freedom, some people need to be killed. Occasionally, these are freelance bandits. But most often, down through the corridors of history, they have turned out to be uniformed agents of a tyrannical central government. That is precisely why the Second Amendment guarantees us that, in America, the government and its agents must *never* be allowed to outgun the common people ... while it says not a word about "legitimate sporting use."

The Founders could not predict precisely when such a time would come again. But they knew for sure it *would* come again. Thus they guaranteed in the strongest terms each citizen his private arms, so that—whenever their treason against our God-given rights leaves us no other choice—we, or our children, or our grandchildren shall retain the ability to shoot government agents through the head, and kill them.

That is what firearms are for. And that is why no people can be without them, and long remain free.

Treason in the Congress

Unless they changed the procedure without telling me, sometime in January 1997 every current member of the United States Congress took an oath, before God and the People, to protect and defend the Constitution of the United States, which still contains the Second Article of Amendment, to wit: "A well-regulated militia, being necessary to the security of a free State, the right of the people to keep and bear Arms, shall not be infringed."

Within hours of swearing that most sacred of oaths, on Jan. 7, 1997, Mr. Hastings of Florida introduced H.R. 186, "to provide

368

for the mandatory registration of handguns."

Then, on Jan. 21, the honorable delegates really got rolling, with Mr. Gutierrez (for himself, Mr. Berman, Mr. McDermott, Mr. Filner, Mr. Wynn, Mr. Miller, Mr. Stark, Mr. Sabo, Mr. Nadler, Mr. Yates, Ms. Woolsey, Mr. Flake, Mr. Abercrombie, Mr. Dellums, Ms. McKinney, Mr. Serrano, Ms. Norton, Ms. Pelosi, and Mr. Engel) introducing H.R. 476, "A BILL To prohibit the possession or transfer of non-sporting handguns."

Across the hall in the Senate, Mr. Moynihan was introducing, also on Jan. 21, S.136, "A BILL To amend chapter 44 of title 18, United States Code, to prohibit the manufacture, transfer, or importation of .25 caliber and .32 caliber and 9 millimeter ammunition."

Always ready with a handy euphemism, the senator advises, "This Act may be cited as the 'Violent Crime Reduction Act of 1997.'"

Busy as a beaver, Mr. Moynihan also introduced, on that same date, S.133, "A BILL To amend the Internal Revenue Code of 1986 to increase the tax on handgun ammunition, to impose the special occupational tax and registration requirements on importers and manufacturers of handgun ammunition, and for other purposes."

Said measure would define as "Articles taxable at 10,000 percent, any jacketed, hollow-point projectile which may be used in a handgun and the jacket of which is designed to produce, upon impact, evenly spaced sharp or barb-like projections that extend beyond the diameter of the unfired projectile."

That is to say, precisely the type of ammunition most states *require* hunters to use and police would continue to be free to use against the citizenry. A mere $1,500 tax on a $15 box of bullets? No, they're not *banning* hunting and self-defense ammunition. ...

• • •

Back in the House, on Feb. 4, 1997, Mr. Manton introduced H.R. 538, "A BILL To require explosive materials to contain taggants to enable law-enforcement authorities to trace the source of the explosive material, whether before or after detonation."

This law would ban the import of surplus military ammunition—since the stuff doesn't contain taggants, of course—as well as civilian possession, use, sale, or disposal of surplus *American* ammunition, though the Department of Defense is conveniently exempted.

Been stockpiling 30.06 and .308 against the day when they might ban further sales of ammo? Gotcha!

Shortly thereafter, on Feb. 13, to express their immense happiness with the way the Bureau of Alcohol, Tobacco and Firearms handled things at Ruby Ridge and at Waco, Mr. Owens (for himself, Mr. Schumer, and Mr. Hastings of Florida) introduced H.R. 788, "A BILL To expand the powers of the Secretary of the Treasury and the Bureau of Alcohol, Tobacco and Firearms to regulate the manufacture, distribution, and sale of firearms and ammunition ..." which the sponsors obligingly advise us "may be cited as the 'Firearms Safety and Violence Prevention Act of 1997.'"

This law would ban anyone new from entering into the firearms business, under Title II Section 201(g): "Stockpiling—It shall be unlawful for any person to manufacture, purchase, or import a firearm product, after the date a regulation is prescribed under this Act with respect to the product and before the date the regulation takes effect, at a rate that is significantly greater than the rate at which the person manufactured, purchased, or imported the product during a base period (prescribed by the Secretary in regulations) ending before the date the regulation is so prescribed."

Look carefully. In order to circumvent the supposedly onerous (though actually only pro forma) necessity that proposed regu-

370

lations be subjected to public comment before going into effect, here is a fine law that would allow proposed regulations to go into effect not when they go into effect, but when they are *proposed*, thus preventing anyone from stocking up on anything that's *about* to be banned.

And what if the ATF just proposed a ban on all firearms, and never got around to issuing any final decision on that proposal? During the endless interim between proposal and "enactment" (since there would no longer be any need to actually "enact" a regulation, since all regulations would go into effect the day they're proposed), what do you suppose would then happen as our existing firearms manufacturers, dealers, and importers either died off or retired? I can't imagine, can you?

But the good works of Feb. 13 weren't over. Oh no. Also on that date, Mr. Owens introduced H.R. 787, "A BILL To prohibit the manufacture, importation, exportation, sale, purchase, transfer, receipt, possession, or transportation of handguns and handgun ammunition, with certain exceptions," which the good congressman suggests "may be cited as the 'Public Health and Safety Act of 1997.'"

Arlynn Afton of the group Families of Michigan for Concealed Carry (see "Appendix II"), which compiled this list of offenses against God and man, says of this one:

"This bill is similar to H.R. 3018, which was introduced by Yates in March of 1996, but this one goes beyond prohibiting the manufacture, importation, sale, purchase, transfer, receipt, and transportation of handguns (except by law enforcement and military, of course) to *banning possession of handguns and ammunition* ... and also gives the Secretary of the Treasury the power to control *use* of the handgun in the only allowable places—government-licensed pistol clubs!"

• • •

371

Article I, Section 6, of the Constitution is very specific: "The senators and representatives ... shall in all cases, except treason, felony and breach of the peace, be privileged from arrest during their attendance at the session of their respective houses ... and for any speech or debate in either house, they shall not be questioned in any other place."

When it comes to the violation of their oaths to protect and defend the Constitution, I fear the gentlemen must answer to a higher authority than can be easily summoned on this Earth.

But it is indeed a felony, of their own enactment, to deprive American citizens of their civil rights under color of law, which would surely be the case if any freeman were debarred the use of arms as a result of the passage of any of these measures.

(Remember that the Fourteenth Amendment, invoked for such a wide range of federal interventions these days, was ratified specifically to prevent local authorities in the South from depriving black Civil War veterans of their arms, including their pistols, without possession of which it was well understood they could never prevail in their efforts to register and vote.)

Still, what about now? Even prior to passage, have the gentlemen already committed any trespass for which they remain subject to arrest, and "questioning in any other place," under the stipulations of Article I, Section 6?

We are left with only one option, though I submit it would serve very well, indeed.

In their proposals listed above, by their blatant, willful, and knowing abrogation of the very terms under which this Constitution was ratified, I submit that the gentlemen who have affixed their names as sponsors of the above measures have committed treason.

And it is on that charge that a free people, at imminent and serious risk of having their God-given right to keep and bear arms infringed beyond what is sufferable (the very right that, once lost, will prevent the people from further defending any other of their supposed remaining rights) should see these men indicted, tried, and—only if convicted by a randomly selected jury of their peers—punished as provided by law.

If this is not done, and if these mincing, posturing, duplicitous scalawags persist in this pursuit, I fear that in a land of men and women grown used to their freedoms, such a lengthening train of abuses and usurpations can have only one eventual result, which is war.

Sean Gabb For President

Sean Gabb, one of Britain's few firearms rights activists (see "Appendix II"), wrote from London in July 1996 that he'd been approached by Simon Wells, a producer for the appropriately named (as it turns out) Chameleon Television in Leeds, about appearing for five minutes on a program about gun control.

"A similar piece would be filmed with a Mr. Bernstein of an anti-gun group. Both pieces would then be shown on the 17th of July and be followed by a studio debate," Mr. Gabb reports.

"Rather looking forward to this, I wrote a draft script and faxed it off to Mr. Wells. He went quiet for a few days, and then came back to me to cancel my appearance."

What was it that Mr. Gabb proposed to say in only five minutes that apparently can't be allowed even on an independent TV station in Leeds?

This:

"Let me begin by saying that I believe in the right of adults to be able to walk into a gun shop and, without showing any licence or proof of identity, buy as many guns and as much ammunition as they can afford. I also believe that adults should be free to keep guns at home and carry them about in public, and use them in defence of their life, liberty and property.

"I am not saying this because I am a gun owner: I am not nor ever have been. I say it because I believe that the right to self-defence is a fundamental human right, comparable to freedom of speech and association. Anyone who is denied this right—to keep and bear arms—is to some extent enslaved. That person has lost control over his life. He is dependent on the State for protection.

"Of course, most people watching me will say that I am mad. Do I want a society where every criminal has a gun, and where every domestic argument ends in a gun battle?

"The short answer is no. The longer answer is to say that more guns do not inevitably mean more killings. ... Great Britain had no gun controls before 1920, and very low rates of armed crime. Today, Switzerland has few controls, and little armed crime. Those parts of the U.S. where guns are most common are generally the least dangerous. ...

"Focusing on professional crime, gun control is plainly a waste of effort. Criminals will always get hold of guns if they want them. At most, it needs a knowledge of the right pubs to visit. All control really does it to disarm the honest public, and let the armed criminals roam through them like a fox through chickens. ...

"But let us move away from armed burglars and rapists and the occasional lone psychopath. We need guns to protect us from the State. Far from protecting us, the State is the main aggressor. A low estimate puts the number of civilians murdered by states this century at 56 million—and millions of these were children. In all cases, genocide was preceded by gun control. How far would the Holocaust have got if the Jews in Nazi Germany had been able to shoot back? How about the Armenians? The Kulaks? The Chinese bourgeoisie? The Bosnians? In all previous societies, guns and freedom have gone together. I doubt if our society is any different.

"Laugh at me. Call me mad. Call me evil. But just remember

me when your loved ones are being raped, or mugged, or dragged off never to be seen again—and you, as an obedient, disarmed little citizen, can do nothing about it."

Don't feel so bad, Sean. I don't think they would have aired it on American TV, either.

Schoolyard Shootings:
Will Gun Locks Prevent Them?

On May 21, 1998, all indications are that a pencil-necked 15-year-old misfit named Kipland Kinkel, younger child (and the only one still living at home) of well-to-do government school-teacher parents, took a .22-caliber rifle, shot his mother and father to death in their home, and then headed down to the school cafeteria to wound 22 of his schoolmates, while killing two more.

What were all the kids in the mill town of Springfield, Ore., doing in the school cafeteria so early that morning? Being taught to expect a government dole and subsidy even for breakfast, it now appears.

At any rate, it was another shooting in the "gun-free zones" that the "send-a-message" liberals have made of our mandatory youth propaganda camps—oops, "public schools." So, needless to say, the Usual Suspects were shortly heard from.

Within days Wayne LaPierre of the National Rifle Association—America's largest gun-control outfit—showed up on Katie Couric's smugly hoplophobic NBC "Today" show, "debating" all-guns-to-the-state Congressman Charles Schumer on a typically heads-they-win-tales-we-lose question: whether it is federal or only local authorities who should "mandate" gun locks.

Mr. LaPierre never asked why they were debating locks for handguns, when all the recent schoolyard shootings were done

375

with long guns.

Since few to none of the recent school killings have been accomplished with handguns (Master Kinkel, like his recent predecessors in Arkansas, carried a handgun for backup, but preferred to do most of his shooting with his more accurate rifle—precisely the type of "sporting weapon" that the gun-grabbers tell us is safer to have around), this opportunistic political carrion-feeding on the young dead to promote bad laws already in the hopper makes about as much sense as fighting highway fatalities by requiring more life preservers on pleasure boats.

Nor did Mr. LaPierre ever call the gun-banner's biggest bluff. He never asked Schumer, "So you're saying gun locks are enough? If you get this law passed you'll never propose another gun control law? This isn't just one more incremental step toward total prohibition?"

After all, once the victim-disarmament gang effectively outlawed machine guns for most Americans, they didn't hesitate to ridicule the real reason we own guns—"a safeguard against tyranny," in the words of Hubert Humphrey—by simpering, "Oh, you and your friends think you can stop the 82nd Airborne with your deer rifles?"

Similarly, once every handgun in the country is required to be double-padlocked inside a time-locked safe, do we think they'll hesitate to argue, "Since you can no longer get the gun out on short notice, it's no good to defend you against a rapist, so how can you argue you still need it at all?"

Advice From the Germans

Highest soprano among the braying state-power bedwetters, as usual, was West Virginia's daily pink sheet, the *Charleston*

Gazette. On May 22, the coaldust daily ululated: "The slaughter of schoolchildren is a price America pays for being a gun-polluted society. ... The recent mass shooting at an Oregon school was the latest in a never-ending string of horrors. This is what happens in a society saturated with 200 million guns. Any child can obtain a weapon and use it in a moment of childish rage. This is what happens in a society where the powerful 'right to bear arms' lobby cows politicians, making them afraid to take any steps to protect people from the gun danger. How long will America endure this madness?"

The fanatical cries to disarm the victims even went international, with Germany's newspaper *Bild* pontificating on May 25 (in the quaintly spastic Associated Press translation): "A 15-year-old murdered his parents in Oregon, shot and killed two schoolmates and wounded 22 others. Again the affected will stand around the coffins, beseech God and bemoan the shameful crime. Probably they will barbarically punish the 15-year-old barbarian. Thereafter they will claim: continuous shooting in television—only a game. The unscrupulous weapons trade—a successful business. And the instructions to build bombs in the Internet had nothing to do with the bloody reality. Really not? High Noon in school. Disarm finally!! Also in television and the weapons closets at home. It's not a pistol that makes a man. Playing with violence is instructions on how to kill."

We don't really have to respond to our Teutonic critics, do we? Their Jewish and Gypsy minorities took their advice to "Disarm finally!!" between 1928 and 1938—gun registration leading to confiscation, just as Mr. Schumer and Mr. LaPierre's backstabbing NRA plan for us here, and is now underway again in both England and France.

They claim European murder rates are lower than ours? Between 1928 and 1945, the German state murdered at least 8 million unarmed civilians from their own and the captured territories (not counting the deaths of men in uniform, though we probably should). Including famines created on purpose for political reasons, Joe Stalin and his Communists during the same years murdered civilians numbering at least 20 million. Even assuming not one single murder has occurred in Europe since 1945—ignoring Bosnia and all the rest—that averages out to 400,000 murders per year since 1928, caused by the citizenry being disarmed, while their governments stayed armed—exactly what's planned for us here.

Or have the brave state socialists like Mr. Schumer or Ms. Feinstein called for disarming the DEA, the ATF, and the FBI—America's SS—while I wasn't listening?

The Government Dispensary

Any death of a child is a tragedy. But if someone has to be callous enough to inject a few facts into this debate, let's start here: Our murder rates are way below the European rate reported above, not in spite of, but *because* we are a well-armed nation, against which the government (up until the past decade, when they started testing the waters with Waco and Ruby Ridge) never dared attempt such atrocities.

(We'll have more now, of course, after federal judge Edward Lodge on May 14, 1998—one week prior to the Kinkel rampage—dismissed all charges against FBI sniper Lon Horiuchi, ruling he was "just doing his job" back in 1992 when he shot away the lower jaw and carotid artery of an Idaho woman named Vicki Weaver, wanted for no crime, whom he found standing in the kitchen doorway of her home, armed with a baby. The fact that Gunner Horiuchi will not even face a manslaughter trial was by far the most important gun-crime-related story of May 1998—yet how much play did it receive in your local newspaper or television station?)

Actually, some excellent commentary moved on the wires in the week following the Springfield high-school-cafeteria shooting, though precious little of this common sense made it through the nation's anti-gun editorial filters.

While "What caused this?" tends to be a rhetorical question, with the inquirer standing ready to answer "guns," isn't it interesting that the day before young Kip Kinkel had his bad day in Springfield, two teens were arrested in Clearfield, Penn., for the 10-days-past murder of 15-year-old Kimberly Jo Dotts, who was dragged into the woods by her teenage friends with a rope around her neck when she threatened to "snitch" about their plans to run away to Florida. There, they hanged young Kimberly Jo by her neck from a tree, before bashing her head in with a rock.

How do the gun-grabbers explain the role of the easy availability of guns in causing *that* schoolgirl murder, in which no firearms were involved? Easy. They just ignore it. In my newspaper, the arrests in Kimberly Jo's death were buried on page 12, on the same day the Kip Kinkel story broke on page one, with photos. And since it didn't fit the anti-gun agenda, Kimberly Jo's horrendous murder was thereafter ignored—even as we heard day after day the anti-gun drum-beating follow-ups about Kip Kinkel's rampage.

But even in the Oregon case, there is a far more obvious suspect than guns, as Maureen Sielaff was quick to detail in the web's *Vigo Examiner* (see "Appendix II"):

"Kip Kinkel had been attending anger-control classes and was taking a prescription drug called Prozac," Ms. Sielaff reported early the next week. "Eli Lilly of Indianapolis, Indiana, was recently sued over the homicidal tendencies this drug is alleged to induce in patients.

"Prozac is commonly given to youth as a treatment for depression. In the book *Prozac and other Psychiatric Drugs*, by Lewis A. Opler, M.D., the following side effects are listed for Prozac: apathy; hallucinations; hostility; irrational ideas; paranoid reactions, antisocial behavior; hysteria; and suicidal thoughts."

The drug's form PV 2472 DPP, prepared by Dista Products Company (a division of Eli Lilly) and last revised on June 12, 1997—the paperwork included in each package of Prozac—lists such other "frequent" symptoms as "chills, hemorrhage and hypertension of the cardiovascular system, nausea and vomiting, agitation, amnesia, confusion, emotional liability, sleep disorder, ear pain, taste perversion, and tinnitus."

If this kid gets a good lawyer, look for a "Prozac defense." And if that happens, my cheery thought for the day is that young Kipland could be looking at as little as three-to-seven on the psychiatric farm.

"Though many are demanding stricter gun control laws as a solution to this sudden increase in homicidal shootings," Ms. Sielaff continues, "these events do not appear to correlate to a sudden increase in firearm ownership. But when the percentage of these killers that are on Prozac is compared to the percentage of the general public on Prozac, a very disturbing pattern emerges. ..."

Meantime, as the religious zealots whoop it up, demonizing every recreational drug of choice but their own, just as fast as they do guns, does anyone really know how many of our schoolchildren (particularly boys) are now doped up with Prozac and Ritalin, relatively new drugs whose long-term psychiatric effects are only now beginning to be discovered?

If you shut up enough animals in a small enough cage, they will eventually start killing one another. Do the mass dopings of kids like Kip Kinkel subdue their "escape" response, and if so are the effects actually worse when they finally break through? Is anyone even tracking the *growth rate* of these mass drug-dosings of our innocent young men by their government wardens? And doesn't this mean our schools' "zero tolerance" drug policies really only mean zero tolerance for *competing* drug pushers?

The Crime Shortage

On May 28, 1998, I published across the top of the *Las Vegas Review-Journal* Op-ed page a piece by James K. Glassman of the American Enterprise Institute, pointing out that the *New York Times* ran the story of the Springfield, Ore., shootings "for three straight days on the front page," while "President Clinton used his Saturday radio address to decry the 'changing culture that desensitizes our children to violence.'"

The only problem is, according to Mr. Glassman, "The truth about violence in America is that it is falling, not rising. From 1993 to 1996, the number of murders fell 20 percent, and just four days before the Oregon shootings, the FBI announced preliminary figures for 1997 that found both murders and robbery down another 9 percent and overall crime off for the sixth straight year. Murders in New York City fell a stunning 22 percent in 1997; in Los Angeles, 20 percent. ...

"You have to wonder about the claims of pop psychologists and of the president himself when he says, as he did Saturday, that the rising tide of murders and mayhem on TV, in movies and on video games is turning kids into killers. *U.S. News* noted that 'juvenile murder arrests declined ... 14 percent from 1994 to 1995 and another 14 percent from 1995 to 1996.'"

But if violence is falling, why do these rare schoolyard incidents get so much media play?

"One answer may be a crime shortage," Mr. Glassman figures. "At a Harvard symposium recently, one panelist pointed out that local TV news shows have to import violent footage now that local criminals aren't turning out enough product (there were only 43 murders in Boston last year, the fewest since 1961). ...

"So, what's the meaning of the schoolhouse slayings? Frankly, not much. The meaning of the hysteria over them ... now, that's worth looking into."

Writing for the Knight Ridder/Tribune News Service a few days later, Vincent Schiraldi, director of the Justice Policy Institute in Washington, D.C., concurred:

"I have now been on television news following every one of the recent school killings answering basically the same question: 'How do you explain the trend of shootings by kids in rural schools?' My answer is always the same: I cannot explain it, because no such trend exists. ...

"In 1992, 55 killings occurred in America's schools—a remarkably small number. By 1997, that number dropped by more than half, to 25. By contrast, 88 people were killed by lightning in 1997.

"The Los Angeles County School System, with about 600,000 students in it, has not had a homicide since 1995. The District of Columbia, with about 600,000 citizens, has had about 600 homicides since that time."

That's not D.C. *school* homicides, you understand. Mr. Glassman's point is that the 600,000 *adults* in the District of Columbia are murdering each other at a rate of one-per-thousand every three years, whereas the 600,000 schoolchildren of the much larger city of Los Angeles are as peaceful as Hindus, despite the renowned presence of the Crips and the Bloods. *What* epidemic of school violence?

"Overall, between 1994 and 1996, there was a 30 percent drop in juvenile homicides in America. Ninety kids were arrested in rural communities for the crime of homicide in 1996, compared to 1,800 in cities. ...

"Between 1992 and 1996, the homicide rate in America dropped by 20 percent. But the number of homicides reported on network news increased by 721 percent. ... Distorted coverage of ... these events has violated recently victimized communities, frightened parents, fomented reactionary legislation and misinformed the public. Worst of all, it may be creating an environment where other troubled youths are copy-catting their well-publicized peers."

Hand Out More Guns

The NRA's standard cry, "Why don't we enforce the laws already on the books?" can get to sound pretty lame through repetition. But remember my interview with Marion Hammer of Florida (since elected to head the NRA in Washington) about one of the tourist murders in Florida five years back, in which she pointed out that the culprit—a young woman—had been arrested for carrying a concealed weapon without a license, robbing a store with a firearm in her possession, and assaulting the officer who was attempting to apprehend her—only a few days before. The authorities let her out due to a lack of jail space (too many victimless dope smokers tying up the cells, presumably).

Similarly, Kip Kinkel was arrested and booked for storing a stolen gun at school the day before his murder rampage ... but then promptly released back into his helpless parents' custody. So, it turns out the NRA's recurrent cry has some specific application: Why push for more gun laws when the cops aren't able to enforce the 20,000 gun laws already on the books? To outlaw everything has the same effect as to legalize everything, except that the cops are thus empowered to harass anyone, any time they want.

The Florida tourist-shooting epidemic is also relevant in another way. Once the airport rental lots started removing their big fluorescent rent-a-car stickers, Florida's "tourist-murder crime wave" disappeared virtually overnight. Similarly, one of the last places a criminal knows he can find unarmed victims in an increasingly well-armed and peaceful America today ... is in the "gun-free school zones" in which the snivelliberals have locked up our children.

In fact, it turns out that if a solution to schoolyard violence is needed, experts with some mighty solid credentials propose that the solution is not to ban guns, but to hand out more.

On June 1, 1998, I published in the *Review-Journal* an excellent piece initially prepared for the *Los Angeles Times* by John R. Lott, Jr., a fellow at University of Chicago School of Law, and author of *More Guns, Less Crime* (University of Chicago Press, 1998), under the headline, "To stop mass shootings, hand out more guns: When Israel armed teachers, the school shootings ended."

In that essay, Professor Lott wrote: "What might appear to be the most obvious policy may actually cost lives. When gun-control laws are passed, it is law-abiding citizens, not would-be criminals, who adhere to them. Police officers or armed guards cannot be stationed everywhere, so gun-control laws risk creating situations in which the good guys cannot defend themselves.

"Other countries have followed a different solution. Twenty or so years ago in Israel, there were many instances of terrorists pulling out machine guns and firing away at civilians in public. However, with expanded concealed-handgun use by Israeli citizens, terrorists soon found ordinary people pulling pistols on them. Suffice it to say, terrorists in Israel no longer engage in such public shootings.

"The one recent shooting of schoolchildren in the Middle East further illustrates these points. On March 13, 1997, seven Israeli girls were shot to death by a Jordanian soldier while they visited

Jordan's so-called Island of Peace. The *Los Angeles Times* reported that the Israelis had 'complied with Jordanian requests to leave their weapons behind when they entered the border enclave. Otherwise, they might have been able to stop the shooting, several parents said.'

"Hardly mentioned in the massive news coverage of the school-related shootings during the past year is how they ended. Two of the four shootings were stopped by a citizen displaying a gun. In the October 1997 shooting spree at a high school in Pearl, Miss., which left two students dead, an assistant principal retrieved a gun from his car and physically immobilized the shooter while waiting for the police."

(That assistant principal had, fortunately for all, violated federal law by bringing that firearm onto campus, even though he left it in the glove compartment of his car.)

"More recently," Professor Lott continues, "the school-related shooting in Edinboro, Penn., which left one teacher dead, was stopped only after a bystander pointed a shotgun at the shooter when he started to reload his gun. The police did not arrive for another 10 minutes. Who knows how many lives were saved by these prompt responses?"

Dr. Lott's exhaustive studies of multiple-victim public shootings in the United States from 1977 to 1995 reveal that "only one policy was found to reduce deaths and injuries from these shootings: allowing law-abiding citizens to carry concealed handguns.

"The effect of 'shall-issue' concealed handgun laws, which give adults the right to carry concealed handguns if they do not have a criminal record or a history of significant mental illness, was dramatic. Thirty-one states now have such laws. When states passed them during the 19 years we studied, the number of multiple-victim public shootings declined by 84 percent. Deaths from these shootings plummeted on average by 90 percent, injuries by

82 percent. ...

"Unfortunately, much of the public policy debate is driven by lopsided coverage of gun use. Horrific events like the Colin Ferguson shooting receive massive news coverage, as they should, but the 2.5 million times each year that people use guns defensively—including cases in which public shootings are stopped before they happen—are ignored. ... Without permitting law-abiding citizens the right to carry guns, we risk leaving victims as sitting ducks."

Sitting ducks like Colin Ferguson's victims on the Long Island Railroad, that is—all forbidden by New York law to carry weapons for their own self-defense.

The gun-grabbers will respond, "A resident of the house is more likely to be injured than an intruder." But only if they cleverly include suicides in their statistics, of course ... as well as gun owners injured with an *intruder's* gun. (It's true—all the statisticians ask is whether the injured party was a gun owner, not which gun injured him.) Besides, you can scare away 100 intruders without ever wounding one, just by showing (or audibly cocking) your weapon. Which makes the minuscule "injury" statistics a red herring.

Crediting Eddie Eagle

All these statistics can get a little boggling, I know. So let's take a specific example. The *Elko Daily Free Press* reports that on April 7, 1998, an unnamed 15-year-old boy in that northern Nevada community tried to stop an intruder from beating his mother, but found he was not strong enough to do so. The lad therefore raced into his mother's bedroom, retrieved a .22 semi-automatic handgun, loaded several rounds into the magazine, inserted the magazine into the weapon, returned, and fired at the assailant three times, hitting him twice and killing him.

"He is credited with saving the life of his mother, and possibly the 3-year-old child also present," the newspaper reports. "The mother suffered a broken cheekbone, a broken nose, several bruises on her body, and a cut to her forehead from the attack."

"It seems to me to be a fairly clear-cut case of self-defense," said D.A. Gary Woodbury, in which case "an inquest is not warranted."

If Congressman Charles Schumer's proposed federal gun-lock bill (just one more of the reasonable moderate little gun-control laws that we'd have to be "extremists" to oppose) had been in effect—or even the non-federal version tacitly OK'd by Mr. LaPierre—the Elko teenager would have done better attempting to whack his mother's assailant with a fireplace log.

Following the successful Israeli example of arming teachers and parent volunteers, Georgia state legislator Mitchell Kaye has now proposed one of the few legislative initiatives likely to directly address the problem: He wants to authorize and encourage Georgia teachers to carry concealed weapons at school. "They know that all the adults in these school gun-free zones are unarmed, and that's the problem," Kaye told CNN the day after the Oregon shootings.

In a carefully scripted line, the gun-grabbers reply that teachers "are supposed to educate children, not execute them."

But we don't give weapons to police officers in the hopes they'll "execute" their suspects, do we? Guns are the great deterrent, preventing crime by their very presence.

The NRA does do *something* useful. The victim-disarmament gang whine that the group's "Eddie Eagle" gun-safety and training classes are nothing but "Joe Camel with feathers." But as it turns out, the parents of the young wrestling team member who finally jumped and subdued Kip Kinkel, 17-year-old Jacob Ryker,

387

credit his firearms training with the fact that he was able to detect when Kinkel's .22 rifle was empty, timing his leap when the assailant had to change weapons.

Linda Ryker also credited her son's familiarity with firearms for helping Jacob deal with the crisis, keeping his wits about him even after he was shot. With his son shot but recovering, Linda's husband Robert, a Navy diver, proudly wore his National Rifle Association cap during the family's press conference.

'They Have Started Mounting Raids to Retrieve Firearms'

Americans who warn that gun registration leads inevitably to confiscation are usually dubbed "paranoid."

In 1992, Australia enacted mandatory gun registration. In 1996, Australia proceeded to enact laws banning all semi-auto weapons of .22 caliber and larger. All such firearms are to be confiscated and destroyed, under a 12-month amnesty program.

Noting that 7,000 United States Marines have been stationed in Australia since July 31, 1995, supposedly for training, one Australian recently wrote me, contending our Marines are there "quite probably to assist the Australian government in forceful and violent confiscation of weapons at or before the end of the amnesty period."

While that fear may be overblown, I did think readers might be interested in this May 9, 1998, posting from Australian Carolyn Dillon:

"Good day to you. ... I am in Australia and the amnesty is finished. Stick up for your rights now! Speaking out is easier than what we now face here.

"Gun owners who did not comply with new regulations in

Australia are now faced with the fact that their name is flagged on government computers, [and] they are liable to four years imprisonment and a fine that is about the cost of an average house.

"Those with firearms licences and those who did not hand in their weapons are liable to search of person or premises without warrant.

"People cannot organize because what the government has done is now legislated, enacted law. Therefore any attempt to communicate or organise is liable to the charge of subversion. If an individual says to another, 'I would suggest that you do not hand in your firearm,' the speaker may be charged with subverting another to commit a criminal act.

"They have started mounting raids to retrieve firearms and this is likely to intensify.

"WHATEVER YOU GUYS DO, FOR GOD'S SAKE DON'T REGISTER YOUR WEAPONS. It really is happening and it seems to be global.

"U.S. brothers, watch your six. If you don't with the politicians, then you will have to watch it for real against your own troopers.

Australia to America: God bless you and pray for us poor bastards down under."

VIII

DEMONIZING THE MILITIAS

Background: The National Firearms Act

Like most government interventions in an otherwise smoothly functioning private market, alcohol Prohibition (1919-1933) was a disaster.

Though proponents celebrated enactment of the Volstead Act as the end of public drunkenness in America, it soon grew apparent it would mean nothing of the sort. Not only did smugglers and bootleggers keep America thoroughly wet, but the incentive they were thus given to make as much profit as possible off each boat- or truckload of illegal hooch permanently changed America from a nation predominately of beer drinkers (low cost per gallon) to a nation swilling distilled spirits. The bad taste of the poorly made hard liquor also needed to be disguised, of course, leading in turn to the rapid growth in popularity of the mixed cocktail.

(After 1934, when Prohibition shifted from alcohol to other drugs, the same phenomenon was observed. Smugglers switched their customers from bulky, smelly, raw opium to far more profitable heroin, and from dilute coca infusions in wine or soft drinks to snorting, smoking, or shooting relatively pure white cocaine— far more profit per ton.)

For the first time, Americans in the 1920s literally went blind from drinking badly made bathtub gin. The profits generated by bootlegging funded the birth of modern organized crime, as the dominant syndicates—largely blocked from investing their profits in legitimate enterprises, where they would have had to explain the source of their newfound wealth to the equally new federal taxmen—branched out into loan sharking, casino gambling, prostitution, numbers-running, infiltration of the labor unions and the entertainment industry, and other rackets.

And since liquor distributors couldn't settle their franchise disputes by going to court, many were forced to use the real-life arbitration method favored by the booze barons of Kansas City and Chicago—the Tommygun drive-by shooting featured prominently in American movies ever since.

(The Hays code of movie censorship was instituted in a vain effort, not primarily to keep America from seeing scenes of sex or drug use—such references remained laughably demure in American films of the 1930s. No, what prompted the Hays code was a demand that gangsters not be glorified, that they always be shown to have paid for their crimes, that they always die in the end. Why? Because Prohibition, by turning the average American into a criminal for merely doing what he'd always done, fostered a lasting hatred for the onetime "peace officers" who now, for the first time, justified their new intrusiveness and clever entrapments under the changed job description of "law enforcement." Overnight, the criminal bootleggers became the good guys of a new urban Sherwood Forest, battling against arbitrary and corrupt authority suddenly trying to restrain, rather than protect, citizens' liberties. Needless to say, Washington didn't like that.)

Most of these problems quickly took care of themselves with the re-legalization of booze by incoming President Franklin Roosevelt in 1933 (and the funny thing is, to date I have never heard anyone accuse FDR of "sending the wrong message to children").

But then, in a classic case of closing the barn door after the horse has gone—in a piece of timing so weird it cries out for further historical study—just as the problem of gangster violence was subsiding, Congress in 1934 enacted the National Firearms Act (NFA), designed to give the FBI another charge on which to hold gangsters, if they were caught in possession of a machine gun without having undergone a background check (which no neckless thug would ever pass) and paying a $200 transfer tax.

Why the tax? This was a tactic borrowed from the then-new regulation of the opiates, actually. Early attempts to control the distribution of such drugs had been thrown out by the courts as unconstitutional. But then the forces of Puritanism stumbled on a 1902 case in which the United States Supreme Court had ruled the federal government is free to regulate anything it taxes.

As an apparent afterthought, at the request of police who were tired of having suspects produce deadly sawed-off shotguns from their coat pockets, shortened shotguns were added to the list of taxed and regulated NFA weapons. And in fact, one of the first recorded uses of the then-obscure Act was to charge an itinerant Missouri moonshiner named Miller with possession of such a shotgun, which had presumably moved in interstate commerce.

The lower courts threw out the charge as an obviously un-constitutional infringement of Miller's right to keep and bear arms. But the federal government, loathe to lose the leverage the NFA gave them over armed perpetrators, appealed to the U.S. Supreme Court.

There, the federals lucked out. Once released from jail, the itinerant Miller disappeared. (This was in the midst of Roosevelt's Great Depression, after all.) So, only one side was represented at the Supreme Court—the government.

The court's logic was simple. The Second Amendment links the right to keep and bear arms with the necessity of a well-regulated militia. Therefore, Miller's possession of the shotgun was protected if it was the kind of weapon a militiaman might find to be of any military use. Was such a weapon of any military use? Had any short-barreled shotguns, for instance, been used in the trenches in the recent Great War in Europe?

The government's attorney, alone before the court and thus without any fear of contradiction, answered with a bald-faced lie. No, your honors, such weapons were not used in France in 1918.

They had been, of course—just as they would prove handy again 30 years later, in the jungles of Vietnam. But the Miller court ruled as a finding of fact that the sawed-off shotgun was of no conceivable military use. Thus, the government was justified in enforcing the National Firearms Act of 1934 by seizing Miller's shotgun.

The court's 1939 Miller decision—no further Second Amendment cases have been heard in the intervening 60 years—is often cited as an anti-gun case, since it upheld the legality of the National Firearms Act. And, in practice, the decision did indeed result in a massive and ongoing crippling of the right of civilians to keep and bear arms.

However, if today's federal officials were to enforce the logic of the Miller court in good faith, there is no way they could require registration, background checks, a $200 tax, or any regulation, restriction, or limitation whatsoever on any civilian wishing to purchase over the counter, for cash, on the spot, fully automatic M-14, M-16, or AK-47, grenade launcher, Bazooka or mortar, 50-caliber belt-fed machine gun, 55mm recoilless rifle, or even a shoulder-launched heat-seeking anti-aircraft missile, since clearly those *are* all weapons that are of current military usefulness: They easily pass the "militia test" of the Miller court.

Nonetheless, the Miller decision is interpreted as the federals see fit, and a federal agent catching anyone cutting down a shotgun below legal length today is considered to have an unbeatable case.

Flexing Their Muscles

Fast-forward to 1991. Even though the Bureau of Alcohol, Tobacco and Firearms is technically a branch of the Treasury Department, the federal agency charged with enforcing the 1934 NFA never has and still does not see its job as merely opening envelopes and processing $200 tax payments.

In fact, this "tax"—set at the 1934 value of 5.7 ounces of gold, or $1,600 in 1998 values—was never meant to be a revenue measure. Instead, it's a way to vastly restrict the availability of the most effective militia-style weapons, especially among politically suspect groups. (The predominately black and Hispanic drug gangs of America's inner cities have far more machine pistols than David Koresh or Randy Weaver—who between them turn out to have owned none; nada; zero; zilch. Those well-armed and well-financed inner-city drug gangs kill an estimated 1,200 people per year. But does the ATF ever raid *their* homes or headquarters? You've got to be kidding. In the first place, they represent no direct political threat to Washington's authority—they do not tend to go on the radio and talk much about the Federal Reserve Board or aid to Israel or the fact that the income tax is not supposed to apply to wages. But secondly, a guy could get *killed* invading the turf of an outfit like that—far safer to launch surprise paramilitary raids on churches full of women and children.)

Anyway, by 1991, the attention of the ATF—now functioning more or less as America's domestic anti-gun Gestapo—had been caught by a gang of white separatists in rural northern Idaho (where white separatism is pretty much de facto, anyway), centered around the Church of the Aryan Brotherhood. Were these characters merely out-of-step loners, or had they actually perpetrated racial hate crimes, like the murder of well-known Jewish talk-radio host Alan Berg in Denver?

Anxious to find out, ATF agents started asking folks around

the fringe of the Aryan Brotherhood if they would infiltrate the group, as paid federal spies. They apparently found no takers.

So, they came up with a plan. One of the nearby neighbors was an out-of-work survivalist and gun nut named Randy Weaver. An undercover agent handed Weaver a couple of shotguns and offered him good money if he would saw them down. Weaver did so, and was promptly busted and charged—with committing a crime completely of the government's invention.

But the ATF didn't really want to jail Weaver, the agents explained. All would be forgiven if he would merely infiltrate the neighboring white-separatist organization and report back.

Weaver refused and retreated to his family's mountaintop cabin. The federals filed their charges. Weaver missed a court date, although it later developed he may have been notified of the wrong date. At any rate, by the summer of 1992 a team of federal marshals was prowling the wooded Weaver property by night in full combat gear, with military M-16s, but without any search or arrest warrant—just to see what kind of resistance agents might confront if they decided to go in and arrest Weaver for failing to appear.

Dawn broke. The Weavers' dog scented the marshals, who retreated down the hill at a run. The tail-wagging dog caught up with one agent, and was machine gunned to death as it turned back and ran—shot through the rump. Fifteen-year-old Sammy Weaver, chasing after his dog, returned fire, and was also shot in the back and killed—on his own property, by trespassing agents in possession of no warrant, who had just shot and killed his dog.

Kevin Harris, a family friend of the Weavers, returned fire into the thick woods. The marshal who had killed young Sammy fell dead. (Since the federal government never produced the bullets recovered in his autopsy, it is unclear to this day whether he was justifiably killed by the fire of Harris, or accidentally by fratricidal fire from the other marshals.)

The federal stand-off on Ruby Ridge had begun. It would not end until FBI sniper Lon Horiuchi had murdered the unarmed Vicky Weaver by shooting her through her kitchen door. (Although Horiuchi was indicted by a local Idaho prosecutor for manslaughter, a federal judge threw out the case, ruling that a federal police agent cannot be charged with a crime even if he kills an unarmed unwanted civilian in her own home, while "following orders.")

Ruby Ridge occurred during the waning days of the Bush administration in 1992. By the time the ATF organized its next public-relations triumph, at the Mount Carmel Church in Waco, Texas, it was six months later and young Bill Clinton had assumed the presidency.

At Waco, nearly 100 ATF agents in full SWAT regalia stormed a church full of women and children just after Sunday services, systematically killing the church's dog and her puppies in their pen, firing through the windows and plywood walls, all supposedly in order to check and see if church leader David Koresh might have any illegal weapons, despite the fact Koresh had earlier cheerfully cooperated with the local sheriff when he had come knocking to check those same weapons—and why not? The sheriff found nothing illegal—and despite the fact Koresh had invited two of the investigating ATF agents to come over and take a look at his weapons right away.

After a two-month siege during which the federals cut off telephone and electrical service to those trapped in the church (though the government's legal right to do so was never made clear), the FBI finally knocked down the walls of the church with tanks (collapsing the stairwell escape routes), injected the nerve gas CS (which is outlawed under the Geneva convention and whose manufacturer warns it can be deadly in enclosed spaces or if set afire), and then torched the plywood building by lobbing incendiary mortar rounds into the corners of the structure. To finish off the job, they hosed down with machine gun fire anyone who tried to escape. Scores of people were murdered—many of the young black and Asian children dying of cyanide-gas poisoning in precisely the same manner as the inmates of Auschwitz.

You can see it all, filmed by the government itself, in the Academy Award-nominated documentary videotape, *Waco: The Rules of Engagement.*

Taking Them at Their Word

For years, those foolish souls who believe their lives will be safer if all civilians are disarmed and only police, soldiers, and professional gangsters retain guns had argued that gun-rights activists misquote the Second Amendment. It doesn't really say, "The right of the people to keep and bear arms shall not be infringed," these wheedlers argue. The right exists only in the context of the introductory phrase, "A well-regulated militia being necessary to the security of a free state ... " There is a right to bear arms only if one belongs to an organized militia, according to the explanation long put forward to explain away the inconvenient Second Amendment by the forces of victim disarmament, led in Congress by New York Congressman (now Senator) Charles Schumer and California Senator Dianne Feinstein.

OK. Following Ruby Ridge and Waco, many gun-rights activists realized they could no longer just sit around writing polite letters to their congressmen and paying their dues to the National Rifle Association (an outfit formed by former Union officers after the Civil War to promote better marksmanship among future draftees, and never a group to resist "reasonable" gun control, particularly if the targets of the next proposed incremental disarmament would primarily be uppity Negroes.)

The forces of victim disarmament were obviously serious,

and actually much emboldened by the success of their two latest monstrous crimes. No federal agents were ever charged, except for the sniper Horiuchi, whose case was quickly dismissed. Many, including the U.S. marshals of Idaho, received awards and promotions.

Clearly, the other side was now willing to send domestic mercenaries to incinerate or otherwise murder harmless law-abiding Americans in their own homes and churches, for the "crime" of merely possessing guns and asserting in speech or writing the right to use them in self-defense against a tyrannical government.

And, what was even more dangerous, a docile public turned out to be willing to buy with wide-eyed credulity the most absurd cover stories, up to and including the government explanation that David Koresh and his followers had all committed suicide by fire like insensate zombies, taking their own young wives and children with them—coincidentally on the same morning government tanks knocked down their kerosene space heaters onto nearby hay bales, while spraying the place full of a flammable gaseous nerve agent. (In other words, a story pretty much as convincing as a contention that the German Jews committed suicide in the Auschwitz gas chambers by rushing in there despite the best efforts of their well-meaning German guards to hold them back.)

The answer to which the gun-rights activists would turn, as it happened, had already been offered up to them by the opposition. "If we're supposedly only allowed to own weapons in the context of forming militias, let's get together and form some organized militias," figured many of those who could see their right to bear arms otherwise slipping away without a fight. "We'll call their bluff. We'll show up at the town green on Sunday for drill, getting folks used to seeing us armed again, as was common in colonial times. Since the other side has argued we *only* have a right to bear arms if we belong to a militia, they'll be hoist by their own petard, and they won't be able to object.

"Furthermore, our very-public militia membership will give us legal standing to challenge various state laws that make it hard to get to militia drills and then home again with our weapons on our persons or in our cars. And, if worse comes to worst and the federals ever try to come and take our guns, at least we'll be as well-organized and trained as the Minutemen were at Lexington and Concord, when government forces came to seize *their* powder and ball."

From the spring of 1993 to the spring of 1995, I watched with interest this short-lived public militia movement taking form. It was a movement born in fear and concern about what the federal government was doing to its own innocent citizens. But it was also a movement born of hope and an old-fashioned American can-do spirit. Don't just talk about a problem: go out and *do* something. Form a club; get on TV; tell all your friends.

I suppose there must have been some racists and wackos who took advantage of the trend to grab a little publicity for their own pet agendas. And from the start, I believe many in what became known as the "patriot movement" made it easy for the anti-gun-rights opposition to discredit and ridicule them, with their willingness to believe and pass along all manner of paranoid conspiracy theories.

But I interviewed a number of militia leaders, and made friends of a few of them. Yes, their political philosophies were often an ill-thought-out mishmash with received elements of protectionism and jingoism that I could not embrace. Yes, there was often in their rhetoric a pathetic and almost existential belief that the dark forces of the Tri-Lateral Commission or the Council on Foreign Relations or the Bildersbergers or the Masons or the New World Order or some other shadowy group of international Jewish banking families in Washington and London and Geneva had been conspiratorially manipulating our fates for centuries. In effect, I was hearing an attribution by relatively unsophisticated rural folk of virtually supernatural powers to their conniving urban opponents, armed with the (not-so-fanciful) spy satellites that can read your license plate, etc.

Nonetheless, I heard no overt racism. I heard no hatred. Defying the imposed stereotypes, a number of the militia leaders with whom I spoke turned out to be black or Jewish themselves. I heard no plans to hurt anyone, unless pushed to the wall.

Over and over again, the plaintive cry was the same: "They take away our kids and won't let us decide how they should be raised up. The kids come home saying everything we taught them out of the Bible is wrong. They came with their environmental regulations and shut down the mill and the mine and threw us out of work; now they come onto our land and tell us you can't cut the wood, you can't dam the creek, you can't run as many cattle, because it's all endangered and protected. And that's what they got away with *before* they started taking away our guns. Why do they want our guns? What on earth do they have in mind for us once we're *disarmed*?"

Every few months, not systematically but whenever an interesting development crossed my desk, I would write an update on the militia movement. More than in any other section of this book, I have found it vital to retain the dates of each of these dispatches and to present them in chronological order, to preserve the coherence of their parabolic curve. You'll notice that the tone of these dispatches changed markedly, over a period of less than four years.

Over those four years, federal police agents systematically destroyed the modern militia movement. Undercover government agents infiltrated the public groups with agents provocateurs, who routinely urged the other members to commit such major felonies as bank robberies to fund their activities. To their immense credit, all the amateur militiamen refused.

But, of course, federal laws now set traps for almost anyone who owns or works on firearms. The militiamen could always be charged with converting a rifle to fully automatic fire without paying the $200 tax (as though you could really get a "manufacturing license" to do so even if you were *willing* to pay the tax— unless your customers are all registered police agencies, of course). Failing that, the militiamen could be indicted for merely buying legal internal parts that they might *later* use to convert a weapon to fully automatic fire. Or, failing everything else, they could be charged with joining in a "conspiracy" to talk about how they *might* someday convert some of their weapons to full-automatic fire.

Ah, that 1934 National Firearms Act. Such a joker.

The change in tone in the following dispatches, from the breezy to the resigned, forms (it seems to me, upon scanning them in retrospect) a part of the story. So I have resisted as much as possible the temptation to clean them up and homogenize them, to change their focus with the benefit of today's 20-20 hindsight.

With many of the most prominent amateur militia leaders of the mid-'90s now in jail—all on trumped-up federal "conspiracy" charges, I hasten to add, none for actually harming anyone—and with their wiser brethren having quietly dropped from view or moved on to other pursuits, I daresay most Americans will breathe a sigh of relief as they read the following postcard history, figuring they've dodged a bullet.

"It's too bad if a few people went away when they didn't really hurt anyone," I can imagine a lot of folks rationalizing, "but isn't it better that the government acted quickly, before any of those guys got carried away and really did do some harm? I mean, they did have guns, and they were organized, right? Would you want the government to just sit by and do nothing?"

Needless to say, my interpretation of what the federal government accomplished, by first demonizing and then destroying in a few short years the fledging public, above-ground, militia movement of the 1990s, is somewhat different.

Three Possible Outcomes

What are the potential results of the current policy of victim disarmament in America today? Here are three possibilities:

1) We can, indeed, become a nation of disarmed slaves. Those who push gun control may not now *plan* for our government to eventually murder its citizens in the numbers disposed of by such previous champions of gun control as Stalin, Hitler, Mao, and Pol Pot. But the Founding Fathers were a pretty smart bunch of guys, and they didn't insist on an armed populace for nothing. They knew the course that any despot will follow, once he realizes his men hold all the cards.

2) The forces of victim disarmament can be defeated in battle. Under this scenario, America will be seized by paroxysms of civil war, revolution, and secession. Eventually, Washington City will either be destroyed or find itself ruling over a pathetic little disarmed socialist slave state extending from Virginia in the south to New York and Massachusetts in the north and possibly as far to the northwest as Madison, Wisconsin. The island plutocracy of Los Angeles could retain some remote degree of allegiance and affiliation to the slave state, like Constantinople to Rome. But as with Albania today, all the best and brightest citizens of the disarmed slave state will flee to the freedom-loving Western Confederacy, and no one will any longer go "back East" on purpose. (For one thing, we wouldn't be allowed to wear our guns.)

3) The third option is the middle course. Peacefully but with impressive demonstrations of resolve and potential firepower, well-armed Americans will gather in public places to seek a redress of grievances, as they are authorized to do by the Bill of Rights, and will successfully demand that America's existing 20,000 gun-control laws be repealed, returning us to the generally peaceful state of liberty and lack of fear of central-government usurpations in which this nation prospered from 1787 to

1912.

What? Of the three options, you prefer Option 3? Oh, too bad. That's the option the federal government just foreclosed. It's gone. The brave souls who might have led those peaceful protests are all in prison. Their surviving friends sure aren't about to step into their shoes. And when the imprisoned militia leaders are released, believe me, they are no longer going to be talking about a "peaceful redress of grievances." Some will be broken men. But those who are not will have a great new strength of purpose, a new bunch of allies and acquaintances with a far more professional outlook on defiance of government decrees, and a brand new plan.

And somehow, I don't think it's going to be Option 1.

That Every Man Be Armed

June 1994—In the spring of 1994, the Santa Rosa County Commission unanimously declared that every able-bodied man, woman, and child of that Florida panhandle jurisdiction was an official member of the local militia. Assigned by the *New York Times* to cover the story, reporter Larry Rohter turned to Dennis Henigan, director of the D.C.-based Legal Action Project of the Center to Prevent Handgun Violence, who declared: "If these folks think this is going to give them Constitutional protection for the ownership of guns as militiamen, it's not going to work. ... You can't avoid gun control laws just by creating some parallel bogus local militia, no matter how many times you get together and march around with guns."

Who needs a militia, anyway? Reporter Rohter responds to his own rhetorical question by playing his trump card, reporting that "some people" have told Escambia County Commissioner

W.A. "Buck" Lee they fear "a secret plan by the Federal Government to bring Hong Kong policemen to the United States to usurp local authority after Hong Kong is handed over to China in 1997."

Unattributed conspiracy theories usually have some trouble finding their way into the pages of the *Times*, but such standards give way, apparently, in the face of the higher goal of discrediting those who cherish the right to bear arms.

What's interesting about the new militia movement is that it proves the gun-grabbers want it both ways. First, those who want only government goons to be armed argue that the second half of the Second Amendment, "The right of the people to keep and bear arms shall not be infringed," does not mean what any school-child can tell us it means, because of the introductory phrase, "A well-regulated militia, being necessary to the security of a free State ... "

But then, when local gun-owners go to the trouble of forming well-regulated militias, the state-power extremists promptly assure us that's not what the Amendment protects, either.

To hear these zealots tell it, what the Founders really meant when they wrote the Second Amendment—having just won their freedom in the field against the most powerful standing army in the world, by dint of the unique historical accident that most American farmers happened to own a hunting rifle superior in accuracy to the British standard-issue "Brown Bess" musket—was that Congress and the president would now be at liberty to arm various new standing armies and SWAT teams, which would then have the right to disarm all the commoners who had just made up General Washington's triumphant Continental Army.

Even Santa Rosa County Commissioner H. Byrd Mapoles, who sponsored the militia resolution, told the *Times* he "does not expect citizen-soldiers to start drills on the courthouse lawn anytime soon."

But Mapoles may not have so long to wait. In southern California, John Wallner, a law student who served two years as a tank crewman with the Marine Corps Reserves and has since run for Congress on the Libertarian ticket, is in the process of founding the San Diego Militia. Wallner's intent is to get together and march around with guns for at least a year, at which point Wallner anticipates filing lawsuits designed to start providing the Second Amendment with teeth.

Wallner figures his first target will be California's Roberti-Roos law, which forbids the transfer of assault rifles like the one-bullet-at-a-time AR-15—a ban that includes letting anyone else so much as touch the weapon.

"I can't let my wife use it," says Wallner. "If my wife is being raped and the only weapon within reach is my Colt AR-15, she has to let herself be raped, because if she picks it up, that's a felony in California."

On what grounds could an active militia claim legal standing to challenge such a law?

"Under Roberti-Roos, I can't let anyone hold my AR-15. It's very hard to enforce firearm safety on the parade ground when the safety officer can't even pick up the firearm to show its proper use."

The organizational meeting of the San Diego Militia was set for 7 p.m. June 14, 1994, at Joe's Restaurant, 3805 Murphy Canyon Road, San Diego. No cloak and dagger—hardly a secret rendezvous.

Meantime, to the north in Hillsboro, Ore., the Washington County Militia has already held its first meeting, a parade drill in a local park to commemorate the victory of a "bogus local militia" over British regulars on the same April date (give or take a day or two) at Lexington and Concord in 1775.

"The reaction has been very muted, which I probably credit to my own underhandedness and PR skills," reports founder Tom Cox.

Cox phoned the local parks department to tell them that "elements of the Oregon militia" would be marching in the park Sunday morning April 17, and that he himself would be carrying a Revolutionary-era black-powder musket. "I didn't bother to mention that one of the guys would have a fully automatic Israeli Galil," Cox admits. "It was perfectly legal; he has a Class 3 license."

The parks department had no objection?

"They asked if we wanted to reserve a picnic table."

Cox says his main goal is to build the group slowly, admitting only those members he is convinced are responsible. "I presented my plan to some veteran friends of mine, and they were real concerned about the risk of one idiot or one malicious person or one agent provocateur screwing everything up, and that's a valid point."

But the main point of the growing militia movement is practical show-and-tell. Politicians, especially in the East, have succeeded in convincing many Americans that an armed neighbor must be either insane or a criminal assailant. The notion that a citizen just walking down the street with a firearm might be a friendly neighbor on his way to militia drill must be reinforced, if the supporters of liberty are to regain any widespread public support against the kind of pathological civilian gun-seizure that has been the precursor to every genocide in this century.

A Significant Event

On April 19, 1995, the second anniversary of the FBI murders at Waco, Texas (the FBI had taken over from the fumbling BATF a few days after the initial February 1993 federal raid, bringing the resulting standoff to a satisfactory conclusion by incinerating most of the church members 60 days later, apparently with some help from members of the Army's Delta Force), the Murrah Federal Building in nearby Oklahoma City—housing on its top floor the BATF office where the Waco raid was actually planned—blew up.

Scores of people died in what is generally described as "the largest terrorist bombing in American history," conveniently ignoring Grant's shelling of the civilian population of Vicksburg. Although the justice dispensed in our federal courts now makes it clear Americans are of two classes (federals, who cannot be charged with any crimes, and serfs, who commit a crime simply by going armed, or teaching others about firearms), the American news media never broke out the Oklahoma City casualties into government employees and their offspring, as opposed to innocent civilians who were in the building because of the requirements of government regulations.

Federal agents quickly arrested U.S. Army veteran Timothy McVeigh, who had never belonged to any civilian militia, and charged him with driving and parking the truck full of ammonium-nitrate fertilizer and fuel oil that exploded in front of the building. Given that McVeigh is reported to have said, "I didn't know about the children" in the building's day-care center—combined with his virtual lack of any organized defense—it is generally believed McVeigh did indeed drive and park the truck bomb.

However, would the single truck bomb—out on the street, beyond the lawn and the trees—explain the registering of two separate explosions on a nearby university seismograph at the time of the blast? Could such a building really be collapsed by such a blast without separate charges being attached to the building's support pillars and detonated simultaneously? (A former Army general who is an expert on demolitions says not.) Isn't it odd that all the ATF agents had been assigned to be out of the office that day, so that none were injured?

Isn't it also odd how federal investigators never looked beyond McVeigh, ignoring reports of more bombs found on the site by rescue workers, as well as eyewitness accounts of strange workmen coming and going from the building's basement the day before? Isn't it odd how quickly and easily McVeigh was caught and then back-trailed, with clues that couldn't have been missed by Mister Magoo?

Although McVeigh may well have been complicit, doesn't this match a pattern of "loner" fall-guys set up to take the blame for crimes that it requires an astonishing suspension of disbelief to credit to one amateur—like the crack marksmanship of Lee Harvey Oswald, with a decrepit surplus Carcano rifle, through the trees, hitting a moving target at more than 100 yards with three head shots, one of them entering the head of President John F. Kennedy from the *front*?

I don't know. Others will presumably write the books about the Oklahoma City bombing. For our purposes here, it's only important to note that it happened, and that although Mr. McVeigh received his demolition training in the U.S. Army and was kicked out of the only militia meeting he is ever known to have attended (in Michigan), U.S. government and press propagandists left the public in no doubt about who was to blame: right-wing extremists, establishment-haters like talk-radio gadfly Rush Limbaugh, and (of course) "the militias."

"Find a Legal Way Around It"

May 3, 1995—The Founders warned against "special militias"—guys who march around in uniform and draw governor's pay. The safest militia, they agreed, was the "unorganized militia"—and boy, are we ever unorganized.

But if Bill Clinton intends to disarm us, decent Americans

face a choice: Either make like Peter the Apostle and deny we've ever met one of these dangerous militiamen or pick up a couple boxes of cartridges for the old M-1 and the SKS, call up a buddy, and spend Saturday sighting them in at 300 yards.

I found a message from a friend on my machine this week, inviting me out to make sure we can still blow up a cantaloupe at combat range. Presumably this will constitute "combat training by non-military groups," which the Anti-Defamation League of B'nai B'rith actually wants banned by federal law.

"In response to the [militia] movement, the heavily government-controlled media of late has been cranking up its propaganda machinery to smear and marginalize the Militia members as malcontents—skinheads, neo-Nazis, child-molesters, vile anti-Semites, whatever," writes Ambrose Evans-Pritchard in a recent *London Sunday Telegraph*. "The Anti-Defamation League ... has published a report on the militias around the U.S. titled 'Armed and Dangerous.' It argues that most militias are filled with fringe malcontents from the Aryan Nation and other white supremacist or neo-Nazi organizations. ... "

"I'm Jewish and I take offense to that," Mark Bowers, a former artillery officer who commands the Montgomery County Militia near Houston, told Evans-Pritchard. "There's nobody of that ilk in our unit. We're trying to recruit blacks, Latinos, Jews, women, anybody who wants to join."

"The American press has been caught off-guard, seriously misjudging the dynamism and scale of the movement," Evans-Pritchard concludes. "In effect, the militias are the shock troops and enforcement arm of the 1994 American Revolution. If the Republicans betray their promises and fail to restore 'constitutional' government, these people could take matters into their own hands."

Military historian Joseph Miranda, writing in the January edition of the *Freedom Network News* (see "Appendix II"), ad-

410

vises, "The militia must determine what the grievances are of mainstream Americans and then promote effective solutions. A major mistake of the militia movement has been the obsession with outlandish conspiracies. The problem facing America is not Russian tanks being transported on rail cars ... or black-painted helicopters. The problem is the government's nonstop violations of the Constitution. These violations include ... the confiscation of firearms and private property, ... documented cases of murder of innocent civilians, and so forth."

Well, yes. Miranda ends up suggesting a new Constitutional Amendment allowing citizens to bring charges against government officials who violate the Constitution. But let's not forget that violating their oaths to uphold the Constitution is already a serious crime, as is violating civil rights under color of law.

That's why "Bill of Rights enforcement"—the arrest, trial, and incarceration of any officeholder who has violated any of the first 10 Amendments—is precisely the mission that Libertarian novelist L. Neil Smith of Colorado has in mind for the Libertarian Second Amendment Caucus he's organizing nationwide.

Meantime, did anyone notice Bill Clinton's response to theSupreme Court decision that the federals may no longer stretch the interstate-commerce clause to justify federal intrusions like the federal ban on firearms within 1,000 feet of a government school?

Baffled Bill called the decision a "threat to children" and gave Attorney General Janet Reno, according to the AP, "one week to come up with a legal way around the ruling."

Since unconstitutional governments have easily killed a million times more children in this century than rogue private gunmen, Congress should respond by coming up with a legal way around allowing Mr. Clinton to complete his four-year term.

Meantime, Rep. Barbara Bailey Kennelly, D-Connecticut, has introduced HR97, which would create a new 2,500-member

FBI Rapid Deployment Force, hereinafter referred to as the "Waffen FBI," while the ACLU warns that under the administration's new Omnibus Counterterrorism Act, a president in a fit of pique could declare the Republican Party a terrorist organization, at which point it would be a crime to contribute to the GOP without a license. "The legislation would even bar the contributor from arguing in court that the GOP is not a terrorist organization," the ACLU reports.

"Eventually We Will Be Free Again"

May 19, 1995—The Clinton administration has always had a strained relationship with the uniformed services. There were young Bill's letters to the Arkansas draft board proclaiming, "I despise the military," for starters, followed (ever since this gang has occupied the White House) by persistent reports of callow young staffers mistaking Marine sentries for bellhops. But at least the president tried to avoid openly ridiculing his troops.

Until May 5, 1995.

You see, the majority of the troops who would respond to the president's call in any real emergency are not the standing army, at all. They are the militia.

Richard Henry Lee of Virginia, who drafted the Second Amendment along with the rest of the Bill of Rights, left no doubt about that when he wrote in 1788, "A militia, when properly formed, are in fact the people themselves. ... [T]he Constitution ought to secure a genuine [militia] and guard against a select militia, by providing that the militias shall always be kept well organized, armed, and disciplined, and include ... all men capable of bearing arms, and that all regulations tending to render this militia useless and defenseless, by establishing select corps of militia, or distinct bodies of military men not having permanent interests and attachments in the community [are] to be avoided."

Founder after Founder stressed the importance of always having the militia constitute the bulk of our armed forces. Samuel Adams warned in 1775, "It is always dangerous to the liberties of the people to have an army stationed among them, over which they have no control," even potentially the Continental army. But, he said, "The Militia is composed of free Citizens. There is therefore no danger of their making use of their power to the destruction of their own Rights."

"Before a standing army can rule," wrote the influential Federalist Noah Webster in 1787, "the people must be disarmed; as they are in almost every kingdom in Europe. [But] the supreme power in America cannot enforce unjust laws by the sword; because the whole body of the people are armed, and constitute a force superior to any band of regular troops that can be, on any pretense, raised in the United States." (That citation, along with others here, are from Stephen Halbrook's profusely footnoted 1984 book, *That Every Man Be Armed*—see "Appendix II.")

Mind you, those who fought the American Revolution did not protest the fact that British troops had been made available to fight the French on the frontier in the 1760s. They happily cooperated with that venture. No, their problem arose from the fact that they saw themselves as full-fledged British citizens, and thus wondered why British (and even mercenary Hessian) troops were still being used to garrison Boston and New York, long after the peace with France was signed.

In this context, today's problem is not that an American "standing army" stands ready to enforce American policy in Bosnia or Beirut, but rather that armed federal "troops" stand ready to barge into our homes and search for weapons the way General Gage's redcoats took to doing in the mid-1770s.

Whether we call these zealots an "army" or a "special militia," make no mistake—today's closest approximation to the kind of occupying army against which the Founding Fathers rose up are the arrogant, "you-don't-dare-prosecute-us," machine gun-toting agents of the FBI, the DEA, the BATF, and the IRS.

It was to the concern that the new army of the United States might take up this *domestic* role that Hamilton referred in Federalist No. 29 when he promised, "That army can never be formidable to the liberties of the people while there is a large body of citizens, little if at all inferior to them in discipline and the use of arms, who stand ready to defend their rights and those of their fellow citizens."

Tench Coxe of Pennsylvania, a friend of Madison and a prominent Federalist, wrote in the *Pennsylvania Gazette* of Feb. 20, 1788, "Who are the militia? Are they not ourselves? ... The militias of these free commonwealths, entitled and accustomed to their arms, when compared to any possible army" (here Coxe specifically meant a repressive army fielded by Congress, not any foreign power), "must be tremendous and irresistible. ... Congress have no power to disarm the militia. Their swords, and every other terrible instrument of the soldier, are the birth-right of an American. ... [T]he unlimited power of the sword is not in the hands of either the federal or the state governments, but, where I trust in God it will ever remain, in the hands of the people."

Tell me Mr. Coxe would have denied every American a fully automatic assault rifle and a shoulder-launched surface-to-air missile, if they'd been invented.

To preserve liberty," wrote Richard Henry Lee in 1788—seven years after the last Redcoat was shipped home in ignominy—"it is essential that the whole body of the people always possess arms, and be taught alike, especially when young, how to use them."

"The great object is, that every man be armed," said Patrick Henry, during the same ratification debates in 1788, with nary a Redcoat in sight. "Everyone who is able must have a gun."

414

If these men wrote a Second Amendment that grants no individual right to own and carry an assault rifle, they appear to have spent endless obsessive hours leaving us false trails.

Yet how did President Clinton, successor to General Washington, address his irregulars in East Lansing, Mich., on May the 5th?

"I say this to the militias and all others who believe that the greatest threat to freedom comes from the government. ... If you say violence is an acceptable way to make change, you are wrong. ... If you appropriate our sacred symbols for paranoid purposes and compare yourselves to colonial militias who fought for the democracy you now rail against, you are wrong."

Interviewed recently by Darrell Rowland of the *Columbus Dispatch*, James Johnson, leader of Ohio's Unorganized Militia, responded to charges that the militias are paranoid white-supremacist groups. "If my ancestors had been armed, they wouldn't have been slaves,' said Johnson, who is black. "That is the genuine fear of many Americans—that they are being led down the path to slavery."

"I think the thing that Easterners ought to understand," agrees Speaker of the House Newt Gingrich, "is that there is across the West a genuine sense of fear of the federal government. This is not the extremist position in much of the West."

Johnson's wife Helen referred to recent warrantless door-to-door searches in federally subsidized housing projects to root out crime. "If they get away with it there, it won't be long before they're knocking on your middle-class door. One of the reasons we [the Ohio Unorganized Militia] exist is to prevent government from using military tactics against civilians in the name of law enforcement. ... I believe the federal government will eventually push the American public to the point of noncompliance."

Sounding like Darth Vader, Clinton warned that modern technology like the Internet—the modern equivalent of Revolutionary-era Committees of Correspondence—has a "dark underside" that leaves the nation "very, very vulnerable to the forces of organized destruction and evil. ... There is no right to kill people who are doing their duty."

Sure there is.

General Washington killed plenty of Redcoats and Hessians who were doing their duty—and in defense of the duly constituted government, at that.

The Jews in the Warsaw ghetto had every right to kill Nazis who were only doing their duty, enforcing duly enacted laws against Jews bearing arms. Our own prosecutions of the Nazis at Nuremberg in 1946 established a lasting precedent that men can and will be legally executed for "just following orders."

Juries good and true have recently acquitted the surviving Branch Davidians of all capital charges in the defense of their church against the 1993 ATF assault. An Idaho jury similarly ruled that neither Randy Weaver nor Harris committed any crime when one or both fired on one of the federal marshals who were in the process of murdering his son and unarmed wife at his remote mountain cabin in 1992 ... even though that marshal died. Those juries ruled the survivors did indeed have a right to kill armed federal thugs who were only doing their duty—didn't they?

Weren't Weaver and Harris and all the Branch Davidian survivors unanimously found innocent on every capital charge, even though they all fired back at trespassing federal agents? Weren't they found innocent? Weren't they?

"How dare you suggest that we in the freest nation on earth live in tyranny?" Clinton demanded in East Lansing.

"Americans have the habit of saying they're the freest nation in the world," answered Canadian tax scholar and author Charles Adams, featured speaker at the annual Ludwig von Mises seminar in Austrian economics at the University of Nevada, Las Vegas, on May 6th. "But they should say 'used to be.' America of all

416

the Western nations is the worst. No one else lets the government go through your bank records, no one else makes you file a form when you hire a babysitter, when you hire a sophomore to mow your lawn. ...

"The IRS used to operate on the honor system, but now it's not an honor system any more," continued Adams, distinguished white-haired author of the current bestseller *For Good and Evil: The Impact of Taxes on the Course of Civilization.*

"The American people don't realize it, but in the last twenty years you've lost all your liberties. ... If it takes a revolution to flush out your tax system, then go for it."

Mr. Jefferson would have agreed. "I hold it that a little rebellion, now and then, is a good thing," he wrote to Madison, "and as necessary in the political world as storms are in the physical. Unsuccessful rebellions, indeed, generally establish the encroachments on the rights of the people, which have produced them. An observation of this truth should render honest republican governors so mild in their punishment of rebellions, as not to discourage them too much. It is the medicine necessary for the sound health of governments."

And later, to William S. Smith in 1787 of armed revolutions. Jefferson wrote, "What country can preserve its liberties, if its rulers are not warned from time to time, that this people preserve the spirit of resistance? Let them take arms. ... The tree of liberty must be refreshed from time to time, with the blood of patriots and tyrants."

"There's no comparison" between the freedoms enjoyed by Americans today and the oppressions suffered by our forefathers in 1775, Bill Clinton and his ilk now insist.

In fact, Americans were enormously more free under King George 220 years ago—*before* the Revolution.

There was no income tax—no levies, seizures, and garnishments, no government snoops demanding to see receipts and bank records, no "money laundering" (since all commerce was considered "clean"), and no robbery of savings through the devaluation of worthless government paper passed off as money. Total taxes were less than one fifth of today's, and no official would ever have dreamed of trying to restrict what a property owner could build on his own land or of carrying off anyone's children to some mandatory government school.

There were no drug laws, with the result that there were no drug gangs and no drug violence.

Yes, publishing sedition against the king was illegal. But since colonial juries were chosen by lot (unlike the pro-government jury-stacking that goes on today), John Peter Zenger was let off with a token fine, even though there was no doubt he was guilty. However, Mr. Washington still took up arms, apparently suffering the delusion that "government was in a conspiracy to take your freedoms away,' in the sarcastic words of Dr. Clinton.

"We will not give the call to action," vows minuteman James Johnson of Columbus. "Our opponents will. But we will not give up the sovereignty of this nation or its Constitution without a fight. There will come a day in this nation when citizens who once thought we were radical will be glad there was an entity called the Ohio Unorganized Militia.

"When this blows, a lot of us will die, a lot of us will be injured for life, and a lot of us will be in jail. But eventually we will be free again."

Liberty, As Sen. Calhoun Said, Is Easier to Get Than to Keep

May 27, 1996—Memorial Day. The bugles blow, laughing children place flags on the graves of the fallen, the surviving comrades of the silent dead squeeze into too-tight uniforms (could they ever really have been so thin?) to march a block or two beneath the flag.

Amidst the picnics and the barbecues, on this first holiday of summer, who can wonder that a peaceful land spares little more thought for those who died to keep it free? Our carefree days, after all, are the very thing they died to protect.

That, and our freedoms.

How safe, today, are the liberties for which so many generations of Americans, in Mr. Lincoln's words, "gave the last full measure of devotion"?

The first Americans to take up arms to protect American liberties were the 70 militiamen who stood at Lexington, Mass., on April 19, 1775, attempting to block Lt. Gen. Thomas Gage from seizing an illegal stockpile of arms and powder at nearby Concord.

The minutemen failed, at first. Eight died and 10 were wounded in the first exchange of fire—a devastating 25 percent casualty rate—without the cost of a single Redcoat. Only after General Gage's troops moved on and searched the nearby village of Concord for hidden arms, and then turned back for Boston, did the colonists exact their revenge, picking off 250 of the 18th century's version of federal gun-control police.

Why were the colonists aroused? The British Parliament in February 1775 had declared Massachusetts to be in "open rebellion"—a declaration that made it legal for government troops to shoot troublesome rebels on sight—precisely the kind of operating orders issued to uniformed government troops at Ruby Ridge in 1992 and at Waco in 1993.

Yet the May 10, 1996, *Boston Globe* reports that Massachusetts state authorities have called on the Bureau of Alcohol, Tobacco and Firearms, seeking high-speed federal scanning computers to help clear up an 11-year backlog of paperwork—800,000 forms in cardboard boxes—generated under a Massachusetts law that now requires the registration of every firearm purchased. The birthplace of the American Revolution also now has a five-year backlog in processing permits required to carry handguns, own rifles, or purchase ammunition.

State legislators say they're worried police officers responding to calls might be unaware which Massachusetts residents have been "stockpiling arms."

"Some guy could be out there buying a hundred guns, but we would have no way to know it," complained Stoneham Police Chief Eugene Passaro.

Someone might ask Chief Passaro how a man with 100 guns can be any more dangerous than a man with two or three (hint: count his hands).

But more importantly, can anyone remember the last time someone tried to ban the civilian "stockpiling of arms" in Massachusetts, and how it worked out?

Of course, no lawmaker or cop who makes it a practical impossibility for the average American to buy, practice with, and carry around a fully automatic M-16 *means* to turn us into a nation of disarmed sheep who hope for the best as they board boxcars for the relocation camps.

They all *believe* they're just keeping us safe from drug gangsters—gangsters who wouldn't need guns to enforce their business contracts in the first place if their products were legalized so they could take their disputes to court ... like liquor distributors.

But as Justice Louis Brandeis wrote in Olmstead vs. the United States, "The greatest dangers to liberty lurk in insidious encroachment by men of zeal, well-meaning but without understanding."

How many times, on sultry Memorial Days, have we listened to the best student in the class strive manfully—or womanfully— to remember Mr. Lincoln's words, without really hearing any personal call to action:

"It is for us, the living ... to be dedicated here to the unfinished work which they who fought here have thus far so nobly advanced ... that we here highly resolve that these dead shall not have died in vain; that this nation, under God, shall have a new birth of freedom; and that government of the people, by the people, for the people, shall not perish from the earth."

Armed government forces "can never be formidable to the liberties of the people," Mr. Hamilton guaranteed in The Federalist No. 29, "while there is a large body of citizens, little if at all inferior to them in discipline and the use of arms, who stand ready to defend their rights and those of their fellow citizens."

Is that the goal of this new Massachusetts law—of all the 20,000 victim disarmament laws that now apply to the common American citizen, but not to the government agent—to make sure the average American is "little if at all inferior in discipline and the use of arms" to the FBI and the ATF?

"What kind of government have you given us?" Mrs. Powel asked Mr. Franklin as he and the other delegates to the Constitutional Convention emerged, at last, from the hall in Philadelphia.

"A republic," he said, " ... if you can keep it."

'Conspiracy to Furnish Instruction in Furtherance of Civil Disorder'

July 17, 1996—Having read the indictments of the dozen people arrested in Phoenix July 1 and charged with being members of the "Viper Militia," I must now report that these government documents contain a startling amount of hogwash.

The Associated Press reported July 8 that an ATF agent, testifying during the second day of hearings to determine whether 11 of the 12 defendants should even be detained pending trial, stated the government had two snitches in the militia unit and "knew it had no immediate plans to attack government buildings."

(The two snitches added up to 14 percent of the membership. We'll shortly see some indication of how active a role one of these characters played in organizing the group's agenda.)

ATF agent Steven Ott testified his snitch "felt there was absolutely no plan to conduct any bombings of these buildings at that time."

What?

From the headlines a few weeks back, one would have thought police stations and TV towers were ready to topple within hours. Wasn't that Bill Clinton himself standing on the White House lawn July saying, "I'd like to begin today by saluting the law-enforcement officers who made arrests in Arizona yesterday to avert a terrible terrorist attack"?

Some of the more paranoid among us even wondered whether the defendants—four of whom are registered Libertarians—were busted just in time to throw the greatest possible cloud over the July 4-7 national convention in Washington, D.C. (televised nationwide on C-SPAN), at which the less-government Libertarian Party nominated financial newsletter editor Harry Browne of Tennessee as its seventh and latest presidential standard-bearer.

(Seven of those arrested in Phoenix were registered Republicans. No reporter that I know of called Haley Barbour, executive director of the national Republican Party, to ask if the GOP is ashamed to be attracting such dangerous radicals, though virtually every Libertarian Party official in Arizona seems to have been asked that question.)

For the record, the Libertarian Party not only opposes the initiation of force, it is the only national party that requires prospective recruits to sign a pledge to that effect before they're enrolled as official members (though of course anyone can register a Libertarian voting preference with the state, without becoming a real party member.)

I called Arizona state Libertarian Party chairman Mike Dugger in Ahwatuckee July 7 to ask for an update. When he told me Arizona's First Amendment attorneys were licking their chops hoping to get a chance to defend this case, I thought he'd made a slip of the tongue.

"You mean *Second* Amendment attorneys," I said, still thinking this was primarily a firearms and explosives case.

"No, First Amendment," he insisted.

Now that I've read the indictments, I see what he means.

To win a conspiracy indictment, prosecutors are supposed to demonstrate to a grand jury that at least one member of the conspiracy has committed an "overt act"—usually interpreted to mean either an outright felony, or an act unmistakably preparatory to the commission of a felony like planting explosives in a bank.

But the alleged conspiracy, in this case, was not planning to blow up any particular building, but rather (Count 1) "Conspiracy to Furnish Instruction in the Use of Explosive Devices and Other Techniques in Furtherance of Civil Disorder," and (Count 2) "Furnishing Instruction In the Use of Explosive Devices and Other Techniques in Furtherance of Civil Disorder."

(Needless to say, this is only a crime for civilians. Sergeants at Parris Island conspire to teach precisely these skills to Marine recruits every day.)

The Phoenix indictment contends the defendants "did knowingly and intentionally combine, conspire, confederate and agree together to teach and demonstrate to each other and other persons the use, application, and making of firearms, explosive and incendiary devices, and techniques capable of causing injury and death ... "

"Teach?" It's now a crime to teach?

Every time your local NRA-affiliated shooting club holds a shooting match and the range supervisor walks down the line, recommending one of the younger fellows wrap his sling around his arm in a way that will steady his rifle better, he is "teaching and demonstrating a technique capable of causing injury and death. ... "

In fact, under the Director of Civilian Marksmanship (DCM) program, any law-abiding American can sign up to shoot in a DCM match. Those who shoot adequate scores are qualified to buy a surplus military rifle, at cost, from the United States government.

Although such rifles will kill a deer, they are fairly cumbersome for that purpose. The main function of the battle rifle is to "cause injury to persons."

The defendants' shoulder patches (yes, shoulder patches— the whole bunch sound more and more like a paintball squad that got carried away) read "Viper Team" only—no mention of any Militia. In fact, by insisting the 12-member Viper Team is or was a militia, it strikes me that the government is stipulating to the very defense most likely to bring an outright acquittal.

For what is a "militia," by definition? It consists of a group of *non*-government employees who gather together to train in the use of military weapons so that they'll be prepared to defend their states' sovereignty should the central government in Washington ever move in to challenge it. That is the stated purpose of the Second Amendment. Thus the famous introductory clause about "A well regulated militia being necessary to the security of a free State" ... remember?

"Free States," each with its own militia—militias not subject to any regulation out of Washington City. That was the promise in exchange for which the Union was ratified.

And "well-regulated" means "well-trained" ... in firing volleys, reloading quickly, and blowing things up. What do you think George Mason and George Washington were up to when they organized meetings of the Fairfax County Militia in the mid-1770s—trading ginger cookie recipes?

The government agents themselves say this rather ragtag bunch was just doing contingency planning for the event of any future federal incursion to take away our rights—hardly a far-fetched concern any longer, after what Americans have seen at Waco and Ruby Ridge and Donald Scott's ranch in the past four years.

As a matter of fact, some could argue that the very arrests in question *constitute* the kind of encroachment on our liberties that Mr. Madison told us (in The Federalist, No. 46) should "provoke plans of resistance" and should be "opposed [by] a militia amounting to near half a million citizens with arms in their hands."

Are we going to arrest all the men in the bowels of the Pentagon who draw up contingency plans for the deployment of U.S. forces to block any Canadian attempt to seize Vermont and New Hampshire? Does the fact that such a plan still sits on some dusty shelf prove those Army boys are engaged in a "conspiracy" to invade Canada? If not, why do they have all those weapons ready to go, when the nation is at peace? Hmm?

"You're talking nonsense," I can hear the statists interjecting. "You're taking about things that only the government has a right to do, as though individual citizens have a right to do the same things."

But where is it these folks imagine the government *gets* the power to do things that individual citizens can't do? Isn't the founding principle of America that all rights start with the people, who then delegate to the government only certain limited powers? The notion of a government that starts out with the power to do anything and everything *it* wants, and then picks and chooses which limited things it will "allow" the individual citizens to do, was surely dreamed up by someone other than Messrs. Jefferson, Washington, and Madison.

Was the Viper Militia "superior" to any band of regular troops that could have been sent in to enforce martial law and seize citizens' guns in Phoenix—to the 82nd Airborne, say? I don't think so, do you? It appears to me they weren't strong enough to oppose a handful of ATF agents accompanied by a TV crew.

To meet the Founders' guarantee, surely the Viper Militia would have needed to be several thousand strong and armed with full-auto 50-caliber machine guns, Apache helicopters, heat-seeking surface-to-air missiles, Abrams tanks, and 155mm cannon, wouldn't you think?

If the contract we made with the federalists in the 1780s is still good, then surely the federal government should be encouraging the Viper Militia to recruit more members and offering to help them buy weapons of the sort listed immediately above— perhaps with no-interest easy-payment plans—not setting them up and arresting them.

• • •

But let's return to the question of what, precisely, were the "overt acts" (necessary to any finding of conspiracy) charged in the Phoenix indictments.

"On or about Dec. 13, 1995," we're told, four of the "conspirators" met and viewed, "for the purpose of training persons in the making and use of explosive devices for use in obstructing the federal government, a videotape. ... "

Oh. Well, then! They watched a videotape!

On the videotape, some members were seen detonating "multiple destructive devices which ultimately created a crater in open land approximately 6 feet in diameter and 3 feet deep. The exercise also included Dean Carl Pleasant discharging an unarmed M-16 type rifle grenade which travelled approximately 100 feet."

That's 30 yards, kids. Ever seen what 10,000 acres of wooded land looks like after the United States Army stages tank exercises? Are Gen. Shalikashvili's armored brigades afraid they might meet a "force superior to any band of regular troops" should they run into defendants Dean Pleasant and Finis Howard Walker, with their 30-yard inert rifle grenade and their capability of blowing a hole six feet wide and three feet deep with "multiple destructive devices" in the Arizona desert?

Oh, and the indictment also specifies that one team member spoke of his attempts to develop a two-foot-long "rocket" made of PCV pipe and fueled with black powder that might soar 200 yards, apparently without any internal guidance system.

Talk about high-tech! This was hush-hush technology, as I recall, when it was introduced to Europe from China in the 14th or 15th century. I remember trying to build something similar— without much success—when I was eight. Good thing there weren't any ATF snitches in my elementary school in Covington, Kentucky.

Were these would-be militiamen foolish to apparently store explosive components in suburban neighborhoods, videotape their experiments in detonating them, and take notes of meetings whose discussions were bound to outrage our federal masters? Probably. Other news reports indicate the leader of the group was so fixated on talking about blowing things up that no other Arizona militia or Second Amendment group would have anything to do with him. Even his Viper Team had shrunk from 43 members a year ago to the 12 peacefully arrested this month.

Did the federals decide to act before they were *all* gone?

Anyway, if the goal here was to protect the immediate safety of the neighbors—rather than staging media-event arrests to generate public outrage against Americans who still dare to bear arms—why wouldn't the authorities approach these fellows openly, politely offering them a safer place to test and store their munitions, rather than sitting by and watching them do dangerous stuff for two years while they tried to build a case? If that failed, why not simply issue a more sensible state or county citation for

427

"reckless endangerment"?

By July 14, reporter Louis Sahagun of the liberal anti-gun *Los Angeles Times* was reporting, "The Viper case now threatens to backfire on federal agencies that heralded it as a breakthrough in the war against domestic terrorists."

Last week, U.S. District Judge Earl Carroll sent six of the suspects home, ruling they constituted no threat to their communities.

In the July 8 hearings that led to those releases, our friend ATF supervisor Steven Ott admitted under oath that his undercover snitch inside the Viper Team had urged the other members to rob banks to further their cause, but that they all refused, Sahagun of the *L.A. Times* reports. Spotting a fellow with initiative who showed up at all the meetings, Viper Team members even proposed that the undercover state Game & Fish officer who infiltrated the group become the organization's leader, Ott testified.

"We told him, 'Absolutely no,'" Ott said.

But the snitch was apparently allowed to provide a place for the group to meet. With free beer and pretzels, I wonder, as an incentive for others to attend? Just who decided to keep this little railroad running, and why?

• • •

In what is probably the most concrete federal charge, one of the members, Gary Curtis Bauer, is also accused of "knowingly and unlawfully possessing one (1) SKS type, 7.62 X 39mm caliber, full-automatic rifle, a machine gun as defined in Title 18, United States Code, section 921(a)(23)," etc. etc.

Plentiful and cheap, the little fixed-magazine SKS carbine may well be the most common weapon of its type in civilian hands in America today. After a brief day in the sun in the 1950s, the

428

Eastern Bloc countries replaced it with the AK-47 and its superior removable magazines, phasing the SKS out of regular service except for guards at remote border posts. Most of the little Simonovs got greased and stacked away in warehouses, which (combined with the fact the SKS fires only one round per trigger pull, thus avoiding the fingerprint-and-$200-tax requirements of our old favorite, the NFA) is precisely why they're now being dug out and sent abroad by former Soviet satellites in need of foreign exchange.

Nor is it illegal for any non-felon to possess an SKS in the United States, even if it includes an extra little piece of metal that allows it to fire its 10 rounds with one pull of the trigger, instead of 10 pulls of the trigger. (The same effect can be accomplished if you purposely break a few internal parts—something the FBI is infamous for doing if it wants to "prove" a seized weapon was capable of firing full-auto.)

All the law says is that you're supposed to pay a $200 tax to possess a weapon that has been converted to full-auto fire—a weapon that happens to sell for $100 to $150 in its semi-automatic (untaxed) configuration, cheaper than any handgun on the market, except for a few recycled Russian clunkers of equally antique vintage.

The ATF, however, tries to make it as onerous and time-consuming as possible to pay that tax and get the required papers, often enforcing an arbitrary six-month wait.

Does this have the effect of maximizing revenue from the tax? It does not. The effect it does have is that many Americans are purposely deluded by the ATF into thinking the possession of such weapons is illegal, as we've seen here.

And does that have the effect of guaranteeing that the citizen militias are "little if at all inferior to [the standing army] in discipline and the use of arms," as the Founders intended and guaranteed? Clearly it does not, since the ATF's arbitrary enforcement methods have actually made machine guns scarce as hens' teeth (except among cocaine wholesalers).

Any legitimate taxing agency—charged with maximizing revenues, rather than a mission far more subversive of our expressly guaranteed freedoms—would be running Public Service spots on TV, urging folks to buy extra machine guns, one for every room in the house, and register them at their new, convenient, 24-hour, drive-through windows.

Any Supreme Court that honored its oath to uphold the Second Amendment would toss out all of this so-called "Title 18" on grounds of these deceptive practices, in defiance of original legislative intent, alone.

But the real point is, the Viper Militia is accused of owning (and failing to pay a $200 tax on) one (1) 30-year-out-of-date burp gun!

Since the seizure reports list several other "machine guns" and "silencers" that do not appear to have brought indictments as separate crimes, one can't help but wonder if most of the firearms possessed by this tiny militia weren't completely legal, with even the $200 tax paid. If so, one wonders if this charge doesn't amount to something more along the lines of a bookkeeping error.

Also seized in the federal raids were "one bag of Viper Militia patches [sic], three magazines, two books" including *Homemade C-4 for Survival*, "one Uzi rifle, two other rifles, silencer, and paperwork for Uzi and silencer, books on silencers, bomb recipes," and the like.

So now we're down to seizing books, readily available through the mail from publishers who advertise openly in national magazines. Books. The conspirators are charged with owning and reading books.

"Teaching"? "Reading"? In the antebellum South, it was against the law to teach a slave to read. Who are the slaves today?

• • •

As if it really needed saying, no one should be planning to blow up any specific occupied buildings, except in defense against overt attempts to deprive us of our Constitutional rights. Innocents could get killed. That would be stupid and immoral.

But totalitarian regimes are not put in place in a single day. They erode our rights a little at a time, in hopes that no single step will be seen as severe enough to cause decent law-abiding citizens to risk their lives, jobs, property, and reputations to say, "That's it, that's the last straw; today we load our rifles and start shooting every government official we see. Where's that damned mailman?"

They count on us saying: "No, not yet, maybe they'll stop with making the Jews sew those silly yellow stars on their clothes. ... "

Or, in our case, "OK, so the Supreme Court ruled last week that the federals can now jail you for years—not just six months any more—without a jury trial. So they're seizing cash from people at airports and at traffic stops without even charging them with crimes. So the IRS can appropriate your bank account and your paychecks without even allowing you a day in court. So I can go to jail if my collectible military rifle has a bayonet lug. But is any single one of these things sufficient reason for me to give up my home, my family, my job, and take to the hills with my rifle?"

In Germany in the late 1930s, precious few citizens chose to take that course. We now sneer at the "good Germans" who whined after the war, "What could I do? What could any one person do? It was the law."

Would history have gone differently if thousands of everyday Germans had taken up arms and begun training in 1935, *in violation of the law*, putting Herr Hitler on notice that any further erosion of personal rights—even those of Jews and Gypsies— would be met with cold steel?

It never happened, and no one now reveres the Germans as a freedom-loving nation and likely never will.

Instead, Americans celebrate each Fourth of July the courage and sacrifice of men like Carter Braxton of Virginia, the wealthy trader who saw his ships swept from the seas and died in rags, and Thomas Nelson, Jr., who aimed the first of Gen. Washington's continental cannon at his own home in Yorktown after Gen. Cornwallis took it over as his headquarters, later to die bankrupt as a result.

We celebrate Francis Lewis of Long Island, who saw his home and properties destroyed and his wife and son die in British prisons.

We celebrate John Hart, who was driven from his wife's bedside by advancing Redcoats as she lay dying. His fields and gristmill laid waste, he lived for more than a year in forests and caves before dying of exhaustion and a broken heart.

These brave men were among the 56 signers of the Declaration of Independence. By doing so, each and every one of them *violated the law*. And when they spoke of risking their lives and fortunes, they weren't just whistling Dixie.

Today, would such men—men who took up arms against the established crown and its mercenaries—be honored in Janet Reno's America? Or would they—along with Mr. Washington—be arrested and charged with "Conspiracy to Furnish Instruction in the Use of Explosive Devices and Other Techniques in Furtherance of Civil Disorder," their homes and farms and firearms all seized and forfeited to the new crown?

Will Ms. Reno's stormtroopers tell us how they believe a civilian militia *should* train to resist oppression? What steps we should follow to legally become adept in the use of heavy machine guns and shoulder-launched surface-to-air missiles—skills now common to the lowliest Vietnamese peasant or free Afghan goatherd—without running afoul of her snitches, spies, and agents provocateurs?

The federal agenda appears to be coming clear. The federals aim to malign, discredit, infiltrate, break up, and arrest all civilian militias until we are, indeed, a nation of disarmed slaves.

The best hope of peace and liberty now lies with the courts and fully informed juries of Arizona, whom I trust will laugh out of court the notion that citizens who never harmed a fly should be jailed for "watching videotapes" of their friends blowing up sand dunes in the desert, no matter how incautious their talk.

Because if the Viper militiamen (and gals) are convicted, the day will have drawn that much nearer—very much nearer—when all Americans will have to decide whether to follow Mr. Madison's advice, to make "plans of resistance" and "appeal to a trial of force," or whether to docilely turn in our deer rifles down at the police station like Good Germans, leave our doors open so the police can enter at their convenience without bothering to knock … and hope for the best.

A Bombing in Atlanta

Aug. 2, 1996—First came the July 17 destruction—possibly by terrorists, possibly during missile tests by our own Navy—of TWA Flight 800 off Long Island, New York. But when this was succeeded by the bombing of an outdoor concert only a mile from the Olympic Village in Atlanta early Saturday morning, July 27 (two dead), the nation's thoughts turned to the proper balance between liberty and safety.

By wide margins, "person-on-the-street" interviews showed Americans anxious to trade even more of their liberties for the promise of greater safety.

Let's assume, for argument's sake, such "straw polls" weren't strongly canted by the predispositions of the TV airheads conducting them, and that this trade-off would stop with a polite "Look inside your purse, ma'am?" The question remains: Are such trade-offs really likely to make us safer?

Thanks to the presence of the Olympic Games—and memories of Munich 1972—Atlanta was already arguably the most security-conscious city in the world by July 26, with parking lots full of trailers housing extra policemen, security experts, and their high-tech gear.

"They that can give up essential liberty to obtain a little temporary safety deserve neither liberty nor safety," Ben Franklin advised us in 1759.

Yes, the apparently random murder of a 44-year-old Georgia housewife by an antipersonnel device was a horrible inexcusable crime.

Meantime, how many innocent Americans were randomly shot July 27 by joy-riding teenage drug dealers? Ten inner-city victims? Twenty? Did any national politician (other than Libertarians, of course) take to the airwaves in high dudgeon, demanding that we end the violence by ending "Prohibition, Part 2," just as alcohol legalization ended the violence of the Roaring Twenties in 1933?

If so, I didn't notice. Yet there were House Speaker Newt Gingrich and his gang on television July 29, saying they regretted having deleted some of the more onerous police-state claptrap from the recent Crime Bill, and would now like to take this opportunity to re-insert chemical tags on all gunpowder, as well as authorizing thousands of FBI roving electronic wiretaps.

Such measures (allowing for technological backwardness) were long practiced in the Soviet Union, where terrorist murder is now the leading cause of death in some professions. Such examples indicate that, when government treats the whole populace as criminals, they do their best to oblige.

434

Meantime Switzerland, where virtually every home holds a legal machine gun, remains among the world's most peaceful societies. As does virtually all of armed America, truth be told, once you leave behind the drug-war turf of the inner cities.

Militia activist Jon Roland reports he was interviewed by the estimable Ambrose Evans-Pritchard of the *London Sunday Telegraph* (now manning that great newspaper's Washington bureau) on these very matters July 30.

"One thing I explained to him that seemed to get his attention," Mr. Roland reports, "is why the Clinton administration is so bent on getting legislation requiring taggants in explosives, and roving wiretaps.

"The main reason for roving wiretaps is not to track criminals or terrorists," Mr. Roland explains. "It is for monitoring political reformers and constitutionalists.

"The main reason for taggants is to make homemade gunpowder illegal. Although most reloaders buy their gunpowder from gun shops, who get it from four main manufacturers, it is easy to make, and many reloaders know how to make it if they had to.

"It would be an easy step to make taggants unavailable to anyone other than those four main manufacturers. Then, perhaps as a condition for selling to government agencies, [the federals could] require those manufacturers to stop selling to gun shops and the public, thus making ammunition unavailable to anyone outside law enforcement."

Paranoid? Leaving aside the mass disarmament of civilians currently underway in Australia (covered in the previous chapter), the conspiracy provisions of the new crime bill have already led to the arrest of 12 gun owners in Arizona, the so-called Viper Militia.

On Monday, July 29, came word that eight more people, including four founding members of the Washington State Militia—with a reputation as one of the most rigorously law-abiding such groups—had been arrested on "explosives and firearms charges." (As usual, the Associated Press dutifully identified the Washington Militia as "an antigovernment group.")

In Atlanta, militiamen Robert Starr and James McCranie sit in a maximum security prison cell, held without bond since their arrests in April, awaiting trial on charges of "conspiracy and possession of an unregistered explosive device [pipe bomb]."

This despite the fact the government's own witness—ATF Agent Steve Gills—has testified that Starr had no knowledge of the pipe-bomb ingredients planted on his property by government snitches and that McCranie told ATF spies he "wanted nothing to do with making pipe bombs."

Is it paranoid to see a government campaign here—with the full cooperation of the lapdog press—to infiltrate, discredit, frame, and imprison the leaders of every locatable civilian militia?

"When conducting an investigation," writes Nancy Lord, attorney for the Macon defendants, "one usually asks the question, 'Who benefits?'"

The pipe bombing in Atlanta during the Olympic Games can only inflame passions against Messrs. Starr and McCranie, Ms. Lord writes, "although they have the perfect alibi [being held for trial without bond in a U.S. pen]."

Meantime, the benefits to those who seek expanded government power are obvious.

"The bombing has led to military personnel on every major street corner in Atlanta," writes Ms. Lord, who has lived in Atlanta since she ran for vice president on the Libertarian Party ticket in 1992 (and presumably knows the kind of troop strength considered normal there, since the last federal occupation ended in 1876), "while government officials call for more money, manpower ... and, yes, authority over our lives. The freedom movement (Militia, Patriots, etc.) has spoken out against this policy for years. Nor would any Georgia militiaman wish to jeopardize the upcoming Macon trial [of Starr and McCrainie]."

It gets more interesting. On May 11—roughly 10 weeks before the Atlanta explosion—the Alabama Constitutional Militia issued a press release as follows: "Through our investigation, we believe the paid government agents" (they proceed to name the two men hired by the government to help frame Messrs. Starr and McCranie) "were attempting to make bombs to stage a terrorist strike at the Olympic Games in Atlanta, Georgia, this summer and blame the Georgia Militia. This clandestine activity is called 'Operation Piedmont.' Piedmont Road is a major thoroughfare in Atlanta which passes Piedmont Park and Georgia State University (Athletics). We have turned this information over to the proper authorities."

Want something stranger yet?

Attorney Lord reports that the U.S. District Court issued a gag order July 26, prohibiting Lord from disclosing more about the government snitches whom the Starr-McCranie defense team suspect of complicity in the Olympic bombing.

The gag order was issued "at 5 p.m. on Friday, approximately seven hours before the bombing," Ms. Lord reports.

"At about 12:30 p.m. on Saturday, July 27, we telephoned the FBI in Atlanta, the Atlanta police, and the federal security agency called SOLEC," she continues, "and told them that we were aware of suspects who know about and have made pipe bombs. We also offered to listen to the 911 tape [of the caller who warned of the Saturday morning blast] and compare it to voice recordings of the individuals, and show our pictures of these men to any eyewitnesses. The FBI official told us they were 'too busy' to speak with us and would not give us any more information.

"On Saturday, we began to observe footage of Bob's [Robert Starr's] arrest [file footage from April 26], and heard that a 'militia connection' was suspected."

Ever since the Murrah Building blast in Oklahoma City (where more damage was done, supposedly with far less explosive, than in Dhahran this June 25), paranoia has run rampant among Patriot activists on the Internet, worrying that this is all an American version of Hitler's famous "Reichstag fire," when the devious fuhrer burned the German houses of parliament so the rump Weimar legislature could not meet to limit his executive power, then proceeded to blame the fire on Jews and Bolsheviks, justifying a further crackdown on his political opponents.

Like most level-headed folks, I tend to take most such speculation with a large grain of salt.

But Saturday, the day after the Olympic bombing, whom did I see on more than one TV "news" broadcast but supposed militia expert Morris Dees of the overwrought left direct-mail fund-raising operation "Klanwatch," arguing from no discoverable evidence that the Atlanta bombing may very well have been the work of skinheads or militia members.

One need only imagine for a moment the networks providing unanswered time for someone to make equally groundless claims that the bombing looked like the work of blacks, Jews, feminists, liberal lawyers, or pro-government extremists, to realize how far we've now come toward transparent undisguised propaganda on our airwaves, so long as the blather fits the pro-government agenda.

As a matter of fact, if we apply the most ancient standard of detective work ("Who benefits?"), as recommended by attorney Lord, we easily see that "pro-government extremists" indeed become far more likely suspects for a lot of these crimes than our much-vilified militiamen and gun owners, who stand to be the first losers (though hardly the last) in the ascendancy of the resultant national police state.

The 'Militia Sympathizer' As Bogeyman

Dec. 4, 1996—One M.C. wrote a letter to the weekly *Mountain-Ear* of Nederland, Colo. (Nov. 14 edition), asking the supporters of fully informed juries a hypothetical question.

"If militia sympathizers wormed their way onto the jury in the Timothy McVeigh case, wouldn't the doctrine of jury nullification allow them to acquit simply because they don't like the federal government?"

Rick Tompkins of Arizona, national spokesman for the Fully Informed Jury Association and runner-up for the 1996 Libertarian presidential nomination, replied via the Internet, where the exchange of letters between M.C. and Paul Grant, attorney for indicted Colorado juror Laura Kriho, had been posted:

"Listen to the buzz words. Are 'militia sympathizers' assumed to be somehow bad by definition? Would M.C. bar militia sympathizers such as Thomas Jefferson, George Washington, George Mason, etc., from jury duty? It seems so.

"Here is my response to his hypothetical question (one that shouldn't be needed for someone who claims to understand the Constitution and the intent of its framers): *yes*, and properly so. Does the concept of a jury of the defendant's peers, randomly selected from the community, have any sensible meaning at all anymore?

"I am a 'militia sympathizer,' in my own way, by my own definitions," Mr. Tompkins continues. "I am also one who is as skeptical and contemptuous of government in general as anyone you could find, and dislike certain specific agencies and their actions to the point of hatred. But if I managed to 'worm my way on the jury' in the case cited, would I acquit mass murderers or indiscriminate killers of children just because I was angry at government? Hardly. Nor do I think the average citizen would do so, 'militia sympathizer' or not. I would, however, require that the

439

case be properly prosecuted, and proved.

"And I find the terminology here quite revealing. 'Wormed their way onto the jury'? Is this a blatant admission of the writer's tacit agreement that it is proper for government to stack juries by whatever means? Also, perhaps, a failure to understand that 'jury nullification,' more properly understood as the 'consent of the governed,' is not just a doctrine, but a fact inherent in the jury system? Without it, there is no true jury, and the sham is revealed."

Novelist Vic Milan then joined the Internet discussion from points east, pointing out the attempt to link suspect McVeigh (still not convicted of any crime, of course) to the patriotic militias.

"Why does M.C. introduce 'militia sympathizers' here? Can M.C. name a militia organization to which Mr. McVeigh ever belonged? With what I think we can safely describe as the worst will in the world, the only contacts between McVeigh and militias that the mass media were able to report resulted in Mr. McVeigh's being asked to leave.

"The closest thing to a 'militia' I know of McVeigh being associated with is the United States Army, in which he served as a non-commissioned officer in combat in Desert Storm," Mr. Milan continued.

"Let me propose a little thought experiment: ... Just replace 'militia sympathizers' in M.C.'s statement with, say, 'Jews.' Or 'gays.' What would we call a person who spoke in terms of Jews 'worming their way onto juries'?"

I would only close by asking, assuming for the moment that the federals have the right culprit in the Oklahoma City (something we plainly cannot know at this juncture), should he or his attorneys be hoping that some "militia members" end up on the jury?

The militia, after all, is the armed body populace as a whole—anyone who would report for duty with a gun if the nation were invaded and the regular army had already been defeated or was busy elsewhere.

Who would likely be the first to show up with their guns, under those circumstances?

Veterans of the armed forces, I would think, followed by policemen both retired and on active duty, hunters, and NRA members.

Do these sound like the kind of folk from which you could expect a "sympathetic" hearing if you had, indeed, blown up a day-care center and killed innocent children?

I don't think so.

Columnist Swallows Fish Story of 'Reservoir Poisonings'

Feb. 5, 1997—Col. David Hackworth, so far as I know (and I've read the highly decorated retired U.S. Army officer's autobiography), has never worked a day of his life at a weekly or daily newspaper. Not as a reporter, not as an editor … not even as an obituary fact-checker.

This does not disqualify Col. Hackworth from writing a newspaper column. The First Amendment happily protects us from ever seeing this profession turned into the exclusive domain of some encrusted and self-protecting guild. In fact, I happen to admire Col. Hackworth's columns, especially when he writes about waste or mismanagement in the Pentagon—a subject he knows something about.

But Col. Hackworth's lack of journalistic experience *might* place a heavier than usual onus on his editors at King Features Syndicate to help guard the colonel against being taken in by fast-talkers with uncorroborated stories to sell.

Recently, Col. Hackworth traveled to Montgomery, Ala., to

consult with one Michael Reynolds, at the self-styled Militia Task Force, an outfit that "operates" out of Morris Dees' Southern Poverty Law Center.

In a Jan. 21 column headlined, "America's most clear and present danger," Col. Hackworth reports that since the bombing of the Murrah Federal Building in Oklahoma City, "terrorist bombings or other terrorist crimes have become almost as common in main street USA as in the British Isles."

Heavens.

"I recently asked Michael Reynolds, an expert on terrorism at the Alabama-based Militia Task Force, who these terrorists are," Col. Hackworth continues. "He says, 'Many of these so-called Patriots advocate nothing less then the dismantling—by force if necessary—of the entire U.S. government and the repudiation of many Constitutional rights.' ...

"Then there are the Lifestyle Patriots, who follow closed-minded anti-government convictions, live as drop outs in isolated communities, home-school their kids and strive for total self-sufficiency while constantly honing their survival skills," Col. Hackworth warns.

"Outlaw Patriots are the ones who collect illegal weapons, resist arrest, run criminal scams and refuse to pay taxes. ... " Col. Hackworth continues.

But then comes the real clincher, as his source Michael Reynolds explains, and Col. Hackworth breathlessly passes the word.

"The most dangerous element of this insurgent movement consists of the Underground Patriots who operate in secret cells of not more then ten people. They're the fanatic, the hardcore, who execute acts of terror against innocent Americans, from exploding pipe bombs at the Atlanta Olympics to bombing federal buildings to poisoning water supplies to robbing banks in order to finance more terrorist acts."

Boy, I'm glad that Atlanta pipe-bombing thing has finally been solved. Funny the FBI never announced any arrests, though. By the way, which are the poisoned municipal water supplies I can no longer drink? Any really big ones? And which bank robberies have been firmly linked to militias? I'm surprised that hasn't gotten more play in the national press. Darn that *New York Times*, always covering up for the Sulzberger family's friends on the Far Right.

Imagine for a moment (I'm trying to come up with the most absurd parallel examples I can think of) a mainstream feature syndicate sending out a column in which the author states, based on a single interview with the head of an outfit calling itself the Negro Watch, or the Task Force on International Jewry, that, "The most dangerous element of this insurgent movement consists of the Underground Negroes/Jews who operate in secret cells of not more then 10 people. They're the fanatic, the hardcore, who execute acts of terror against innocent Americans from exploding pipe bombs at the Atlanta Olympics to bombing federal buildings to poisoning water supplies to robbing banks in order to finance more terrorist acts."

Don't suppose that would bring a phone call from the editor, do you? "Hack, I think we may have a little problem here, unless you can get us some independent corroboration. Now, which water supply is it this 'Jewish Cabal' is supposed to have poisoned?"

Morris Dees, Col. Hackworth concludes, "is on target when he says, 'States with laws against militia and paramilitary training should vigorously enforce them. States without such laws should enact them.'"

Leaving aside for the moment the clear fact that America is *not* being wracked by a paroxysm of terror bombings and reservoir poisonings ... leaving moot the question of whether militias are responsible for crimes that haven't even occurred ... what on earth does the colonel mean?

It's not clear to me how we could even operate a state or municipal police academy if the good colonel and his new friends succeeded in banning all "paramilitary training." I doubt we could teach firearm safety to kids at NRA rifle ranges.

And as for "outlawing the militia," what can that mean, except a total ban on the possession of firearms by anyone who is not a full-time government soldier—precisely the level of personal freedom enjoyed by the residents of Mao's Red China, Pol Pot's Cambodia, and Hitler's Germany?

And here I thought *I* was a bit radical.

Most Americans Should Be Ashamed to Celebrate the Fourth

July 3, 1997—What an inconvenient holiday the Fourth of July has become.

So long as we stick to grilling hot dogs and hamburgers, hauling the kids to the lake or the mountains, and winding up the day watching the fireworks as the Boston Pops plays the "1812"— written by a subject of the czar to celebrate the defeat of our vital ally the French—we can usually manage to convince ourselves we still cling to the same values that made July 4, 1776, a date that continues to ring in history.

Great Britain taxed the colonists at far lower rates than Americans tolerate today—and never dreamed of granting government agents the power to search our private bank records to locate "unreported income." Nor did the king's ministers ever attempt to stack our juries by disqualifying any juror who refused to swear in advance to leave their conscience outside and enforce the law as the judge explained it to them.

The king's ministers insisted the colonists were represented by Members of Parliament who had never set foot on these shores. Today, of course, our interests are "represented" by one of two millionaire lawyers—both members of the incumbent Republicrat Party— between whom we were privileged to "choose" last election day, men who for the most part have lived in mansions and sent their kids to private schools in the wealthy suburbs of the imperial capital for decades.

Yet the colonists did rebel. It's hard to imagine, today, the faith and courage of a few hundred frozen musketmen, setting off across the darkened Delaware, gambling their lives and farms on the chance they could engage and defeat the greatest land army in the history of the known world, armed with only two palpable assets: one irreplaceable man to lead them, and some flimsy newspaper reprints of a parchment declaring: "We hold these Truths to be self-evident, that all Men are created equal, that they are endowed by their Creator with certain unalienable rights, that among these are Life, Liberty, and the Pursuit of Happiness— That to secure these Rights, Governments are instituted among men, deriving their just Powers from the Consent of the Governed, that whenever any Form of Government becomes destructive to these Ends, it is the Right of the People to alter or abolish it. … "

Do we believe that, still?

Recently, President Clinton's then-Drug Czar, Lee Brown, told me the role of government is to protect the people from dangers, such as drugs. I corrected him, saying, "No, the role of government is to protect our liberties."

"We'll just have to disagree on that," the president's appointee said.

The War for American Independence began over unregistered untaxed guns, when British forces attempted to seize arsenals of rifles, powder, and ball from the hands of ill-organized Patriot militias in Lexington and Concord. American civilians shot and killed scores of these government agents as they marched back to Boston. Are those Minutemen still our heroes? Or do we now consider them "dangerous terrorists" and "depraved government-haters"?

In Phoenix last week, an air-conditioner repairman and former military policeman named Chuck Knight was convicted by jurors—some tearful—who said they had no choice under the judge's instructions, on a single federal conspiracy count of associating with others who owned automatic rifles on which they had failed to pay a $200 transfer tax. This was after a trial in which defense attorney Ivan Abrams says he was forbidden to bring up the Second Amendment as a defense.

Were the Viper Militia readying plans of resistance, as recommended by Mr. Madison in The Federalist No. 46? Would the Constitution ever have been ratified at all had Mr. Madison and his fellow federalists warned the citizens that such non-violent preparations would get their weapons seized and land them in jail for decades?

Happy Fourth of July.

Driving the Militias Underground

July 16, 1997—An anonymous correspondent from AOL-land writes:

"Vin, I read your [July 4] piece. It's certainly thought-provoking. ...

"You've claimed that the paramilitary groups are there to defend democracy. You've also claimed that the government should not be employed to protect us from drugs, but to ensure freedom.

"What would your response be if, in a fit of anger because his son or daughter died from a drug overdose, a leader of a paramilitary group decided it was time to move against the government because it had failed in its job of keeping drugs out of America?

"I would like to expand on this idea. At the time of the American Revolution, the leaders did all they could to rally the colonists behind them. They published papers, like Tom Paine's *Common Sense*, held rallies, and went before the people. The paramilitary groups of today operate in secret, keeping their political agenda hidden from the people. ... Who knows what their political agendas are, and if the group that emerges on top will represent your view, or my views, or anyone else's? Revolution has often led to dictatorships and repression ... Napoleon, Lenin, Mao Tse-Tung, the Khmer Rouge. ...

"I do not disagree with everything you said. But I also think you do not recognize some situations that are potentially very dangerous. ... "

I responded:

Greetings, unnamed correspondent—

I carry no portfolio for "democracy"—the pernicious doctrine that three wolves and a sheep should take a majority vote on what's for supper.

I am far more interested in the God-given liberties that the Bill of Rights assures us no government can infringe ... even by a vote of two hundred million-to-one.

In answer to your first question, I don't know. What would your response be if, in a fit of anger, the leader of a left-wing environmental group (or an armed government police agency, for that matter) decided it was time to move against the lumber companies because they had provided the wood that made the ladder off which the leader's child slipped and fell to his death?

In your rather bizarre hypothetical example (I would think vigilante justice against drug dealers would be more likely than against narcotics agents), I suppose his fellow patriots would promptly lock him up in a nuthouse or turn him in (far more likely than in a government agency, where the chain of command is all). Or, as your hypothetical militia leader drew a bead on a government agent, I assume he'd be either shot, or arrested and put on trial. I'd *like* to think the same thing would happen to a bureau chief of the FBI or EPA, should he or she decide to murder a lumber executive.

However, given that no FBI or ATF agent has ever been so much as put on trial for the murders at Waco or Ruby Ridge, I kind of doubt they'd face such justice, don't you? Wouldn't we be far more likely to hear that the lumber guy had been shot "in full accordance with the rules of engagement in force at that time, and in full compliance with departmental procedures and regulations"?

We could construct "lone-nut" hypotheticals all day. What's the point? What's your proposed solution? For the federal government to seize and destroy every hunting rifle in America? Now there's an idea. Can we seize and destroy the arms of every federal police agency first? Why not? Because they've "never murdered anyone"? You might want to check on that with Sammy and Vicky Weaver, and a few dozen Seventh-day Adventist children in Waco, Texas, and Donald Scott on a hill above Malibu, California.

Anyway, up until a year ago, it was not true, as you contend, that "The paramilitary groups of today operate in secret, keeping their political agenda hidden from the people." The Viper Militia in Phoenix held meetings, and took minutes. They videotaped their activities. The leaders of the militias in San Diego and Washington state called me up regularly until last spring, giving me their names and numbers and asking me to help announce the times and public places they would be meeting to drill. (I don't think I ever did—but it was nice of them to keep in touch.)

The fellow in San Diego was (is?) an earnest young lawyer, who hoped to get his militia well-enough established to bring lawsuits challenging California laws that now make it illegal to even hand your legal gun to another person (that's considered an "illegal transfer"), since this obviously makes it hard for a drill instructor to instruct a recruit in the safe and proper use of a weapon.

Then, starting a year ago, the federal government started infiltrating and busting the militias: first in Macon, Georgia; then the Vipers in Phoenix; then similar groups in West Virginia, New Hampshire, and Washington state. Most of those dozens of defendants have now caved in and accepted plea bargains, pleading guilty to the made-up crime of "conspiracy" to teach others how to use weapons, etc. Why? Because they realized they would never be allowed by federal judges to even mention the Second Amendment in court as part of their defense.

(In the Georgia case, a defendant was convicted even after government snitches admitted under oath they had buried bomb makings on his property without his knowledge. In the West Virginia case, the *Washington Post* reports a government agent provocateur approached a militia leader with blueprints to a nearby government computer facility, offering to help arrange a sale to a fictitious international terrorist. In New Hampshire, the government informant appears to have actually stolen night-vision equipment from a government armory, proceeding to deliver it to a surprised militia leader. Did the accused behave foolishly, in all these cases? Probably. But the common thread is that it was always the busy government informant thinking up the "crimes.")

These Draconian prosecutions will likely have the effect of *driving* militia groups to keep their activities secret, since many who most prominently tried to organize forthrightly and publicly now face five to nine years in prison. This is entirely the doing of the federal government.

But what right is it of yours or mine to know their "agendas," anyway? If they choose to own machine guns—a right guaranteed them in the Second Amendment—and to meet together without telling anyone else what they're up to—as guaranteed in the First and Fourth Amendments—so what? I'm far less afraid of an armed neighbor than a Ninja-clad ATF or DEA agent coming through my door with guns ablaze because his warrant has the wrong address. Ask Donald Scott. Ask Samuel Weaver. Ask the black and Asian mothers and their innocent babies (never named on any warrants) at Waco.

Ask the retired black preacher who died of a heart attack while handcuffed to his bedframe in his Boston apartment last year because the local drug police busted the apartment one floor *above* the one their secret informant told them to hit.

Tyrants like Lenin, Stalin, Mao, and Pol Pot insisted that private citizens be disarmed, so that the central government and its army would have complete control. Revolutionists and rabid government-haters like Washington, Mason, Paine, and Patrick Henry, on the other hand, insisted that the common man *must* retain his arms, and always be better armed than the central government authorities, in order to resist tyranny, whether galloping or slinking in slowly on its belly.

By their fruits shall ye know them. Who is a more vocal spokesman for the common man retaining all his military-style arms: my friend, militia spokesman J.J. Johnson (whose credentials as a white supremacist are marred only by the fact he happens to be black), or Bill Clinton, Charles Schumer, and Dianne Feinstein? Who is more likely to lead us into tyranny?

How many members of active militia groups have you met and chatted with? How many active gun owners and shooters? If the government started telling you that the biggest danger to your safety was the "dirty Jew," would you accept that at face value, rather than ask a kindly rabbi or Jewish family in the neighborhood whether you could spend a weekend with them, to see what kind of people they really are?

I hope not.

450

'The Fight's over. There's No One Left to Fight.'

Aug. 15, 1997—In July 1997, Lew Rockwell of the Ludwig von Mises Institute in Auburn, Ala., took note of my reporting on the Viper Militia case and asked me if I could sum up the affair in one wrap-up article for publication in the September 1997 issue of *The Rothbard-Rockwell Report*, targeted at professional economists with a free-market bent.

As it turns out, that essay also serves as a final obituary for the attempt to develop a healthy, open, public-militia movement in America the 1990s—and as a close for this discussion.

Here it is:

"There's no way to rule innocent men. The only power any government has is the power to crack down on criminals. Well, when there aren't enough criminals, one makes them. One declares so many things to be a crime that it becomes impossible to live without breaking laws."

—*Ayn Rand,* Atlas Shrugged

On June 4, 1997, the trial of the only Viper Militia defendant to face a jury—after months in jail, 10 have pleaded guilty to one charge or another, while one still awaits trial—got underway before Judge Earl H. Carroll in the federal district courthouse in downtown Phoenix.

At the end of the two-week trial, late on the afternoon of June 18, the jury began its deliberations on the single charge of "conspiracy to make or possess unregistered destructive devices" against 47-year-old air-conditioning installer and Vietnam-era Army veteran Chuck Knight.

The "overt acts" Knight was accused of committing as part of the Arizona militia group? Standing guard while other militia members practiced blowing up sand dunes with homemade explosives out in the desert and participating in a discussion during which the Vipers agreed to buy some blasting caps.

Charles Knight was never alleged to have owned or handled explosives, nor any illegal or untaxed firearm. He never fired a gun at anyone in anger, is never alleged to have harmed anyone, nor stolen anything, nor threatened anyone with harm—unless, of course, we count the government, which obviously feels *very* threatened by the existence of groups like the Viper Militia, despite the fact no militia group can be shown to have killed anyone in recent years—compared to the estimated annual death toll of America's inner-city street gangs, now hovering around 1,200 corpses per year.

After taking off a three-day weekend, the jury trooped back into the courtroom on Tuesday June 24, to report they were hopeless deadlocked. The judge asked them whether, with further deliberations, they might reach a verdict. The foreman replied, "No."

But Judge Carroll was not satisfied. He sent the 12 back to the jury room, instructing them that they would not be released until they had reached a verdict, and that the verdict must be unanimous.

Ninety minutes later they returned, and found Chuck Knight guilty.

The Viper Militia case may be a watershed in the struggle to preserve the right of private Americans to bear arms.

Following the original July 1, 1996, bust of the 14-member outfit (two "members" turned out to be paid government informants), President Clinton made a Rose Garden announcement, saying, "I'd like to begin today by saluting the law-enforcement officers who made arrests in Arizona yesterday to avert a terrible terrorist attack."

The initial government spin was that the Vipers had specific plans to bomb government buildings and commercial television towers, some of which they had actually videotaped from the outside. But that story started to erode almost immediately.

By the time ATF case agent Steven Ott was testifying at a pre-release hearing in Phoenix July 7, he told the court his snitch "felt there was absolutely no plan to conduct any bombings of these buildings at that time," which is why the ATF never informed occupants of those buildings that they were in any danger.

Judge Carroll let half the defendants go home "on their own recognizance" that day a year ago—no bail required—and Chuck Knight still drives around Phoenix a free man today, running what's left of his air-conditioner business, as he awaits sentencing Sept. 8.

Is this the way we treat dangerous terrorists?

• • •

I called Chuck Knight, father of four children aged 16 to 26 (and stepfather of two more boys), in Phoenix July 8, and asked him why he thought the jury finally voted to convict.

"The jury was convinced by the tantrums thrown by the prosecutors that this was a dangerous group. There was hardly any mention made of Chuck Knight. Mostly that these guys had machine guns, and that Gary Bauer had, unbeknownst to most of the rest of us, built seven hand grenades."

(Bauer, Vietnam veteran of both the 101st and 87th Airborne Divisions, recipient of the Purple Heart and both the Bronze and Silver Stars, pleaded guilty to multiple counts of owning weapons the government taught him to use, and is now serving nine years in the Federal Correctional Facility in Sheridan, Oregon.)

Defense attorney Ivan Abrams objected to the government's hauling machine guns belonging to other Vipers into the courtroom, since Knight was not charged with owning any such weapons. Objection overruled.

I told Knight I'd heard that some of the "unregistered machine guns" presented by the prosecution had actually been built by the government out of spare parts found at the homes of the various militia members.

"This is the way the law reads: If they can take parts and with eight hours of professional work by professional gunsmiths working full time in Washington, D.C., make it fire more than one round, then its a machine gun. There was a guy who published a magazine piece on this a couple of years ago, a guy who took a wrecked Volvo and in about seven hours made a weapon that would fire four or five rounds. So by the legal definition used in this case the Volvo was, technically, a machine gun. We're talking about professional gunsmiths, with access to sophisticated machine shops."

Surely the best defense, then, would be to challenge the law as ridiculous, to ask the jury to acquit based on the statute or ATF regulation being unconstitutionally broad?

"The attorney is not allowed to challenge the law. He's there to prove I didn't violate the law. Judge Earl H. Carroll said, 'There won't be any Constitutional issues discussed in this court.'"

Why does Knight think 10 out of his 12 fellow militiamen took the plea bargain?

"You don't have a clue to the terrorist tactics that were employed. ... Hank [decorated veteran Henry Oberturf] was beat up while in jail and Rick Walker nearly died because they would not give him his medicine—he's a diabetic with a heart problem. ... "

Still, the average citizen assumes the jury gets to weigh all the issues, that the defense is free to present its explanation of how the Second Amendment renders the law in question null and void.

"No, you absolutely can't present any defense you want," Knight protests. "There are so many things you're not allowed to say."

Knight, himself, would have faced a lesser sentence had he

taken the plea bargain.

"I'm so glad I'm a Christian. I don't want to end up standing in front of God someday and saying, 'I didn't believe, so I took a plea bargain and lied about my whole life to get out of trouble.' I think my actions are telling Him loud enough that I trust Him. ... "

Although Knight was a deacon at his last church, "Folks at the church didn't even bother calling me" after his arrest, he explained.

A friend invited Knight to visit the First Institutional Baptist Church, in downtown Phoenix, instead. At first, Knight didn't understand why his friend laughed that the reporters wouldn't follow or bother him there. He did once he arrived.

"This new church is mostly a black church—there are maybe six white people—and these people have been just wonderful. They've welcomed me with open arms. ... I have three hundred little aunties that come over and pinch me on the cheek and tell me how proud they are of what I'm doing. One of my friends there took me aside and said, 'You know, Chuck, black people understand, more than you can know, what it is to be falsely arrested, to be falsely accused and convicted.'

"To be amongst them and to hear the stories, and have these people reach out to me like they have, they have literally saved my life. I was suicidal when I went there. I was rescued from the brink, and I don't say that lightly. This coming Sunday will be my one-year anniversary. The only Sunday I missed was the weekend we took Donna to California to surrender" for his wife's one-year term in the women's federal prison in Dublin, California.

What was his wife's offense?

"They had nothing on her except that she knew these people and she knew they were making explosives to go blow up out in the desert, and she spoke Politically Incorrectly and talked about what we should do if, if, if. ... There was never any plan. Under the law, you have to have a plan for an explosive to become a destructive device, and without that plan ... "

"My argument centered around the fact that there was no plan to harm anyone," explains Knight's defense attorney, Ivan Abrams. "Who was the target of these weapons of destruction? Where were they going to be used and when and how? And every one of these questions resulted in the answer, 'I don't know.' So there was no plan and no intent. And if intent is required for a criminal conspiracy, there's no crime. Is it a crime to bury ammonium nitrate, to have these devices ready to go in case of emergency? No."

I asked Chuck Knight what he believes the government's real goal is, in pressing such prosecutions.

"Their goal is to disarm the public. This is to make sure everyone knows that if they can put me in prison for five years for going out to two field exercises in six months, after fifteen years in business in this town, meeting the public all day every day, a church-going guy, a good father—if we can throw this guy in prison, think what we can do to you.

"If we tell you you can't have any guns, you better get all the guns out of your house right now, law or no law. If they can terrorize my wife into taking a year—she pled guilty to the same charge I'm up on, she took a plea bargain and got a year and a day—I've got to be made an example of. You just don't fight it when the government comes after you; that's not allowed."

"It's hard to tell what crime Chuck has committed," writes his attorney, Ivan Abrams, in a personal note to me dated July 4. "The conspiracy charge is so broad that he may be 'guilty' of associating with machine gunners, thinking too much about fresh fertilizer, camping in the desert while dressed in cammies, or, worst of all, having a friend who had a friend who had a wife who bought a nasty book."

The jurors "said after the fact that they didn't feel I was guilty," Knight reports, "that the law was too broad. [Juror] Chuck Wahn said that in a broadcast interview. He's a fifty-ish guy, he was almost in tears. But it doesn't help me any. ... It would have been nice if I had a juror or two with some guts. The jurors in the William Penn case [London, 1670] were tortured by the judge, and they still refused to convict."

"The jurors are quoted in the newspaper down here as saying we thought Chuck Knight was a nice guy, but there just wasn't any choice, the judge said you have to ignore your hearts and enforce the law," explained defense attorney Abrams in a telephone interview two days after the verdict. "I even dropped in [a reference to] the Fugitive Slave Act at that point, but the judge had ordered us not to discuss jury nullification, and I saw him coming up off the bench at me. ... "

Yet, surprisingly enough, Abrams says the jury included gun owners. "It was much better than what you usually get in Phoenix. We had people who shoot recreationally and have been to gun shows. But what they were afraid of was this really bad compound word called 'ammonium nitrate.' Our timing couldn't have been worse, thank you Mr. McVeigh—he went on trial the same time." Abrams says he moved for a mistrial on the grounds that the ongoing McVeigh trial in Denver (for the 1996 bombing of the Murrah federal building in Oklahoma City) was coloring the atmosphere, "but it was not granted."

• • •

"Aren't they just speeding up Darwinism?" I asked attorney Abrams of the government's prosecutions of these highly visible public militia units. By shutting down the goofier militias, the guys who parade around in public in camouflage fatigues, aren't they just teaching those who profoundly fear and distrust the government how to be more secretive, more serious, more professional ... and simultaneously walling them off from the influence of more moderate voices?

"But that's what they want to do," the self-described liberal Democrat replied. "Look at the War on Drugs, which is dependent on evil men with evil-sounding Hispanic names: Marcos Fernando Guzman. And the more of them we can create, we have our enemy and our target and then we can create our government agency. It is to the government's advantage to make more and badder militias, because the worse they are, the more agencies like the ATF can come out and say, 'We are the first line of defense, we are saving the nation from ruin, we need money from Congress.'

"We're in a terrible state as a nation in that we have no enemies. So what better enemy to create than ugly guys in ugly clothes, redneck racists running around killing people with stinking bags of fertilizer?

"Sadly, Chuck Knight ain't no racist; he ain't no white supremacist; he's no Christian religious fanatic. I'm a Jew; I don't think he's going to eat me. I respect Chuck and we will remain friends.

"Some of these guys from New York, you bring them out here where the real disaffection is, and they'll be shocked first of all at the depth of it. I'm shocked at the depth of the disaffection, but also at the way it permeates all layers of society.

"I really do think the government wants to encourage the militias, which is why you get agents provocateurs like [John 'Doc'] Schultz." Here, Abrams was referring to Private Investigator Scott Jason Wells, the former Colorado state trooper who infiltrated the Vipers on his own initiative after taking a job at the Phoenix gun store they frequented. He then shopped his "undercover" services to numerous agencies—he was reportedly turned down cold by the FBI—for five months before attracting the attention of the Arizona Department of Game & Fish, and then the federal Bureau of Alcohol, Tobacco and Firearms, which eventually paid him $12,000 for his services.

When infiltrator "Schultz" proposed to the rest of the group that they rob banks, and Chuck Knight replied, "That's the last thing we'd ever do," Schultz's testimony for the government "was that they were just prioritizing," Abrams laughs. "I thought when he said that we were home free—if anything would show the absurdity of the case, that would be it. I asked, 'What was the second-to-last thing they were going to do?' but the question was thrown out."

I asked former federal prosecutor Abrams if he was ready to join a militia, himself.

"I'm going to keep practicing with my Winchester Model '94 in 30-30, and my Glock 23, and keep buying as much ammunition as I can possibly afford. ... I think we have to stand up and thumb our noses at the tyrannies of government, and not be like this jury and say, 'We didn't want to convict him, but we had to; we didn't have any choice.' I'm just appalled at the ability of the American people to turn over authority to the central government. ... "

"The conspiracy laws are an obscenity," says Chuck Knight. "You can hammer anyone with a conspiracy, all they have to do is talk. The way I read the Constitution, if no one has been hurt, if there is no victim, there is no crime. ...

"They've all but put me out of business. ... I have clients that are afraid to have me there because they're afraid they'll be put under surveillance. The guy who's most terrified is an orthodontist who's had some run-ins with the IRS. He said, 'Chuck, I know they're out to get anything they can on you, so I just can't have you around. I just can't stand to go through all that again. ... ' That's the saddest thing I've ever heard, that's how close we are to Hitler's Germany. America is like ancient Rome. This is bread and circuses now. ... They're trying to make everyone a federal felon so we'll all lose our firearms rights.

"The fight's over. There's no one left to fight. You may be allowed to store food and keep a weapon, but you're not allowed to talk to anyone about it. ... If a police officer stops you for a traffic offense they can now search your car. So many of our Constitutional rights are gone, I'm heartsick."

IX

IT KEEPS COMING
BACK TO WACO

Let's See Them Use *This* as Another
Excuse to Expand Federal Power

On Feb. 28, 1993, 76 agents of the federal Bureau of Alcohol, Tobacco and Firearms, garbed all in black, stormed the Branch Davidian church in Waco, Texas, machine pistols ablaze. Since the ATF's search warrant—acquired by presenting a local magistrate with eight-month-old information blatantly false on its face—allowed only a peaceful knock at the door, this assault was illegal.

The ATF raid, planned and led by agents Phillip Chojnacki and Chuck Sarabyn from the ATF office in the Murrah Federal Building in Oklahoma City, was conducted under rules of engagement that required the agents to withdraw and not return fire blindly into the building if any resistance was met—according to the sworn court testimony of agent Barbara Maxwell, who took part in the assault.

Yet when the Davidians returned fire, the agents fired blindly for hours into a wooden building they knew contained unarmed women and children, killing at least one 2-year-old baby. They broke off their attack only when they ran out of ammo and sought to recover their wounded. In the course of this atrocity, it now appears several of the ATF agents also shot either themselves or each other.

None of the ATF agents were ever charged with any crime. Instead, the surviving *Davidians* were put on trial and imprisoned, for the crime of "resisting." The two leaders of the ATF raid were restored to full duty and full pay.

When the ATF couldn't resolve what quickly became a stand-off with the surviving Branch Davidians in their church, the FBI was called in to lay siege to the Davidians. The FBI cut off utilities to the building, an act for which they never explained any legal basis. This forced the occupants to turn to kerosene space heaters to warm the children and nursing mothers in the building. This was a direct and predictable result of the FBI's illegal termination of utility services to the church.

Finally, sensing that public opinion was starting to shift in favor of the Christians they held hostage in the church, the FBI decided on April 19, 1993—with the specific approval of Bill Clinton and Janet Reno—to end the siege. The federal agents sent in battle tanks (illegal for use against civilians on this continent —an inconvenience the government got around by euphemistically dubbing them "armored personnel carriers" after removing only their longest-range guns) to knock holes in the walls of the wooden church and to thus collapse the interior stairwells. These tanks then sprayed CS gas (illegal for use in war, much more disabling than standard tear gas, and considered potentially deadly in enclosed spaces by its manufacturer) into the building.

At that point, with their surviving victims prostrate and convulsing in their own vomit and with the stairwells collapsed, the federal government became an accessory in the deaths of all 86 who perished in the ensuing inferno, even if that fire was set by Davidian leader David Koresh, which is unlikely for three reasons:

1) The tanks could hardly have knocked down the walls *without* knocking over at least one space heater and thus starting the

fire, while the occupants hunkered down to avoid the covering machine gun fire from government snipers at the rear of the building, snipers whose muzzle flashes are visible on overhead infrared government film of the engagement since made public under the Freedom of Information Act; 2) The FBI said it would present, at the trial of its surviving victims, proof positive that Koresh started the fire, but never did so; and 3) the FBI quickly bulldozed the rubble so no one could conduct an independent forensic investigation, which might have turned up (according to the author of an Academy Award-nominated documentary on the subject) such evidence as spent government incendiary mortar rounds.

If the Bureau were blameless, surely it would have done the opposite—preserve the site until independent forensic teams could be brought in to confirm the FBI's story. (Even though the wreckage of the blown-up Murrah Building in Oklahoma City was similarly leveled before an independent, non-government, forensic probe was possible, it took weeks to get clearance to bulldoze that site; the church at Waco was leveled within days.)

• • •

On April 19, 1995, the two-year anniversary of the Waco murders, the Oklahoma City command posts of the Bureau of Alcohol, Tobacco and Firearms and the Drug Enforcement Administration blew up. (Curiously, it appears the FBI had quietly moved its offices out of the building about a month before.)

A number of children of government agents in a day-care center in the building—probably about the same number as the 18 children murdered by the ATF and FBI in the Waco holocaust—also died in the blast.

(The collateral slaughter of children is, of course, a tragedy. Let's merely stipulate for the record that no death penalty was sought, nor anyone branded an "evil coward" by the sitting president of the United States, after Wounded Knee, Dresden, Hiroshima, or any of the scores of incendiary bombings of Japan that at times killed 100,000 women and children in a single night. No yellow roses for them ... nor for the Davidians.)

No one, of course, should endorse, encourage, support, or justify the Oklahoma City bombing. The fearfully stupid and indiscriminate act has set back the cause of liberty in this country no one yet knows how far. The problem with vigilante justice is that it deprives us of the presumption of innocence and virtually every other protection against miscarriage of justice.

But when we warn against vigilantism, we almost always make the point that those tempted to take the law into their own hands should be patient—that they should await justice from prosecutors and the courts.

Can we really say that in this case?

Did President Clinton call the ATF and FBI agents who murdered the Branch Davidians "evil cowards" and "animals," as he did the Oklahoma City bombers? Did he apply those terms to FBI sniper Lon Horiuchi, who shot the unarmed Vicki Weaver through the head, killing her instantly as she held a baby in her arms in her cabin in rural Idaho in the fall of 1992? Did he so brand the drug police who murdered the innocent Donald Scott in his Malibu ranch house? Did anyone seek the death penalty against any of the culprits in those killings, as Janet Reno promised to seek it against the Oklahoma City bombers?

Of course not. When government agents kill commoners these days, there's not even the kind of token indictment and mock trial that the Founders complained about in the Declaration of Independence. They're just let go with a wink and a commendation.

It's only when commoners dare to kill the occupying swarms of officers "sent hither to eat out our substance" in their federal colonial headquarters that such terms get bandied about.

What chance would a citizen have today, walking into a federal court building and trying to file a suit demanding that the ATF be disbanded, since its very existence violates the Second Amendment by infringing the right to bear arms? How about a citizen of Oklahoma, seeking to file suit to have the local federal building closed and all its swarms of bureaucrats sent packing back to Washington?

Such suits would be thrown out in the blink of an eye under "sovereign immunity" or "lack of standing" or whatever. The federal judiciary these days is not a competing power, anxious to keep the executive and legislative branches hemmed inside Constitutional bounds. It is a co-conspirator, sternly holding the people down while allowing our voracious oppressors to commit unbridled mayhem any way they please.

So, whether we lament the results or not, if the courts no longer provide a peaceful avenue through which citizens can enforce the Constitution and Bill of Rights, should we really be surprised that some folks—more and more—give up in frustration and take the law (however foolishly and tragically) into their own hands?

The day after the Oklahoma City bombing, White House chief of staff Leon Panetta said he had sent word to the 6,000 federal buildings around the country to beef up their security.

Why are there 6,000 such federal facilities within the several states—at an average of 120 per state? The Founders promised the Washington government would be a small and puny thing, concerned only with "external affairs."

Why were hundreds of armed federal police and other federal parasites busying themselves in Oklahoma City on April 19, 1995? This wasn't some branch post office. There are no naval facilities in Oklahoma, nor any customs houses. What were all those people *doing* there?

Now, our TV commentators work to spread panic in order to justify further crackdowns on gun owners and other "right-wing" groups, although no guns were used in this bombing. They ask, "Whatever can we do so we and our children can again be safe in our places of work?"

Um, let me think here … avoid placing day-care centers inside armed ATF, FBI, and DEA command centers?

The ATF did not start its murderous war against American gun owners in 1993. It's been going on for 25 years. They maimed Air Force veteran Ken Ballew in Silver Spring, Md., in 1971; they murdered Craig Davis in Chicago in 1989. The standard method of operation of these domestic Gestapos is to descend in massive force on American families late at night or at dawn, catching them at gunpoint while in their pajamas or showers, and shooting them if they resist. (Even Democratic Michigan Congressman John Dingell recently called the ATF "jackbooted American fascists.")

Did these bullies-with-badges really believe they would forever be able to choose the time and place of their battles, that no one would ever turn the tables, counterattacking when the federals least expected it, at a place where the agents' children—rather than the citizens'—were at risk for a change?

What idiot starts a war—complete with massacres and tens of thousands of POWs—and thinks no one will ever counterattack?

The American Revolution started—and cost the British their colonies—when the redcoats attempted to seize the arms and powder of law-abiding Americans at Lexington and Concord in 1775.

The bombing in Oklahoma City in 1995 occurred because the ATF in 1993 raided a Texas church, attempting to seize the arms and ammunition of law-abiding Americans.

A government that trusts its people is no threat to its people and need not fear its people. A government that treats its populace the way the Germans treated the occupants of the Warsaw ghetto (the Waco raid occurred on the 50th anniversary of the last great "sweep" to disarm the Jews there, and ended about the same way) will eventually share the fate of all tyrants.

If the federal government wants to end the violence, the solution will come not from more oppressive laws, more metal detectors, and more doomed attempts at victim disarmament. (What will we ban next—fertilizer and fuel oil?) All Bill Clinton has to do is disband the prototype "domestic fringe hate group"—the ATF—and stop trying to disarm a free people.

Have you heard a single TV or government "expert" suggest that? Of course not. That's because the terms of our so-called national debate are now predetermined for us. We will only discuss to what extent the latest crisis justifies further expansion of federal power; never the opposite.

Start By Closing Down These Three 'Dangerous, Armed Cults'

Treating Attorney General Janet Reno like Cleopatra on her barge, a select committee of Congress ended 10 days of hearings into the government murders at Waco on Aug. 1, 1995, having examined no evidence and convinced no one.

Ms. Reno said again that she accepts full personal responsibility for everything that happened, both at the start and at the end of the 51-day Branch Davidian siege, when more than 80 people burned to death.

But it's a funny kind of "responsibility."

If a bank robber embarks on his crime with no intention of killing anyone, but one of his hostages dies of a heart attack—or even from police fire—during the holdup, Ms. Reno would be the first to explain that the bank robber must be charged with murder: his intentions count for nothing.

In the final assault, Ms. Reno's FBI cultists punched holes in the walls with tanks (she compared them to "rent-a-cars" in her Aug. 1 testimony) and inserted poisonous flammable gas without a care in the world for the fact this must inevitably knock over some of the kerosene lanterns and space heaters onto the bales of hay that were piled up against FBI small-arms fire—on a day with 40-mile-per-hour winds, while they held fire-fighting equipment many miles away.

How can anyone claim responsibility for these acts without indicting herself on a charge of multiple negligent homicide (at the very least) as her last official act before resigning?

The problem with these Waco "hearings" is that no one asked the kind of questions that could at least form the basis for later perjury prosecutions.

The government bragged—before the Davidian survivors went on trial in San Antonio—that they had a videotape proving that the Davidians fired first. No one has ever seen it. Why wasn't each government witness asked in turn, "Is there such a tape? Was it, to your knowledge or belief, erased, destroyed, or hidden away?"

Bullet holes in the metal-sheathed Dutch door that David Koresh held open while the ATF cultists opened fire (the Davidians' dog and her four still-chained puppies died first, typical of a pre-emptive strike, not the actions of men trying to extricate themselves from an unexpected "ambush")—would reveal whether the shots were incoming or outgoing. It's doubtful that door was destroyed by fire, but it's never been found. Every government witness could have been asked, "Do you have knowledge of anyone having carried away, destroyed, or hidden that door so this committee cannot examine it?"

Ms. Reno says she lay awake at night before the final raid, wondering, "What about the children?"

Others have doubtless lain awake with similar questions on

their lips. "What about the children?" we can imagine Dr. Mengele murmuring. "Are we using too much Zyklon B on them?"

Even more absurdly, Ms. Reno testified the final burnout had to be done in a hurry, because she feared that a single Internet posting by some unidentified attorney, calling for America's un-organized militia to descend on Waco, might brings hordes of gunmen to break the siege.

There was also a missed opportunity for the question of the decade: "Did you assume then, Ms. Reno, that if a number of armed American civilians drove to the scene, they would take David Koresh's side against your men? Why? What were you and your men doing that led you to believe that over time, as they found out what was going on, an ever-increasing number of gun-owning Americans—for that's what the militia is—would take up arms on Mr. Koresh's behalf, and against you? What were you afraid of people seeing there? Why were the press and the fire engines held back, miles from the scene? What other bodies of federal troops were present? Were members of the Delta Force on the scene, Ms. Reno? Did any of them have sniper rifles or mor-tars capable of firing incendiary projectiles? Why?"

Most hideous, of course, were the Democratic questioners, anxious to express empathy for poor Janet. "Can you tell us what you have learned that will help us in future dealings with danger-ous, armed cults?" one sniveled.

The phrase brought to mind a report by S.K. Bardwell in the July 27 *Houston Chronicle*.

It seems the owner of a Houston topless club called the Ritz Plaza was shot five times by a man named Pete Sinclair, who grew irate when the owner told him he and the other drunks bar-hopping with him in a chartered bus for his bachelor party could not enter the club without paying a $5 cover charge.

At first, Houston police could not find Sinclair's 9 mm Glock at the scene. It was turned in to police the next day by federal agents who had apparently removed it from the scene.

Why federal agents? Pete Sinclair and all the other drunks on his bus turned out to be members of one of the three most "dangerous, armed cults" to which Ms. Reno could possibly turn her attention—the Drug Enforcement Administration.

Speaking the Unpalatable Truth

J.K., an editor at a newspaper in west Texas, responded to my column of Aug. 30, 1996, which dealt primarily with the Chechen freedom fighters. He argued that column was "reprehensible and irresponsible," because in the final paragraphs, "You say flat out that federal agents fired on the Branch Davidians in Waco; that is unproven stuff of conspiracists. You also then recommend Chechen-style retaliation against federal agents."

This "betrays an attitude that goes way beyond what I consider to be reasonable, rational dissent," he concludes.

I find it interesting that J.K. didn't bother to call me (he has my number) to ask how I determined that federal agents shot into the Waco church complex from the circling National Guard helicopters. (These helicopters were only acquired, let us remember, when the ATF mission commander lied outright to the Texas National Guard, claiming he believed David Koresh was operating a methamphetamine lab—the only circumstance under which such military equipment is supposed to be available for use against U.S. citizens on our own soil.)

How is it that any fact is determined to be solid enough to be reported in any respectable newspaper, eventually passing into the history books? Do reporters just happen to be on the scene of most of the holdups, plane crashes, or other unscheduled events that fill the bulk of our news accounts?

Of course not. They interview eyewitnesses when they can, or experts who have sifted the forensic evidence when they cannot. Then, when accounts disagree or seem hard to believe, they seek corroboration from other witnesses. They hammer away at or finally dismiss the accounts of those who turn out to have some strong motivation to lie, and especially of those who keep changing their stories, who can be demonstrated beyond a doubt *already* to have lied.

How do I know ATF agents fired from the helicopters at Waco? I interviewed, face-to-face, Waco survivor Catherine Matteson, a 72-year-old Christian lady of clear eye and calm demeanor. I didn't merely talk to her over the phone, watch edited portions of her statements on videotape, or hear her when she spoke on a panel surrounded by other Branch Davidians with whom she might have wanted to stay on good terms (although those means of acquiring information are generally accepted for newspaper publication, if that's all that's available.)

No, I asked her face-to-face, one-on-one. She told me she saw the helicopters firing down through the walls and roof of the church at Waco on Feb. 28, 1993.

"Now, Catherine," I said, not wanting to let such an important point go by without a little more poking, "it was real noisy. There was gunfire down at the front of the building. The helicopter rotors themselves are pretty noisy. Probably you heard gunfire while the helicopters flew by, and you just *assumed* there was fire coming from the aircraft, right?"

"No," said the 72-year-old Christian lady, looking me straight in the eye, calm and serene as if she were reporting what kind of bird she saw on the bird feeder this morning. "The helicopters were firing at us. I saw the yellow flashes. We had to get down on the floor, because the bullets were coming in the window and through the walls."

"The yellow flashes" is what experienced interviewers call a significant corroborative detail. How many 72-year-old ladies who have never been in combat, do you suppose, know that a machine gun makes a yellow muzzle-flash that can often be seen, even in daylight … especially if it's firing directly at you?

Catherine Matteson was never put on trial. She faced no charges when I spoke with her, and doubtless never will. While she is indeed inclined to think well of her fellow church members, I submit there is no reason to assume she is lying, especially when her account is substantially corroborated by 12 other Davidian survivors, many of them under oath.

I have also spoken to Dick DeGuerin, one of David Koresh's attorneys, face-to-face. He told me that—long before the church at Waco was burned to the ground and bulldozed to destroy the evidence, just as the Branch Davidians feared the government would do—he was in the building, trying to negotiate a surrender. The occupants took him up to the third floor, where he saw many bullet holes in the ceiling.

Mr. DeGuerin told me he knows enough about the behavior of bullets coming through wood that he recognized the downward-pointing splinters as a sure sign that these were exit holes caused by gunfire from above. He could not have been fooled by bullet holes "planted" by someone firing upward from inside. He also stated there was no high ground near the Waco church building from which any such fire could have come—it had to be from the helicopters.

Attorney DeGuerin—who had no reason to lie to me on behalf of a client long dead—has also repeated this under oath.

Another Waco survivor with whom I have spoken in person, David Thibodeau, is a stocky direct fellow who retains a hint of his native "down-Maine" accent. He confirmed for me what he testified to before Congress, and also stated in a signed affidavit—that during the initial ATF attack of Feb. 28, 1993, church member Winston Blake was killed by a bullet that—from its trajectory through the wall—could only have come from a helicopter above.

There are also strong indications that Jaydean Wendell, an Asian-American, was killed instantly by a single bullet that penetrated downward to her second floor bedroom that day, piercing her brain as she lay on the bed in full view of her small child, playing in the same room.

The government contends Ms. Wendell must have been firing a rifle if she was shot—as though bullets fired in blindly through walls and roofs can distinguish the armed from the unarmed.

(At the Branch Davidian trial, a female ATF agent testified that the invaders' standing orders were to withdraw if fired upon, and *not* to return fire through the plywood walls. Although she and her partner were apparently the only agents to obey this order, no ATF assailant has ever been disciplined for raking a plywood building full of unarmed women and children with penetrating rifle fire.)

• • •

On the other hand, let us look at the government denials.

Initially, the government contended such fire was an impossibility, because the helicopters in question were unarmed.

(These denials, mind you, tend to be institutional. My attempts to reach individual ATF agents for interviews have always been diverted to professional public information officers who were not on the scene and who specialize in non-denial denials, answering with such rhetorical questions as: "Do you really believe trained government agents would behave that way?")

Reporters like myself are carefully prevented from looking individual agents in the face to see if they sweat, dart their eyes, or display short tempers or frustration under the kind of probing questions to which the Branch Davidian survivors and attorneys happily—and voluntarily—subject themselves.

However, during the recent House Waco hearings, BATF agent Davy Aguilera, who rode in one of the helicopters, testified that BATF agents in the Blackhawks had their automatic weapons with them, loaded, during the raid. Although he answered, "No," when asked whether he had fired, he did disclose that agents had been told they were allowed to fire in self-defense.

So, to get the helicopters, they lied about the "methamphetamine lab." To get the search warrant, which they never tried to serve, they lied about the Rev. Koresh and his parishioners having fully automatic weapons, while also purposely concealing the fact that the Rev. Koresh had invited them (in the hearing of a witness) to come inspect his weapons any time.

Later, the FBI lied about the urgent need to knock down the walls and staircases (with tanks) and feed in the toxic, flammable, CS gas to "end the child abuse."

What else have the federals done to encourage us to believe they're telling the truth ... this time?

An unsigned Treasury Department memo turned over to congressional investigators, referring to helicopters as "HCs" in its discussion of the dress rehearsal for the Waco raid at Fort Hood, Texas, reads: "HCs as a diversion. Simultaneous gunfire. Worked in Seattle. Three to four hundred meters from boundary. Hover. Practiced at Hood."

Yet, although the agents who first denied being armed now admit they carried loaded machine guns in the helicopters and were authorized to fire, we are expected to believe they saw gunfire from the church, saw four of their buddies below being hit and falling in a wild firefight, but still refrained from firing?

To believe this, mind you, we would also have to believe that all the video cameras recording the raid just happened to run out of tape at the point where the helicopters swooped near the building, since that's the point at which the videotapes are interrupted. Every single one of them.

On the audio tape of the second Branch Davidian 911 call of that day, still early in the raid, now-deceased Davidian Wayne Martin can be heard shouting excitedly: "Another chopper with more people—more guns going off. They're firing! That's them, not us." The voice identified in court as church member Steve Schneider then adds: "There's a chopper with more of them. Another chopper with more people and more guns going off. Here they come!"

Throughout, the government machine guns (the church members had none) can be heard firing in the background.

Such voice recordings, made while an event is actually taking place and before anyone has time to reconstruct a better story later on, are generally considered to be excellent evidence. Against this we have only denials by federal agents who—if they said anything else—would be exposing themselves and their comrades-in-arms to indictment for cold-blooded murder.

Now *there's* a motivation for deception.

So, in answer to editor J.K.'s assertion that my reporting is "the unproven stuff of conspiracists," I can say this much: Before I reached my conclusion of fact, I personally investigated this matter more fully than 90 percent of the stories that appear as factual accounts in any daily newspaper in America. An award-winning professional reporter and editor of more than 20 years experience, now writing full-time for a newspaper of more than 150,000 circulation, my sole stock-in-trade is my credibility, my insistence on reporting the truth as best I can discover it.

That does not mean I'm infallible. I'm as capable as any human being of misunderstanding something. On such rare occasions, I file a correction as timely as possible.

But I submit that "believing in conspiracies" does not prove one a fruitcake.

Yes, some "conspiracists" are certifiable. If the transmission drops out of your neighbor's old truck and he blames it on space-alien radio signals or a secret 300-year-old plot by a small cabal of international Jewish bankers, he's nuts.

But federal prosecutors charge people with "conspiracies" all the time. One assumes they "believe" in all these conspiracies, yet no one seems to dismiss all federal prosecutors as fruitcakes, even when juries finally throw out large numbers of these conspiracy indictments as unprovable or unfounded (read: nuts).

A conspiracy is a plan between two or more parties either to commit a wrong or to cover up wrongdoing after the fact. Conspiracies happen all the time. Government agents conspire to keep us from finding out about their terrible fatal screw-ups, caused by cranking up the adrenaline levels of too many ill-trained and overarmed agents in circumstances where such tactics are totally uncalled for —like Waco.

But when an editor like J.K. says that my reporting of such facts is "the stuff of conspiracists," what he really means is that he has forgotten his duty to thoroughly investigate and then present all the facts, no matter how uncomfortable they may make him, his bosses, or those readers who hope to cling to their comforting delusions just a little longer.

The obvious truth about our government's murderous behavior at Waco and Ruby Ridge and Donald Scott's ranch is being self-censored by less-than-courageous news editors who know there is a national disinformation campaign afoot to brand anyone who expresses concern about such matters as "black helicopter conspiracy nuts."

That such men and women are more interested in preserving their own careers than in reporting facts that have met every standard and common-sense test of corroboration, but which are simply too disturbing to consider, should perhaps not surprise us. But it does make me ashamed to share their profession, one that in this country once went by the shining motto: "Print the truth and raise hell."

· · ·

As to whether I "recommend Chechen-style retaliation against federal agents," I believe we move here beyond matters of professional judgment and into purposeful misrepresentation. The word "retaliation," I believe, has been carefully chosen by editor J.K. alone. I myself never used the word, which is completely inappropriate to the actions of the Branch Davidians at Mount Carmel—though perhaps not to the eventual burnout by the federals.

If a federal agent wrongs me or mine, and some months later I "retaliate" by ambushing or harming that or some different federal agent at a different place, at that point I am fighting a guerrilla war of resistance. "Retaliation," by definition, always occurs considerably after the triggering event, and with forethought.

While I do indeed fear it may eventually come to a war of retaliation—should our out-of-control government keep systematically usurping the rights of a once-free people, stripping us of our arms and numbering us like cattle—I consistently advise against such measures.

But let's remember, the Branch Davidians who fired back at government agents charging their home and church with guns ablaze—who did not "retaliate" at some later time, but rather immediately defended themselves and their families under extreme duress—were unanimously found innocent by an American jury of all the capital charges.

The San Antonio jury ruled their shooting of those federal agents was justified and acquitted them of any wrongdoing in shooting those federals (just as Randy Weaver and Kevin Harris were unanimously acquitted of killing the trespassing federal marshal at Ruby Ridge), finding them guilty only of some relatively minor weapons charges.

A jury of 12 Americans good and true has spoken unanimously—despite all kinds of hooting and hollering for blood by the pro-government extremist press. The shooting of the federal agents at Waco was justifiable self-defense, not "retaliation."

The forewoman of the Branch Davidian's jury in San Antonio, Sarah Bain, told me the jury was shocked when the judge sent the defendants up for years on those minor charges. This was done over her written protest, in a letter in which she told the judge that the jury assumed the defendants would be released for "time served."

So, American law says we are justified in firing back at men in black ninja suits who come running onto our property firing their guns, just as every major Western religion tells us that this is not just our right, but our duty.

Russian helicopters fired at the Chechen rebels, attempting to kill them in their own land. The ragtag Chechen teenagers shot down eight. They had every right to do so.

If a helicopter swoops over my property and opens fire at me and my family, unannounced and unprovoked, I will use every means I have available (as pitiful as those are, under current legal restrictions) to try to shoot down that helicopter and kill everyone aboard, and I don't care what color uniforms the occupants turn out to be wearing. Even the Talmud instructs us, according to my friend Aaron Zelman of Jews for the Preservation of Firearms Ownership, "If a man comes and attacks your family, you shall rise up and smite him."

I wonder what alternative plan J.K. in Texas has to defend himself and his family if the time ever comes. Will he go home to his wife and kids tonight and say, "Now listen kids, honey, this is important. If government men come in a helicopter and start shooting in through the roof and windows here and trying to kill us, I want you all to know that I've decided we're not going to resist in any way. We're not going to fire back, even in an attempt to scare them away. Instead, I expect every one of you to follow my example, as I drop my trousers and kneel down on the floor with my butt up, to provide them with a large soft target."

Alternatively, I suppose he figures he can always dial 911. We're always assured that, after we're disarmed, we can count on the local police to protect us. Like any law-abiding citizens, the Branch Davidians dialed 911. They died two months later, still waiting for the sheriff.

I have not been alone in reporting—after documenting as best I can—the real significance of Waco. Rebecca Wyatt's "Vantage Point" column in the August 1996 issue of *Guns & Ammo* magazine argues that Waco is "but a glimpse of our future" if the federal government continues to seize "illegal powers as [the] Constitution gathers dust."

And the Gun Owners Foundation published Carol Moore's book *The Davidian Massacre* (see "Appendix II"), including her latest research on the topic, drawn from interviews with the participants, as well as trial and congressional transcripts.

James Bovard, the eminently respectable Cato Institute scholar, frequent contributor to the *Wall Street Journal's* op-ed page, and author of the book *Lost Rights: The Destruction of American Liberty*—whom I personally know to be a decent and common-sense fellow—describes the author:

"Carol Moore has done more research on Waco than anyone else. Her book pulls together many of the most shocking details of government abuses that a reader cannot find anywhere else. Anyone interested in Waco should learn much from her book."

As I ordered my copy, I was tempted to order one for J.K. in Texas.

But for some reason, I doubted he would bother to read it.

Gen. Custer Victim of Dastardly Indian Ambush

I enjoyed the multi-part 1996 PBS series on *The West*, produced by Ken Burns of *Civil War* and *Baseball* fame.

Of course, bubbling up through the episodes came the enervating political worldview we've come to expect from the government propaganda channels.

Don't get me wrong. The vicious racism so casually inflicted on Native Americans, Chinese immigrants, and even the descendants of the original Mexican settlers was real. The series dealt quite well with the treatment of the Indian, even if a certain blissful revisionism could be detected in the notion that a Stone-age nomad culture could long have held vast acreage against more efficient systems of food production on this continent, had only their competitors been more "compassionate."

Has such a situation ever prevailed, anywhere but on the most remote geographical fringes? Go to Europe. Ask to see the lands that have been set aside so the wandering Picts and Celts might pursue their Stone-age lifestyles without so much as encountering a fence. Do the Europeans contemplate paying any reparations? Do they lose any sleep?

The mining industry, predictably, was portrayed in the documentary as a plague upon the land, darkening the sun, stripping the ground bare, exposing men to insufferable dangers.

Why, then, did these men travel halfway around the world to land these jobs? Why no mention of the fact that, thanks to their hard work and sacrifice, their grandchildren now enjoy a standard of living never dreamed of in homelands like Wales and Czechoslovakia?

Nor was there a single mention of the benefits of abundant and cheap electricity, moving on transmission lines spun of the copper those brave men hewed from the earth.

And as for the mighty Columbian Exposition of 1893, the

scriptwriters put on their best little sneers, ridiculing the California pavilion for displaying life-size Greek statuary built entirely of figs and prunes.

Surely only a generation that has never known hunger could mock the pride of a nation that—through hard work—had created a land of agricultural bounty for all.

All that said, however, I thought the strongest insight came during the reportage on Buffalo Bill Cody's Wild West Show, with its repeated and crowd-pleasing Indian attacks, ending in every case with the endangered white settlers being rescued from the savages.

The history of the West is a history of conquest by the European peoples. Yet our myth of the West always has the European settlers *defending* themselves against attack. What a *reluctant* conquest!

To imagine an equal absurdity, I can only speculate what kind of action adventures we'd be seeing out of Germany now, had Hitler managed to win a negotiated settlement and the Reich still occupied the Ukraine. The great popular heroes, presumably, would be courageous but outnumbered SS men, riding in each episode to the rescue of another poor outnumbered homestead full of blond-haired Aryan settlers, under attack by a savage band of hairy murderous Jews.

In an even more current example of the same phenomenon, young S.H. writes me from Texas:

"I read your recent article on Waco and I must tell you I am dismayed. ... You are willing to allow for the honesty of the Davidians in every instance but allow for none from the ATF. ...

"My father is an ATF agent. He was at Mount Carmel. He fired his 9mm pistol and his HK-MP5 rifle (also 9mm and not of the penetrating power that many who are not familiar with the weapon might at first believe) from the ground. ...

"The agents in the helicopters did have their weapons with

481

them. They had their 9mm pistols. If you really want a story, find somebody who can shoot through a window, let alone at a target in the window, from inside a moving helicopter with a pistol. ... That would be a story! ...

"Let me ask you; if you were going to a gun fight, if you were intending to engage in trading fire, would you wear a red baseball cap? I know an agent who went to Mount Carmel that did. ...

"The long and the short of it was that the ATF was there to serve an arrest warrant and to seize the illegal weapons. If the Davidians had not opened fire, if they had not sought to ambush federal agents, the ATF would have arrested two men, taken away some weapons that were illegal, and the rest of the Davidians would still be there, worshiping just as they pleased. ... "

Here we have it again, taking root before our very eyes, the notion that 76 combat-clad government agents, with orders to shoot anyone spotted with a gun, armed with German automatic submachine guns firing especially lethal hydroshock bullets as they stormed a church full of women and children, shooting five tame dogs in their pen as they headed for the front door, were in fact the defenseless *victims* on Feb. 28, 1993, caught with nothing but inadequate little Heckler & Koch 9mm popguns that they happened to be carrying the way you or I might carry a pocket knife, "ambushed" by vicious Christian cultists intent on mowing down innocent ATF social workers as they happened to stroll by, carrying picnic lunches, on their way to a softball game.

I responded:

Dear Mr. H—

I understand how the fact that your father was involved in the government homicides at Waco may make it hard for you to consider what happened there objectively.

However, if you've had military service, I'm sure you understand the reluctance of any member of a tightly knit unit to turn snitch and expose his fellow officers to prosecution for a capital crime. You surely know the ease with which it can be rationalized, that "Maybe things went wrong, but we didn't start out meaning to do wrong. We were just following orders. You have to follow orders. Things happen, and it could have happened that way to anyone. It doesn't mean me and my buddies are bad. ... "

Remember, both ATF Director Higgins and Secretary Bentsen admitted to congressional committees and on television that these men could and should be charged with "wrongful homicide" if they lied about who fired first, and/or if they in fact fired indiscriminately into the building.

Well, I'm sorry to ruin your day, young Mr. H., but they did lie, they did fire indiscriminately, and many of them have already admitted doing so, under oath.

You say the ATF agents were armed "only" with their 9mm pistols and H&K submachine guns. If I were caught in possession of a Heckler & Koch MP-5 submachine gun today, I'd be put in jail. TV comentators would pout and scowl as this "fully automatic destructive device" was displayed on a table which would also contain my kitchen butcher knives, the souvenir Zulu spear that my mother once sent me from her African vacation, and whatever cash I had on my person, as evidence of my obvious intent to stage some kind of assassination or major rebellion.

One MP-5, Mr. H.—not 76.

Yet you imply the fact that they only carried such puny popguns proves the combat-clad ATF raiders, in their bulletproof vests and Kevlar army helmets, were caught completely unawares by the Davidian "ambush" as they just happened to be peacefully passing Mount Carmel on their way to some kind of Sunday afternoon softball game.

The hydroshock bullets the ATF employed that day are defined as "highly penetrating rounds." Although they could (and did) easily penetrate the windows and plywood walls at the church at Mount Carmel, they expand when they hit the human body, tearing out large areas of flesh, as opposed to passing through as would usually be the case with a fully jacketed standard military round. In fact, use of such bullets in war may well be against the Geneva conventions.

It's also worth noting that such bullets are actually larger around *before* they expand than the 7.62mm bullets fired from an M-60 machine gun, the usual weapon of the Huey waist-gunners who combat veterans tell me were the source of the most accurate and destructive strafing fire in Vietnam—despite your contention that no one can possibly hit anything from a hovering helicopter.

At the Davidian trial, in answer to defense questioning, FBI agent James Cadigan said of the special hydroshock bullets in use by the ATF (and the ATF alone) that day, "They're designed to kill, disable, wound, destroy whatever they hit" (trial transcript page 1235). Yet you tell us these pitiful little peashooters are so much weaker than what we might think ... sort of like the rubber bullets used in "crowd control," perhaps?

Care to stand still while someone pumps four or five 9mm hydroshocks into you, Mr. H.? Tell you what—we'll even let you hold up a sheet of normal construction plywood to stop the rounds. OK?

• • •

Agent Sprague, when asked at trial and under oath to define the "threats" at which he shot that day, described a pair of hands at a window, a pair of arms, and curtains moving. He said he fired at all of them (trial transcripts, page 2241-2 and 2252-3).

Agent Timothy Gabourie admitted that since he was not wearing a helmet and didn't want to raise his head above the side of the truck behind which he was hiding, he drew his 9mm pistol and fired 25 to 30 shots into the building *without looking*. Agent

Barbara Maxwell admitted under oath that agents were firing indiscriminately through walls and windows.

But of course, it's *not* true that the 76 attacking agents were armed only with weapons shooting 9mm handgun rounds. BATF Chief of Special Operations Richard L. Garner admitted to a congressional committee that the attacking agents were also equipped with numerous .308- (7.62 NATO) caliber high-power sniper rifles, eight military-style AR-15 rifles (bottlenecked .223, as you know), and 12 large-gauge shotguns.

At the trial, Texas Rangers testified that they collected more than 70 used shell casings in and around the undercover house, from which ATF snipers were firing into the building that day with their .308 rifles. That's more than 300 yards from a church full of mostly unarmed victims.

Yes, a good sniper can hit quite precisely with a scoped .308 rifle at 300 yards. But not through walls and curtains. Nor would any responsible police officer ever take such a shot, if he knew (as all the ATF agents knew) that there were also unarmed women and children in the building, possibly directly behind their shadowy curtain-moving targets.

Yet they fired more than 70 rounds of .308 NATO.

Do you consider the bottle necked NATO .308 cartridge a round "not of the penetrating power that many who are not familiar with the weapon might at first believe," Mr. H.? I'll expand my offer. You stand 300 yards away from a marksman of my choice, holding up a piece of standard construction plywood— the same stuff the walls at Mount Carmel were made of—as a shield. We'll put 10 or 20 rounds of .308 NATO into the plywood, which you apparently believe will stop each and every round of the type fired by government marksmen at Waco. You'll be fine ... won't you?

As for agents firing machine pistols from helicopters, they wouldn't need to be good shots to score kills inside a building containing dozens of people if they fired in enough random rounds through the roof, walls, and windows.

Given your familiarity with weapons, would you really fire a 9mm handgun loaded with *any kind* of live ammo at a target pinned up to the side of your own house, when your family members were inside, based on your confidence that 9mm rounds won't penetrate the walls of the average civilian dwelling?

But, in fact, it's highly unlikely the firing from the helicopters *was* with 9mm H&Ks or sidearms—it's far more likely, given the eyewitness testimony, that it was with fully automatic M-16s or even M-60s. Since you seem to have such good contacts inside the agency, why don't you find out for us precisely what kind of weapon each agent fired from the helicopters (I'd love the names and current addresses and phone numbers, with the weapon fired by each); they won't tell us.

You criticize those who are not willing to accept the truthfulness of the ATF at face value. Maybe that's because they've been shown to lie, over and over again.

In fact, they lied for months, contending the helicopters were unarmed, before they finally admitted they carried loaded weapons with them. They called the newspaper and TV reporters who said they saw the choppers circling the building multiple times liars, even though some of the videotape later proved those reporters were correct.

They lied about the suspected drug lab to acquire the helicopters, remember? They lied in the affidavit filed to obtain the search warrant. They invented lies after the fact about being there to "prevent child abuse" (a charge that had already been checked out and dismissed by the proper Texas state authorities—and no responsibility of any federal agency, in any case). They lied about believing the Davidians had illegal 50-caliber machine guns.

There were no 50-caliber machine guns. ATF commanders finally had to admit under oath at trial that the Davidians owned only two perfectly legal single-shot bolt-action 50-caliber *rifles*, and that none of their shells showed any firing-pin impressions. They only "cooked off" in the final fatal fire, two months later.

• • •

The ATF routinely and famously lies about how weapons they seize are "full-auto," altering them after seizure till they'll fire a two-round burst even if they then jam—all that's required to meet their definition of an illegal, fully automatic machine gun.

They're *instructed* to lie under oath at trial about their third-class tax and permit records being 100 percent accurate, and they dutifully do so, every time, when they know actual accuracy has only recently been improved, after considerable effort, from 50 to perhaps 70 percent. They lied to Randy Weaver, who had never committed any known crime, to entrap him in hopes of turning him into a snitch on the activities of an Idaho church.

The whole claim that the Waco raid was necessary *in any way* is a lie. When BATF investigators Davy Aguilera and Jim Skinner visited local gun dealer Henry McMahon on July 20, 1992, to ask about David Koresh's gun purchases, McMahon called Koresh on the phone. Koresh said, "If there's a problem, tell them to come out here. If they want to see my guns, they're more than welcome."

Mr. McMahon walked back into the room where the ATF agents were waiting, carrying the cellular phone. "I've got him [the Rev. Koresh] on the phone," he said. "If you'd like to go out there and see those guns, you're more than welcome to."

Growing quite agitated, Agent Aguilera responded, "No, no!" The agents "didn't want to do it that way."

At the trial of the surviving victims in San Antonio, Judge Walter Smith allowed Mr. McMahon's business partner and friend, Karen Kilpatrick, who is not a Branch Davidian and who witnessed this incident, to describe it *under oath*. When she got to the point where she waved her hands over her head and shook her head in imitation of Agent Aguilera, the whole courtroom burst into laughter (trial transcript, page 4904).

At that point Judge Smith, no friend of the defense, who had previously stated he was "not going to allow the government to be put on trial here," refused to allow McMahon himself to take the stand.

• • •

So the ATF went to Waco to serve an arrest warrant. Since young S.H. also reports his father was there on the government side, I asked him, "Perhaps your direct sources in the ATF can finally tell us: Which officer had the arrest warrant in his possession?" No ATF agent has ever been able to provide that name at trial or to any congressional committee.

The nation desperately needs the specific name of the person who had that printed warrant on his person, and meant to serve it. Will he or she now confirm this for reporters? At what phone number can we reach the agent who physically had the written search or arrest warrant with him or her at Mount Carmel at the beginning of the assault on Feb. 28, and who will so swear under oath?

Obviously, he must have been in the lead, with the document out in plain sight of David Koresh when the latter opened the door. His account would be *crucial* to anyone hoping to believe the ATF's version of events. *Please* identify him and arrange for us to speak to him.

Then let's all ask him if, in their initial attempts to make a peaceful entry, the ATF agents shot the five tame family dogs where they stood in their pen (as planned and practiced) before or after he tried to hand the warrant to David Koresh. Let's also ask him how the noisy and intimidating "helicopter diversion" you're so fond of was supposed to facilitate the peaceful service of this warrant.

But then, if there was *any* plan to peacefully serve a warrant, why attempt to spring a surprise attack by 76 ninja-clad agents pouring out of cattle trailers, at all? Was a surprise attack necessary because David Koresh or his followers had ever drawn guns or resisted visits by the local police, by Texas child welfare inspectors, or anyone else? When? Why weren't any such incidents cited on the affidavit seeking the search warrant?

Nothing in informant Aguilera's affidavit indicated any reason to expect the Rev. Koresh or his followers to use force to resist. That's why the magistrate did not issue a so-called "no-knock" warrant. Title 18, USC 3109 states that an officer must give notice of his legal authority and purpose before attempting to enter the premises. Only more than a year after the fact did any ATF agent change his story to claim he yelled "Search warrant!" a few seconds after the firing began. Specifically asked at trial whether they ever rehearsed a peaceful unresisted entry, Agent Ballesteros said, "No, we did not."

If a peaceful service was intended, why—when David Koresh opened the door, held up his empty hand, and said "Wait, let's talk, there are women and children in here"—did agents immediately open fire, critically wounding his father-in-law who stood behind him?

Why did the ladder team place their ladders against the side of the building and begin their illegal entry even as this was happening? How would this have facilitated giving anyone inside the opportunity to peacefully comply?

At the trial, Agent Bill Buford, who was on the team that climbed to and entered the second-story window, testified that those agents had been authorized to shoot anyone inside who they saw with a weapon—even though those agents had not announced they were police or that they were serving a search warrant.

In fact, Agent Buford testified that he did so shoot a Davidian who approached him carrying a gun—inside that gun owner's private dwelling (trial transcript, pg. 2732-33).

If you, Mr. H., were a Branch Davidian planning an ambush, wouldn't you put some men in trenches or behind other cover in outlying positions, to achieve a crossfire?

How was an ambush of the BATF possible, when every BATF commander knew they were expected? The Rev. Koresh, having been informed of the upcoming raid by the local mailman (a Branch Davidian), told undercover agent Robert Rodriguez, "Robert, they're coming. Whether BATF or FBI or whatever, they're coming." The undercover agent shook Koresh's hand, left, and informed the agents in the undercover house that the raid was expected, in plenty of time for ATF commanders to have called it off if they'd wished.

Instead, co-commander Chuck Sarabyn decided to proceed, rushing out to the staging area and shouting, "Get ready to go! They know we're coming!" and "Koresh knows the ATF and the National Guard are coming!" This incident is reported on page 91 of the Treasury Department report. More than 60 agents have reported they heard Sarabyn give this warning.

"Ambush"?

In fact, the jury in San Antonio specifically rejected charges that the Davidians ambushed anyone. Juror Teresa Talerico later commented, "They had 45 minutes to get their people positioned, to get the guns all passed out. It seems to be quite apparent that there was no such plan, because of the hustle-bustle to get guns, even after the ATF drove up."

Waco Herald-Tribune photographs, which reporter Marc Masferrer testified were all taken within the first 20 to 30 seconds of the raid, show windows intact with screens in place and no one visible at the windows, even as agents are firing at and into the church.

During the trial, Agent Roland Ballesteros was asked whether it wouldn't have made more sense for anyone planning an ambush to remove the screens and place gunmen at the windows. Agent Ballesteros acknowledged the photos show the screens in place and no one returning fire from the building, even though they clearly show his own men firing into the building.

The photographs from the early moments of the assault show agents kneeling in plain sight in front of the building with no cover, firing into the building. No ATF agent has ever been able to explain why anyone would take up such firing positions if there was or had been *any* return fire at that point, let alone why these men were not instantly killed if there was any kind of Davidian ambush.

Justice Department outside expert Alan Stone, M.D., wrote in his Nov. 8, 1993, report to the Justice Department on Waco: "The BATF investigation reports that the so-called 'dynamic entry' turned into what is described as being 'ambushed.' As I tried to get a sense of the state of mind and behavior of the people in the compound, the idea that the Davidians' actions were considered an 'ambush' troubled me. If they were militants determined to ambush and kill as many ATF agents as possible, it seemed to me that given their firepower, the devastation would have been much worse. … The ATF agents brought to the compound in cattle cars could have been cattle going to slaughter if the Davidians had taken full advantage of their tactical superiority."

Again, this is from an official government report.

Within one minute after the raid began, Davidian Wayne Martin, a Harvard-educated attorney, reached the McLennan County Sheriff's office by dialing 911. He immediately shouted, "There are about 75 men around our building shooting at us in Mount Carmel. Tell them there are children and women in here and to call it off! Call it off!"

Why would suicidal militants, anxious to kill as many government agents as possible, make such a call?

Section 9.31 of the Texas Penal Code states: "The use of force to resist an arrest or search is justified: (1) If, before the actor offers any resistance, the peace officer (or persons acting at his direction) uses or attempts to use greater force than necessary to make the arrest or search; and (2) When and to the degree the actor reasonably believes the force is immediately necessary to protect himself against the peace officer's (or other person's) use or attempted use of greater force than necessary."

The San Antonio jury, even after being stacked by prosecutors to eliminate any gun nuts, militia members, or folks predisposed to be suspicious of the ATF, found there was no ambush. The only convictions were on the minor, Constitutionally dubious, gun-law violations.

Yet the pro-government extremists continue to parrot this long-discredited nonsense about an ambush of the government storm troopers, when in fact it was the ATF that was trying to pull off an ambush ... and merely bungled it.

It must be appalling, Mr. H., to realize that you were nourished, clothed, and raised up with money looted from unwilling taxpayers at gunpoint (government guns, of course, which remain unrestricted), and paid to your father for a life's work depriving honest, law-abiding Americans of their Second Amendment right to bear arms. For this is the overwhelming mission of the current ATF, a supposed "tax-collecting agency," which in 1993 handled 10,818 cases in which they sought the arrest and imprisonment of gun owners (not people who use guns in the commission of violent crimes—that's a different agency entirely), while their criminal referrals on alcohol and tobacco matters totaled only 38 (source, ATF internal case summary reports, counts are number of defendants).

I can understand, to some extent, how hard it must be for you to contemplate that your father engaged in a completely unjustified, unnecessary, and illegal paramilitary action that resulted in the death of five to 10 innocent Branch Davidians from wounds inflicted that day, as well as the deaths of four ATF agents, most probably from friendly fire. (The government claims never to have checked the bullets from their wounds to match them against either Davidian or ATF weapons ... an odd omission.)

It must be even harder to realize that the actions of your father and his agency on Feb. 28, 1993, eventually led to the government's toxic gassing and incineration of more than 60 additional innocent persons—half of them women and young children—as other government agencies attempted to cover up the evidence of the initial ATF bungling in a raid that Col. Charles Beckwith (U.S. Army, ret.), founder of the Delta Force, told the *Houston Post* on March 4, 1993, was "very amateur" in both planning and execution.

They knew perfectly well they could have arrested an unarmed David Koresh any time he went jogging—they had undercover operatives in place who reported how often he went jogging, or into town for supplies ... alone or with only one companion, and unarmed.

The ATF knew perfectly well they could have called David Koresh on a cellular phone and said they'd like to drop by in 10 minutes to inspect his weapons for any violations (leaving no time for anyone to go out back and bury anything), just as the local sheriff had gone calling in the recent past. They were actually *invited* by David Koresh, months before this unnecessary raid.

Yet they decided against these options. Instead, the publicity-hungry BATF piled 76 pumped-up (though inexperienced) fully armed agents in cattle trailers, raced to the scene, and sent them charging the building in a planned assault.

Even if the deaths were not specifically "planned," legal doctrine usually dictates that deaths, which occur during the commission of some other premeditated felony such as depriving citizens of their civil rights under color of law, are chargeable as murder.

I believe these killings should be indicted and brought to trial as murders.

So far, I still have a right to say so.

And, of course, the tragedies spreading like ripples on a pond from these government crimes at Waco in 1993 are still expanding.

Unless some faction of the government itself blew up the Murrah building in Oklahoma City to destroy all the Waco-raid planning documents which were stored in the ATF office there, we're left to assume all *those* deaths were in reprisal (however misguided the perpetrator in his selection of tactics) for the ATF-FBI murders at Waco.

Eventually, unless the uniformed liars confess, accept their punishment, and do their penance, I suspect the brand of their guilt will burn its way to the surface of the Washington government's flesh, like the scarlet letter "A" on the preacher's chest in the famous novel, in a level of violence and insurrection that will make what we've seen to date look like Sunnybrook Farm.

APPENDIX I

The Odds of a Randomly Selected Jury of 12 Failing to Convict, Charted by Percentage of Population That Stands in Opposition to a Given Law

I was lucky enough to elicit an intriguing mathematical analysis of just how our system of trial by jury—presuming a *randomly selected* jury of 12 free and private citizens, any one of whom can block conviction—works to prevent enforcement of laws that fail to retain overwhelming public support.

Interestingly, the analysis developed in correspondence after I made a mathematical mistake.

In autumn 1997, a young man wrote in from the Pacific Northwest, asking my help and advice for a class paper. His assignment? Propose ways to increase voter turnout.

I pointed out that before we try to increase voter turnout, we should ask why so many politicians and bureaucrats are working so hard to accomplish this goal. It certainly can't be because they believe higher voter turnout will result in more of them being kicked out of their tax-paid jobs.

In fact, their problem is just the opposite. Around this time, the United Nations threw out the result of supervised elections in occupied Bosnia when voter turnout failed to reach 50 percent. Too many voters had obviously been intimidated into staying away from the polls and the results were therefore invalid, ruled the U.N. high command.

How do you think American politicians liked that word: "invalid"?

As more and more Americans realize that nothing will change whether they vote for Tweedle-Dumb or Tweedle-Dumber—that the whole ball game is rigged from the moment the government decides whose names shall be allowed on their ballot and which candidates will be "allowed" into the TV debates—fewer and fewer people are heading to the polls to cast a "vote of confidence" for the current con game.

This is a good thing, in many ways. Our nation was never meant to be an outright "democracy," where a majority could "vote" on whether you have a right to Ninth Amendment medical liberty (self-prescribing codeine or marijuana), First Amendment religious liberty (belonging to the Peyote Way Church of God, the Branch Davidians, or the local Wiccan Temple), or to keep and bear arms (belt-fed 30-caliber Browning 1919s, without any government permit). Those things are all *rights*, not subject to an up-or-down vote by anyone. When we're duped into voting for lawmakers who claim a right to study and decide such issues, we only endorse their claim of some authority to legislate away the Bill of Rights.

So, unless there's a solid Libertarian on the ballot or you can figure out a way to use your vote to sow confusion among the enemy, my advice on election day was and is: Stay home. Don't vote. *Certainly* don't endorse with your vote the "lesser-of-two-evil" statist collectivist looters-at-gunpoint. It will not achieve "peaceful change." When was the last time you cast a straight up-or-down vote on whether you can own a machine-gun collection or an opium plantation without the government's permission, or whether the IRS and its income tax shall end tomorrow? If you *were* allowed to cast such a vote and the initiative passed two-to-one, do you think our government would honor the will of the majority any more than it allowed the voters of Arizona and California to legalize medical marijuana, by *their* two-to-one majority votes in 1997? Don't vote. It only encourages them, and allows them to claim your *personal support* and endorsement for their tyranny.

Furthermore, increasing numbers of former voters are listening to such common-sense advice, which creates a problem for our masters: How are they going to claim a "mandate" for their latest schemes, once the total turnout of obedient slaves falls permanently below 50 percent?

However, having said all that, I still wanted to give the young man a substantive response to his inquiry. So, if for some reason we *really* wanted to get more people to the polls (I told the young man), one idea might be to let voters do what jurors used to be able to do: repeal any law that fails to gain 92 percent support.

After all, one juror in 12 represents 8.3 percent of the population, I reasoned. And one juror can stop any prosecution from succeeding. Therefore, no law should be allowed to stand unless it can garner 92 percent public support. Let's allow the voters to vote up or down at the polls on drug laws, gun laws, tax laws—and any law that receives *only* 91 percent support or less will be promptly repealed—with the Legislature banned from enacting it again for 99 years.

(Mind you, no one was proposing that 8 or 9 percent of the populace be allowed to create new enactments or prohibitions or taxes or laws—only that existing laws be *repealed* if they failed to achieve 92 percent support. Nor would any group of racist extremists comprising 9 percent of the local voting populace—already a pretty far-fetched hypothesis—be able to "repeal the law against lynching Jews or Negroes," as one rather wild-eyed correspondent objected. I know of no jurisdiction in America that has a specific law against killing Jews, blacks, or any other minority member. Any such rabid and depraved hatemongers would have to convince 9 percent of the populace to vote with them to repeal the existing criminal statute against murder, period—hardly a prospect worth losing much sleep over. In fact, *no* sensible criminal law against assault, armed robbery, or rape sensibly defined would be in any danger from this proposal, though the War on Drugs and a thousand other post-1912 bureaucratic edicts of the *malum prohibitum* variety would promptly shrivel, blacken, and die like weeds after a hard freeze.

My proposal of such a "9 percent rule" brought e-mail responses from two gentlemen with a superior grasp of statistics, cheerfully correcting my amateur calculation. Electrical engineer Steve Mahan of Panama City, Fla., wrote:

"Vin—[Your] statistical analysis of the percentage of the populace disagreeing with a given law in order to have a 50 percent chance of a 'not guilty' verdict is in error.

"The actual chance for a number of jurors to not convict (one opposed out of N jurors) is the probability of each juror voting to convict raised to the power of the number of jurors. With the percentage given in your article (8.3 percent of the populace opposing the law), one prosecuted under an unsupported law faces a $\{1-(1/12)\}$-to-the-twelfth probability of conviction, or 35.2 percent.

"The correct value to assure an even chance of conviction with a 12-member jury drawn from a random jury pool is about 94.5 percent general support (for the law in question) among the population.

"This, of course, leads to an even higher level of support for the points raised in your article.

"Just as an academic exercise, consider: 99 percent popular support for a law renders an 88.6 percent chance of conviction.

98 percent support? A 78.4 percent chance of conviction. 97 percent popular support for the law? A 69.4 percent chance of conviction."

By the time a mere 5 percent of the populace actively opposes a law, according to the calculations of engineer Mahan, the chance of a unanimous conviction by a jury of 12 drops to 54.04 percent. Under a law with 90 percent popular support but 10 percent of the populace opposed? Only a 28.2 percent chance of conviction. 85 percent support for the law? 14.22 percent. 75 percent popular support for the law in question? Only a 3.17 percent chance of conviction.

Of course, since our ambitious district attorneys want a conviction rate of *at least* 90 percent, we see just how quickly a principled jury pool will squelch prosecutions of even marginally unpopular laws.

Software developer Thomas Junker of Houston, Tex., responded similarly:

"Most people grossly underestimate the positive effect of the 12-man jury in controlling the exercise of the government's ultimate weapon: the criminal law. This is because many presume that there is an intuitive relationship between the number of jurors and what people commonly consider to be 'odds' or 'percentages.'

"The marvelous and very well-kept secret of the jury system is that the percentages work many times more effectively to protect individuals against unpopular prosecution than almost anyone understands. That assumes, of course, that the system is not otherwise tampered with (which it is), and that jurors are selected randomly (which they are not).

"One might think, for instance, that the fact that there are 12 jurors means that one may correctly compute the odds of a jury containing someone disposed for or against some law on the basis of twelfths. Reasonable enough, but entirely incorrect. Happily, the mathematically correct analysis of such things reveals why the 12-man jury is such a powerful mechanism to thwart tyranny, when allowed to function as it was intended.

"The question at hand is this: Given a level of support for a law in the general population, what is the probability that a given jury will be 'uncontaminated' by at least one opponent of that law? For instance, if 99 percent of the population supports a penalty for murder, what is the probability that the government can empanel a jury, all 12 of whom are disposed to punish a defendant well-proved to have committed murder?

"In probability analysis, a decidedly non-intuitive field, we can calculate that quite simply. It is the probability of juror 1 being in support of the law (a number between 0 and 1, in this case .99) multiplied by the probability of juror 2 being in support, and so on through juror 12. This is the same as raising the probability, .99, to the 12th power, which yields a very different result than intuition tells us. The answer is .89, or 89 percent.

"(.99 x .99 x .99 x .99 x .99 x .99 x .99 x .99 x .99 x .99 x .99 x .99 = .8864).

"How fascinating! A loss of support for a law of 1 percent in the general population drops the government's chance of finding a 'pure' jury by 11 percentage points. In actual fact, of course, support for punishing murder exceeds 99 percent by a good margin and comes very very close to 100 percent. That is not the case for political and bureaucratic crimes, however.

"Now we're beginning to reveal how the jury system protects minority political views against being steamrollered by the entrenched powers as long as those powers are not permitted to violate the Constitution.

"Say there is a committed minority opposed to the income tax. Say it constitutes 4 percent of the population and is vehemently opposed on principle to any and all prosecutions for income tax offenses. What is the probability that the government could find a jury free of such people? 'Pretty good!' you might answer, '96 percent of the population is in support, or at least not opposed.' How good? 96 percent? Wrong. 90 percent? Wrong. 80 percent? Nope. Let's see how it computes:

".96 x .96 x .96 x .96 x .96 x .96 x .96 x .96 x .96 x .96 x .96 x .96 = .6127

"Interesting! If a minority political view such as opposition to the income tax is held by as few as 4 percent of the people, and held strongly enough that they would refuse to convict anyone under the income tax laws regardless of the facts of the case, the government would lose almost 40 percent of jury trials in such cases! Unless, of course, the government cheats by violating the Constitution and stacking the jury by filtering out those with a view opposed to the law at hand.

"Here we see the beauty, the almost artistic perfection, of the 12-man jury. When jurors are truly selected at random (and that was the way it was done when the word "jury" was written into our Constitution), the system provides significant protection for minority political views, even to the range of a mere few percent of the population, while assuring that virtually all juries will likely be disposed to punish those who commit universally recognized wrongs.

"It is doubtful that even 1/10th of 1 percent of the population would ever condone murder, while it is quite likely that severe differences of political opinion can and do involve 10, 20, even 50 percent on one side of an issue or the other.

"What the jury system does, in effect, is guarantee that if someone stands accused of committing an act universally considered to be bad, he will be judged on the facts of the case, but if someone is accused of an act that at least a few percent of the population thinks should not be punishable, the government will have a hard time finding a jury that doesn't have at least one person who will vote 'Not guilty!'

"Just *how* hard a time will the government have in finding a jury free of your sympathizers? Ah, the exquisite perfection of it all! As opposition to a law passes 5 percent, the government's chances of finding a "good" jury fall below 50 percent. When opposition rises to 10 percent, the government's position falls below 29 percent. When opponents of a law constitute 20 percent of the people, the government has a dismal 7 percent chance or less of finding a jury willing to convict.

"As opposition rises past 32 percent the government's position falls below 1 percent. This means that if the population were divided into three camps on some controversial issue, no law enforcing the views of any of the three camps could be effectively enforced. Meanwhile, though, all the murderers, thieves, and other miscreants against whom the government could make a sufficiently strong factual case would continue to go to prison."

The obvious question, since most surveys show at least 33 percent of the populace already in favor of legalizing marijuana and generally ending the War on Drugs, is why—under the numbers so ably explained here by Mr. Junker and my previous respondent on this topic, Steven Mahan of Florida—99 percent of such cases don't *already* result in either acquittals or hung juries, *as the Founders obviously intended.*

That result would force Drug War prosecutors to fold up their tents, the same way 23 hung juries in a row ended the Salem witchcraft trials three centuries ago. The nation would return to its previous peaceful state, depriving the would-be fascists of their greatest single excuse for wiretapping, surveilling our bank accounts, searching our cars and luggage, seizing the property of innocent persons before trial, borrowing military equipment to raid and immolate suspicious churches, etc.

Unfortunately, the answer is equally obvious. The judges are stacking the juries, by dismissing anyone who will admit to opposing the law in question, thus artificially keeping the whole vicious machine in gear, rather than allowing it to run out of steam, as the Founders intended *any* unpopular witch-hunt or pogrom to grow quickly unsustainable in the face of the properly functioning jury system that they guaranteed us in no fewer than three of the first 10 Amendments.

Mr. Junker continues:

"Understanding [these numbers] makes it blazingly clear why the 12-man jury was found in antiquity to provide a fully functional balance between acquiescence to punishment for things that are wrong in and of themselves and things that are held to be wrong by the government merely because the government says so. The one system allows real wrongs to be effectively prosecuted while providing a powerful tool for throwing out stupid and harmful prosecutions like yesterday's trash."

However, Mr. Junker then follows with a warning about "The 6-Man Jury":

"Once you understand the beauty of the mathematics of the 12-man jury and compare the numbers with those of the six-man jury, it becomes all too clear why government has been agitating and itchily trying to change the system from 12 to six.

"Simply put, the six-man jury thoroughly undermines the protection of the jury system for minority political views. It doesn't just change it a little, it demolishes the numbers shown above for the 12-man jury.

"Interestingly, the reduced jury size benefits the government more in the unpopular cases than in the cases involving no political controversy. At 99.99 percent agreement that murder is bad, the chances of having a murder advocate on the jury don't change noticeably for 6 or 12 jurors. But at 50 percent popular agreement that involuntary military service is Constitutional and that resisters should be punished, the government has a *sixty-four*-times greater chance of finding a "good" jury willing to convict resisters if only six jurors are required.

"The six-man jury is government's way to hang onto its power to throw people into prison under bad laws even as its popular support falls to levels at which the 12-man jury would thoroughly nullify the bad laws.

"It has taken over 700 years since the Magna Carta for political shrewdness and the manipulation of public opinion and the legislative process to sprout malignantly and grow to the point at which the jury system is finally being undone. Those who would undo it should beware, because it is the penultimate peaceful defense of those who would be free before they have no choice but to take matters into their own hands ... as happened in the 1770s."

Mr. Junker can be reached at tjunker@phoenix.net; Mr. Mahan in Florida at stevem@digitalexp.com.

APPENDIX II

Chapter I—Where We Went Wrong

The Myth of the Robber Barons, by Burton Folsom, is available for $9.95 plus shipping from Laissez Faire Books, 938 Howard St., San Francisco, CA 94103, tel. 800/326-0996.

Heritage Foundation, 214 Mass. Ave. NE, Washington 20002.

Chapter III—Voir Dire

Darlene and Jerry Span can be contacted at 110 N. 24th St., Phoenix Ariz. 95034.

For a more detailed analysis of the history of jury rights, see the well-researched article "Jury Nullification: Empowering the Jury as the Fourth Branch of Government," by retired—now the late—justice of the Washington State Supreme Court William Goodloe, in the Summer 1996 edition of the FIJActivist. The quarterly newsletter is available for $25 per year from the Fully Informed Jury Association, P.O. Box 59, Helmville, MT 59843, tel. 406/793-5550.

New Jersey Libertarian, 37 Malvern Place, Verona, NJ 07044.

Chapter IV—Public Schools

For information on the progress of the Parental Rights Amendment in your state, contact Executive Director Greg Erken at: Of The People, 2111 Wilson Boulevard Suite 700, Arlington, VA 22201; tel. 703/351-5051.

For information on the Separation of School & State Alliance, contact Marshall Fritz, 4578 N. First No. 310, Fresno, CA 93726; tel. 209/292-1776; email sepschool@psnw.com.

Dumbing Us Down, available for $12.45 from New Society Publishers, 4527 Springfield Ave., Philadelphia PA 19143, and Laissez Faire.

The Education Liberator, 4578 N. First, Fresno, CA 93726; tel. 209/292-1776.

Chapter V—Why People Hate the Government

Unless it's been mysteriously removed, the essay "Assassination Politics" used to be available on the Internet at http://jya.com/ap.htm. The federal complaint against Mr. Bell was available at http://jya.com/jimbell3.htm.

Chapter VI—The Courtesan Press

To really weed out the Libertarians from the authoritarians, you need the diamond-shaped "World's Smallest Political Quiz," sold at $13.45 for 200 copies by the Advocates for Self-Government, 269 Market Place Boulevard, No.106, Cartersville, GA 30120. Call for the Advocates' catalog, or to order toll-free, at 800/932-1776.

Subscriptions to *The Free Market* run $25 per year (tax-deductible); write Ludwig von Mises Institute, Auburn, AL 36849-5301, tel. 205/844-2500.

For further information on *Positively Healthy*, write P.O. Box 71, Richmond, Surrey TW9 3DJ, U.K., tel. (011-44) 01-940-5355.

Chapter VII—All God's Children Got Guns

Lethal Laws, by Jay Simpkin, Aaron Zelman, and Alan M. Rice, Jews for the Preservation of Firearms Ownership, $28.95 postpaid, 2872 S. Wentworth Ave., Milwaukee, WI 53207.

Gateway to Tryanny, by Jay Simpkin and Aaron Zelman, $22.90 postpaid, Jews for the Preservation of Firearms Ownership, $28.95 postpaid, 2872 S. Wentworth Ave., Milwaukee, WI 53207.

Second Amendment is For Everyone (SAFE), 10412 N. 8th Ave. No. 3, Phoenix, AZ 85021; http://www.indirect.com/www/safe.

Families of Michigan for Concealed Carry, tel. 616/243-4790, email gunlist@wings.net.

Sean Gabb's e-mail address is cea01sig@gold.ac.uk.

Vigo Examiner's website: http://www.Vigo-Examiner.com.

Chapter VIII—Demonizing The Militias

Freedom Network News is available for $35 a year from the International Society for Individual Liberty, 1800 Market St., San Francisco, CA 94102.

That Every Man Be Armed by Stephen Holbrook is available for $16.95 from The Independent Institute, 134 Ninety-Eighth Ave., Oakland, CA 94603.

Chapter IX—It Keeps Coming Back to Waco

Autographed copies of *The Davidian Massacre* by Carol Moore are available at $9 book rate ($11 first-class or Canada) from Carol Moore, Box 65518, Washington, D.C. 20035, tel. 202/635-3739.

ABOUT THE AUTHOR

 Vin Suprynowicz grew up in a nice Politically Correct Democratic family, fine folks who taught him that it was wrong to steal or to hate people for being different from them. He still feels that way, but has expanded his idea of who those people are from merely homosexuals and members of racial minorities to machine-gun owners, militiamen, folks who choose to vote their conscience in the jury rooms in defiance of the judge's instructions, who use intoxicants other than those approved by the current government, who decline to contribute any portion of their income to support the welfare/police state, and the like.

He landed his first newspaper job at the alternative *Hartford Advocate* in 1972 after graduating from Wesleyan University. He went on to become the star reporter at the daily *Willimantic Chronicle*, wire editor of the *Norwich Bulletin*, managing editor of the daily *Northern Virginia Sun*, and founder and publisher of the weekly *Providence Eagle*. Suprynowicz was named three times to the Golden Dozen (the top 12 weekly editorial writers in the U.S. and Canada) by the International Society of Weekly Newspaper Editors.

He finally migrated west to Phoenix, then moved to Las Vegas. He's currently an editorial writer for the *Las Vegas Review-Journal*. He also pens a twice-a-week syndicated political column that runs in 20 or so daily newspapers around the country.

NO "LIBERTARIAN" IN YOUR
LOCAL NEWSPAPER?

Many fans who use the Internet to access Vin Suprynowicz's twice-a-week syndicated column, "The Libertarian," ask, "How can I get the editor of my local newspaper to run this stuff?" Here's how to try.

Photocopy a small section of this book—just a sample, no more than six pages. Or download a few vintage installments of The Libertarian from one of two web sites:

the Vinyard at http://www.infomagic.com/liberty/vinyard.htm, or the Vindex at http://www.nguworld.com/vindex.

Then call your local newspaper and ask for the name and mailing address of the editorial-page editor. Send the samples (or the whole book, if you prefer) with a brief signed letter politely stressing that you're a regular reader of the newspaper and a patronizer of its advertisers. Inform the editor that Vin Suprynowicz's twice-a-week columns are syndicated via Mountain Media, a six-year-old syndication service listed in the annual Editor & Publisher Syndicate Directory. The columns are available via e-mail, snail mail, fax, or AP wire. Pricing information is based on newspaper circulation; quotes available from Mountain Media at P.O. Box 4422, Las Vegas, NV 89127-4422, or via e-mail at vin@lvrj.com.

Place a follow-up telephone call to the editor a day or two after you expect the sample columns to arrive. Ask if they were received and read. Point out that the Libertarian point of view differs considerably from those of traditional liberal or conservative columnists. Therefore, the editor might consider running the column to provide readers with a more complete spectrum of current political thought, whether he or she personally agrees with the column or not.

In many cases, you'll hear, "We don't have any room; our

editorial and commentary pages are already full."

Well, duh. You didn't think they were running large swatches of blank white space. Obviously, some existing columnist would have to be replaced, or run with less frequency.

But to stand a chance of helping, sarcasm should be a bit subtler. Instead, try: "Well, of course, if you're already filling up your page with the likes of Doug Bandow, Steve Chapman, Jim Bovard, Sheldon Richman, Lew Rockwell, Thomas Sowell, Joseph Sobran, Walter Williams, and Phyllis Schlafly, Vin doesn't mind waiting in line. While few of those columnists are actual capital-L Libertarians, at least they offer your readers *some* version of the philosophy of smaller government and laissez-faire.

More often than not, your editor will sputter: "Who? Never heard of any of those people, either."

What? The editor declines to run *anything* but defenses of the Cult of the Omnipotent State by aging Republicrat hacks?

Admittedly, the chances of succeeding with this strategy drop precipitously as one approaches the politically correct Washington-New York-Boston corridor. But anywhere else, it's worth a shot. Especially if you're not the *only* reader the editor hears from ...